Watercolour
AND BEYOND

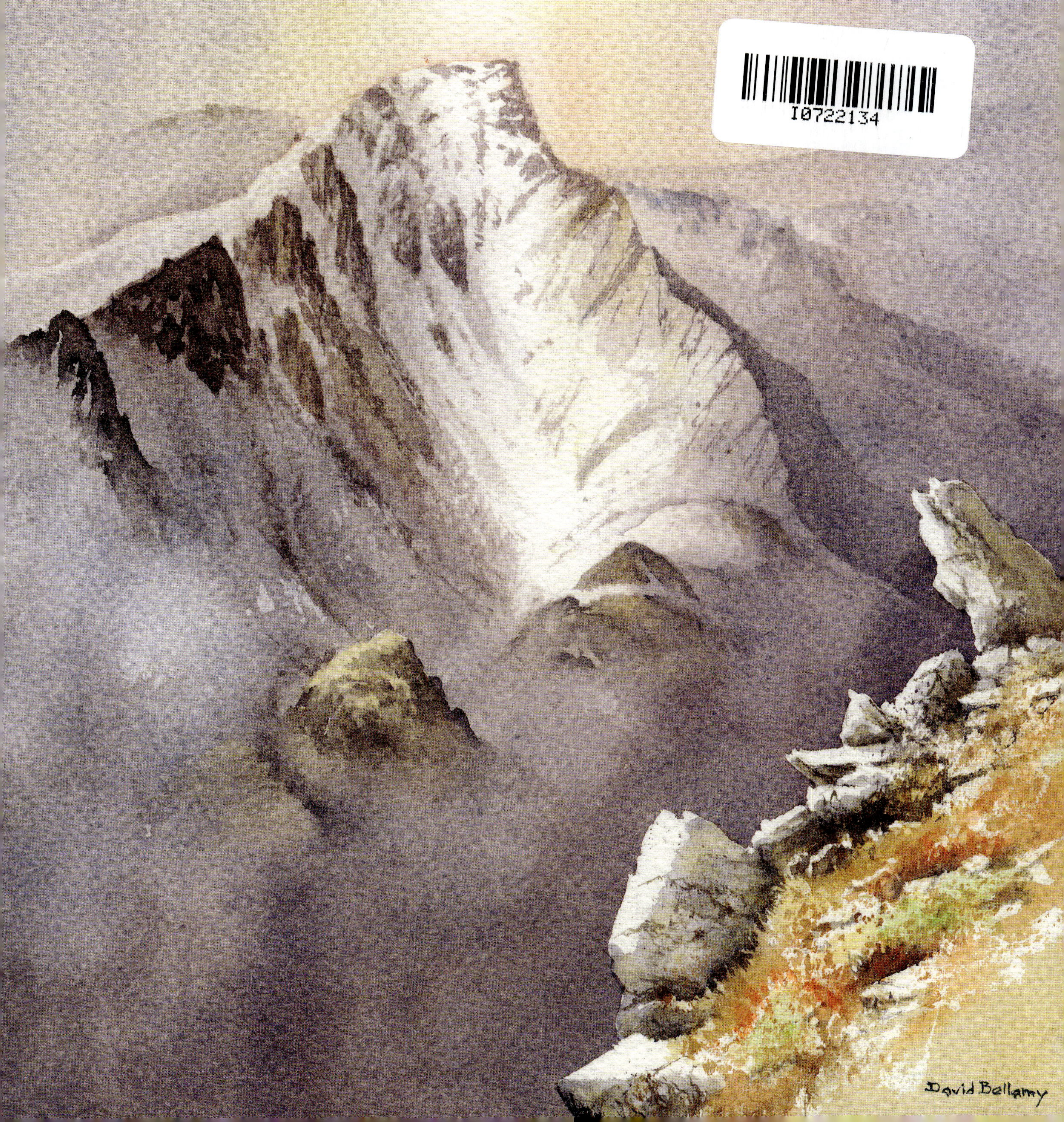

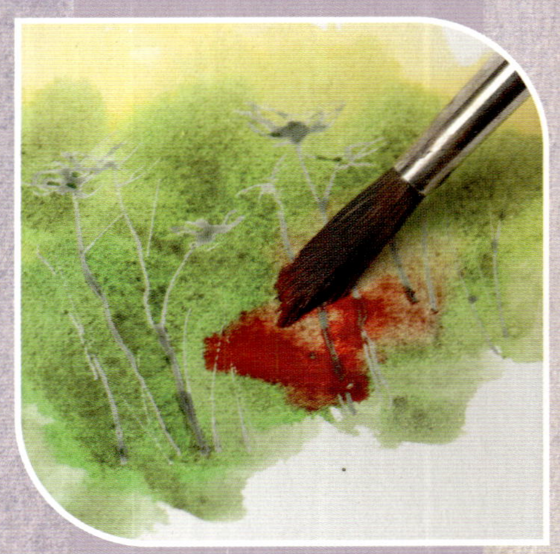

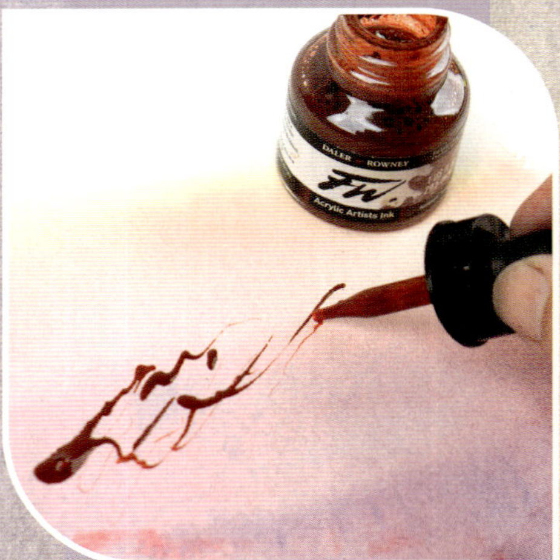

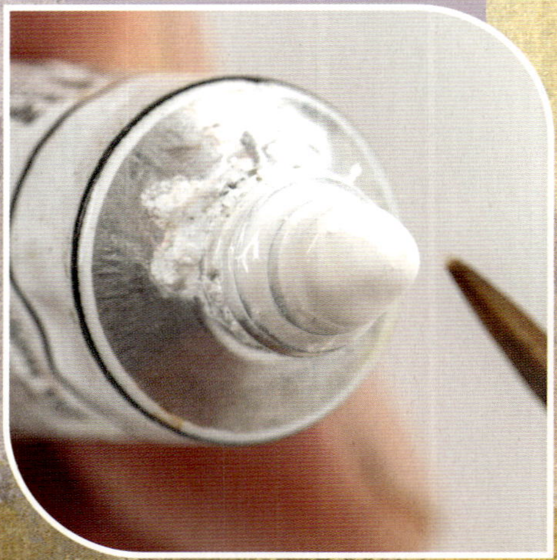

DEDICATION

To my dear Bibi, who at three years old is already displaying the absurd sense of humour associated with her grandfather.

ACKNOWLEDGEMENTS

I would like to thank Edward Ralph for editing the book, Juan Hayward who did the design, Mark Davison for his photography, Jenny Keal for checking my manuscript, and Andy Hughes for her help with information on the Mid-Wales railways.

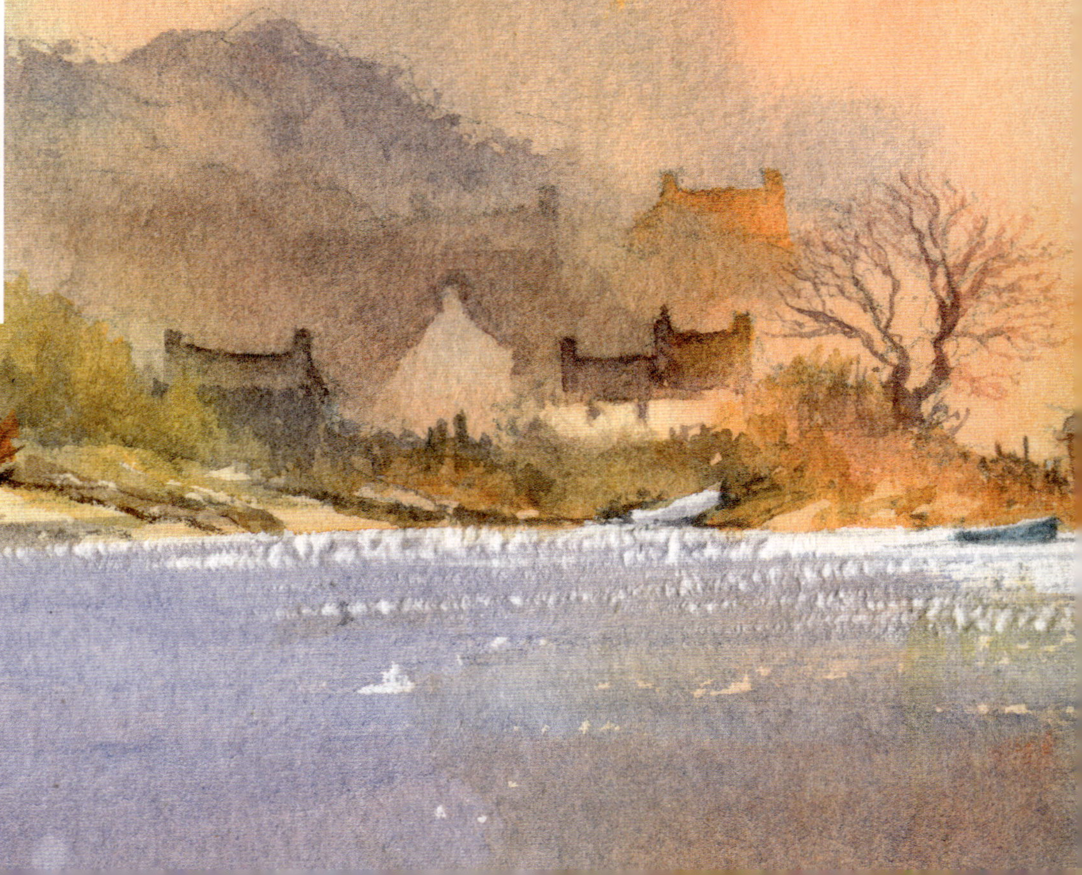

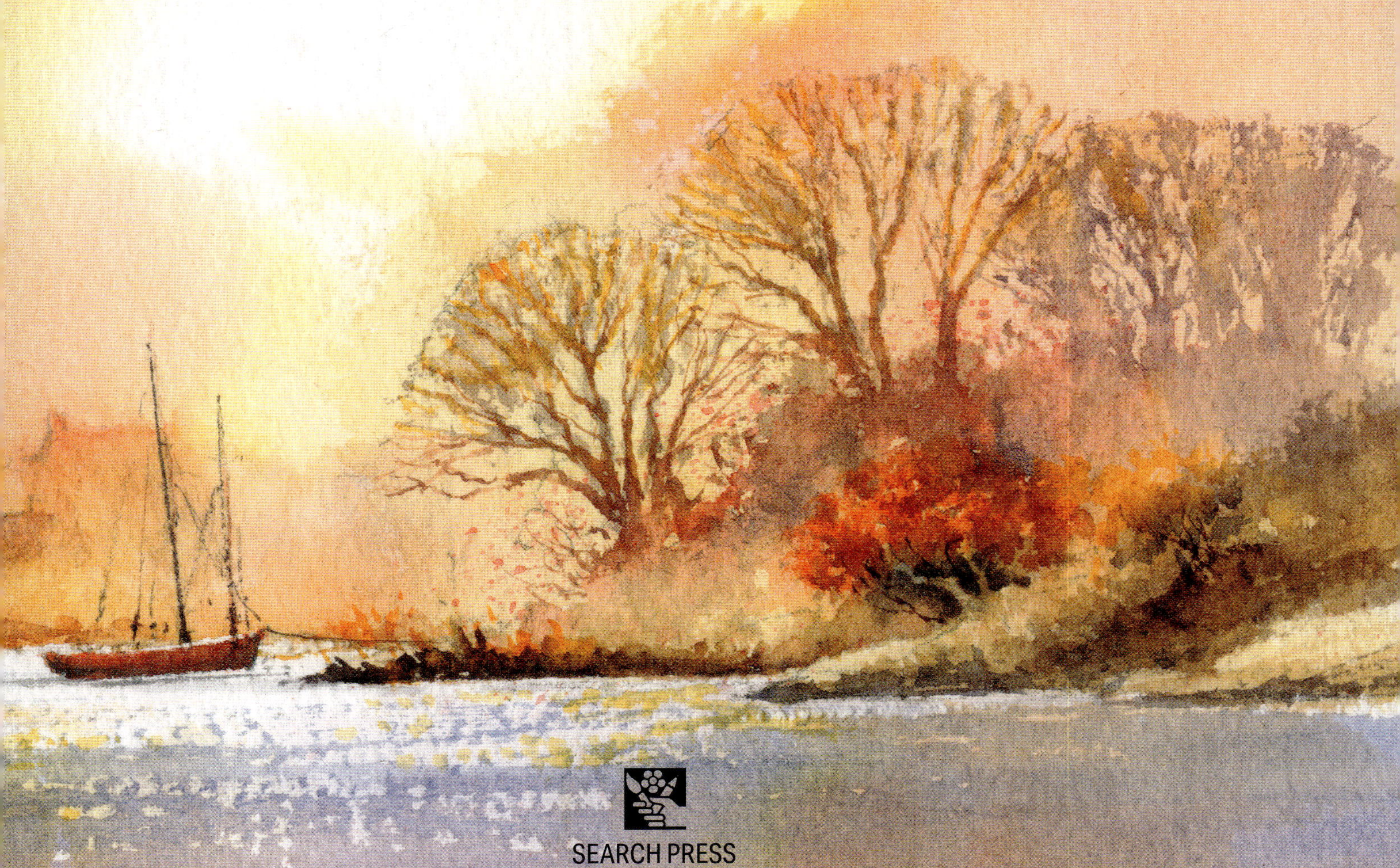

Watercolour
AND BEYOND

Exploring the frontiers of landscape painting

DAVID BELLAMY

SEARCH PRESS

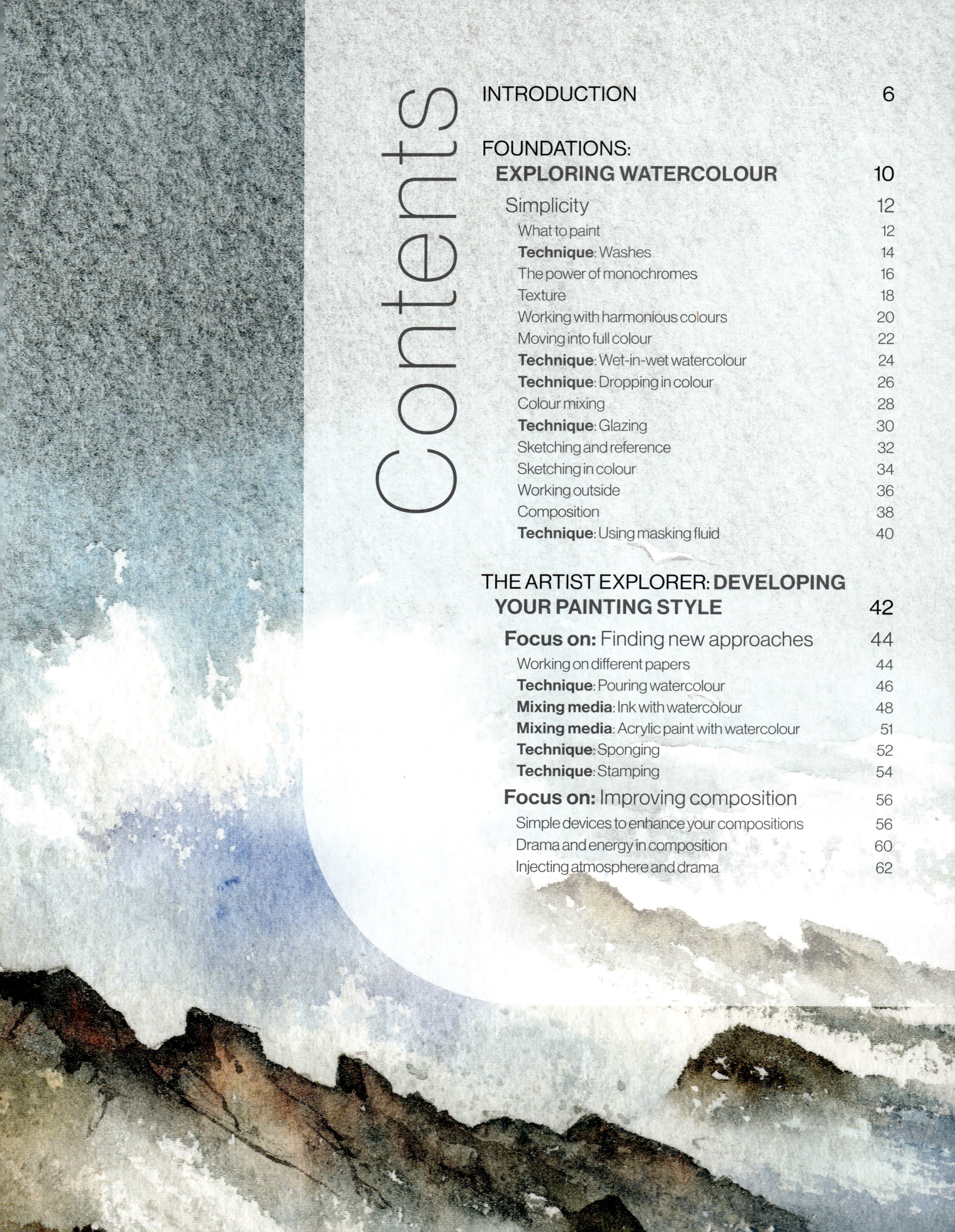

Contents

David Bellamy

Introduction

For some time now traditional watercolour painting has been relegated to 'lesser medium' status by many galleries and artists who see acrylics and oil painting as more exciting. Yet watercolour has a vibrancy and new opportunities of its own, as well as a host of new colours to excite the artist. While I am mainly a traditional watercolourist, I also experiment a lot; for the medium to flourish it needs to keep abreast of innovations.

In this book I aim to illustrate ways in which to make your watercolours glow with excitement; to offer you new methods of working and new ways of using familiar materials – and at the same time make the whole experience great fun. After considering traditional ways of working with watercolour for landscapes, we will explore more innovative techniques and materials, then go on to look at options for how to combine and use these techniques effectively.

Although this book is aimed mainly at those with a little experience, beginners can get enormous benefit from many of the approaches shown here: concentrating on simple but effective landscape subjects, learning how to correct mistakes, introducing new materials, and much more.

> *While I am mainly a traditional watercolourist, I also experiment a lot; for the medium to flourish it needs to keep abreast of innovations.*

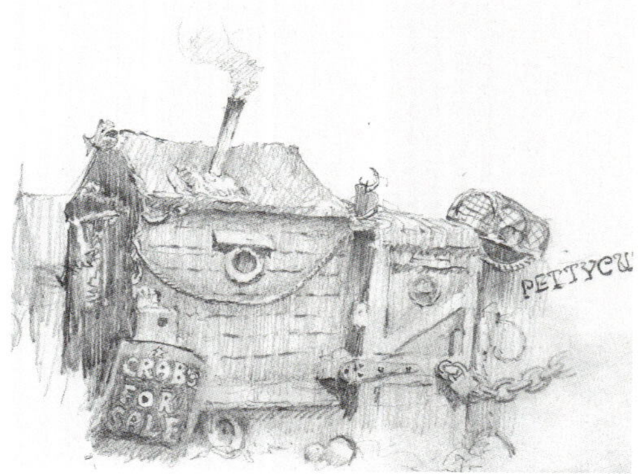

Fisherman's Hut, Pettycur
This gem of a subject on the coast of Fife simply had to be sketched. I only wish that I had had time to render it in colour.

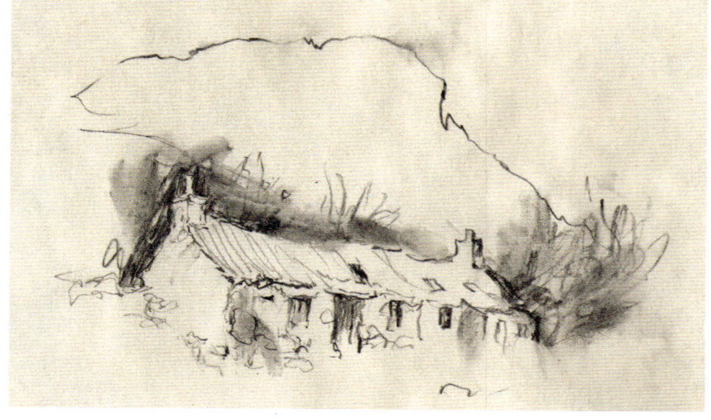

Cottages at Shieldaig, Scottish Highlands
This two-minute sketch was made using a stump of a water-soluble pencil during a slight pause while walking past the subject. A few swipes of my finger helped to create a little tone in places. It's a rough rendition of a charming subject, made when I had little time — yet it is sketches like this that inspire my best paintings. You don't need to draw in vast amounts of detail, and with sketching, speed can often be a distinct advantage. I always carry around a few pencil stumps in my pocket for instant action.

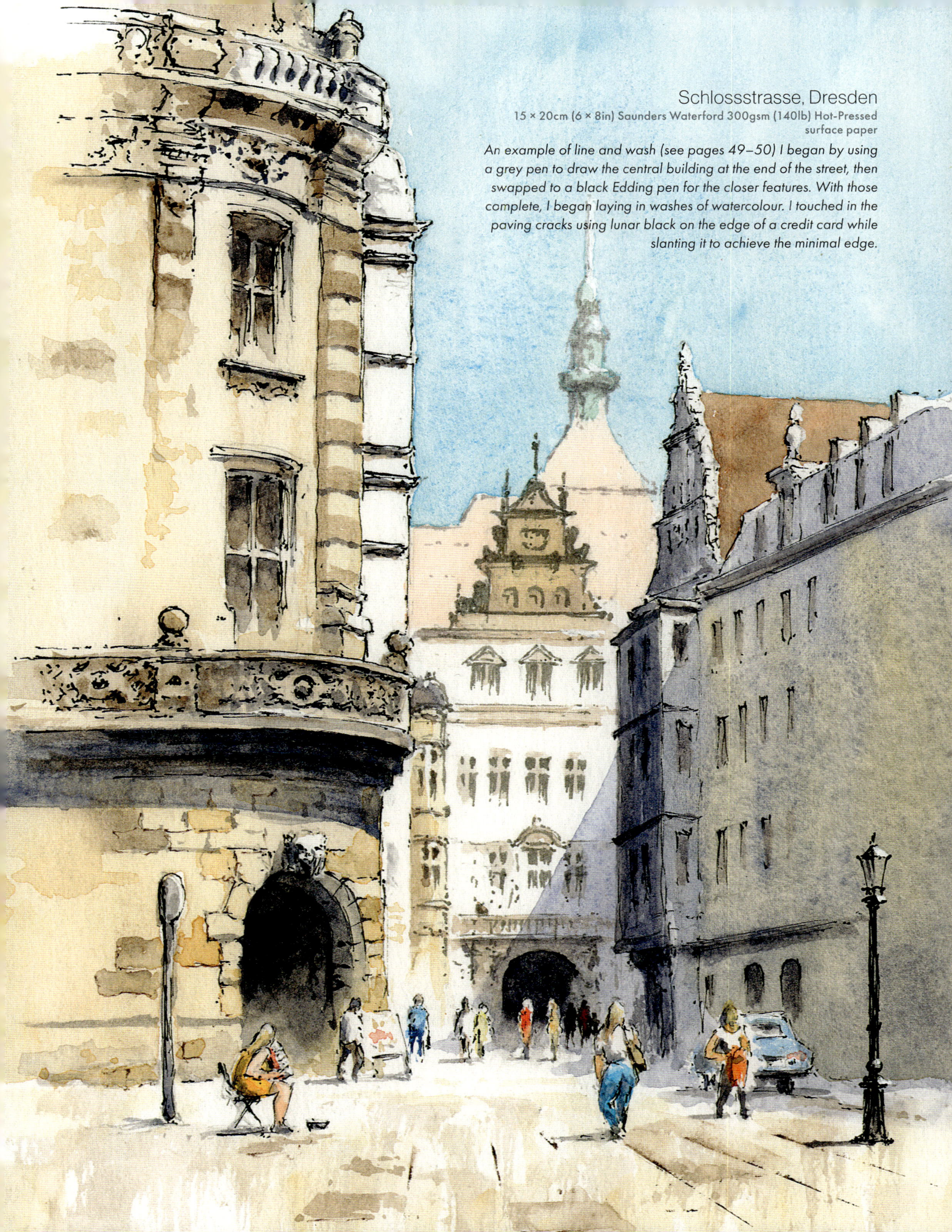

Schlossstrasse, Dresden

15 × 20cm (6 × 8in) Saunders Waterford 300gsm (140lb) Hot-Pressed
surface paper

*An example of line and wash (see pages 49–50) I began by using
a grey pen to draw the central building at the end of the street, then
swapped to a black Edding pen for the closer features. With those
complete, I began laying in washes of watercolour. I touched in the
paving cracks using lunar black on the edge of a credit card while
slanting it to achieve the minimal edge.*

Variety will help you to loosen up and to get out of that artistic rut
that seems to affect us at times. You are encouraged not to paint a
landscape exactly as it stands before you, but to create an illusion
of the scene.

Many artists are put off watercolour painting because they
find it difficult to master the techniques involved, or perhaps
want instant success. This difficulty is usually because they take
on subjects that are too challenging for their level of experience
and they have not been shown how to develop their expertise
gradually. It is for this reason that the stages shown with some
of the paintings are included: they illustrate critical points in the
process where essential aspects might otherwise be overlooked.

Slavish adherence to the colours present in a scene is
discouraged, so while colour is a personal choice, I have
included some suggestions and attractive combinations of
colours for you to try. Likewise, injecting light into a scene is
vital, especially so when we are confronted by a dull day, and
there are examples of how to improve this from photographs of
gloom-ridden landscapes.

For those of you who are fed up with stacking and storing
finished paintings with nowhere to hang them, at the end of the
book I have included some suggestions for other forms of painting
besides pieces intended to hang on the wall – which will also help
you expand your painting creativity into new areas.

Throughout the book I have endeavoured to introduce a sense
of fun into the learning process, as I strongly feel that art is to be
enjoyed, whether you are creating it or simply studying the work
of other artists. Painting is a powerful antidote to depression and
illness, and can take us away into far-off lands, often at times
when we need a distraction. Like nature, art has a therapeutic
effect on our well-being and stress levels. It has been a great
solace to me that I can paint scenes from my past travels – to
visit my studio and be suddenly transported to somewhere like
the Andes in South America by painting from those sketches and
photographs – sheer gold. Hopefully the joy you share through
these pages will enable you to create new ideas and ways
of working.

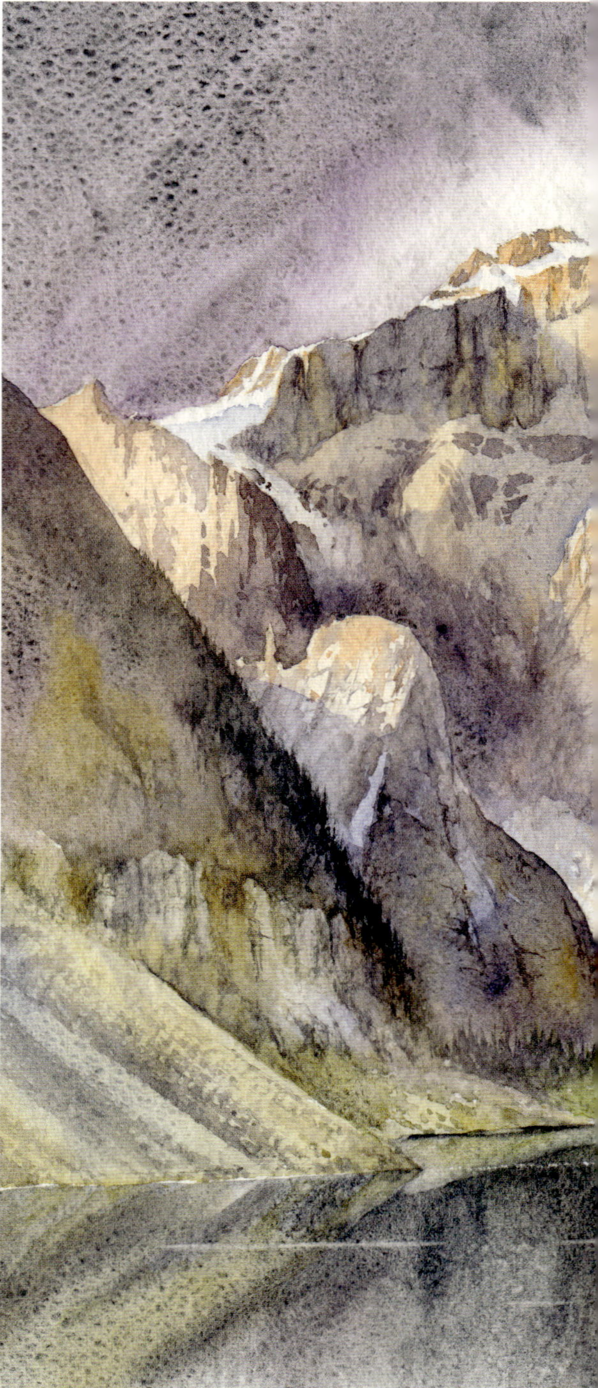

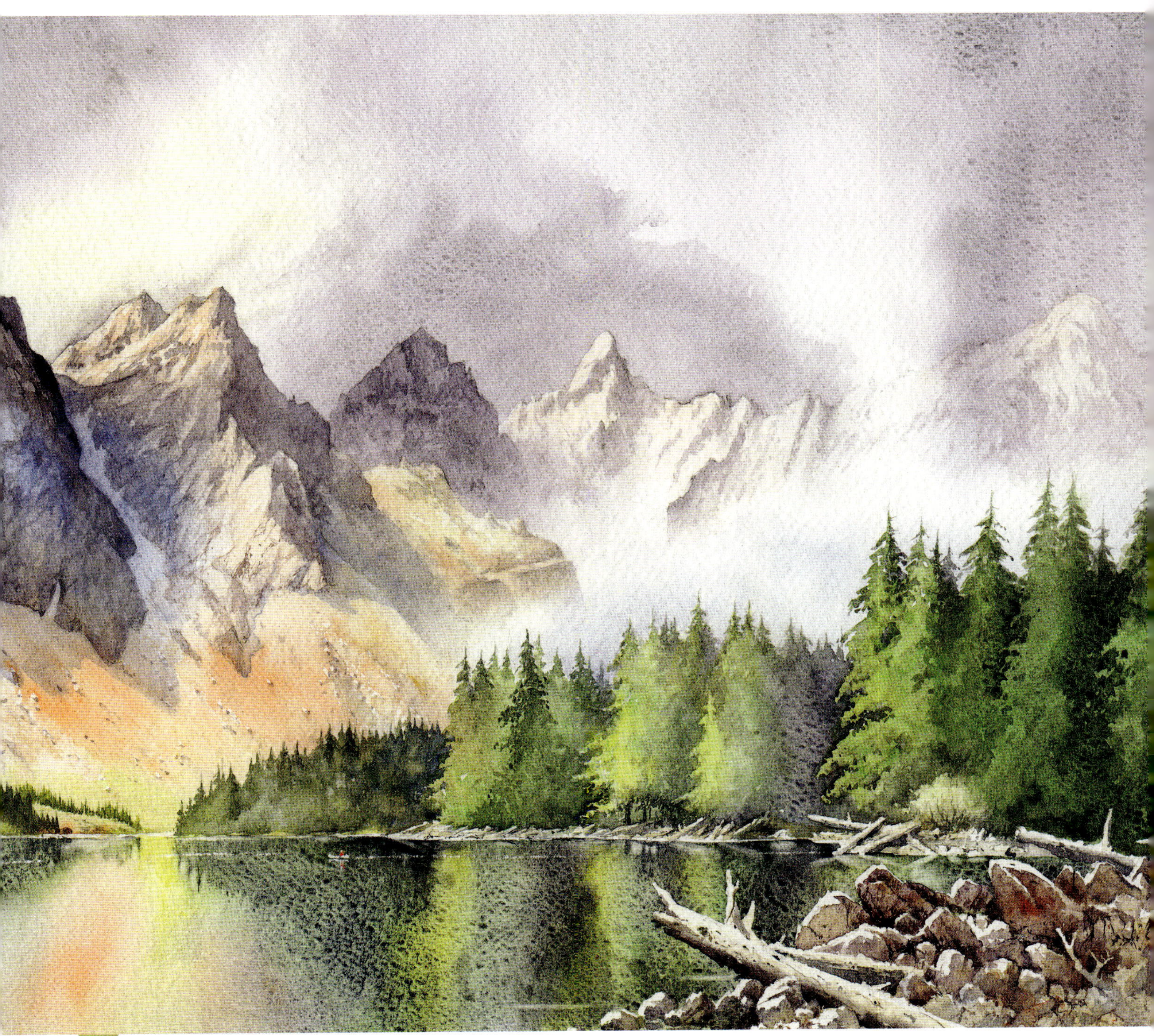

Moraine Lake, Canadian Rockies

51 × 30.5cm (20 × 12in) Fabriano 300gsm (140lb) Rough surface paper

Detail on the striking cirque (a bowl-shaped valley carved by glaciers) fades as the peaks recede into the right-hand distance. This is in stark contrast to the powerful textural granulations in the foreground, which were produced by laying green apatite genuine onto a very rough paper surface.

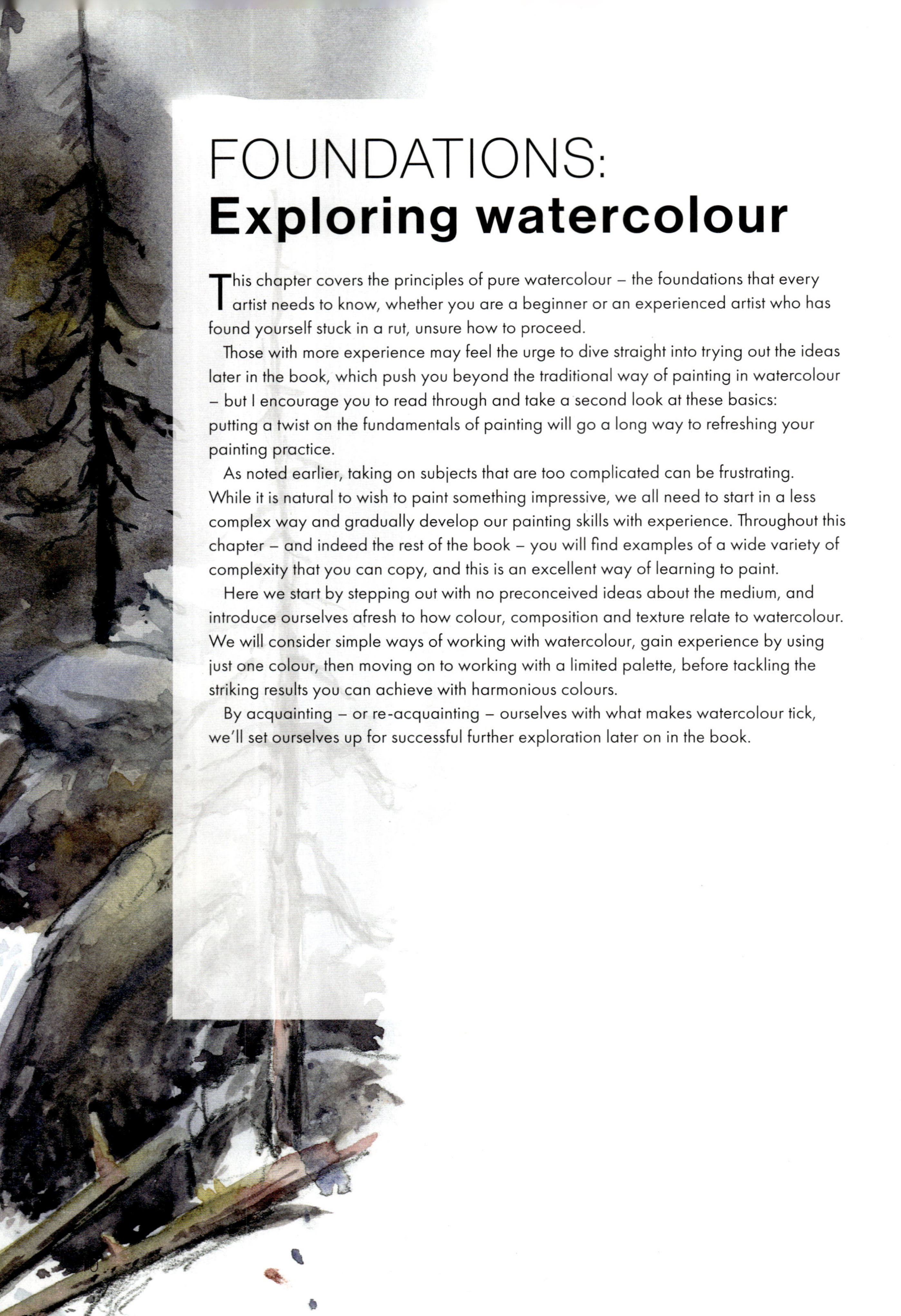

FOUNDATIONS:
Exploring watercolour

This chapter covers the principles of pure watercolour – the foundations that every artist needs to know, whether you are a beginner or an experienced artist who has found yourself stuck in a rut, unsure how to proceed.

Those with more experience may feel the urge to dive straight into trying out the ideas later in the book, which push you beyond the traditional way of painting in watercolour – but I encourage you to read through and take a second look at these basics: putting a twist on the fundamentals of painting will go a long way to refreshing your painting practice.

As noted earlier, taking on subjects that are too complicated can be frustrating. While it is natural to wish to paint something impressive, we all need to start in a less complex way and gradually develop our painting skills with experience. Throughout this chapter – and indeed the rest of the book – you will find examples of a wide variety of complexity that you can copy, and this is an excellent way of learning to paint.

Here we start by stepping out with no preconceived ideas about the medium, and introduce ourselves afresh to how colour, composition and texture relate to watercolour. We will consider simple ways of working with watercolour, gain experience by using just one colour, then moving on to working with a limited palette, before tackling the striking results you can achieve with harmonious colours.

By acquainting – or re-acquainting – ourselves with what makes watercolour tick, we'll set ourselves up for successful further exploration later on in the book.

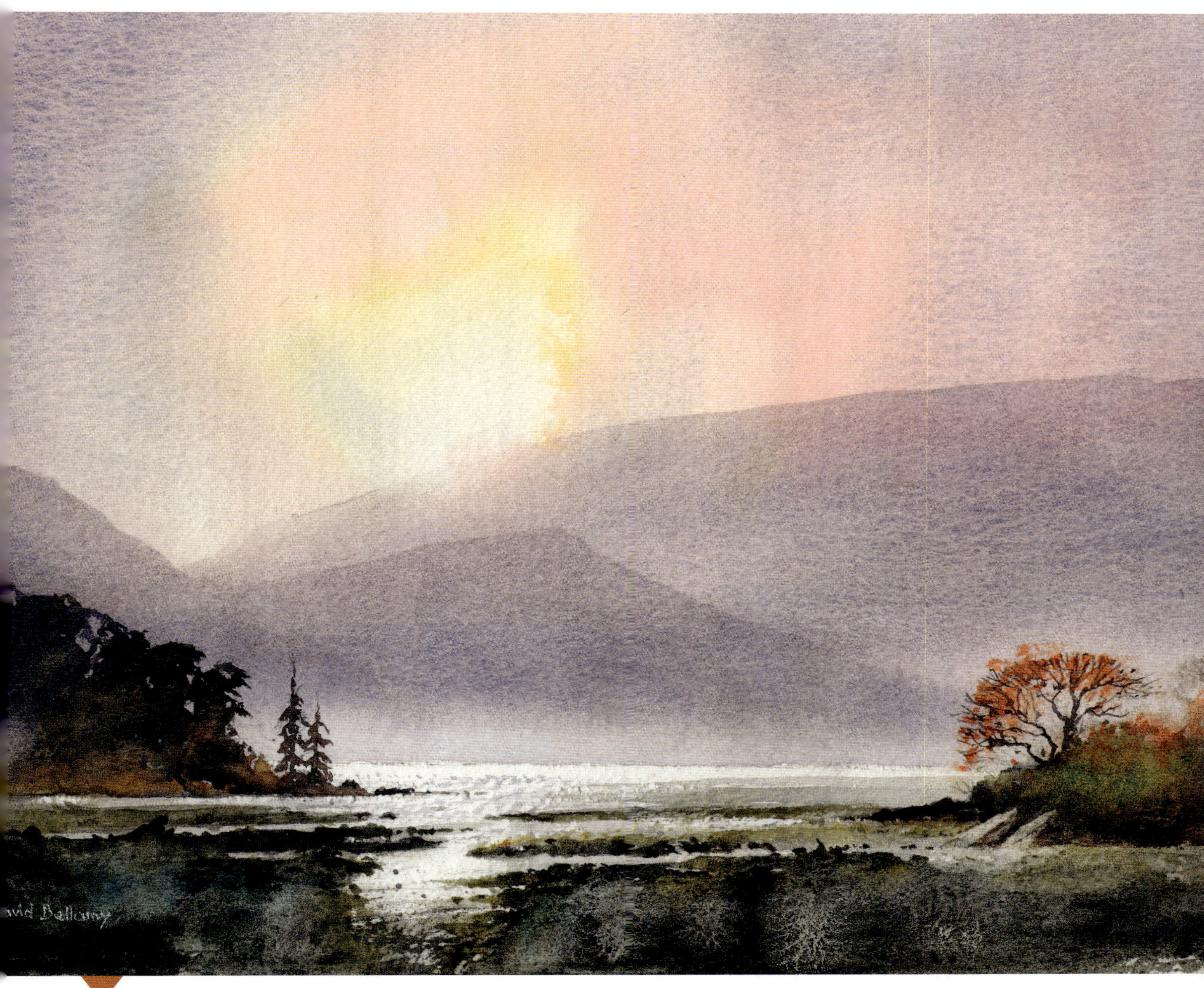

Midim Khola River, Nepal

30.5 × 20cm (12 × 8in) Saunders Waterford 300gsm (140lb) Rough surface paper

A few trees, strong light and sparkling water is all you need for a beautiful subject, and although I could see vague detail on the far mountains, I used only slight changes in tone to hint at them.

The sparkling water was achieved by horizontally dry-brushing French ultramarine with a touch of burnt umber in a narrow band just below the far shoreline. The rough paper helps with this and it works best if you have little water on the brush. Test it on the side of the paper first. I also dabbed a few spots of the same mixture across and just above the rocks beside the trees. I resisted the temptation to add more detail. Using a limited palette in this way is a good step up from the monochrome (see pages 16–17).

Simplicity

Even the simplest landscape is complicated – and frighteningly so to the inexperienced.
As with all our paintings, we need to modify what we see before us in order to create a
decent finished result. With that in mind, let's have a go at some simple subjects, fundamental
techniques and key concepts that will give us foundations to build upon.

What to paint

The first question, of course, is simply 'what should I paint?' There are a great many beautiful
landscapes out there, but some can lack a centre of interest, which will make painting the scene
more of a challenge. We will look at adapting our compositions later on; but for the moment,
start with a clear, simple subject that appeals just as it is.

Preparing paint

*In general, you should prepare each colour or mix of colours
freshly, just before you begin a particular area of your work.*

*Put out as much paint as you think you might need. For a
typical wash, squeeze 15mm (½in) or so of paint into your
palette, then use your mixing brush (an old painting brush is
fine) to lift over clean water from your water pot and gently mix
to combine the water and paint.*

*How much you dilute it will depend on the task at hand. For
most purposes you want a pool of very fluid paint, with plenty
of water. Watercolour paint goes a long way, so you can add
a lot of water to surprisingly little paint.*

Starting points for picking a scene to paint

- Choose a subject with a definite and prominent
  centre of interest, such as a building, bridge,
  shapely crag or mountain.

- When you look at a landscape subject, observe
  it through half-closed eyes. This eliminates
  much unnecessary detail, and helps you to see
  the most important tones more clearly. In turn,
  this will let you assess whether the scene is
  likely to be a good subject.

- Bodies of water can be difficult unless kept
  as a simple flat wash, and while mature trees
  make excellent centres of interest, they
  can be complex to render in watercolour.
  These subjects are best left until you are
  more confident.

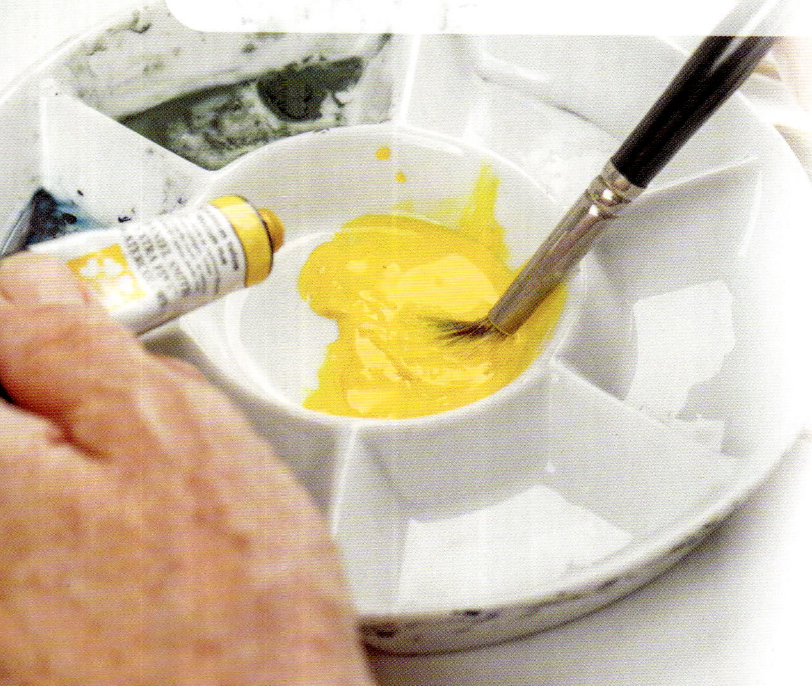

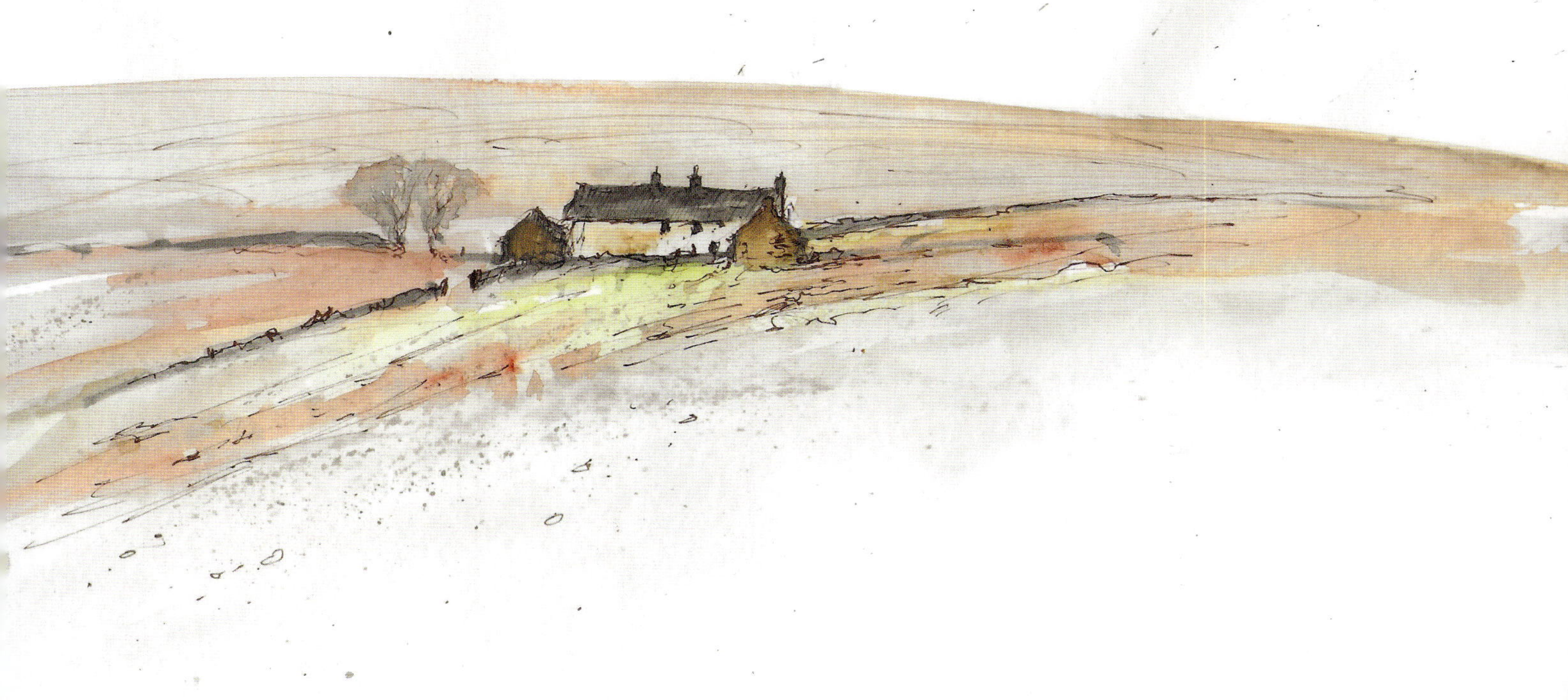

Painting *Houses on Carleton Moor*

This simple subject, carried out on site as a watercolour sketch, is ideal for beginners to landscape painting as it illustrates buildings that form a strongly defined, yet uncomplicated centre of interest.

- I began with a drawing using a fine pen. Note that the sky area has been left completely untouched – choosing what not to paint is an important lesson for success in watercolour.
- Loose washes (see overleaf) of cadmium yellow pale, followed by a mixture of yellow ochre and weak light red were used to cover the ground area. You can see where variation in the ground cover has been achieved by laying on a slightly stronger application of the main wash to the left of the buildings.
- The watercolour washes were applied horizontally across the paper, with plenty of water on the brush to make them weak. Laying a weak wash of colour, such as yellow ochre (or perhaps light red, well watered-down to be almost pink), and letting it dry before working over it with a stronger colour (such as raw umber) to cover only parts is an easy way to give your ground interesting variation.
- Some light grey spatter (see right) was applied to the foreground to hint at detail without being unnecessarily complicated.

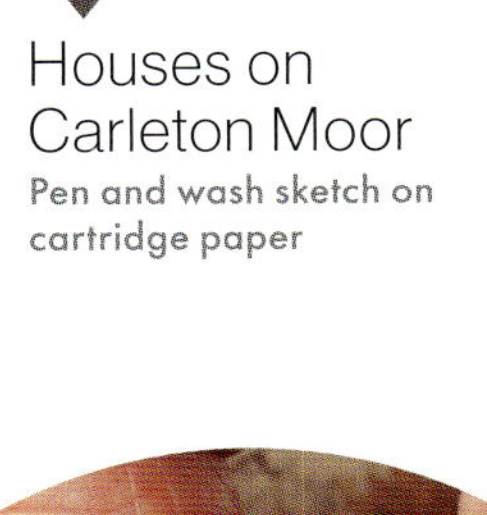

Spattering
This is a speckled effect created by drawing a finger over a loaded brush to flick paint onto the surface.

Washes

The ability to handle your washes with dexterity is crucial to good watercolour technique. The traditional way of laying a wash is to apply it in horizontal bands with a large brush while keeping it fluid down the paper, and ensuring the paper is at an angle to achieve this flow.

However, you can also work your washes vertically or diagonally in order to achieve a more dynamic result, especially where your washes vary in tone and graduation. If you find it easier you can tilt the paper to one side while laying such a wash.

Examples of vertical washes can be seen in *Woodland Cascade* on page 45 and *Dollar Cove, Cornwall,* on page 77; while *Sunshine & Mist on the Wye* on page 95 demonstrates the strengths of diagonal washes well.

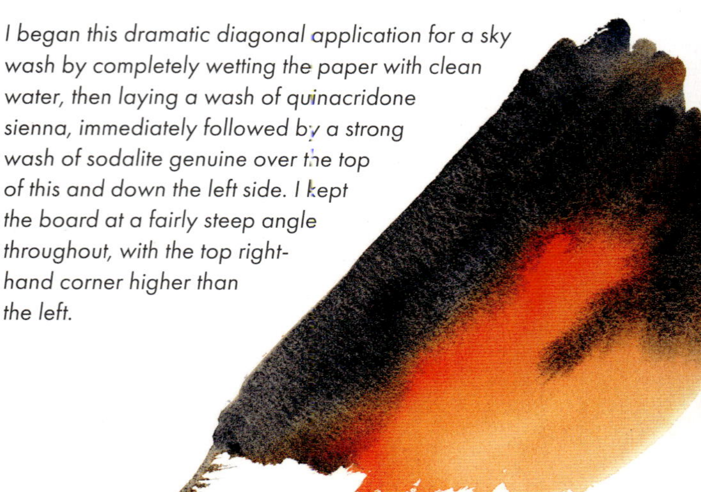

I began this dramatic diagonal application for a sky wash by completely wetting the paper with clean water, then laying a wash of quinacridone sienna, immediately followed by a strong wash of sodalite genuine over the top of this and down the left side. I kept the board at a fairly steep angle throughout, with the top right-hand corner higher than the left.

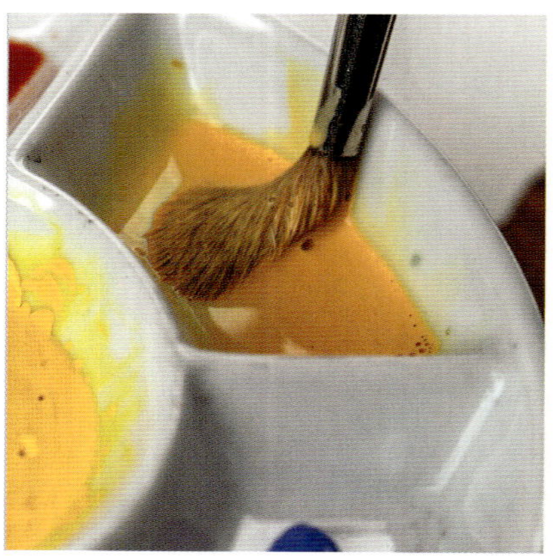

Plenty of water The paints should be prepared to be very fluid, with lots of water. Make sure you make enough of each colour – running out halfway through is frustrating.

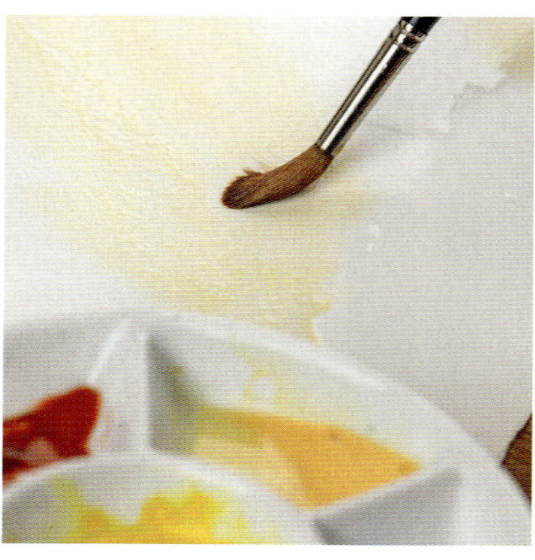

Wet paper Washes flow more easily if you lay a wash of pure, clean water across the paper beforehand. Using a large brush, apply the paint into the wet surface, starting from one edge of the area you want to cover.

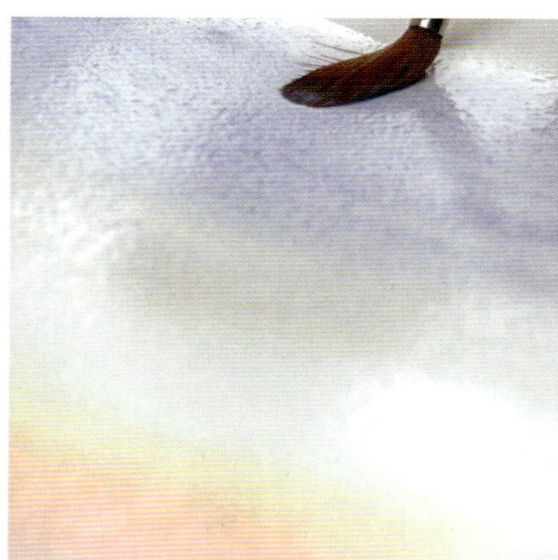

Work into the wet area Continue working across the area while the paint remains wet. Work as quickly as possible – this keeps things spontaneous and will give a smooth result.

The keys to success with washes

- Laying a wash of clean water across the paper first is especially advisable when using Hot-Pressed (smooth) paper as it dries so much more quickly.
- Use as large a mop brush as you can confidently handle.
- Test your mix on scrap paper to check both that the colour is the right strength of tone, and that the wash is fairly fluid.

- Prepare the paint mixture in a palette well and ensure there is sufficient to cover the area to be painted. It is better to mix too much than too little.
- With a vari-coloured wash, make sure that the second colour is also mixed and ready for application before applying any paint to the paper.

Incorporating watercolour pencils into washes

Drawing into a wet watercolour wash with sharp-pointed watercolour
pencils (see right) is a fascinating way of creating images. It can also be
used to rescue a painting that has not quite worked. Take a few of these
pencils out sketching with you.

  I suggest you take an old piece of cartridge paper, or perhaps the back
of another piece of work (not your best!) and test out a few washes on it.
Draw into it with a dark watercolour pencil without being too particular,
and see how you get on.

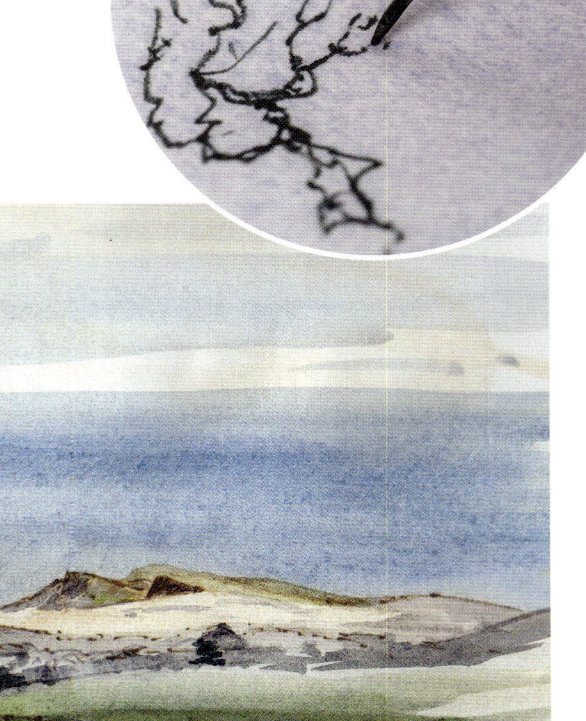

Dryslwyn Castle
Sketch on cartridge paper

*This is a watercolour sketch with details outlined with dark watercolour pencils used
for drawing rather than for their colour, to enable an extremely rapid sketch. This
shows the scene with the River Towy in flood and the Carmarthen Fans caught in
distant sunlight.*

*I've done some of my best work on scrap paper, simply because I am less inhibited.
You will probably notice an improvement simply because you are more confident with
no concern about wasting good paper, or having to get everything perfect. Repeat
this and simply enjoy the freedom this approach gives you.*

*See more on
watercolour pencils
on pages 96–97.*

The power of monochromes

You will probably be eager to work with a full colour palette, but I highly recommended that you carry out a number of monochromes first. Working in just one colour will ensure a marvellous sense of unity in your painting, and help you to get to grips w th the intricacies of watercolour painting. It frees you from having to choose your colours, and allows you to think of each part of the composition in simple terms of how light or dark they are.

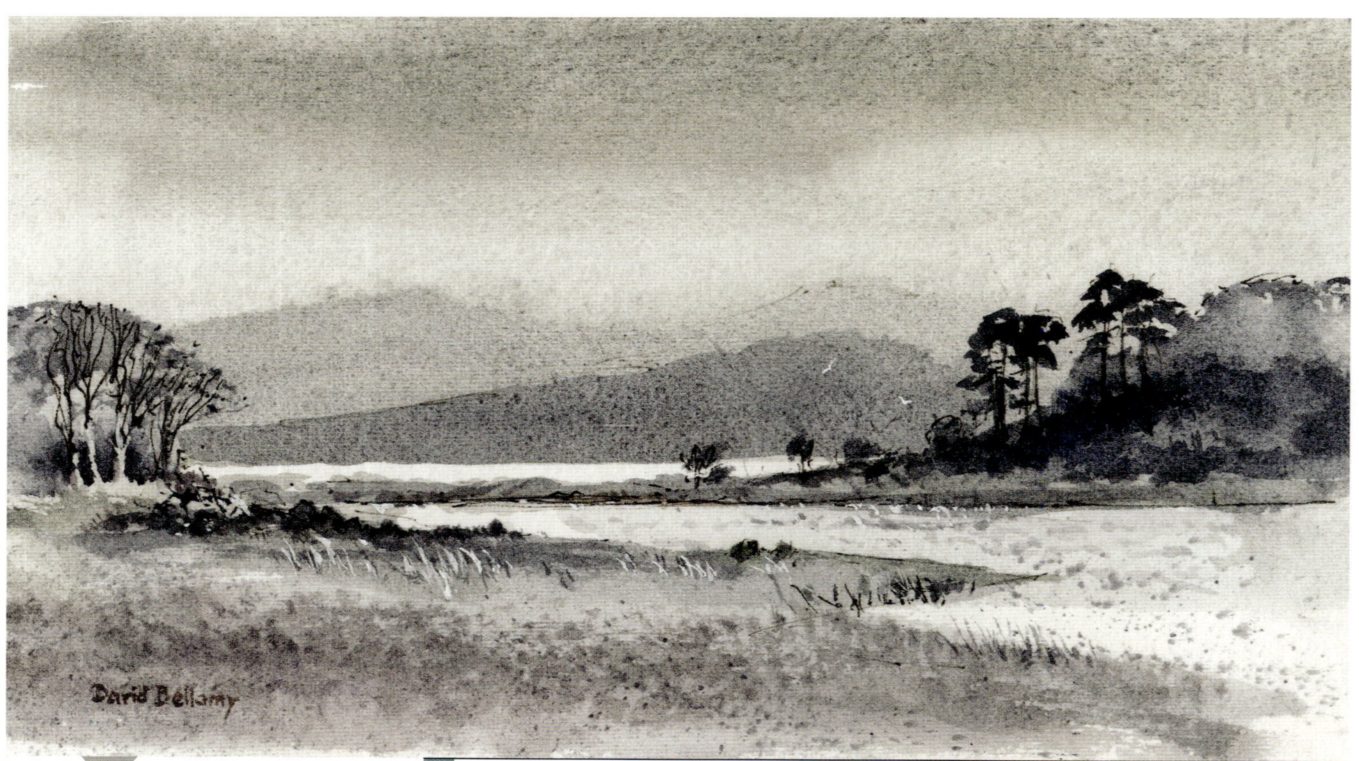

Kent Estuary, Cumbria

18 × 12.5cm (7 × 5in) Saunders Waterford 300gsm (140lb) Hot-Pressed surface paper

This has been painted on Hot-Pressed paper, the smoothest of the watercolour papers. While excellent for detail, paint dries quickly upon it – bear this in mind if you decide to try it out.

Painting *Kent Estuary, Cumbria*

Painted entirely with indigo, this scene shows how effective using just one colour can be. Painting in watercolour, without the need to concern yourself with the problems of choosing and mixing colour, is very enjoyable.

- Note the importance of tonal values in the sketch: the water is mainly the white paper, while the lower sky is extremely light with just a hint of the weakest tone of indigo.
- The distant hills were introduced while the sky was still damp, but the lower hill with stronger tone was added when the paper had completely dried.
- The Caledonian pines were rendered in just about the strongest tone you can achieve with indigo. This strong value brings them forward, creating a sense of quite some distance in front of the hills. It also ensures that they become the focal point.
- Try painting a monochrome similar to this with burnt umber (as shown opposite) or burnt sienna instead of indigo – any of these three paints will give you access to a wide range of tones.

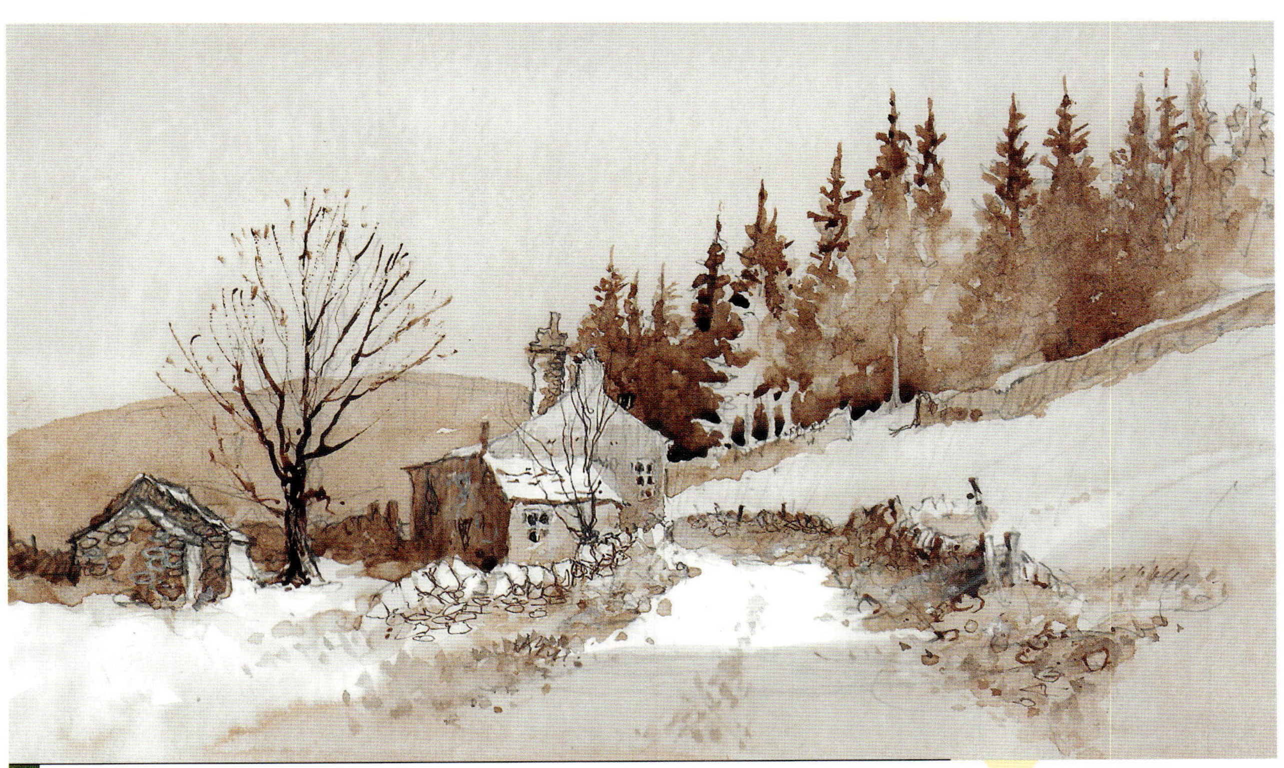

Painting *Yorkshire Lane*

Made in a cartridge paper sketchbook, this landscape was achieved with just burnt umber, and you can see the rich variety of tonal values that can be obtained from this colour.

- The outbuilding roof, the left-hand capstones on the wall and the further part of the lane are the white of the untouched paper, while the sky and fields are very weak burnt umber.
- Strength of tone can be altered simply by diluting your paints – the more water, the paler the result. Once dry, tone can be strengthened by laying down further washes over the top.
- Try a number of sketches and/or paintings in this way and your watercolour painting will improve considerably. Critically, this will improve your understanding of tonal values immensely.

Yorkshire Lane
30 × 21cm (11¾ × 8¼in) sketch
on cartridge paper

Texture

Textures can come in visual form, where we create an illusion by adopting certain techniques, or in physical form where we introduce additives and various materials to create an almost 3D effect. Here I want simply to introduce the concept and look at how the emphasis on granulations can make life a little easier for the watercolourist.

The visual texture created by granulating colour can be used to suggest the roughness of tree bark or rock structures, for example, or simply to suggest a hint of detail in a feature, and this latter use can be a powerful aid to simplification.

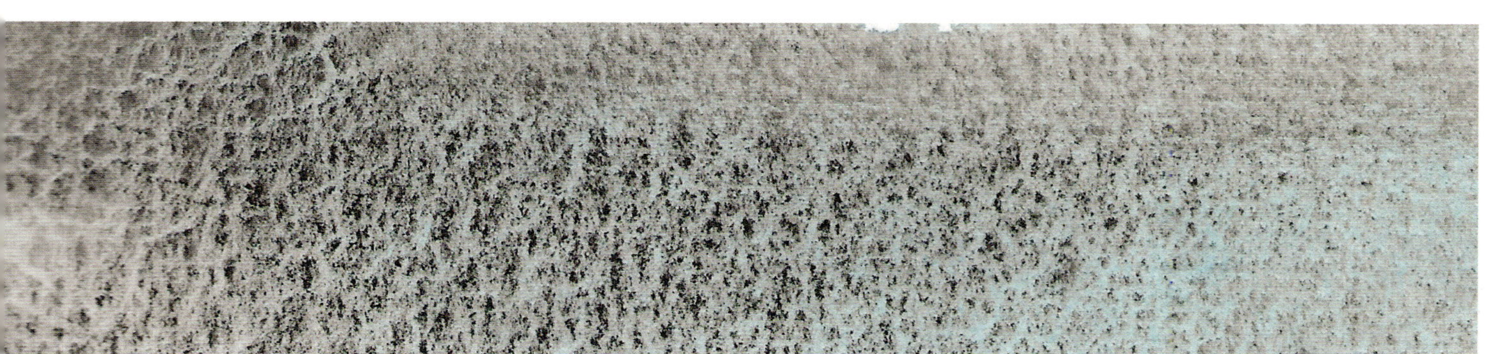

Granulation and suggested detail

Many colours on the market incorporate highly granulating pigments, which create an attractively speckled, gritty appearance as the particles of pigment sink and gather into the recesses of the paper texture.

Granulations can enhance a painting, provide texture without any effort on the part of the artist, and – as in the case of *Marloes Beach*, opposite – they can substitute for detail.

Examples of
extreme granulations
Lunar blue was used in both these examples, with some lunar black added to the lower example. Both colours granulate strongly, which is why I enjoy using these Daniel Smith watercolours.

There is more about visual texture on pages 94–107, and we look at physical texture on pages 108–123.

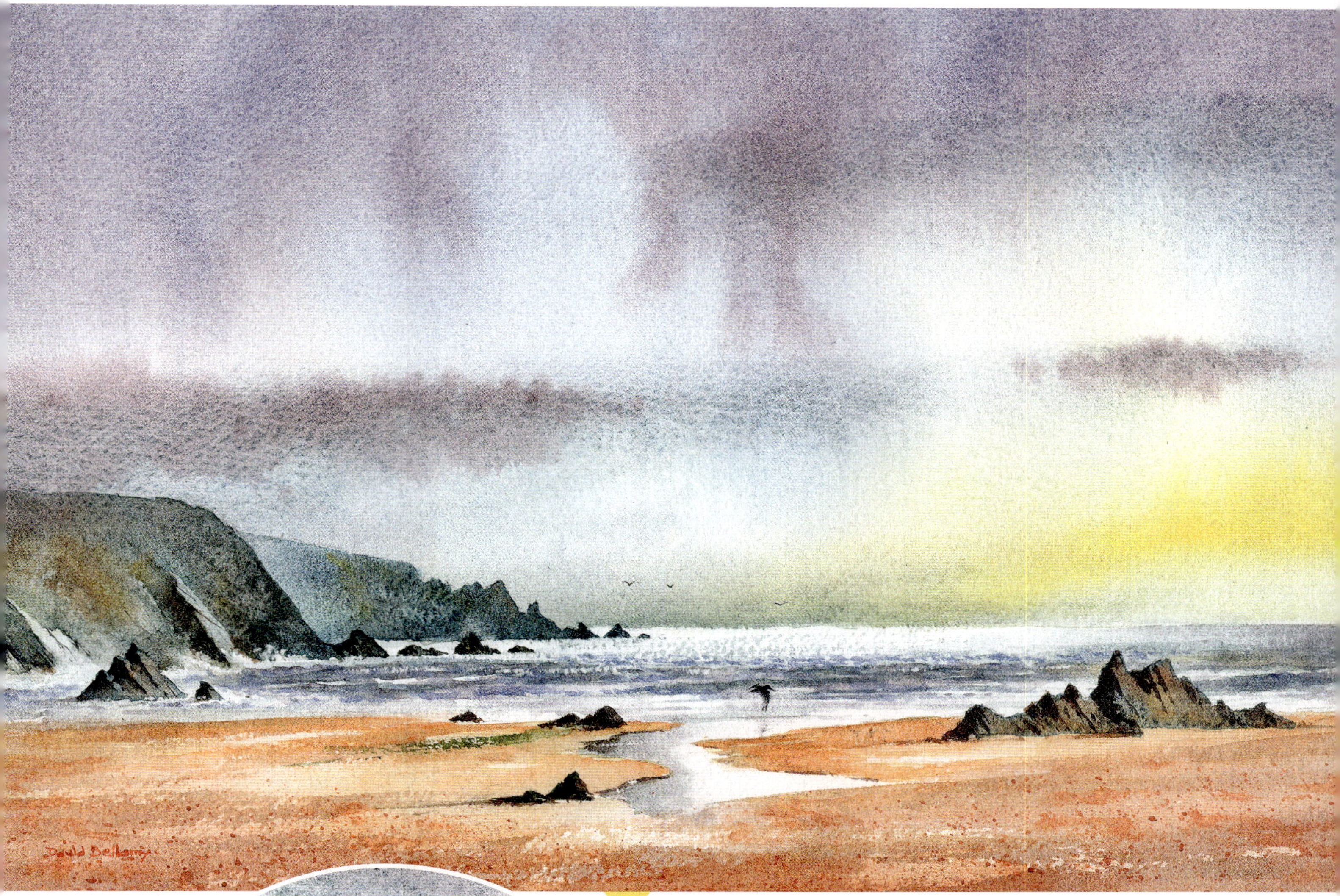

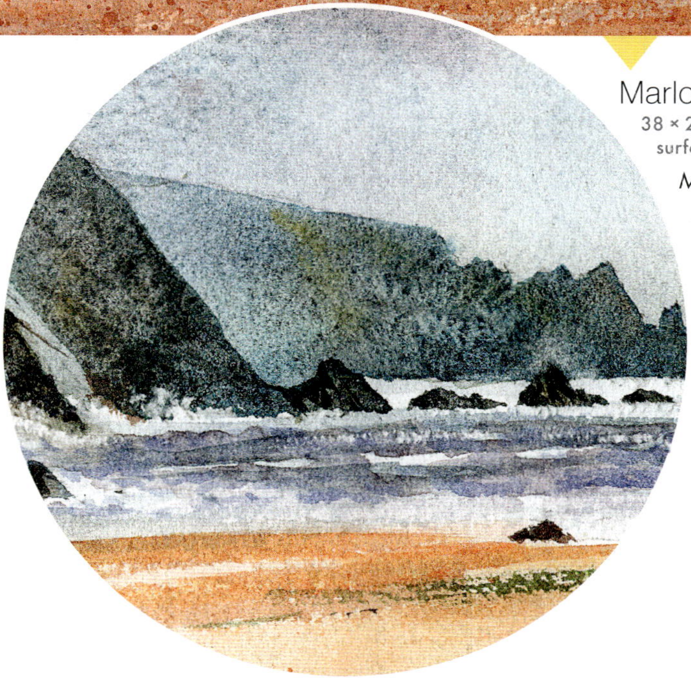

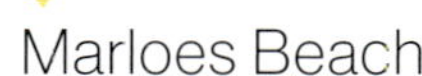

Marloes Beach

38 × 23cm (15 × 9in) Saunders Waterford 425gsm (200lb) Rough surface paper

Much of the colour was lost in the back-lighting, but this imparted a more dramatic mood. I kept the sea simple – you don't have to paint in great crashing waves, especially if you find them difficult to render.

For the cliffs I used lunar blue. This is a fabulous colour, though unpredictable at times. I love it for its often irregular granulations (see detail, left) which in this case have provided some good texture, thus creating interest without me having to add detail.

Working with harmonious colours

From monochromes, it is just a short step to introducing one or two more colours. Keeping the number of colours limited and in harmony will help to retain this unity and build your skills.

Harmonious colours are those that are found close together in the same quadrant of the colour wheel. For example, if you have been painting solely with burnt umber, then add colours like yellow ochre, raw sienna, light red, cadmium orange, quinacridone gold, or any colour that has a tendency towards warm earth colours. Likewise, if you choose to use indigo, for example, you can add cool colours such as French ultramarine, cobalt blue, phthalo blue, or perhaps a green.

In the example on this page, I have added a small amount of French ultramarine, which is not in harmony with the other colours I have used, but is included solely to darken the tones in places. Its use in this way has not detracted from the sense of colour harmony.

Naples yellow

Burnt umber

Cadmium red

French ultramarine

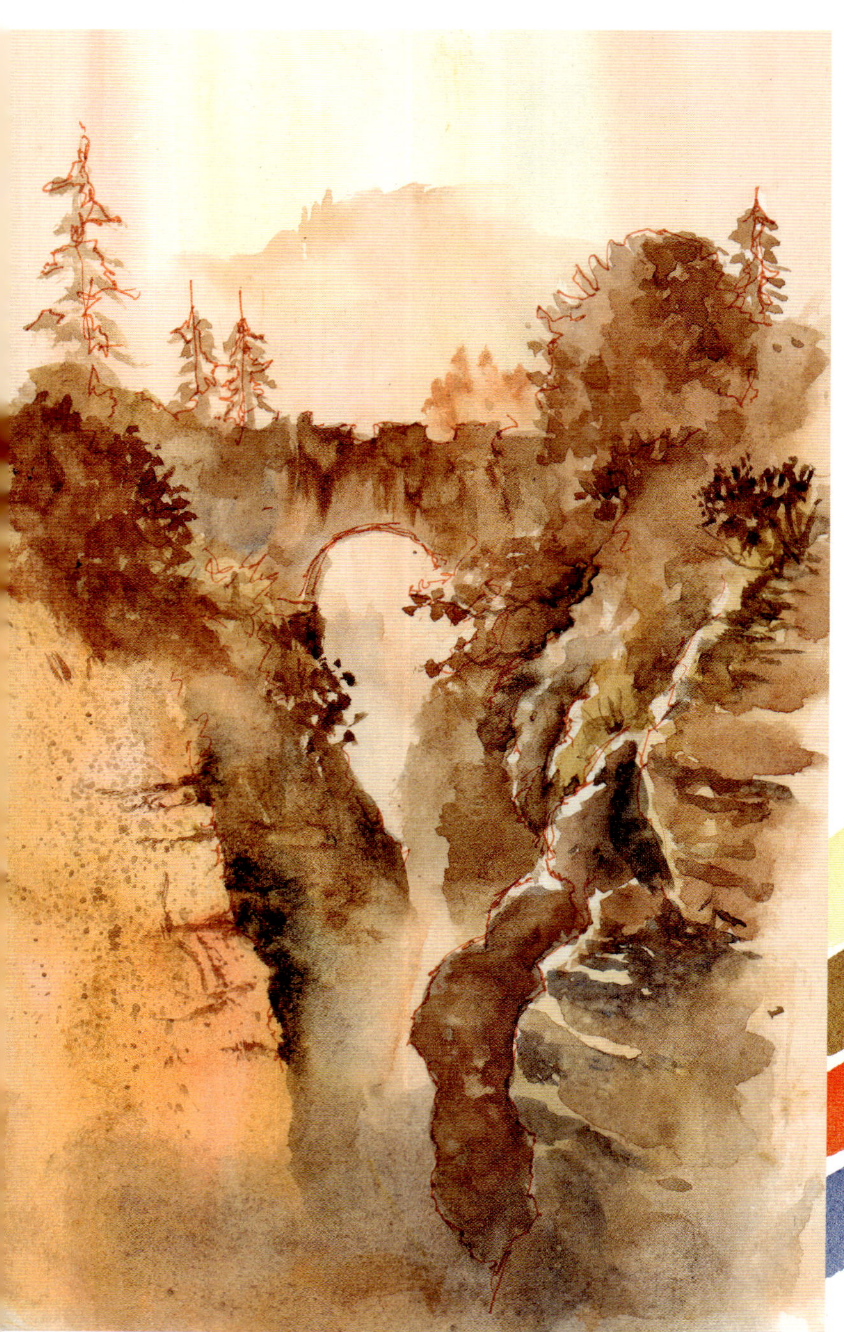

Puente Viejo, Ronda
A4 (21 × 30cm/8¼ × 11¾in) cartridge sketchbook

I began by drawing the outline in sepia ink, then washed Naples yellow into the sky. Most of the rest of the sketch is painted with burnt umber with a few touches of French ultramarine mixed in for the darker shadows, and some cadmium red added to the burnt umber on the left-hand cliff. The chasm drops down a long way, creating a dramatic setting for this lovely old bridge.

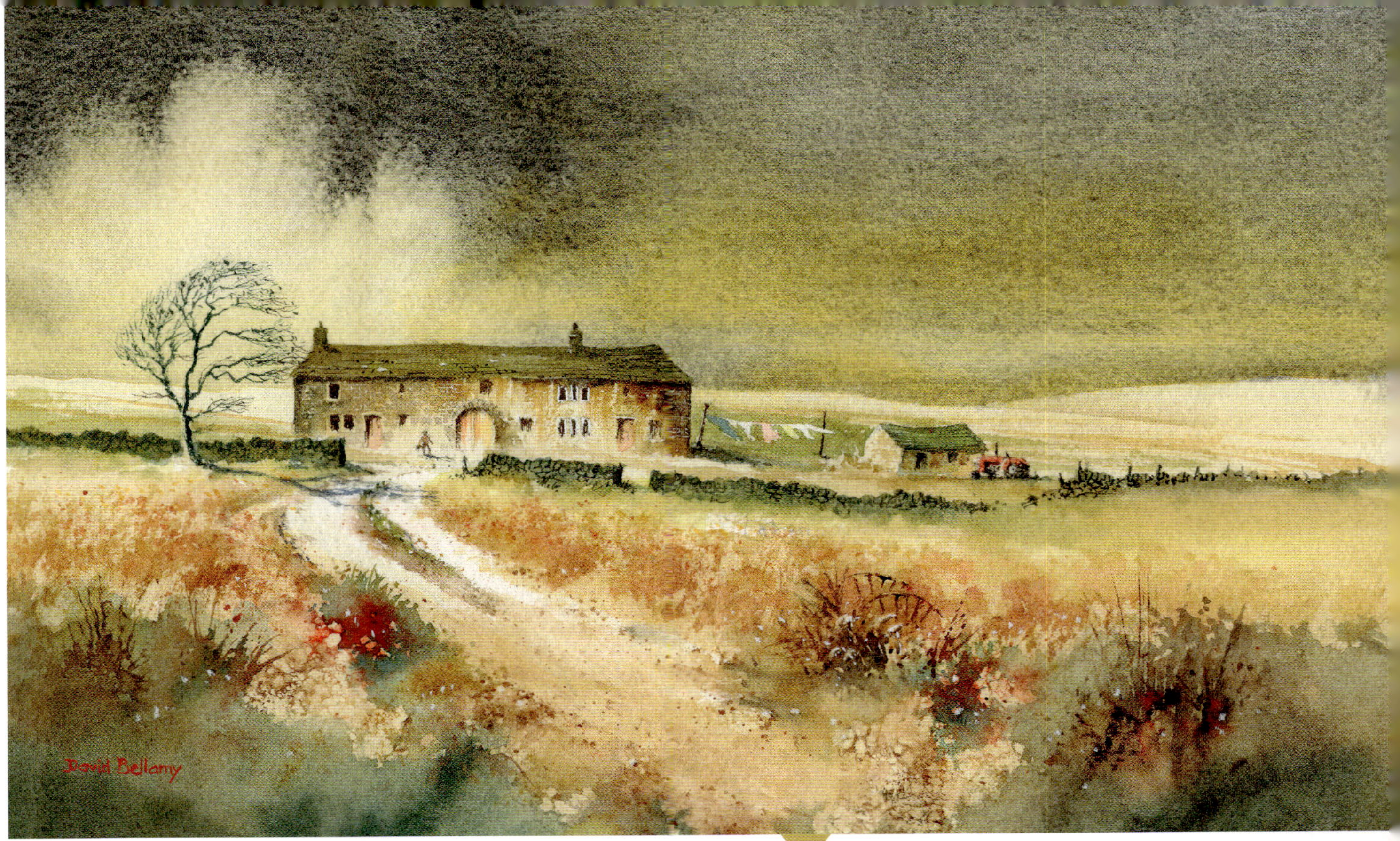

Harmony for effect

In the main I have painted *Windy Day in the Pennines* dominated by warm, harmonious colours in an attempt to create a pleasant aspect to counter the bleak, wind-ravaged situation. I have used lunar black in the sky and French ultramarine in the darker mixes of the buildings, drystone wall, tree and foreground vegetation to create greater strength, but this does not detract from the overall harmonious effect. Often, small introductions of a non-harmonious colour can provide an excellent accent to a focal point.

For *Farm in the Crags*, I employed harmonious colours in the cool spectrum; although note that I have mixed cadmium red into French ultramarine for the crags, roofs and bushes. As the red is weak, the coolness dominates. I have painted the foreground with a mixture of French ultramarine, weak burnt sienna and touches of yellow ochre, using downward strokes of a 12mm (½in) flat brush, while suggesting an intermittent lead-in with a path.

Adding an accent in a complementary rather than harmonious colour is the next step towards working in full colour.

Windy Day in the Pennines
30.5 × 20.5cm (12 × 8in) Saunders Waterford 300gsm (140lb) Not surface paper

Note the varying tone on the building and the lack of a strong definition between the bottom of the house and the ground. Too many strong lines tend to detract in a painting.

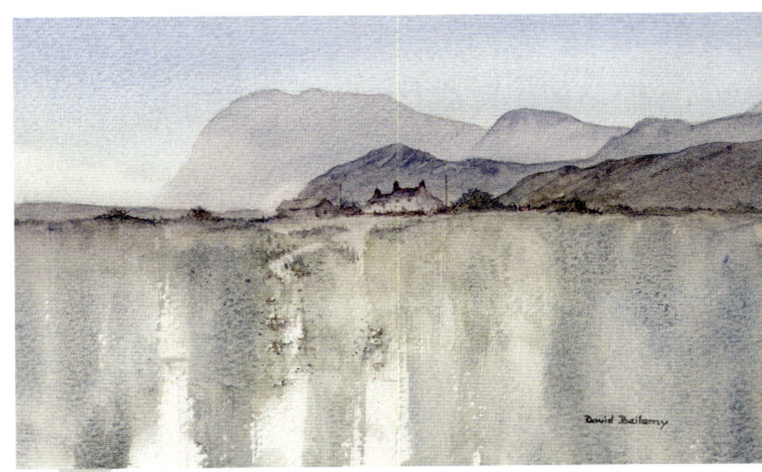

Farm in the Crags
25.5 × 15cm (10 × 6in) Saunders Waterford 300gsm (140lb) Not surface paper

Moving into full colour

We now look at tackling a painting using many colours. Don't try to include every colour you see before you in a scene. I normally use a base colour for many of my colour mixes in a work as this helps retain a feeling of unity. French ultramarine works well for this as it is a good mixer and can produce a wide range of tones; whether mixed with cadmium red for a roof, alizarin crimson for clouds, burnt umber for the really dark shadows, or with a yellow to produce a green.

How do you determine the colour to use in the main passages of the composition? Start by considering how light or dark a tone will make it most appealing; do you want to create a moody, subtle effect, or perhaps prefer a bright, colourful scene? Is the overall scheme to be cool or warm? Are bold and dramatic colours to be the order of the day?

Once you have established these aspects you are in a better position to choose your colours – cool, warm, vibrant or whatever. There is no need to strive hard to replicate the colour in the actual subject, unless you particularly like it – it's far better to stamp your own authority on a painting by deciding which colours you wish to use. You will see how I tackle this by comparing those paintings that are accompanied by photographs of the scene.

Starting points for full colour

- Even in full colour, it is best to keep to a fairly restricted palette to avoid making the scene too garish – unless that is your aim, of course.

- Decide on a mood or theme, and use this to help determine your base colour.

- Lighting and atmosphere can alter local colours drastically. Take advantage of this by imposing your own choice of colours on the work, even to the degree of introducing a complementary – a red instead of a green hill, for example.

- It is essential to work out the main overall colour combinations before you begin a painting.

- Decide whether you intend to make it a high-key painting (where you don't include strong, dark tones), a low-key one (where the dark tones dominate), or somewhere in between.

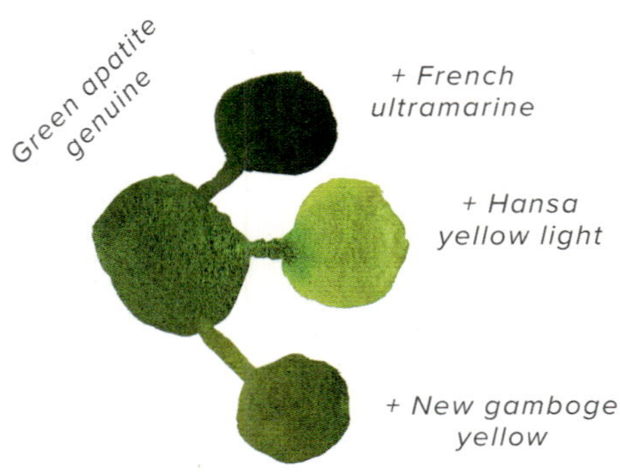

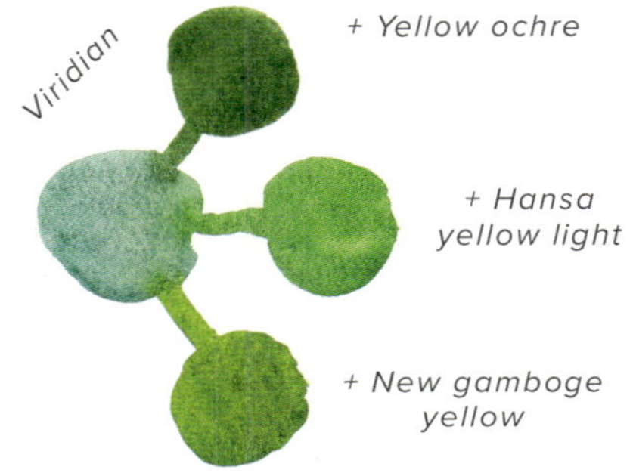

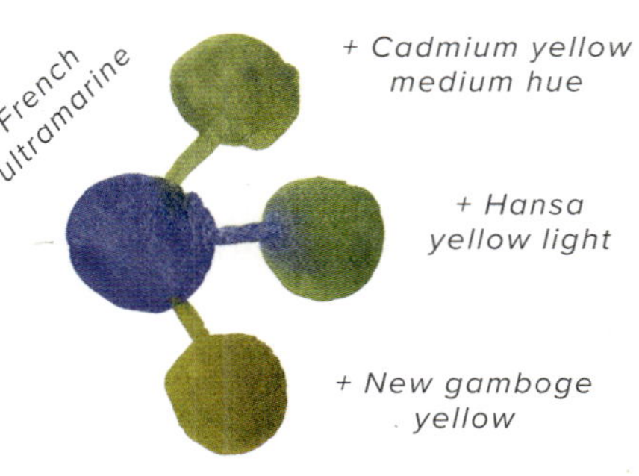

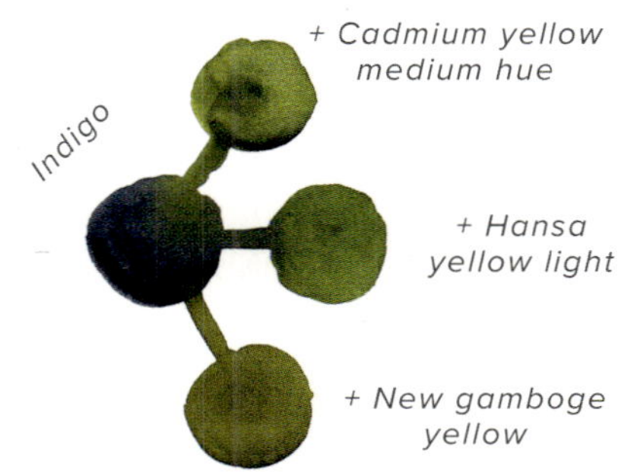

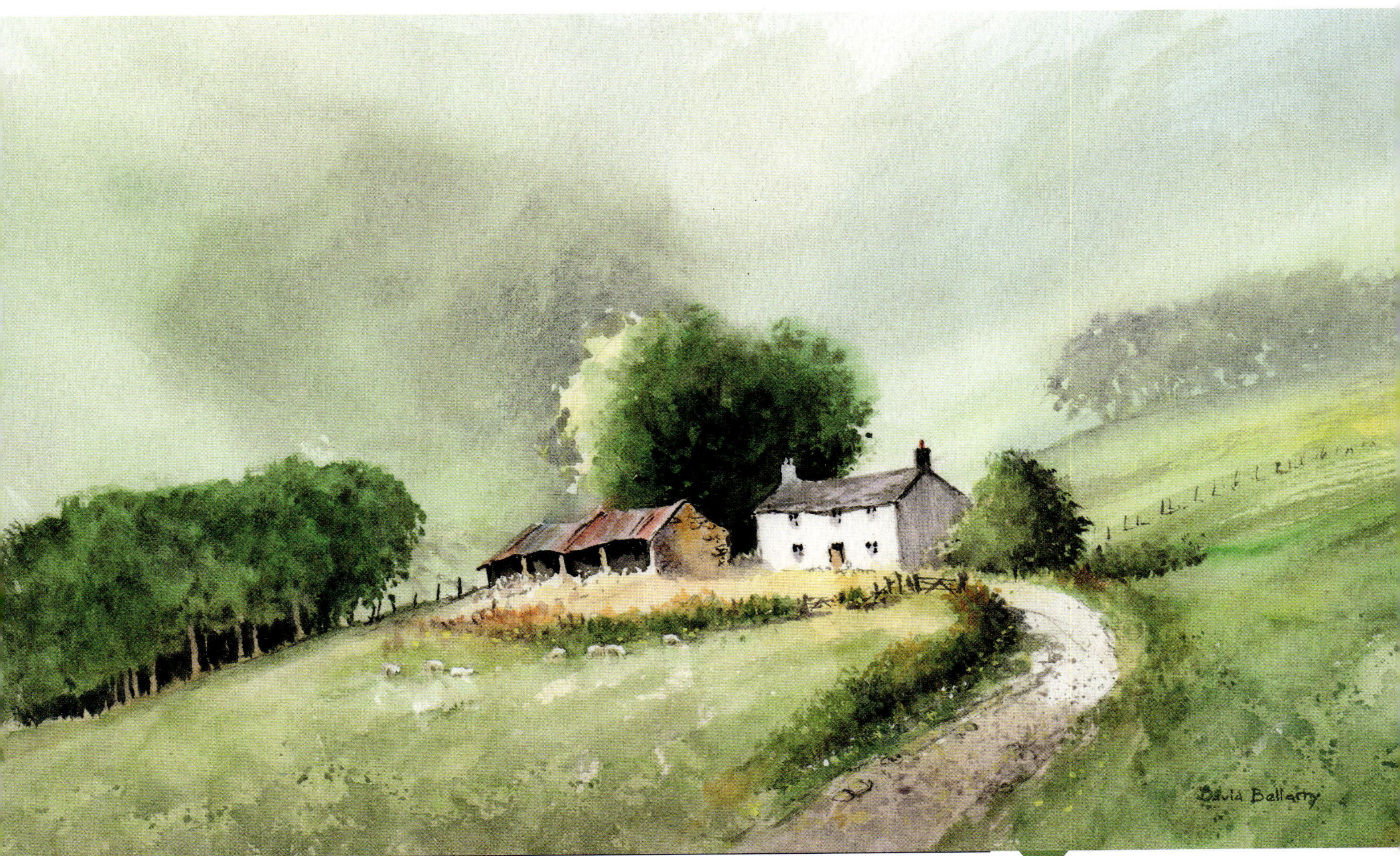

Painting *Summer in the Wye Valley*

This painting offers a great opportunity to explore how to tackle summer greens.

- I began with an ink drawing of the buildings, something I rarely do in a painting, but an approach that works well on structures like this. The indefinite background (perhaps sky, perhaps a misty hillside: sometimes it works well to retain this sense of mystery) was created with a mixture of cobalt blue with a touch of green apatite genuine.

- The central group of trees behind the buildings was started with nickel titanate yellow on the left side, and when this was dry the background wash of green apatite genuine and cobalt blue was laid down. Above the outbuilding this wash describes the left-hand edge of the trees by painting around the yellow.

- Because this painting is full of summer greens, I have used green apatite genuine as my base colour. This is used in the mixes for all the trees and bushes, and in extremely weak form over the fields.

- Don't try to include every green you can see.

- It's an excellent idea to counter over-all greenery with touches of red, its complementary colour. Here I have included red in the roof of the outbuilding and on a small patch on the ground below. This red injection is best located on or near the focal point to draw the eye of the viewer.

Summer in the
Wye Valley
30.5 × 20.5cm (12 × 8in)
Saunders Waterford
300gsm (140lb) Not
surface paper

Wet-in-wet watercolour

Another key technique, working wet in wet – that is, adding fresh paint to an area of wet paint on the surface – enables you to create a misty effect by brushing a colour into a damp area. This might be used to lay a wash into a damp surface, as in *Wye below Erwood*, where I used the wet-into-wet technique to add the misty background hill while the underlying sky wash was still damp; or to suggest details of misty trees, rocks and other features, as in *Little Neath River*, opposite.

The skill lies in knowing when the already-laid wash is ready to accept the second application of paint.

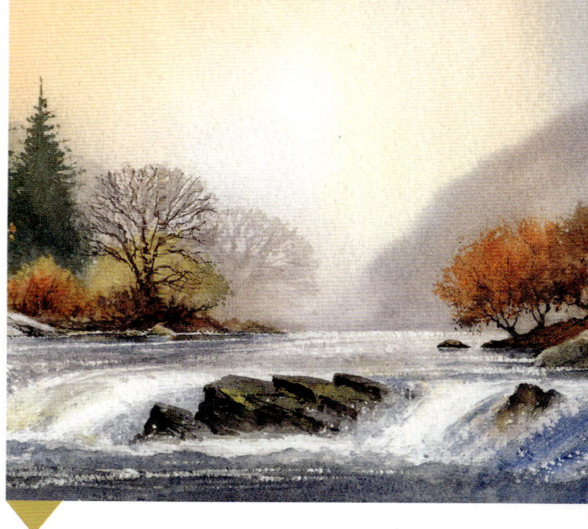

Wye below Erwood
33.5 × 24cm (13¼ × 9½in) Saunders Waterford 640gsm (300lb) Rough surface paper.

Applying the wash After applying a dilute wash, wait for the paper to dry out a little. Load the brush with your second colour while you wait.

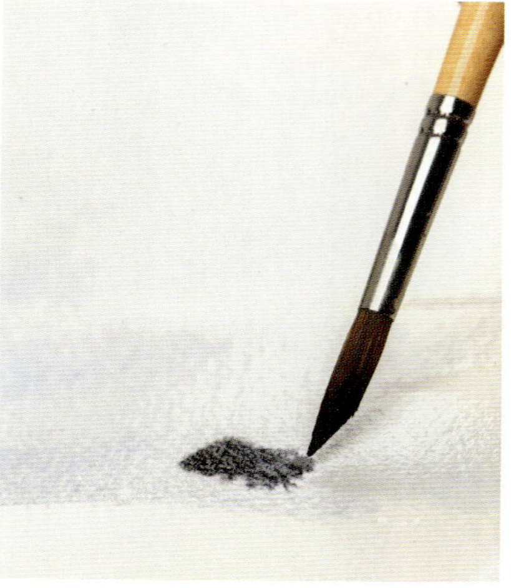

Judging the timing Test the paint by touching the brush down within the composition. It should spread slowly. If the paint flows out too quickly, wait a little longer and try again.

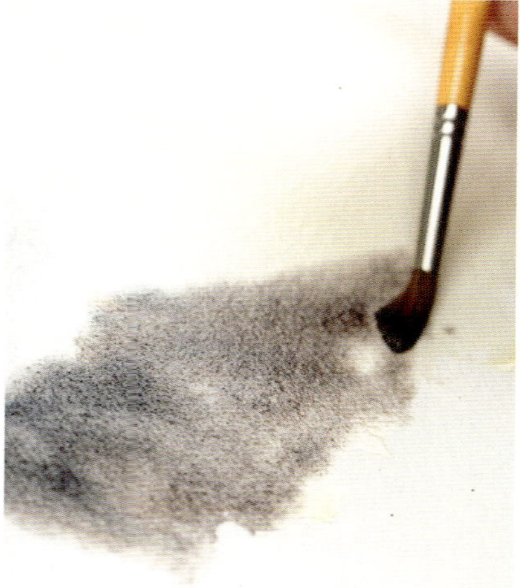

Adding the next colour If the paint diffuses well, creating a soft-edged feature as intended, then go ahead and paint in that feature.

The keys to wet-in-wet success

- Timing is critical. It takes experience to get it right every time.
- Doing your test in the centre of where a feature will appear means that the eventual application will cover the test.
- When working into the damp area, do so with as little water on the brush as possible, otherwise cabbage-like run-backs are likely to appear in your wash.
- Very large areas are difficult to complete in time. If you feel the paper is drying out, stop, let it dry completely, then rewet with clean water and carry on.
- As the paper dries, the effect will be less diffuse; so you can add finer detail – just stop before it is too dry.

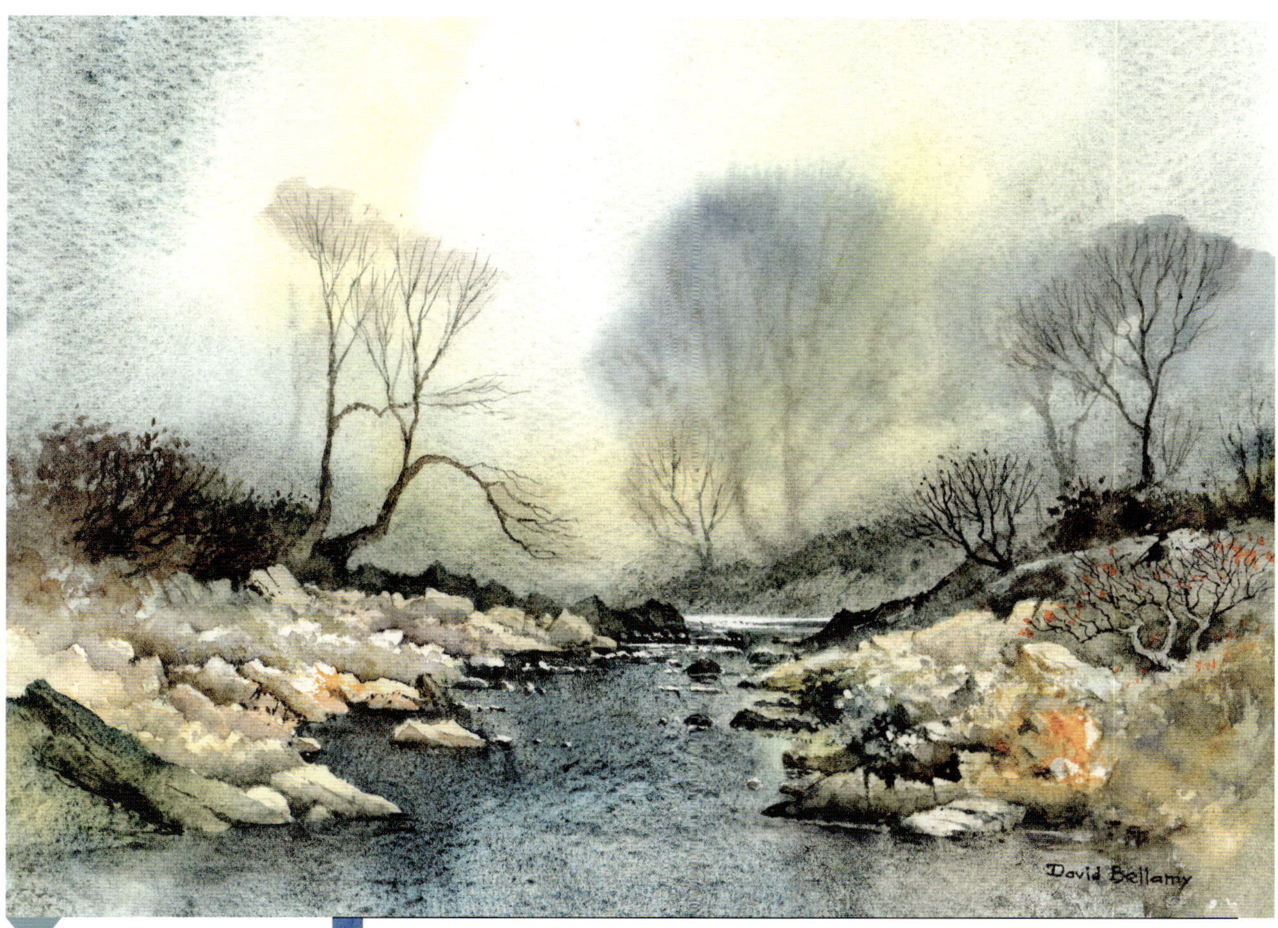

Little Neath River

25.5 × 20.5cm (10 × 8in)
Saunders Waterford
425gsm (200lb) Hot-Pressed
surface paper

Painting *Little Neath River*

Simplification has been achieved in this painting by three methods:

- First, the number of background trees has been reduced by suggesting some with the wet-in-wet method, stroking in a few tree trunks while the wash was still damp.

- Second, through describing the shapes of the rocks and stones mostly by where the tops catch the light. This was achieved by painting the shadow areas on the far side of the stones.

- Third, by using lunar blue, a strongly granulating pigment, to create the water, with touches of lunar black in places. The granulations in the lunar blue suggest ripples in the water without having to define them with a brush.

Wet-in-wet for distance

Some of the background trees are hardly perceptible. Wet-in-wet is the ideal tool for this effect – the wetter the wash is when the tree is added, the more it will diffuse, and the paler and softer the result in the finished painting.

Negative painting, explained on pages 68–69, is useful for rocks like those in this painting.

Dropping in colour

Dropping a colour into a wet wash is a technique I use in almost every painting. It is a way of mixing colours on the paper rather than on the palette, and can range from a small dab of colour dropped into a wash to a much larger introduction of colour. It's an extremely effective method that is often ignored by artists.

I often use dropped-in colours in lieu of detail; the soft effect suggests detail to the viewer where little exists.

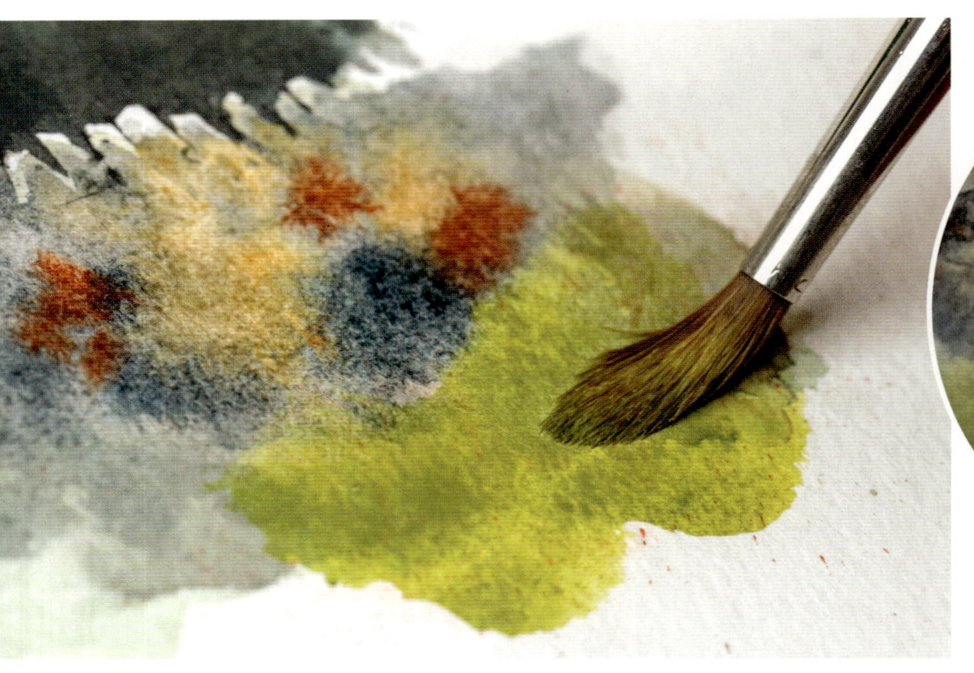

Drop in early Working wet in wet, add touches of the other colours into a base wash. The colours you add work best when they contrast with the base wash – on this grey wash example, I'm using relatively bright colours: yellow ochre and burnt sienna. Note how they push the underlying wash away.

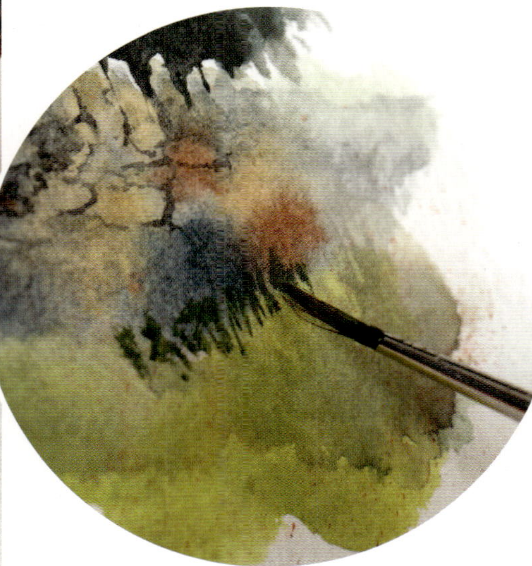

Don't fiddle Leave the paint undisturbed to dry – after which you can work over the top with darker details.

Keys to success with dropping in

- You need to drop in the added colour to the wet wash as quickly as you can for best effect.
- Yellow ochre is one of the most effective colours for this as it is an aggressive colour that pushes other colours aside, but I also drop in cadmium red, light red, phthalo blue and other colours at times.

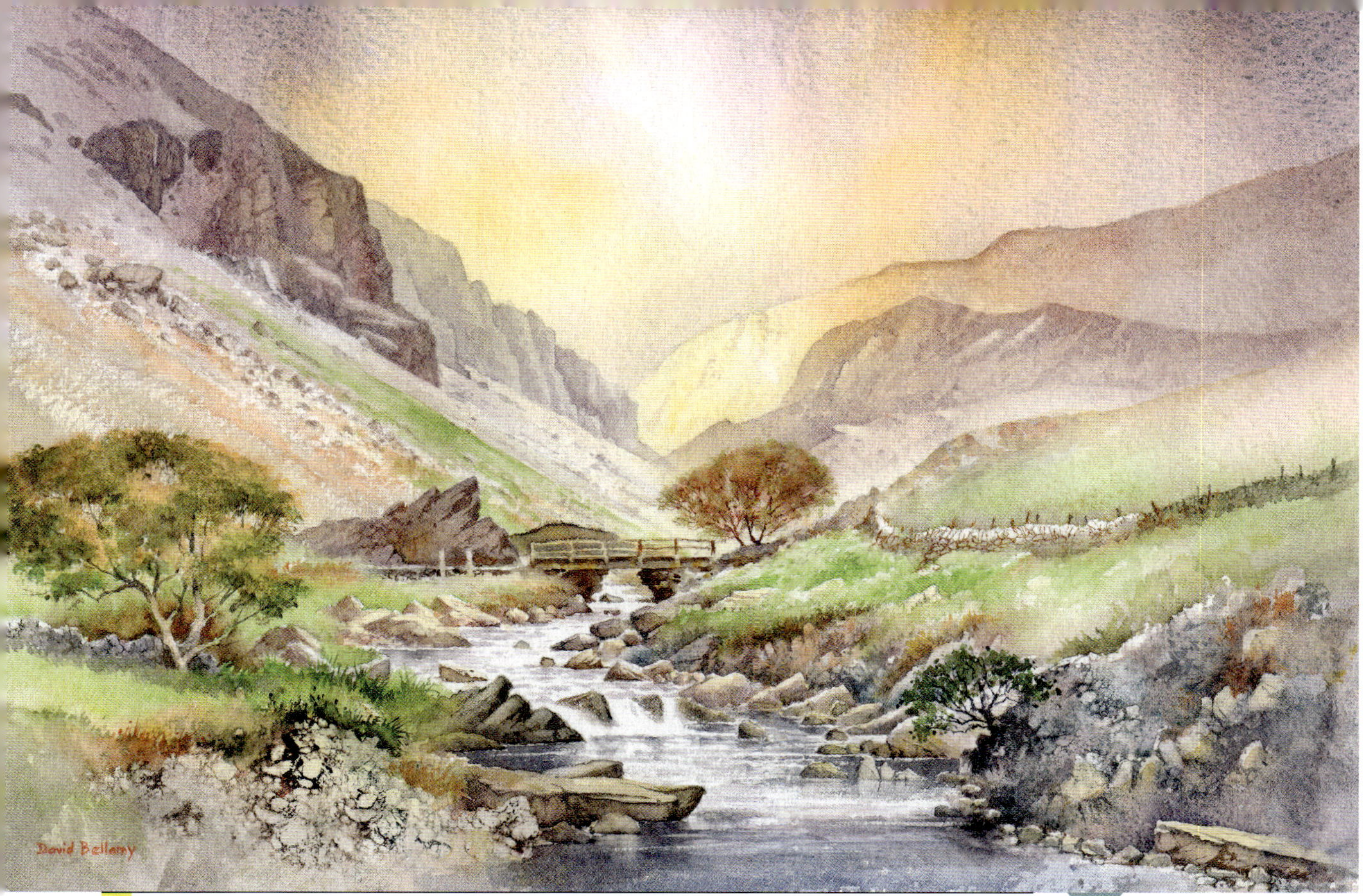

Painting *Bridge in the Llanberis Pass*

- The sky wash comprises French ultramarine and cadmium red, letting it run down into the quinacridone gold below.
- For the cliffs high above the bridge, cobalt blue and yellow ochre created a cool overall appearance in keeping with the more distant position. Once dry I suggested crag detail with cobalt blue and a touch of cadmium red.
- For the closer, darker cliffs I reverted to the French ultramarine and cadmium red mix, dropping in a little more cadmium red in places to add variety.
- The riverside rocks were painted with cadmium red and yellow ochre, and their shadows with cadmium red and French ultramarine. I blended edges where I wanted softer lines.
- For the flatter rocks on either side of the river in the foreground I dropped in Naples yellow while the rocks were still wet, to suggest reflected light.
- I used a cosmetics sponge to dab colour into the riverbanks on either side. The left-hand one is more prominent, and in this case, I have dabbed it into just one colour.

*Bridge in the
Llanberis Pass*
35.5 × 30.5cm (14 × 12in)
Saunders Waterford 425gsm
(200lb) Rough surface paper

*The use of French ultramarine
as the base colour ensures an
overall feeling of unity.*

*The sponging technique
is explained on page 52.*

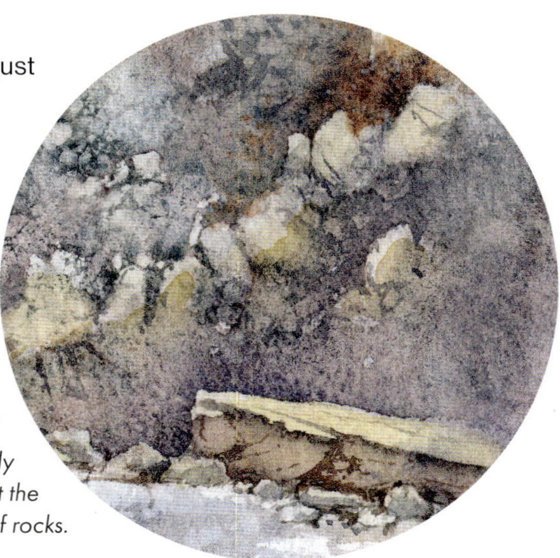

Detail of dropping in

*This shows clearly the effects of dropping
in Naples yellow into the underside of
the flat rock: a lighter area caused by light
reflecting off the water. Once the wash had
dried, these dropped-in shapes were partially
outlined with darker details to draw out the
shapes and create the impression of rocks.*

Colour mixing

As you will have seen in *Bridge in the Llanberis Pass* on page 27, colour mixing is not just about combining paints on the palette, but dropping colours into wet washes to create variegated colours that are mixed on the paper.

Laying a wash with one colour and then floating in other colours is a further way of mixing colour on the paper – and extremely useful where you wish to warm up a sky towards the sun, for example. In this case you need to work quickly and keep the washes really fluid. Wetting the paper first will help.

Some of the following colour combinations might be useful for you, but you should always experiment with colour mixtures to find out which ones suit you best.

Cadmium yellow pale and phthalo blue (red shade)

Keys to mixing success

It's essential to experiment with mixing on your own to see what particularly interests you. This is the only way to learn about colour mixing, and I hope I never stop learning.

- There are many combinations of colours that produce greens, purples, greys and so on.
- Add more water to weaken the result, and more paint to strengthen.
- Different paints have different strengths. Try varying the proportions of each colours in a mix to explore further.
- In the past, I rarely used black, as it is such a dead colour, but the Daniel Smith lunar black transformed my attitude, as its granulations simply knocked me out. Combining it with other colours – a yellow perhaps, for a dark green suitable for the shadows in foliage – can be extremely effective.

Moonglow and quinacridone sienna

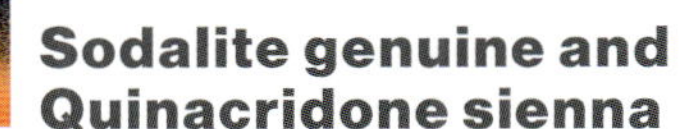

**Pyrrol red and phthalo blue
(red shade)**

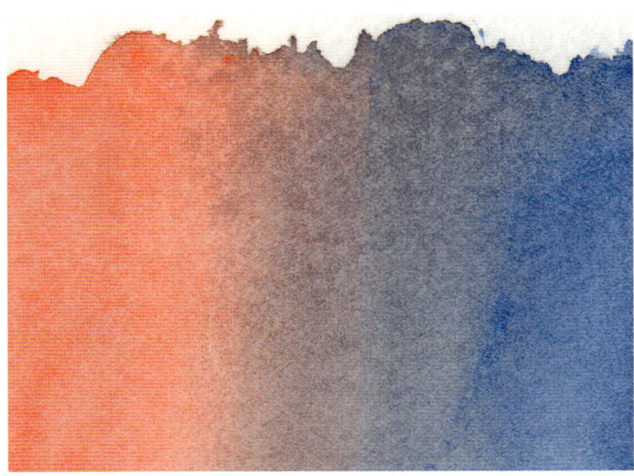

**Sodalite genuine and
Quinacridone sienna**

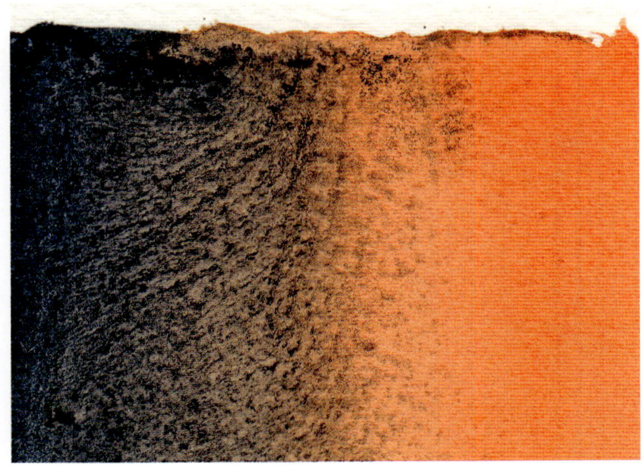

Exciting colour mixtures

*A few examples of some useful colour mixtures in which I have floated the colours
together and mixed them on the paper. All the paints are from Daniel Smith's Extra Fine
range of watercolours.*

**Quinacridone gold and
green apatite genuine**

**Sodalite genuine and
green apatite genuine**

Glazing

A glaze is a transparent wash laid over part of a composition that has already been painted and allowed to dry. It can be extremely effective as a means to suggest falling rain over part of a distant ridge, for warming up or cooling down part of the work, or for creating shadow areas to subdue a feature. It should be applied with copious amounts of water.

The magic of a glaze

To illustrate how a glaze can affect a painting I decided to change the painting on the right by giving more prominence to the shepherd's hut. You can see the results opposite.

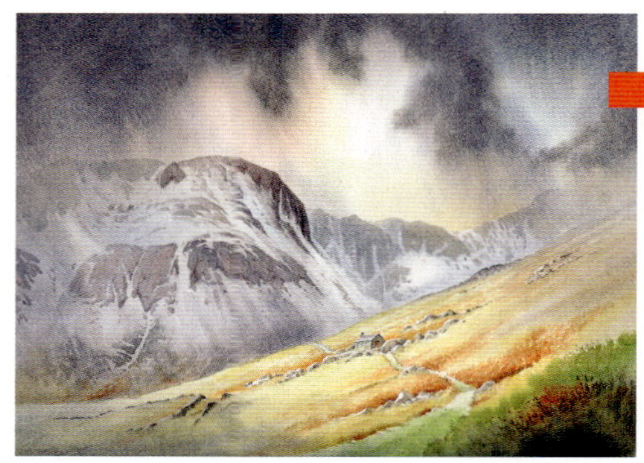

Pen-yr-Helgi-ddu – original painting

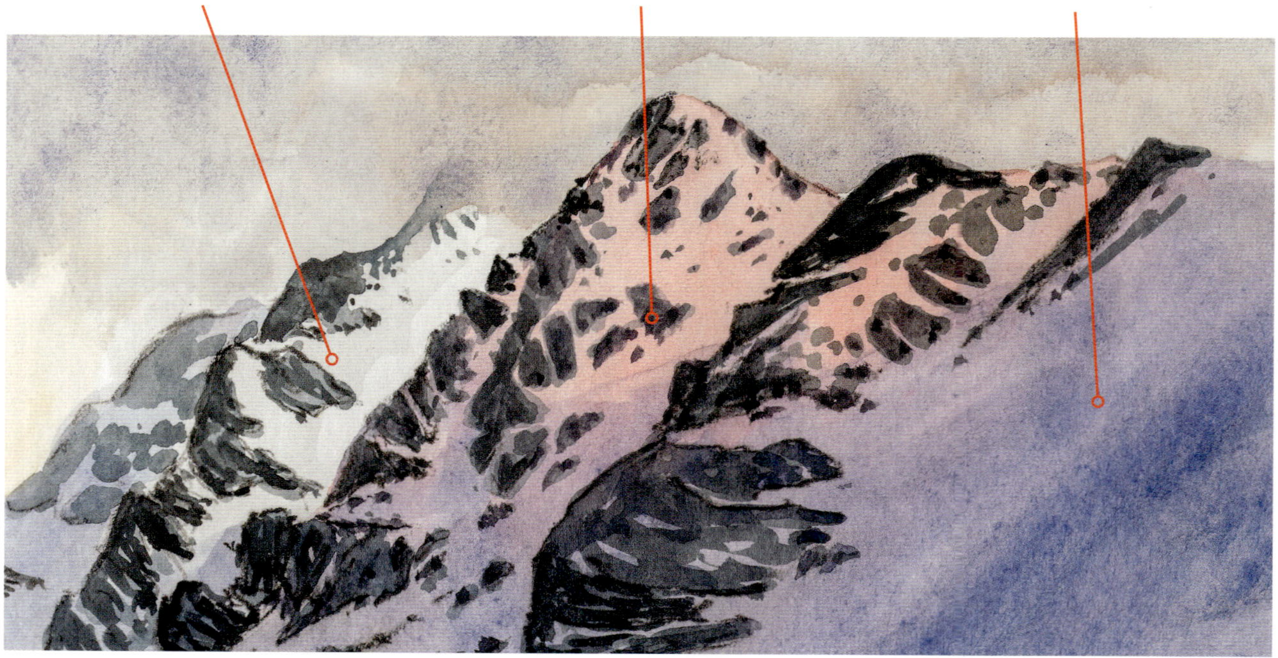

Keys to success with glazing

- Glazing can be a hazardous technique as it can mess up your painting if it goes wrong, so practise on old paintings that haven't quite worked out before you try it on one that you are pleased with.

- The glaze technique is excellent for introducing a strong sense of atmosphere and losing or subduing a feature.

There are more techniques for altering paintings on pages 142–149.

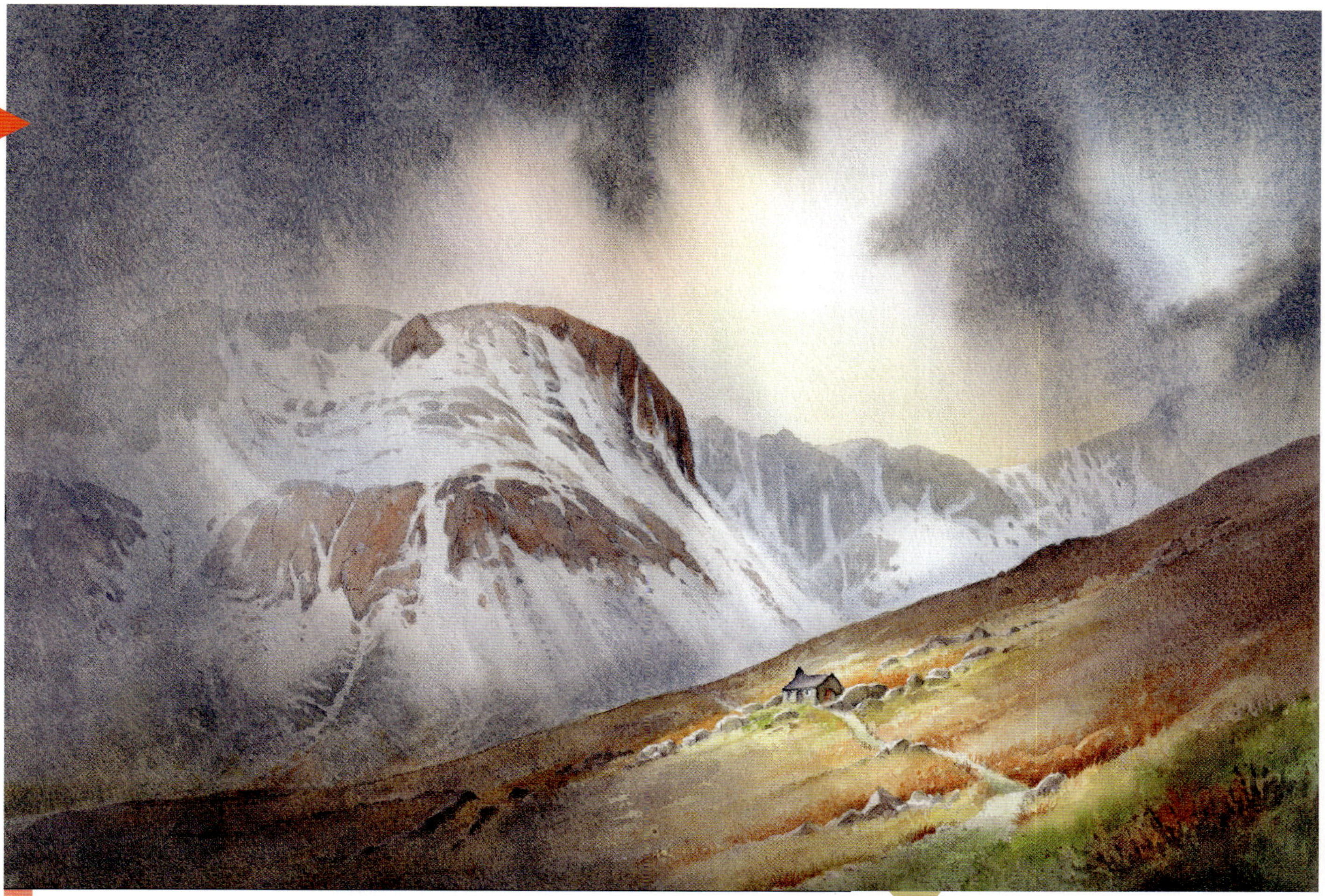

Repainting *Pen-yr-Helgi-ddu*

This painting was done many years ago, but I was not satisfied with the result, shown opposite. It had been hidden away out of sight, but I decided to try glazing to improve it.

- I completely re-wet the paper, then applied a strong mix of French ultramarine and cadmium red over the area around the hut, leaving the hut itself clear.
- I also took the glaze up into the mountain area on the left to lose some of the detail there.
- On the extreme left and right of the composition, you can also see original glazes over the mountain ridges, where I had suggested a rain squall coming in once the ridges had dried.

Pen-yr-Helgi-ddu
40.5 × 30.5cm (16 × 12in) Saunders Waterford 300gsm (140lb) Not surface paper

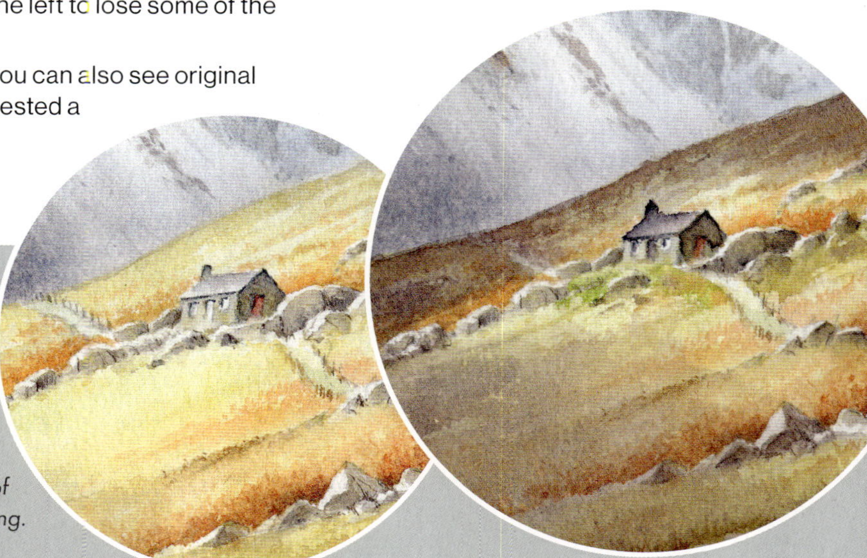

Before and after
Glazing allowed me to surround the shepherd's hut with shadow, leaving it alone bathed in warm sunlight. The increase in contrast creates a stronger focal point and sense of narrative, making for a much more successful finished painting.

Sketching and reference

You will by now have carried out several watercolours copying my examples, or working from other images you may find appropriate. Before we go further, we should look at how we acquire our source material.

Reference and copyright

Ideally our source material should be from our own sketches and photographs done on location, although many artists like to work from books, magazines, calendars and other sources, especially those who are unable to get out into the blue yonder.

Be aware that you might be infringing someone's copyright if you copy their painting or photograph and exhibit the result in public. There are sites on the internet where you can obtain copyright-free images from which to work. If you copy another artwork and wish to exhibit it, sign it and annotate it *'After JMW Turner'*, or whoever did the original.

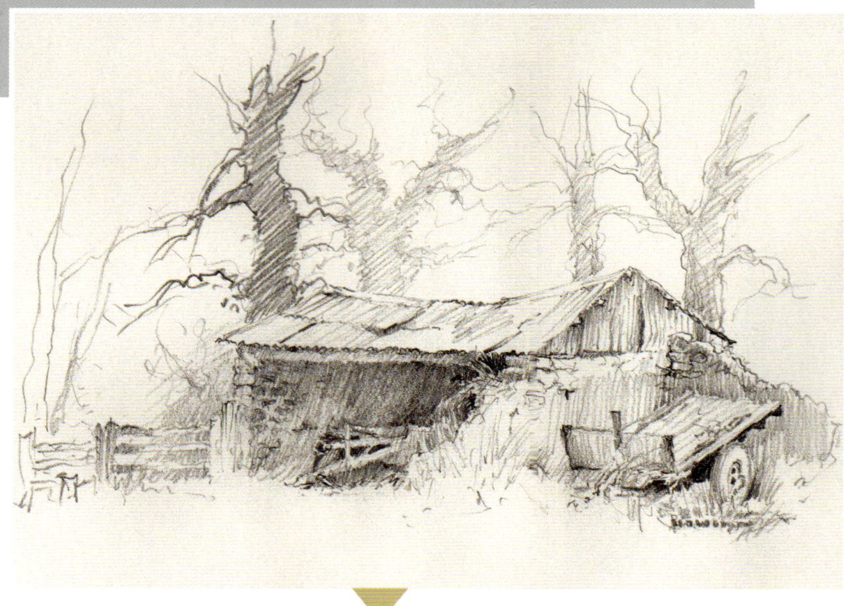

Barn at Kilkerny, Radnorshire

This small pencil sketch explores the intricacies of the subject, and has the advantage over a photograph in that I gain a much better understanding of the scene, and can check every important aspect before I leave the location. I usually back up the sketches with photographs and like to make colour notes if working in monochrome.

Supporting reference

Photography has never been easier, as smartphone cameras make it easy to record your subject.

- When you photograph a subject, capture it from different angles to collect as much information as possible, and if necessary go in close to ensure you get the details.

- Including a large area of bright sky in a photograph may cause the ground area to appear too dark, making it difficult to ascertain details when you are working from the image. Take additional photographs of the subject without much sky so that the automatic system gives you a better exposure.

Sketching tools

Once you know the sort of subjects you would like to paint it's good to get out into the landscape and try sketching. Since I first began sketching the amount of new materials on the market has mushroomed, and it can be quite daunting for newcomers to choose what to take out sketching. Here are the essentials:

- The **pencil** has never been superseded, so make sure you take along a few, from 2B to 7B as you wish. Most of my sketching is done with a 3B or 4B.
- A small **cartridge sketchbook** – I favour an A4 (21 × 29¾cm/8¼ × 11¾in) or A5 (14.5 × 21cm/5¾ × 8¼in) format.
- One or two **water-soluble graphite pencils** are excellent for creating washes of tone, either using a normal **paintbrush** or the handy **water brush** like Pentel's Aquash brushes. These contain water in their handles so you don't need a **water pot**. If you prefer to use a water pot, get one with a screw-on top (or otherwise sealable).

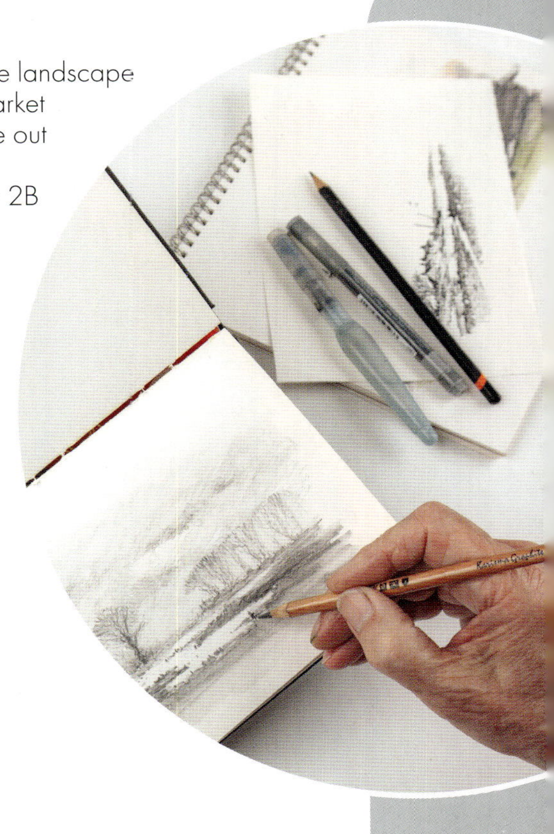

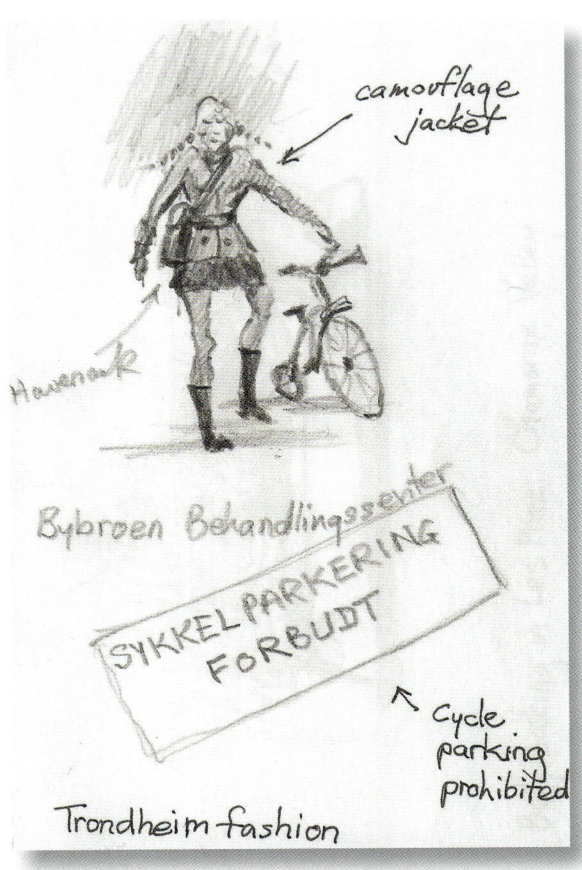

Trondheim Fashion

This rapid pencil sketch was done in my pocket sketchbook, which is mainly devoted to figure work snatched when the opportunity arises, and is heavily biased towards caricatures. It's sometimes rather fun to include some humour in your work.

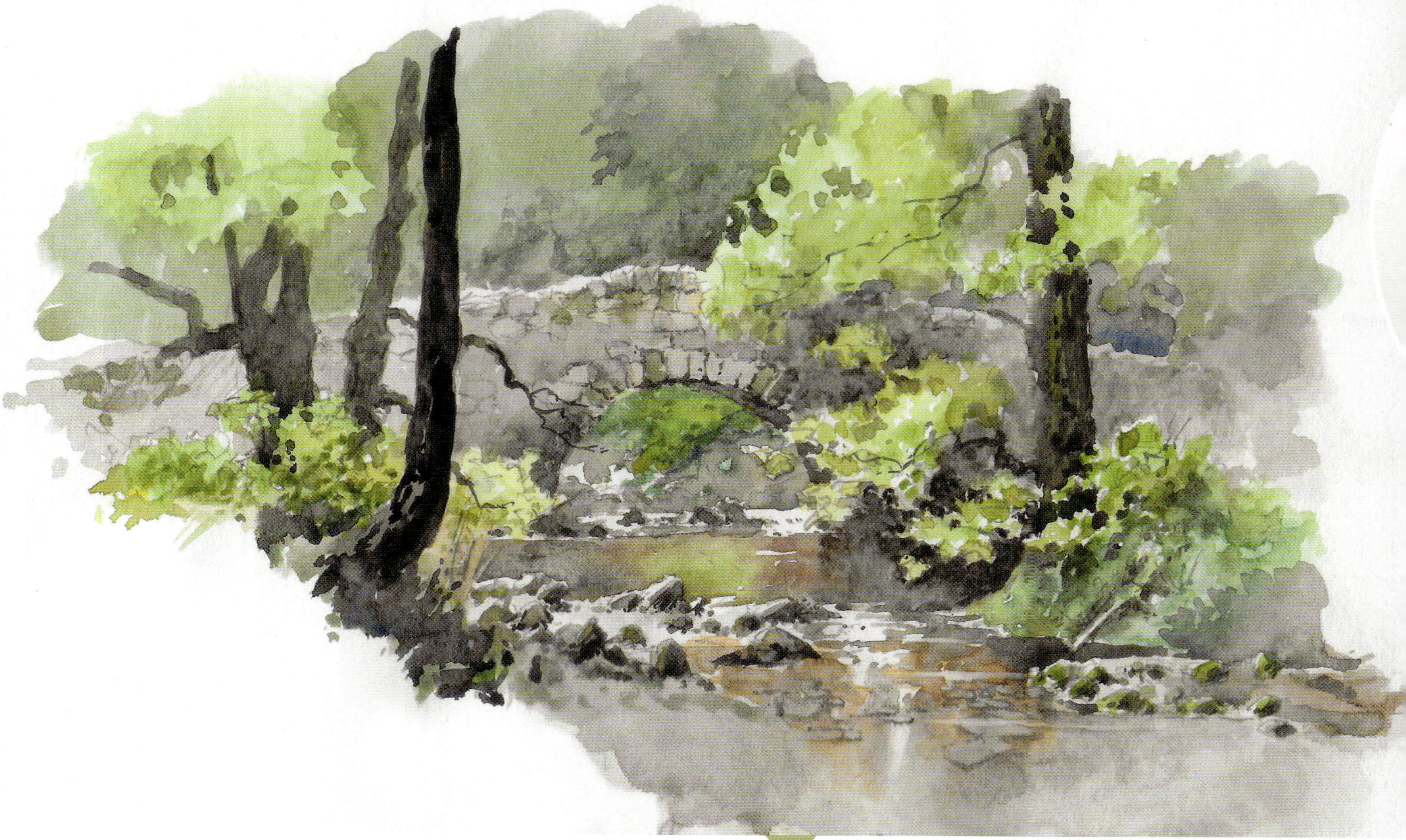

Sketching in colour

The beauty of sketching in colour is that you are not only recording the colour, but at the same time learning to apply watercolour, and this was the way I learnt to paint in watercolour.

If you are not working in colour, it is useful to note down the colours on the side, rather than rely on the photograph.

Rhydywernen Bridge
Watercolour sketch on cartridge paper

It's easy enough to simply take a photograph of a scene like this, but you learn so much more about the subject by sketching. Equally important is the fact that you are enjoying yourself amidst nature, under no pressure to achieve a master painting – and if things go wrong, you can blame the wind, the cold, an aggressive sheep or whatever. Remember that no-one need see it. This is a powerful way of learning to paint in watercolour.

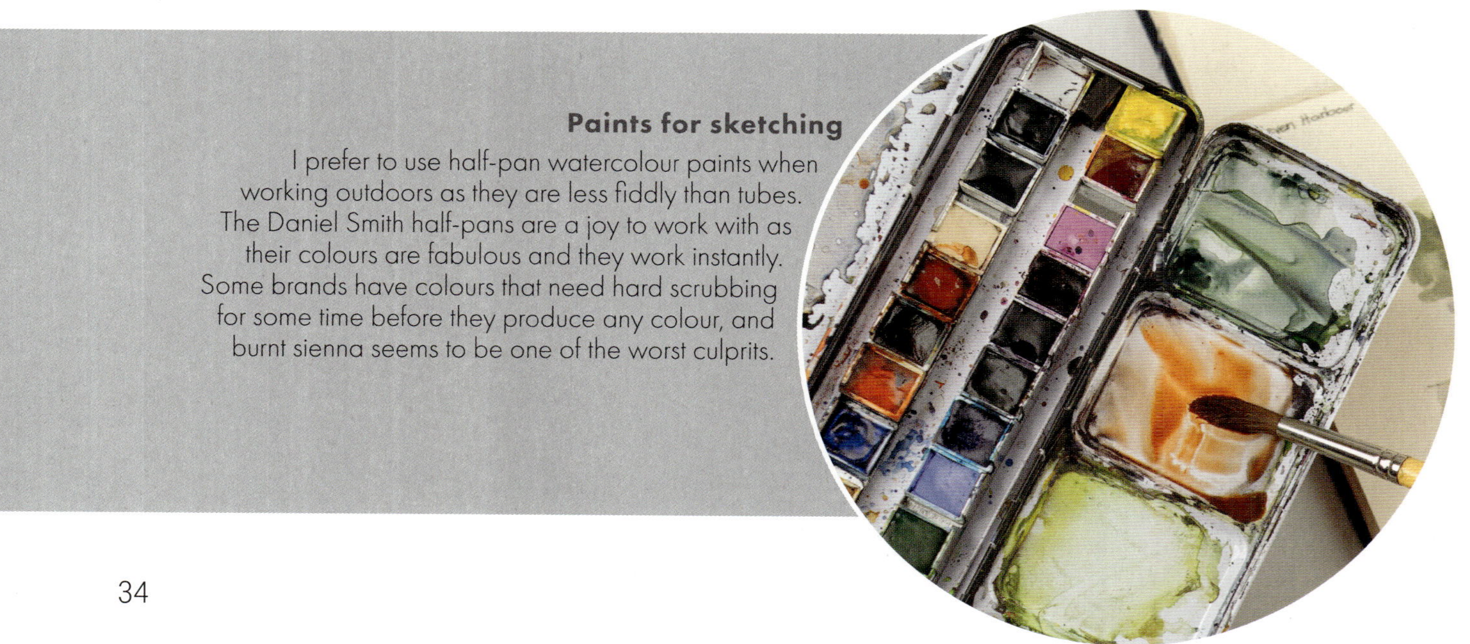

Paints for sketching

I prefer to use half-pan watercolour paints when working outdoors as they are less fiddly than tubes. The Daniel Smith half-pans are a joy to work with as their colours are fabulous and they work instantly. Some brands have colours that need hard scrubbing for some time before they produce any colour, and burnt sienna seems to be one of the worst culprits.

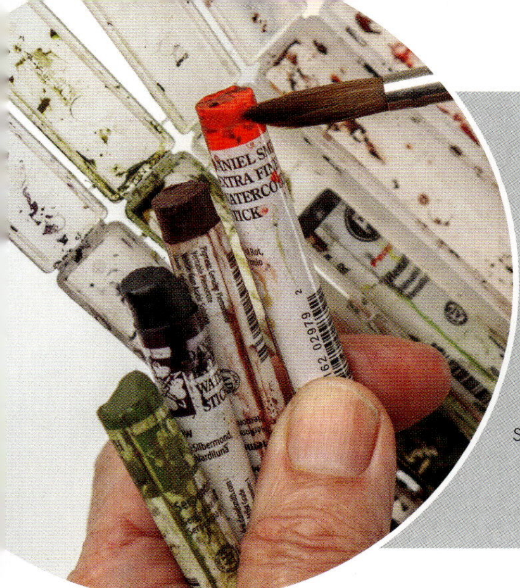

Watercolour sticks for dynamic sketches

Recently I have been using the Daniel Smith watercolour sticks. These little gems hold beautifully intense colours and are so easy to use – you can hold a few of them in one hand and pick up the paint with a brush or water brush, mixing them on the side of your sketch or on scrap paper, or whatever is convenient, and apply the paint. You can also lay the stick across the paper while it is dry or wet, mix in other colours and then wash over the passage. This approach tends to show up more of the stroke marks, which can impart a sense of dynamism and movement in a work.

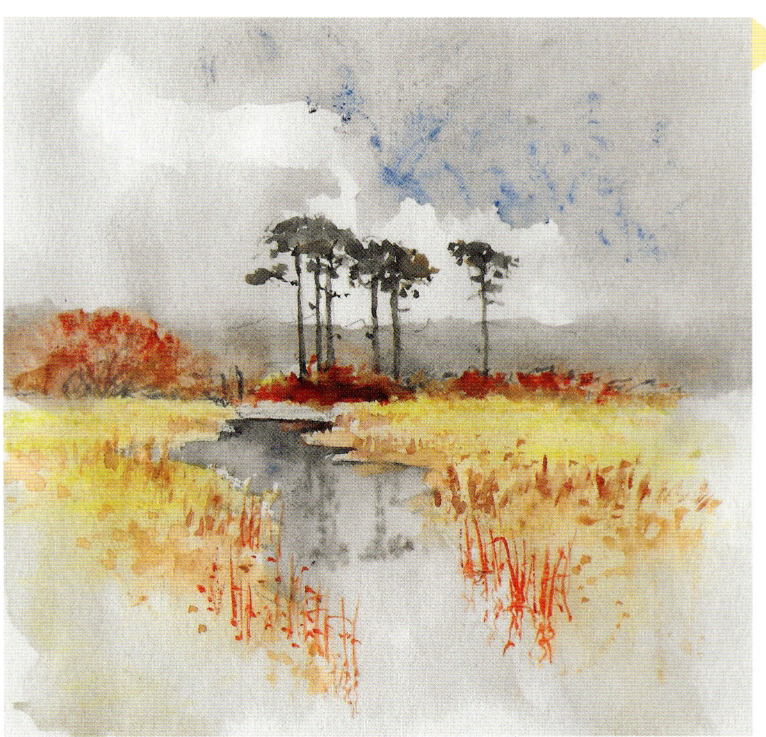

Pool on Thursley Common, Surrey
Watercolour sketch on cartridge paper

This brief sketch shows two ways of working with watercolour sticks. Firstly the blue part of the sky was rendered by rubbing a stick of French ultramarine over the paper, then washing over with water. While this method works well, the rubbed marks show faintly in places. This may not be a problem in certain parts of the work.

Normally I prefer the second method where I apply the paint with a brush, picking the paint up directly from the stick, or mixing two colours and then laying on the colour. That is how the rest of this sketch was accomplished.

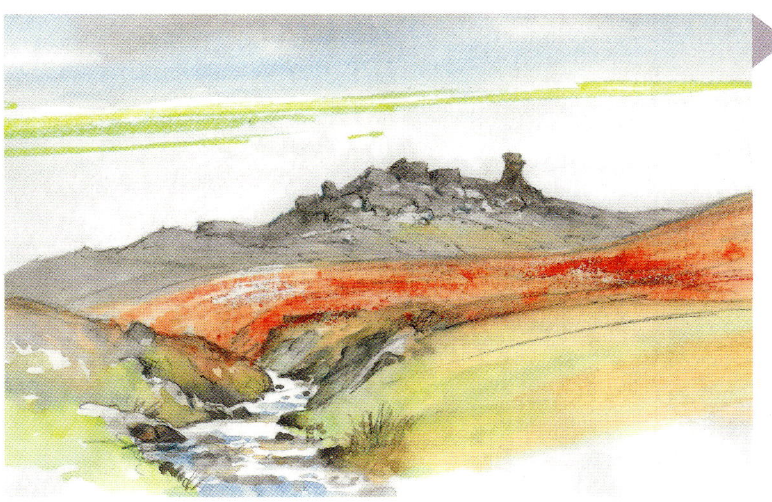

Bald Stone, North Staffordshire Moors

This is another sketch on cartridge paper using the watercolour sticks, and the technique to point out here is where I laid weak but fluid quinacridone sienna across the central part with a brush, then when the paper had dried I drew the quinacridone sienna stick across the same area to create a rough-looking texture suggestive of the moor.

By all means use these sticks for finished paintings. This over-laying technique would be even more pronounced on a Not surface, and is difficult to replicate with traditional paints.

Working outside

You will find sketches and alfresco paintings made using various materials throughout the book, including line and wash sketching.

Painting directly from nature can be very rewarding. There is no need to completely finish the work out of doors, so long as you have all the most important details rendered, and perhaps a photograph or two to back it up when you want to finish it back home. There is often more of a sense of urgency about working outside, which encourages you to concentrate on the most important features.

Sketching and painting from life

The difference between painting and watercolour sketching outdoors can be blurred. I normally carry around sketchbooks as well as a selection of watercolour papers in a folder, the latter for more finished work that I regard as a painting.

In some landscapes colour can be vital in describing the nuances of a colourful feature: glaciers and arctic ice, for example, have a myriad of subtle colours which are impossible to describe without using paints, and much is often lost in photographs (especially if I am the photographer!). Likewise, when capturing colour variation, as in the yellow wall at the rear of the sketch in Perpignan, it is often quicker to lay washes than to draw out the scene in pencil and attempt to indicate the extent of the colour variations with arrows.

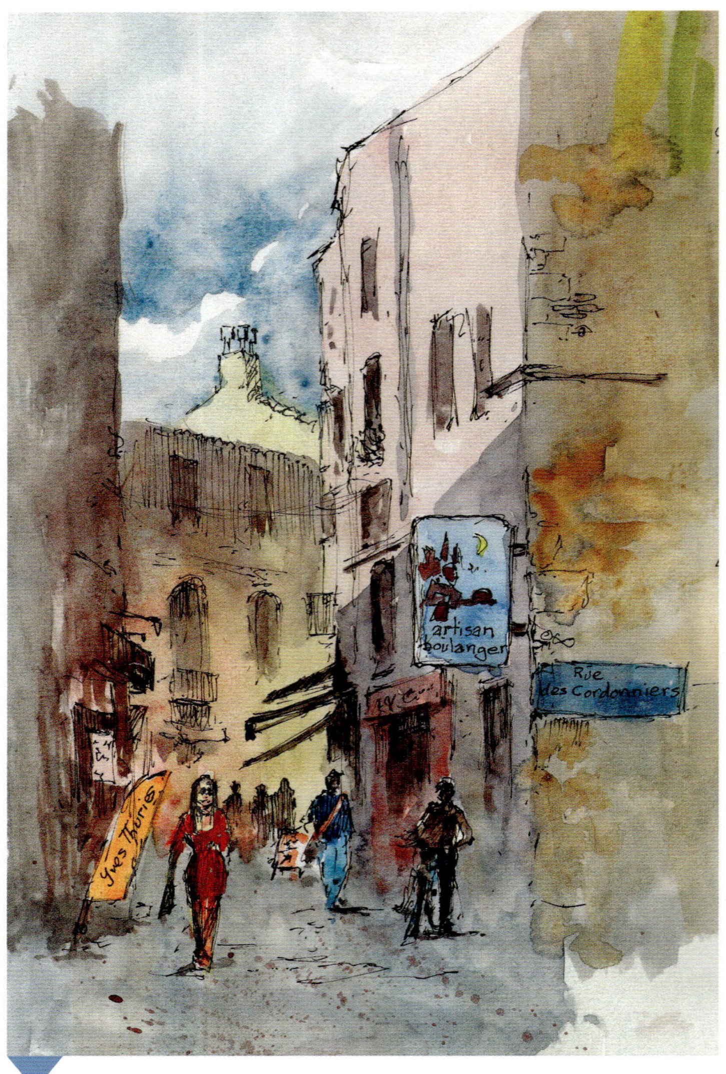

Alleyway in Perpignan
Watercolour sketch on cartridge paper

I positioned myself at a table outside a café in the Place de la Republique so that I could sketch this alleyway leading off the square. To my delight a small lady, not unlike the diminutive singer Edith Piaf, was well into Je Ne Regrette Rien in the middle of the square as I began drawing. I took my time over my cappuccino, using the last dregs to lay initial washes over the alleyway.

The reflected light in the distant part lent a striking accent to the composition, and while it is not easy sketching figures that constantly move and are gone in moments, it's always worth a try: you become more proficient if you keep practising. If you enjoy working in towns, seek out these pleasant cafés in good locations and you too will experience such blissful sketching.

There is more about line and wash on pages 49–50, and on including figures on pages 84–87.

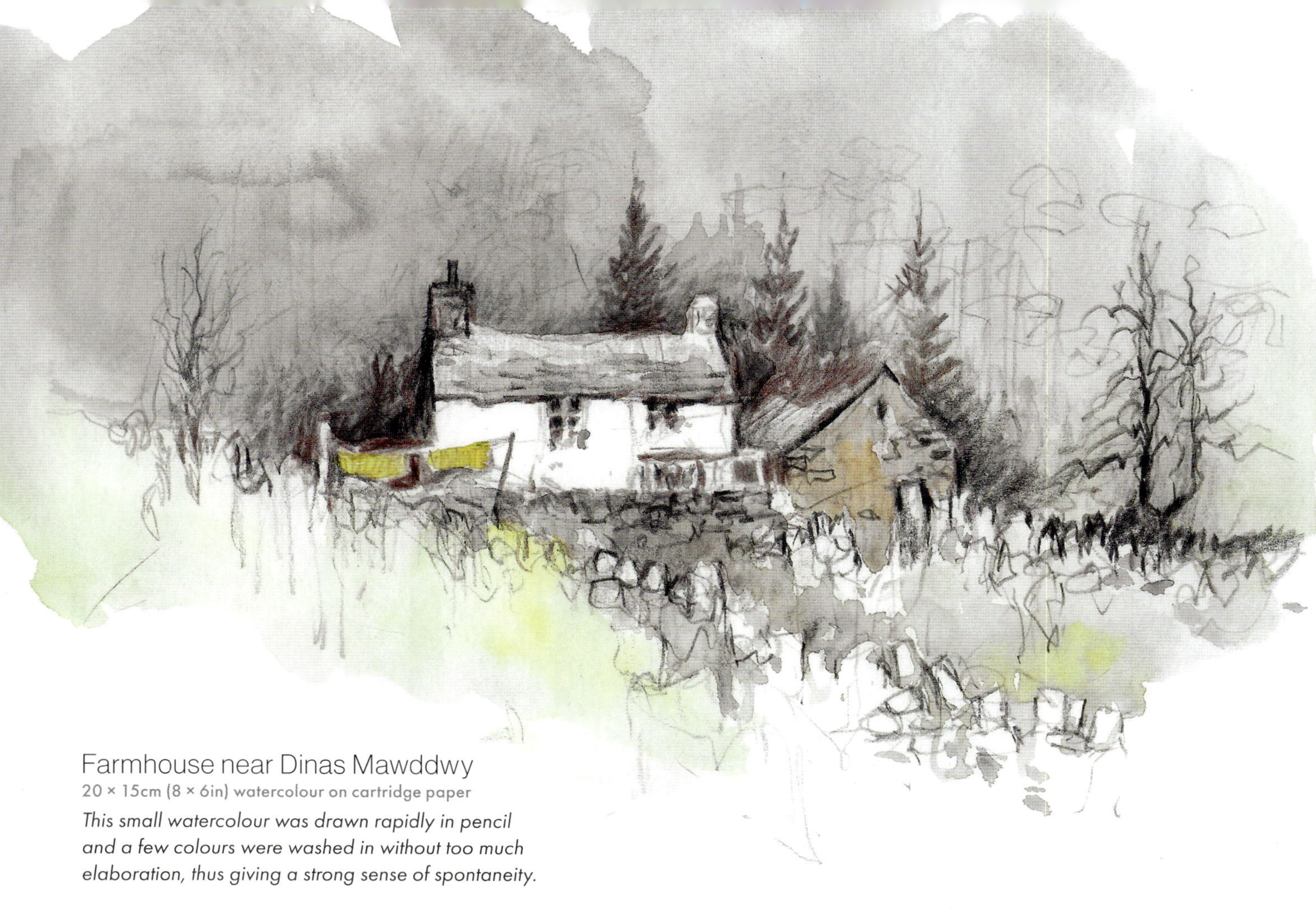

Farmhouse near Dinas Mawddwy
20 × 15cm (8 × 6in) watercolour on cartridge paper
*This small watercolour was drawn rapidly in pencil
and a few colours were washed in without too much
elaboration, thus giving a strong sense of spontaneity.*

Key points for successful outdoor painting

- By all means use an easel for outdoor painting, but I mostly sit on a rock, toadstool or whatever is convenient with the painting across my knees. Lightweight drawing boards are available if needed.

- Before starting, carefully observe the scene and note the critical points you wish to emphasize, then make sure you prioritize these ahead of the more mundane features.

- Unless the subject is really simple it is best to begin with a sketch of the scene to establish the scale and where the main features will appear. You can embellish the sketch while waiting for the washes to dry on the painting.

- I often lay washes for the sky before finishing the drawing of foreground detail so that the sky is drying as I continue working.

- Don't try to rush a painting in the face of an approaching blizzard or other potential discomfort. It is much better to concentrate on getting the important elements right than to create a finished painting. You can complete it back at home, especially if you have a sketch and photographs.

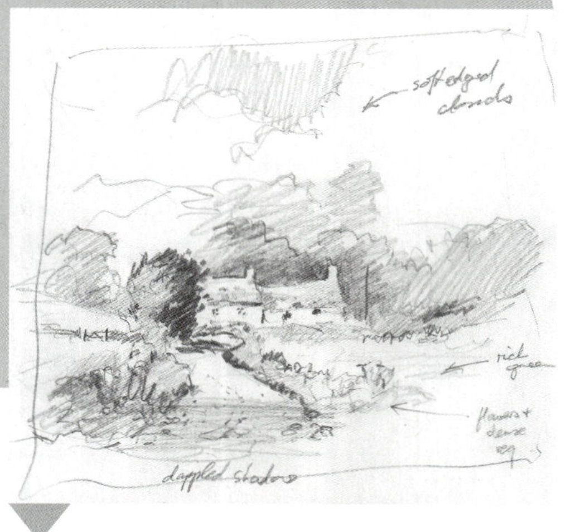

Cottages in sunlight

A typical studio sketch done in preparation for the finished painting. I make notes on the sketch regarding colours and tones, as well as various other notes to remind myself of my plan.

Composition

Rarely will you find a landscape scene as you would ideally wish it to be (see page 12), so making changes to the scene before you is a vital procedure if you want to make your paintings interesting and stamp some of your own creativity on it. Altering and adapting a scene is a key part of composition.

Studio sketches

Sketching and composition are closely linked; the former is a great way to learn about the latter. Sometimes you will return with several sketches or photographs of the same scene, and you may wish to introduce elements from one image into another. so to piece these together into a strong composition it's best to carry out one or two studio sketches – that is simply a sketch made back at home, away from the scene, that relies on using your reference and memory.

You don't need to slavishly copy the scene, either in terms of features, tones or colours. You may wish to make the scene more dramatic; perhaps change the time of day and introduce long cast shadows in the foreground to suggest evening; build up heavy storm clouds in the sky; or have little or no sky at all. It is with the studio sketches that you sort out your final approach.

Key points for composition

- As noted on page 12, make sure you have a strong focal point or centre of interest. If you find a beautiful scene with no obvious focal point, emphasize one of the trees, boats or whatever is present by strengthening the detail on it, warming up the colours and improving the light around it.

- Alternatively, you could introduce a feature appropriate to the location, such as a figure, an animal, or perhaps a tractor. Such elements always attract the eye to become an immediate centre of interest. It helps to support this focal point with subsidiary features such as a gateway, tree, or whatever seems appropriate.

- It is useful to include a lead-in to the focal point, in the form of a path, road, stream or hedgerow. In the case of a boat, a rope or similar feature can serve as a lead-in.

- Avoid putting a hedgerow or fence across the foreground unless you include some sort of break, as this gives the impression of cutting off the centre of interest.

- Traditionally the centre of interest is best positioned one-third of the way into a composition from one of the sides and either top or bottom, but with many modern works it could be anywhere.

- Try observing the scene through a rectangular hole cut in a piece of card – it will make working out the composition easier by removing distracting extraneous details.

See pages 56–59 for more examples and tips on how to improve your compositions.

Windy Day, Trelerw

25.5 × 15cm (10 × 6in) Saunders Waterford 300gsm
(140lb) Not surface paper

*It's worth considering a different format to
your original sketch or photograph in order
to emphasize the foreground, perhaps, or to
enhance the sense of calm by extending the
rectangular format horizontally.*

*Equally, you may settle on a format on a whim.
This painting shows the subject as I saw it – a
large expanse of field with the tiny cottages at the
far end, and I felt this format would bring back
that sensation.*

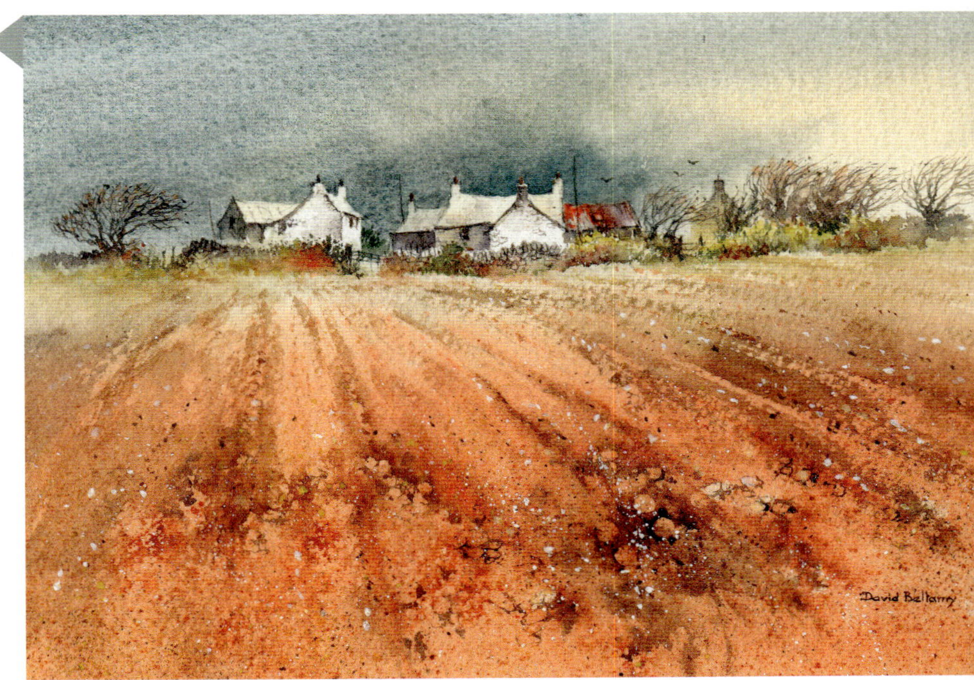

Barn by the Towy Estuary

28 ×23cm (11 × 9in) Saunders Waterford 300gsm
(140lb) Hot-Pressed surface paper

*This watercolour illustrates some of the classic
conventions of composition. The barn is the
centre of interest, supported by the large tree
and pheasants. The track provides a lead-in to
the barn, while the gap in the ground cover in
the foreground allows the viewer to observe
the focal point unobstructed. On the right, small
trees provide balance. The background ridge
disappears into the cloud, creating mood and
avoiding a long boring line of the ridge.*

*While the right-hand small trees were exactly
where I have placed them, and the background
ridge could indeed only be seen vaguely through
the December gloom, much of the rest of the
composition has been adapted: the tall tree, the
track leading in, and the pheasants were not
present and the roof was grey, not red.*

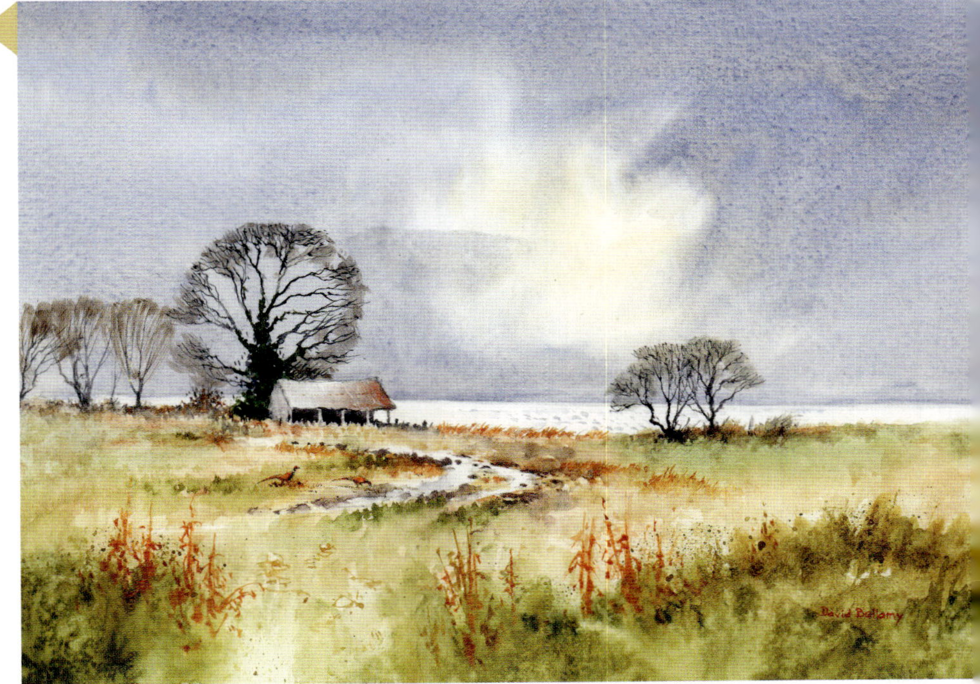

*The barn roof here has been gradated from
light on the left to a darker tone on the right
so that it stands out against the background:
a useful technique called counterchange that
you can adopt to suit the subject. Page 67
explores counterchange in more detail.*

Using masking fluid

Masking fluid is extremely useful for reserving white passages. My preference is for Pebeo Drawing Gum, a grey solution that is gentle on the paper and enables you to lay a light colour – a yellow, for example – allow it to dry and then paint the fluid over the yellow area. When the gum is later rubbed off using a clean finger, it will leave the underlying paint intact, unlike some masking fluid solutions which remove the colour.

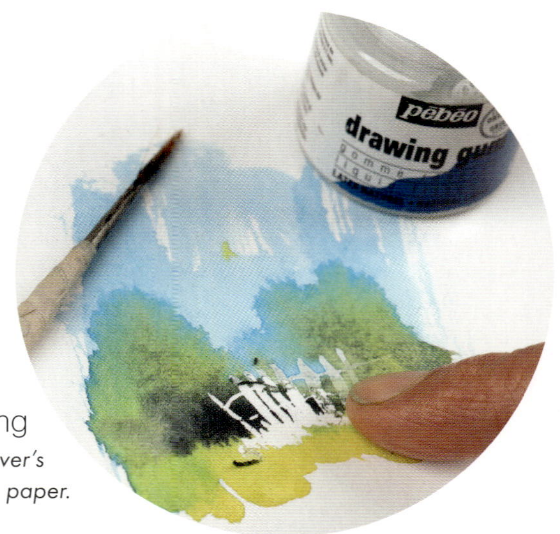

Masking

Removing masking fluid will reveal whatever's underneath; in this case clean paper.

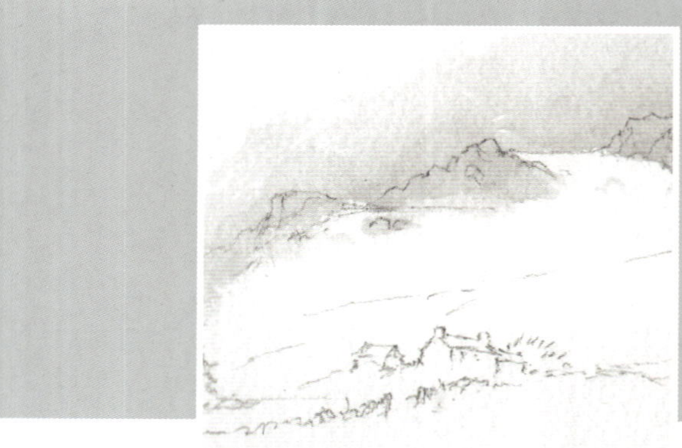

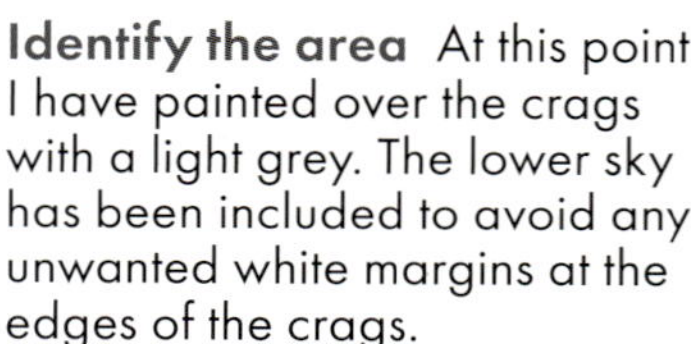

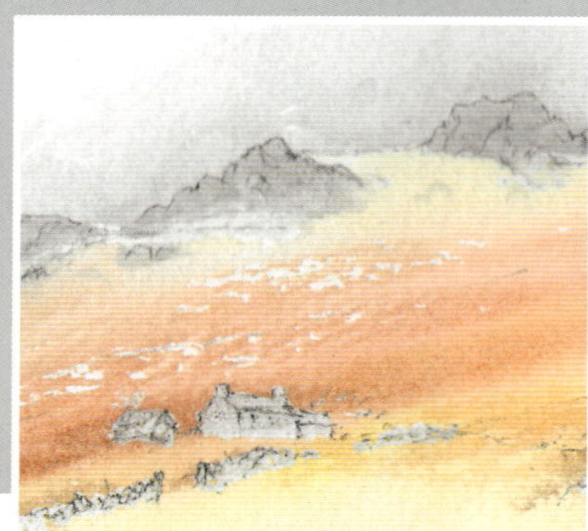

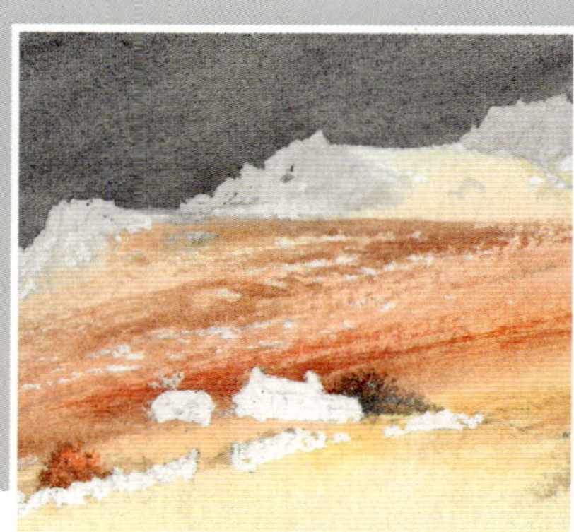

Identify the area At this point I have painted over the crags with a light grey. The lower sky has been included to avoid any unwanted white margins at the edges of the crags.

Apply the masking fluid Here the crags have been over-painted with the darker grey of the drawing gum (masking fluid) once the crags had dried, as well as the buildings, many boulders and the dry-stone wall. When the masking fluid had dried washes of Naples yellow and transparent red oxide were applied.

Remove the masking fluid Before removing the masking fluid a stronger mixture of burnt Sienna was brushed across the slopes to vary the effect. The dark sky wash comprised Payne's grey and a little lunar black. Once the paper had completely dried the masking fluid was removed by rubbing with a finger.

Keys to success with masking fluid

There is more about using masking fluid on page 88.

- Some watercolour papers do not take well to masking fluid and may tear when you attempt to remove it.

- Test your masking fluid on part of the paper you will be using before committing yourself, to ascertain whether it tears the paper when being removed.

- Keep an old brush aside purely for use with masking fluid, as it can spoil good brushes. Clean the brush well afterwards using either one of the cleaning fluids made for the purpose, soap and water, or (as I do) by dipping the brush into the residue of the small shampoo bottles you find in hotels.

- Masking fluid can leave a stark, hard-edged outline that in places may appear too harsh, so you may need to soften these with a damp brush. You may also need to re-shape an area where the fluid has gone slightly awry.

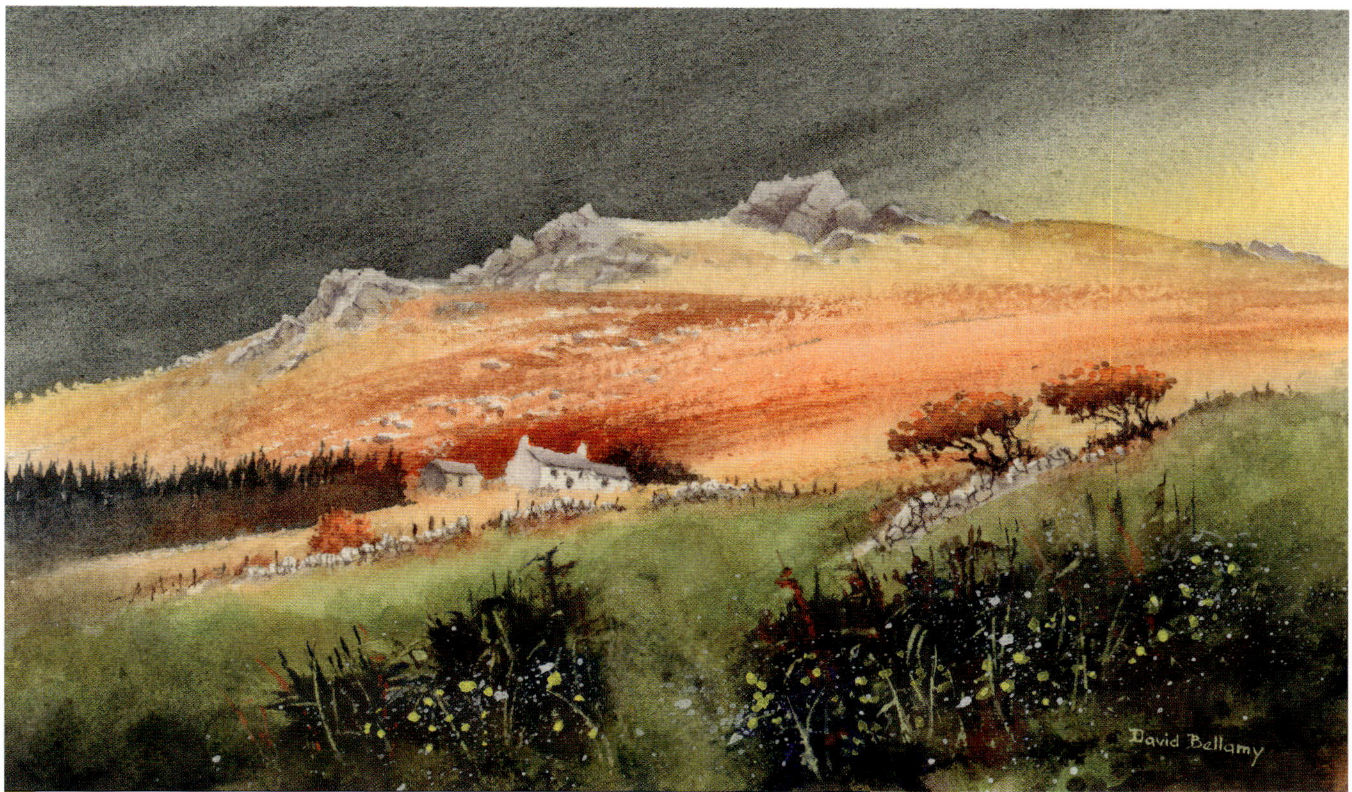

Painting *Cottage Below Carn Ffoi*

- A light grey comprising a mix of French ultramarine and burnt sienna was painted onto the crags and allowed to dry. Before tackling the rest of the painting, I applied Pebeo Drawing Gum over the crags, boulders, buildings and dry-stone walls.

- Once dry, I washed in Naples yellow at the top of the ridge between the crags, cadmium yellow pale over the right-hand trees and below the cottage, and transparent red oxide over the buildings. Higher up I laid on some burnt sienna.

- Mixing Payne's gray with a little lunar black, I swept a dark wash across a pre-wetted sky area so that the dark wash would blend in on the right. I left the brush-strokes visible as they impart a sense of energy and movement. Note the counterchange, with the hill being darker than the sky on the right.

- I dragged burnt sienna across the moor to suggest rough ground, the impression helped by the spots of masking fluid, all of which was then removed, revealing the underlying grey on the crags, which shows up well against the dark sky.

- After detailing the building, crags and dry-stone walls, I introduced the band of conifers with French ultramarine and raw umber. For the small trees on the right I worked with a mix of French ultramarine and burnt umber, with transparent red oxide for the foliage. I then scraped out stalks with a painting knife. Finally I spattered white gouache into the dark passage and used a fine brush to suggest some yellow flowers using a mixture of white and yellow gouache.

Cottage Below Carn Ffoi
25.5 × 16.5cm (10 × 6½in) Saunders Waterford 640gsm (300lb) Rough surface paper

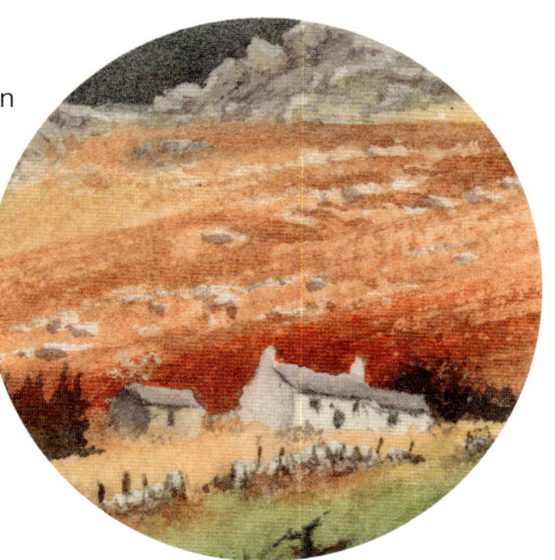

This close-up shows previously masked-out areas after being painted. Some edges have been softened with a damp brush to prevent them looking too hard.

You can read about scraping out on page 108, and spattering on page 13.

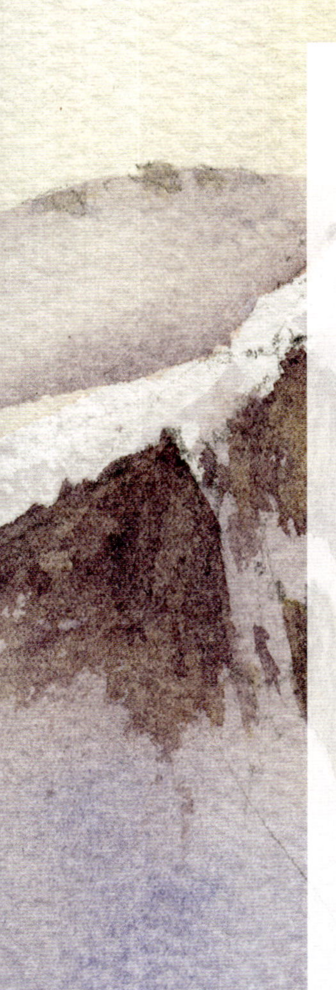

THE ARTIST EXPLORER:
Developing your painting style

Time to explore the unknown. In this chapter you will find a range of more innovative techniques, materials and experiments, such as combining watercolour with gouache, inks, collage, pastels, gesso, watercolour ground and more, as well as introducing found materials alongside those not normally associated with watercolour painting. We'll also look at how to combine these different media and techniques, to give you more starting points for your own exploration.

Experimenting with these methods will provide you with new ideas for working, and at the same time be fun. Once you get into this way of working it encourages you to explore further, so don't limit yourself to what you see in this book: there simply isn't the room here to show the many possibilities you can try.

Make notes as you progress with each technique: which colours you use, the order of working, how an additive may have been applied, and anything else that will help you recall how you did it. There is nothing more frustrating than looking back at a superb effect you have created and being unable to remember how you did it, or what colours were involved. I keep a book of watercolour paper for experiments – but you could instead maintain an exercise book showing the title of each painting and your notes on the way it was produced.

Watercolour painting can be challenging, but it should also be great fun. Whether we are trying to loosen up, or continue in a more methodical way, I firmly believe that if we are enjoying the process then we are more likely to end up with a better result.

> *Watercolour painting can be challenging, but it should also be great fun.*

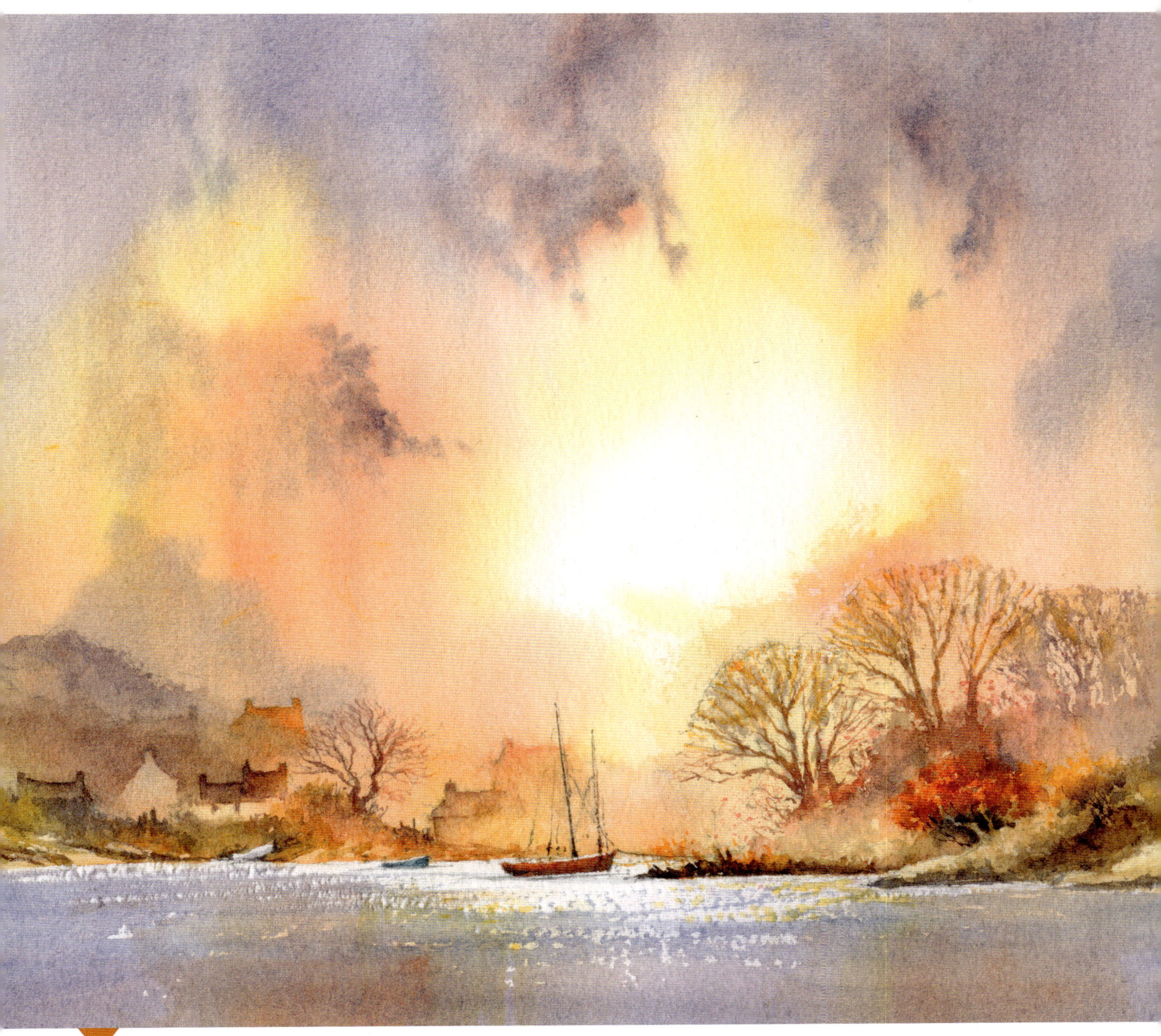

Llangwm, Pembrokeshire
38 × 25.5cm (15 × 10in) Saunders Waterford 640gsm (300lb) Rough surface paper

This was sketched on a dull day, so I was keen to inject atmosphere and intense light into the painting to lose some of the detail. The sky was created by working nickel titanate yellow round the white patch above the main boat, immediately adding quinacridone gold to the outer rim, and then laying a broad wash of lavender over the upper part of the sky and down both sides. Quickly I brought in some French ultramarine and permanent alizarin crimson, jiggling it in to create the squiggles of purple dripping out of the clouds. I also added Aussie red gold in places, bringing it down to water-level in the centre. Using mainly transparent red oxide and French ultramarine, most of the buildings are mere suggestions, their detail lost closer to the brightness.

Finding new approaches

There are new ways to work with traditional materials that can create fresh results and a dramatic change of style in your work, and it can be rewarding to experiment with this in mind. This can be an extremely useful process when you feel you are in a rut and don't know which avenue to pursue. Such experiments do not need to be complicated or intimidating. The easy methods shown here can add excitement and vigour to your work.

If you are reluctant to change your style, consider using these new methods for different purposes, such as creating greetings cards, or artwork that is not aimed at hanging on walls. See pages 150–159 for more on this.

Loosening up

Adopting a looser style in your paintings is a common desire. This will develop with experience, and actively re-assessing your approach will help things along:

- Suggest detail, rather than including every brick, stone, leaf, fencepost (or whatever) in the painting.
- Vigorous handling of the brush, knife, or whatever instrument you are using, will impart energy into the work.
- Allow accidents such as run-backs to happen when applying washes, rather than trying to create a perfect result.
- Make a feature of the white paper by vignetting your composition, or simply leaving parts of it untouched.
- Choose an uncomplicated subject and limit the time you take to complete the painting. This will help you to look for the essential elements and ignore parts that are not important.
- Painting outdoors is another excellent way of learning to loosen up, as you are often battling against not just time, but the weather as well.

Working on different papers

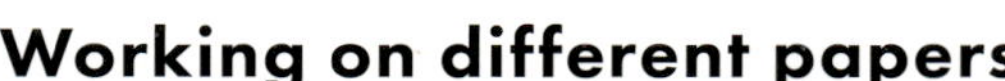

Something as simple as using a different type of paper surface can change the character of your work. Rather than the textured Not surface I usually favour, the paintings opposite are worked on an untextured paper designed for illustrators. Its extreme smoothness creates a really different feel to watercolour paper. Although it is not the easiest of papers to handle with watercolour, working on very smooth paper is an enjoyable change of pace that comes with its own advantages as well as challenges. Pulling out colour (see page 64), for example, works extremely well on extra-smooth paper, as does spattering (see page 13). Laying a preliminary wash of clean water over the paper before applying the actual colour wash is essential for a smooth result.

Daler-Rowney manufacture Bristol paper which has a very smooth surface, ideal for illustrators and produced in pads in different sizes. There are many other similar papers on the market.

Woodland Cascade

I began with vertical strokes of lunar blue with nickel titanate yellow in the centre, and touches of burnt sienna. The trees were created wet-in-wet with lunar blue and burnt sienna. Before the wash dried, I spattered water over parts of the wash. Once dry, I continued with lunar blue and burnt sienna, the paper surface encouraging sharp edges to the boulders, and I pulled out colour easily with a small flat brush.

I left the falls as pure white paper, but dabbed in a few spots of white gouache to indicate splashes. Falling water is best kept as simple as possible, as it is easy to make it look overworked.

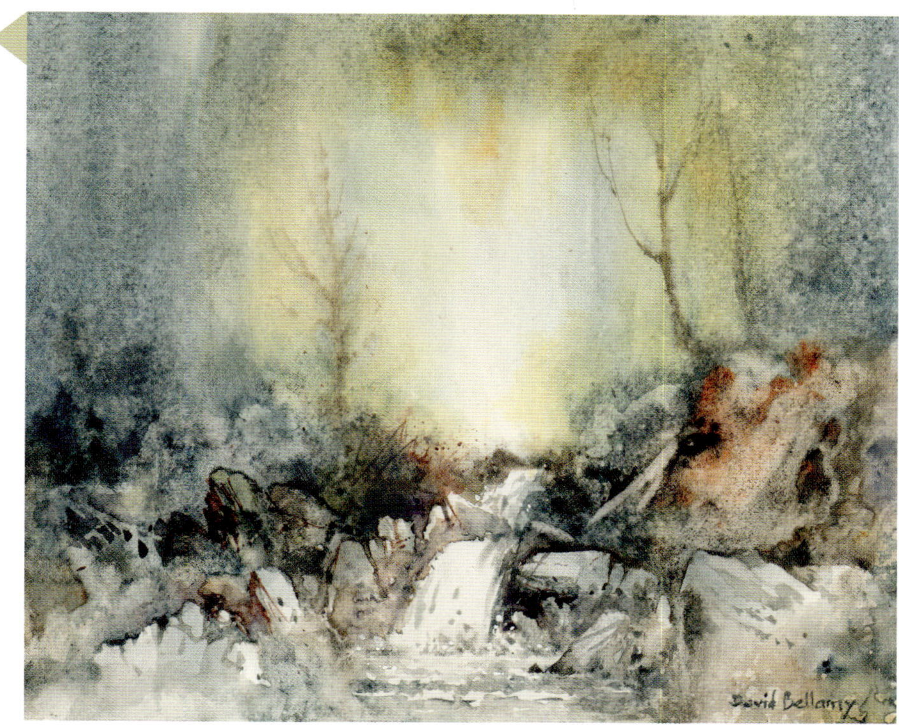

Tree Fantasy

15 × 12.5cm (6 × 5in) Bristol board

Here I was playing with extra-smooth paper, creating something that appeared to be half-beast, swirling a variety of colours onto the paper, dropping in others and spattering with water while it was wet. Halfway through the painting I turned it upside-down to finish it as you see it.

Trying out new surfaces to take your watercolours can be great fun, especially as in this case I had no idea what the subject might be. Having an artistic 'fun day' in this way can be truly therapeutic, and even lead to some exciting revelations. Such paintings can be cropped to be made into a greetings card, gift tag or artistic masterpiece.

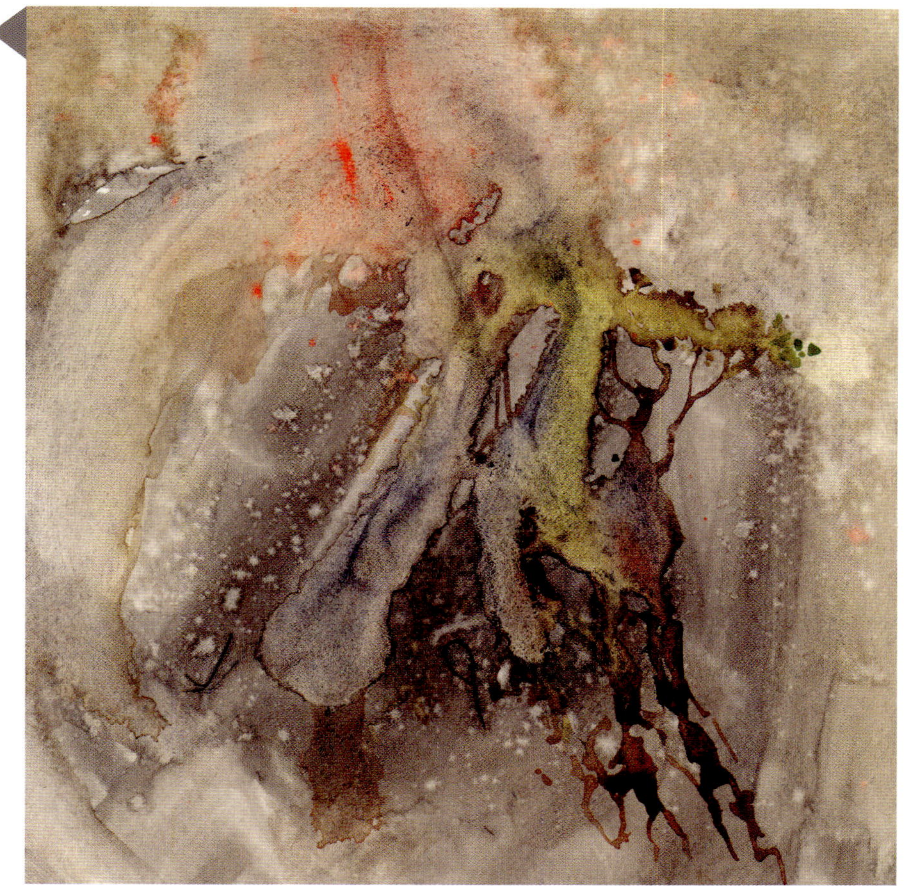

TECHNIQUE
Pouring watercolour

Pouring paint has recently become more popular as a technique, but it is usually done with acrylics. As you can see here, this fluid, flowing technique is ideally suited to watercolour, too.

  Pouring is an alternative to the traditional manner of laying washes (see page 14), and can create some dramatic effects. Pouring a strongly granulating colour onto a Rough paper surface is a simple way of enhancing textures in a passage, for example.

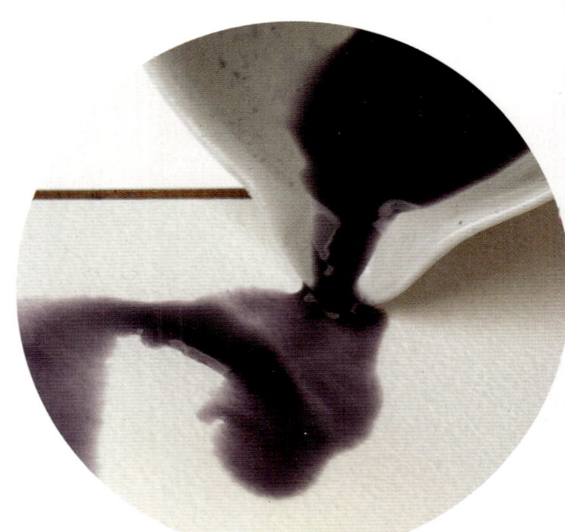

Pouring
Prepare your paint in a container like a small jug, and pour it onto the paper, tipping the board to get it to flow as you wish.

Keys to success with pouring

- Test the process a few times before trying it for real.
- Be prepared to tilt the paper in a direction that will attain the most promising result.
- Keep a spray diffuser handy to spray into the wet, flowing wash where you may need to weaken the tonal strength, or create a shaft of light.
- If things go wrong, immediately blast the wash with a stronger spray of clean water and try again.

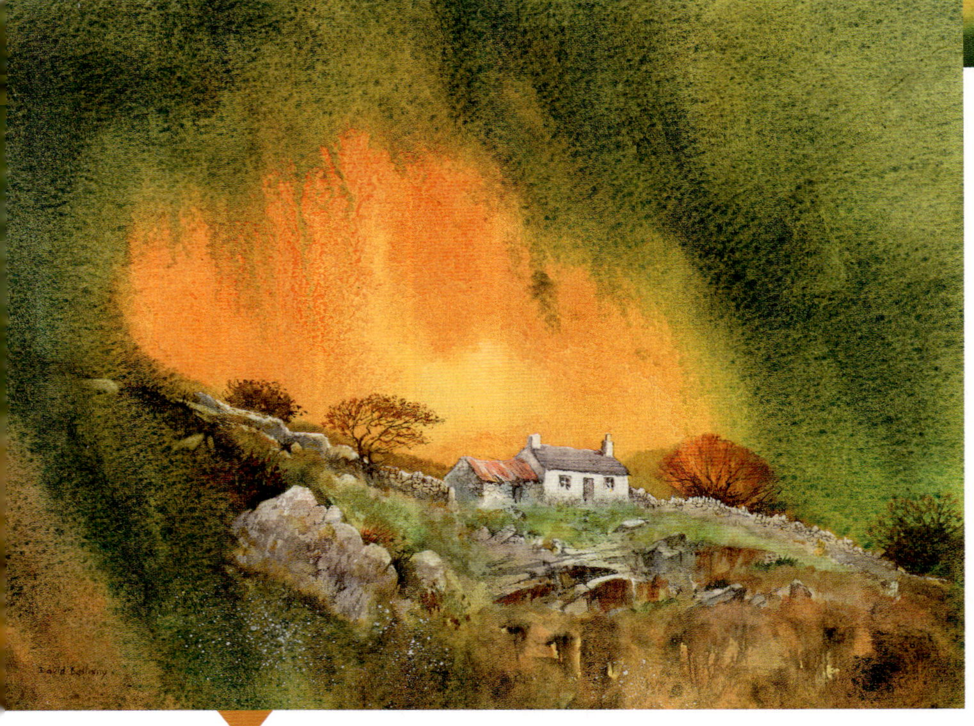

Mountain Retreat
30.5 × 23cm (12 × 9in) Saunders Waterford 300gsm (140lb) Not surface paper

Painting *Mountain Retreat*

Based on a pencil sketch, much of the composition is from my imagination. This way of working can be very liberating.

- Note the intense brightness of Aussie red gold, which I washed over the central sky before pouring a strong mix of hematite violet genuine and lunar blue over the top, with more on either side than in the centre.
- I held the board at a sharp angle for a few moments to encourage a wild, windswept atmosphere.
- The cottage, walls and rocks were all protected from the downpour with masking fluid applied beforehand.
- The branches of the tree to the left of the cottage were rendered with a fine dip pen charged with a watercolour mix of French ultramarine and burnt umber.

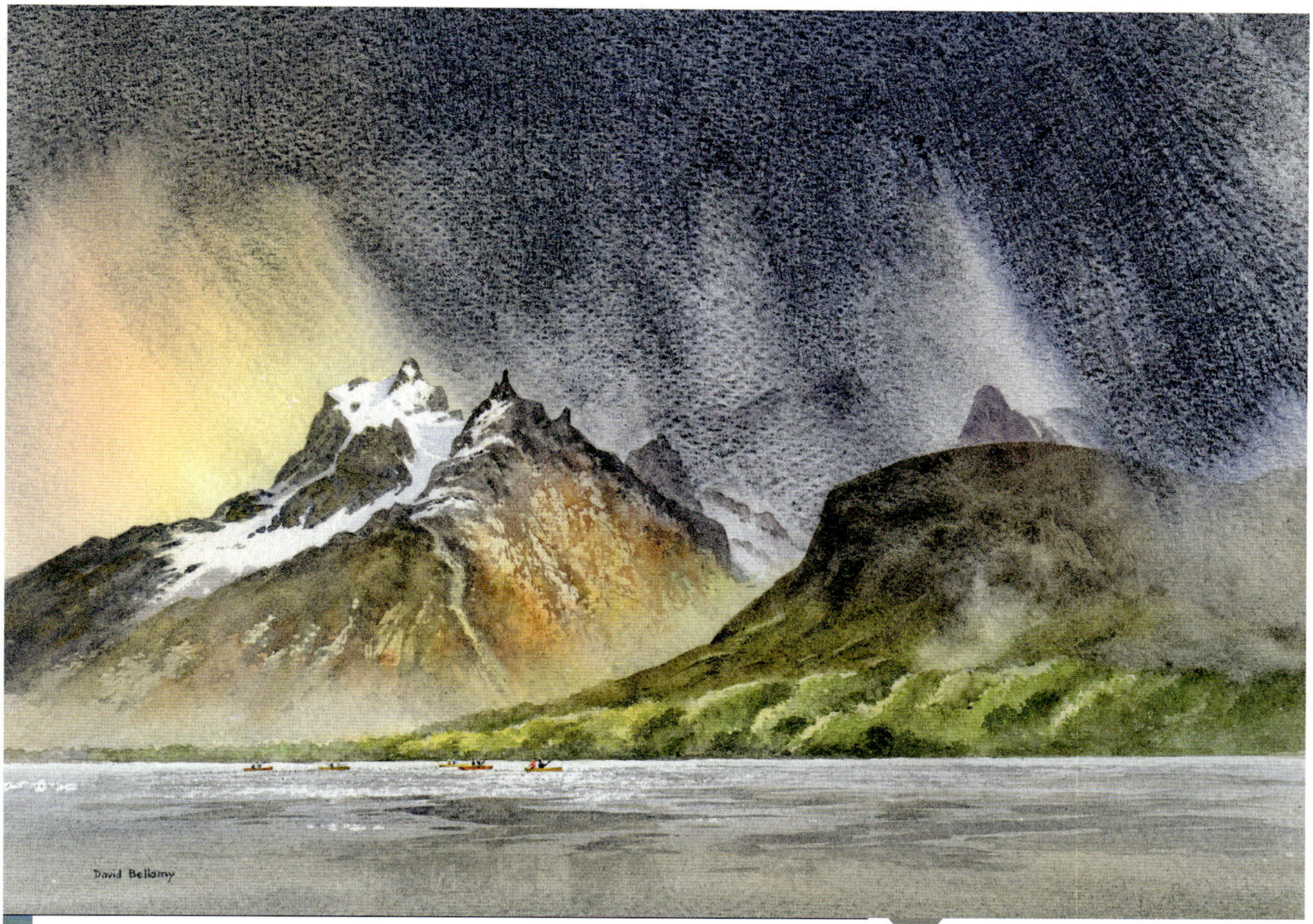

Painting *Kayaking down Rio Serrano, Chile*

- I began by applying masking fluid (see page 40) over the snow areas. For the wild, stormy sky, I wetted the whole sky and applied a wash of Naples yellow and some alizarin crimson for the left-hand sky, and lunar blue to render the far distant peaks.
- Once dry, I re-wetted the whole sky and held the paper at a steep angle, slanting to the right, then poured on a strong mixture of very liquid sodalite genuine. I applied less paint over the left-hand part of the sky to avoid losing the warm colours.
- The wash flowed down over the peaks to allow them just to be made out through the atmosphere, while the texture on the central peak was achieved by scumbling transparent red oxide across the paper with the side of a rigger brush, adding some details with burnt umber.
- The river was rendered firstly with a dry-brushed half-inch band of light sodalite genuine below the far shore, and then a fully wet wash below it. Once dry I used the edge of a 12mm (½in) flat brush to create the darker patches of swirling water.

Kayaking down Rio Serrano, Chile
38 × 25.5cm (15 × 10in) Saunders Waterford 425gsm (200lb) Rough surface paper

This scene was originally sketched from a canoe as we made our way down the Rio Serrano swollen with glacier-melt while on one of my adventure painting holidays with a group.

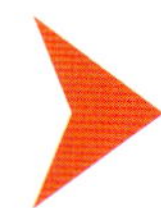

See pages 92–93 for more on scumbling, and 90–91 for dry brush.

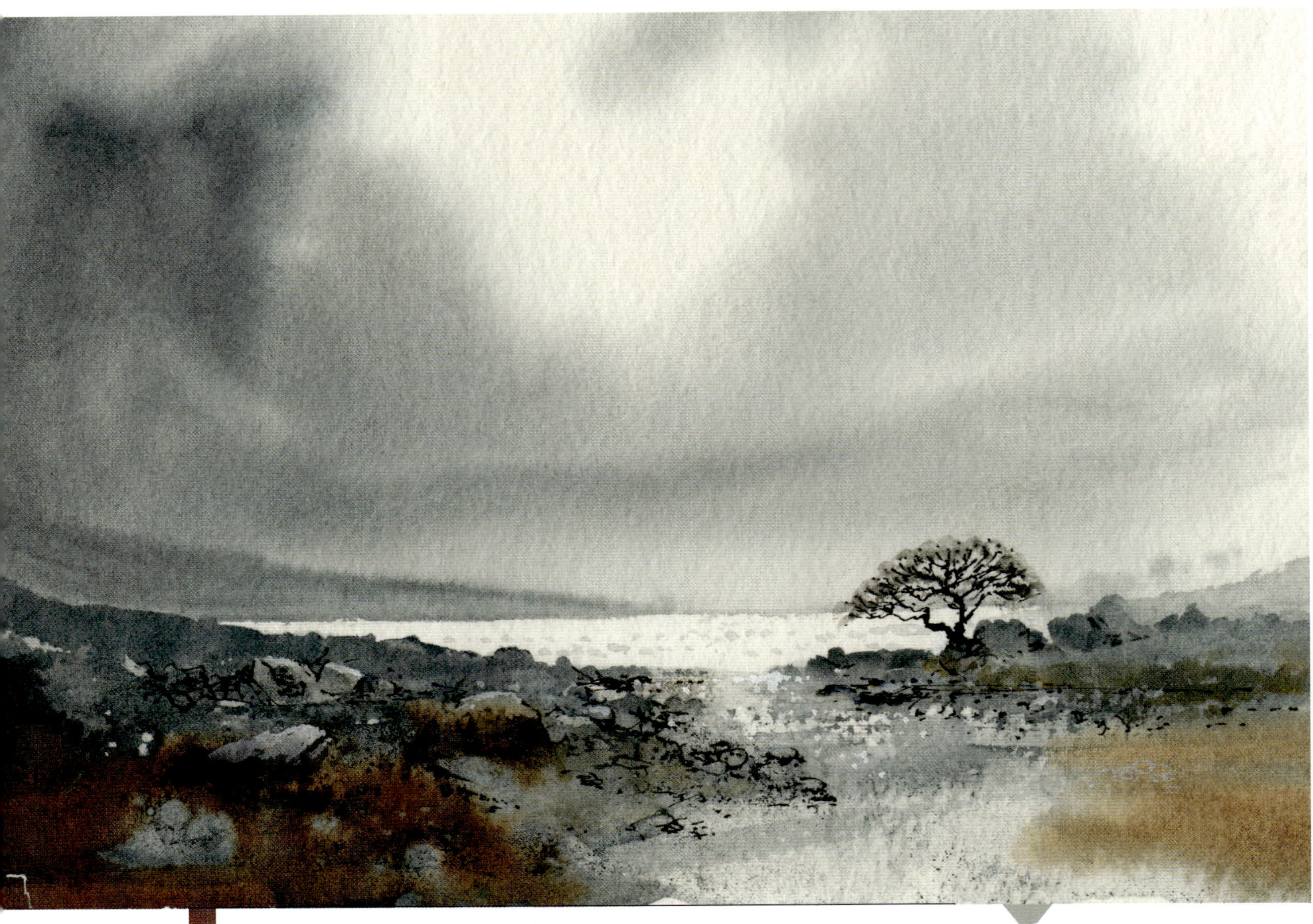

Silver Tarn
25.5 × 17.5cm (10 × 7in) Saunders
Waterford 640gsm (300lb) Rough
surface paper

Painting *Silver Tarn*

- I began with a wash of clean water across the sky and then applied Payne's gray FW acrylic ink (see opposite) with a swirling motion to suggest clouds. I brushed in the sloping far shore on the left-hand side with a stronger application of the same colour.

- I dabbed some small blobs of weak Payne's gray on the water and then continued down into the foreground with weak colour at first, then stronger colour to create detail once it had dried.

- On the nearest part of the foreground I introduced some Daniel Smith walnut ink, and then added a few highlights on rocks and the outlet stream with white gouache.

Ink with watercolour

In the early days, Indian ink was not permanent and faded with time, but the advent of acrylic inks now gives us a permanent result for ink drawings and working in line and wash. As the following pages illustrate, you can use them simply to draw, or lay them as washes, diluting them with water as you wish, to create a weaker wash.

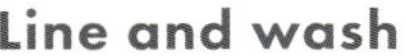

Dropper bottles

These Daler-Rowney FW acrylic inks are excellent for laying in washes, as they come with their own pipette attached to the cap. This can be used to dispense the ink into the palette to produce a wash, or to directly apply the ink to the paper.

Line and wash

Also known as pen and wash, this usually involves making a pen drawing, then laying on watercolour (or diluted ink) washes to add colour and tone. A looser approach may be achieved by beginning with the washes and then drawing into this once the wash has dried.

There are many ways of working in line and wash. It's a lovely medium and well worth spending some time experimenting with different ways of working.

West Hoathly Village, Sussex

I drew this sketch with a sepia pen on cartridge paper while sitting in the car and coloured it in later with FW acrylic inks: red earth, antelope brown, a touch of yellow and Payne's gray. I wanted to retain a light, airy feeling with no strong darks.

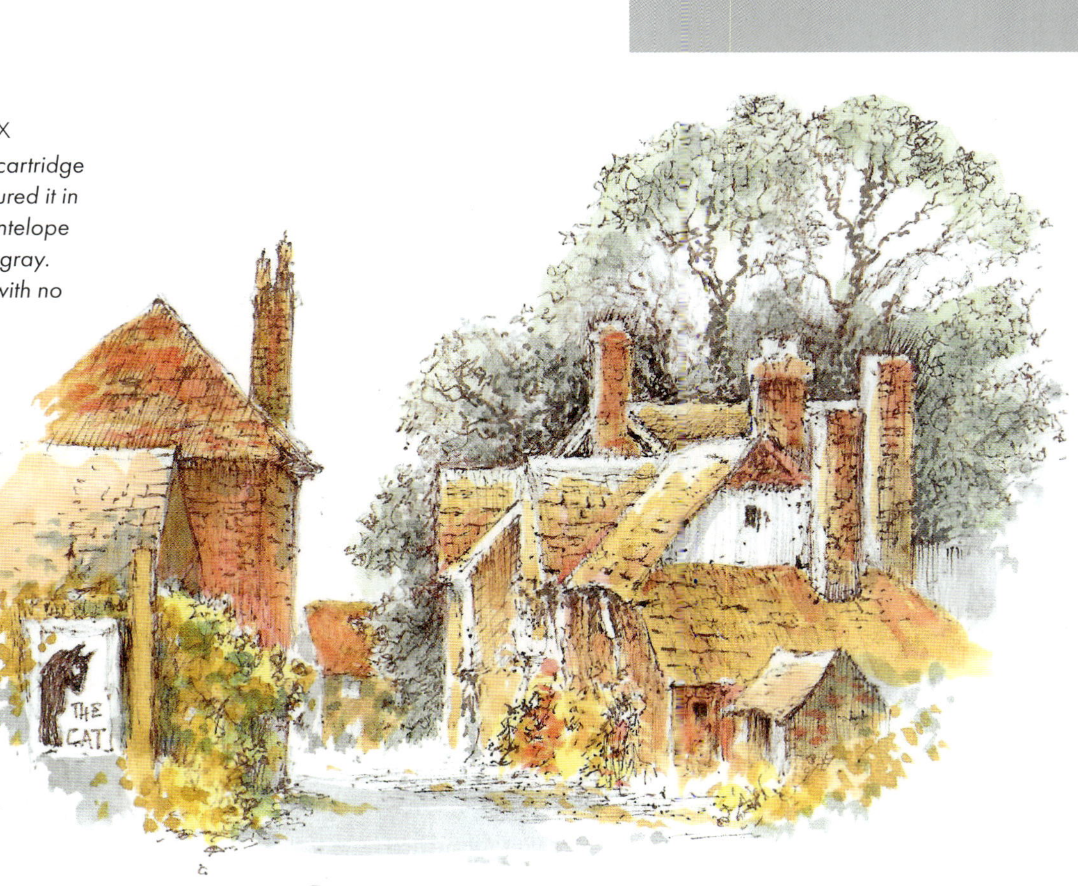

Exploring line and wash

I use pens mostly for sketching buildings, sometimes adding colour.
A fibre-tip pen will produce an even line, while a dip pen is more expressive
in creating more variety in the line. It is, however, a pain to carry around
bottles of ink if you are working outdoors. I particularly like applying
ink lines with a rigger brush as it can impart real character to a line
and easily work on Rough paper, but this takes some practice.

In this scene a dip pen was used to describe the features, and
this is excellent for varying the strength of the line, as you can
especially see on the rocks beneath the cottage in the detail.

Initial ink drawing

Pen Porthclais, prior to watercolour washes. These
monochrome washes were laid with diluted black acrylic ink.

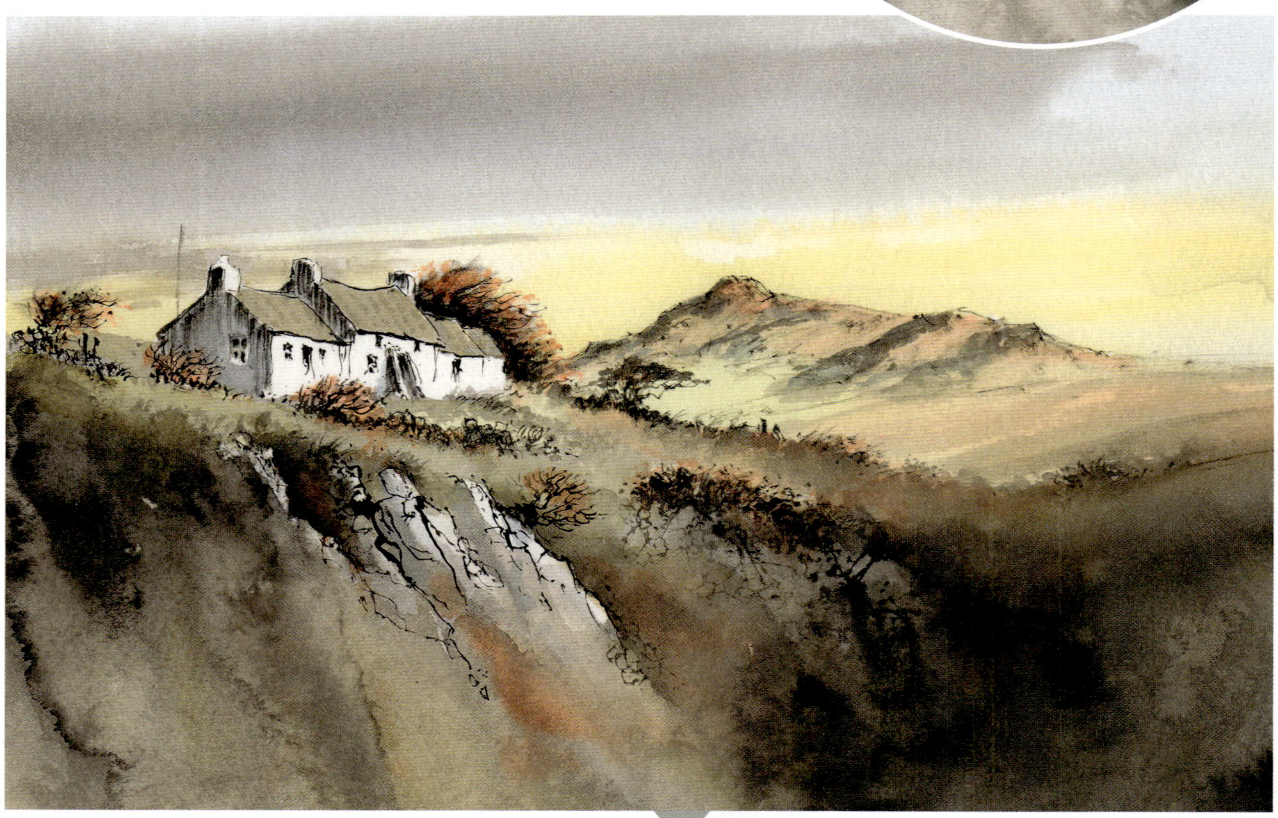

Pen Porthclais

23 × 12.5cm (9 × 5in) Saunders Waterford 425gsm (200lb) Not
surface paper

Weak washes of watercolour were laid across the composition.
Creating the tones at the earlier stage with ink diluted to various
degrees is a useful alternative to mixing various tones for
the colours.

Acrylic paint with watercolour

Working with acrylics would need a whole new book, but here I just want to point out the possibilities for bringing in little touches of acrylics to enhance or rectify a problem in watercolour. This obviates the need to use masking fluid or negative painting to get light areas on top of dark.

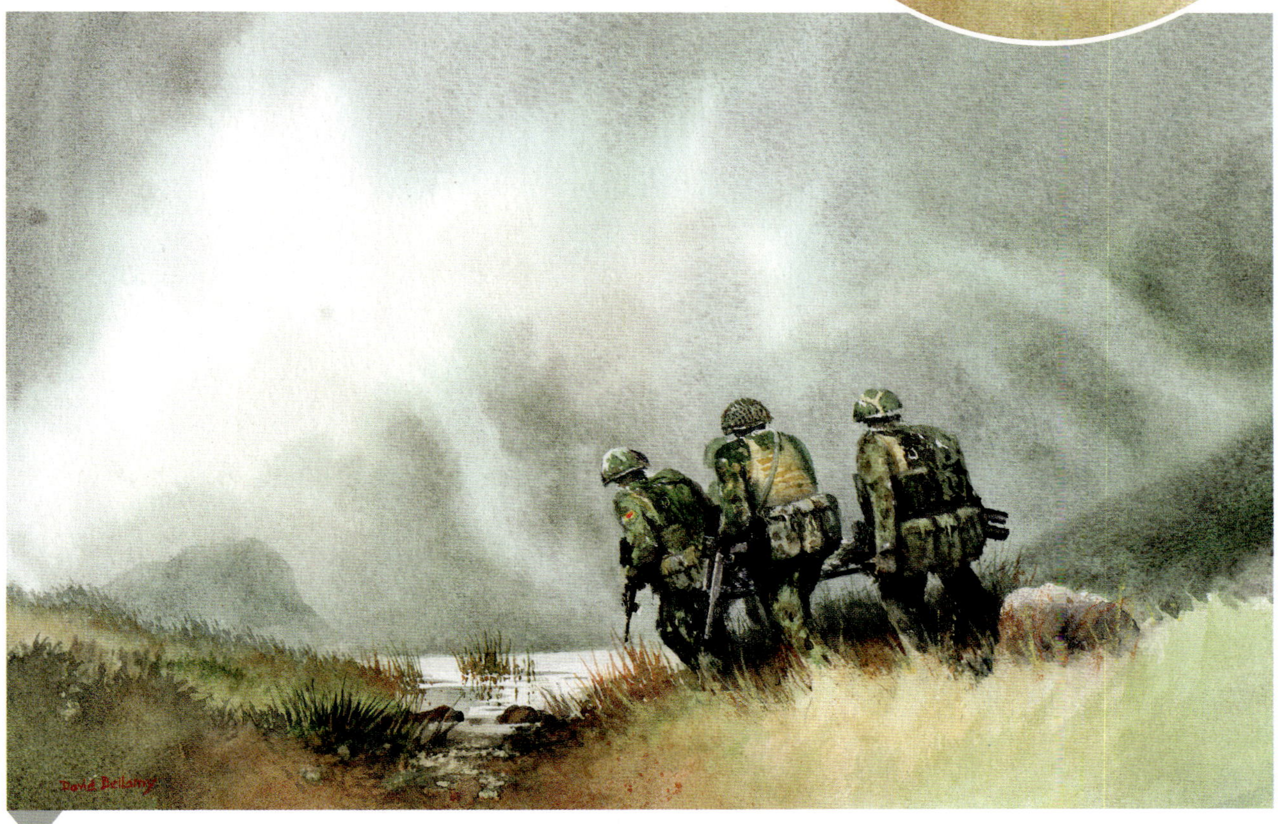

Detail of acrylic paint
Here I found Naples yellow acrylic paint excellent for feathering in the light-coloured reeds beneath the stretcher-bearers.

Casualty Rescue
30.5 × 23cm (12 × 9in) Saunders Waterford 300gsm (140lb) Not surface paper

I did the original sketch during a battle exercise – and used the smoke of battle to isolate the stretcher-bearers as they struggled across rough ground.

TECHNIQUE

Sponging

Flat cosmetics sponges, which can be found in supermarkets and high street shops, have varied and interesting surfaces scored by holes of various sizes. When these are dipped in paint and applied to a painting they can produce the most fascinating effects.

Sponging is a fantastic technique for pebbles, walls and foliage. Sometimes I bend the sponges and cut larger gaps to further vary the resulting marks.

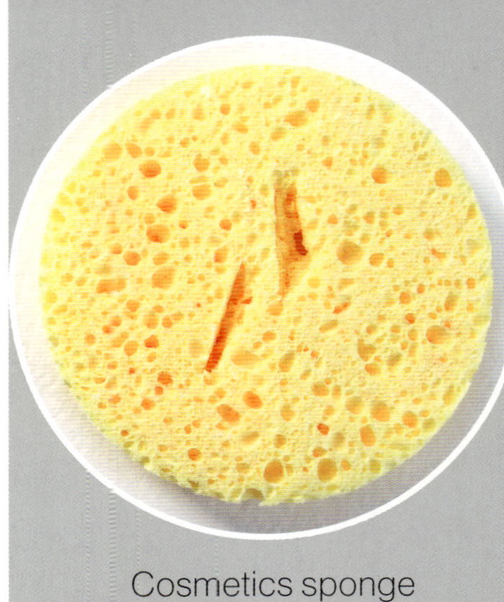

Cosmetics sponge

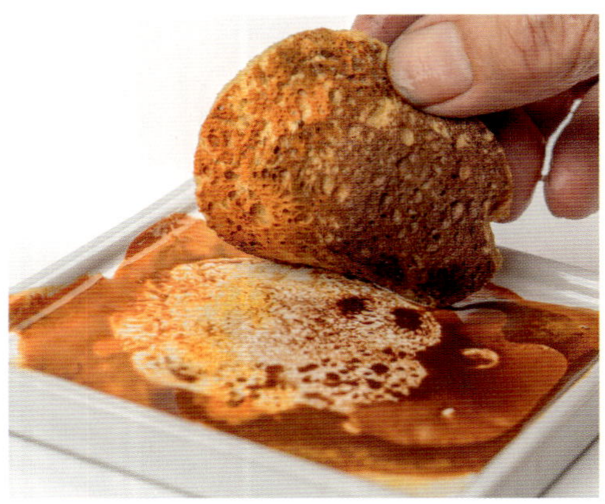

Load the sponge Prepare your paint in a flat palette or saucer, and simply dip the sponge in to load it.

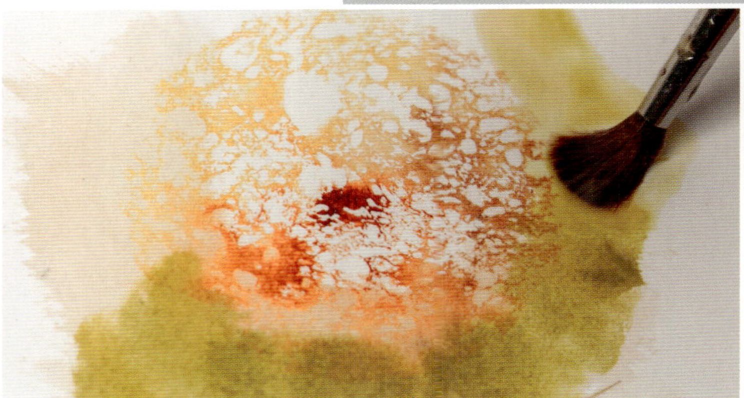

Hiding the circle Once you have applied the sponge to the paper you need to blend in the edges to avoid a harsh-edged circle remaining. You can achieve this by washing over the edge with a large brush or sponge, or prior to applying the effect wet the area where the edge will appear.

The keys to sponging success

- It is always best to test sponge-dabbing out on scrap paper first to ensure you have the right consistency of paint.
- Try dabbing the sponge into two or three different colours to create a more varied result.
- A creamy consistency usually works best, but you will find it best to test the effect first on spare paper.
- This technique has been used in the paintings of *The Tranquil Wye*, opposite; *Bridge in the Llanberis Pass* on page 27; and *Solva Moorings* on page 137.

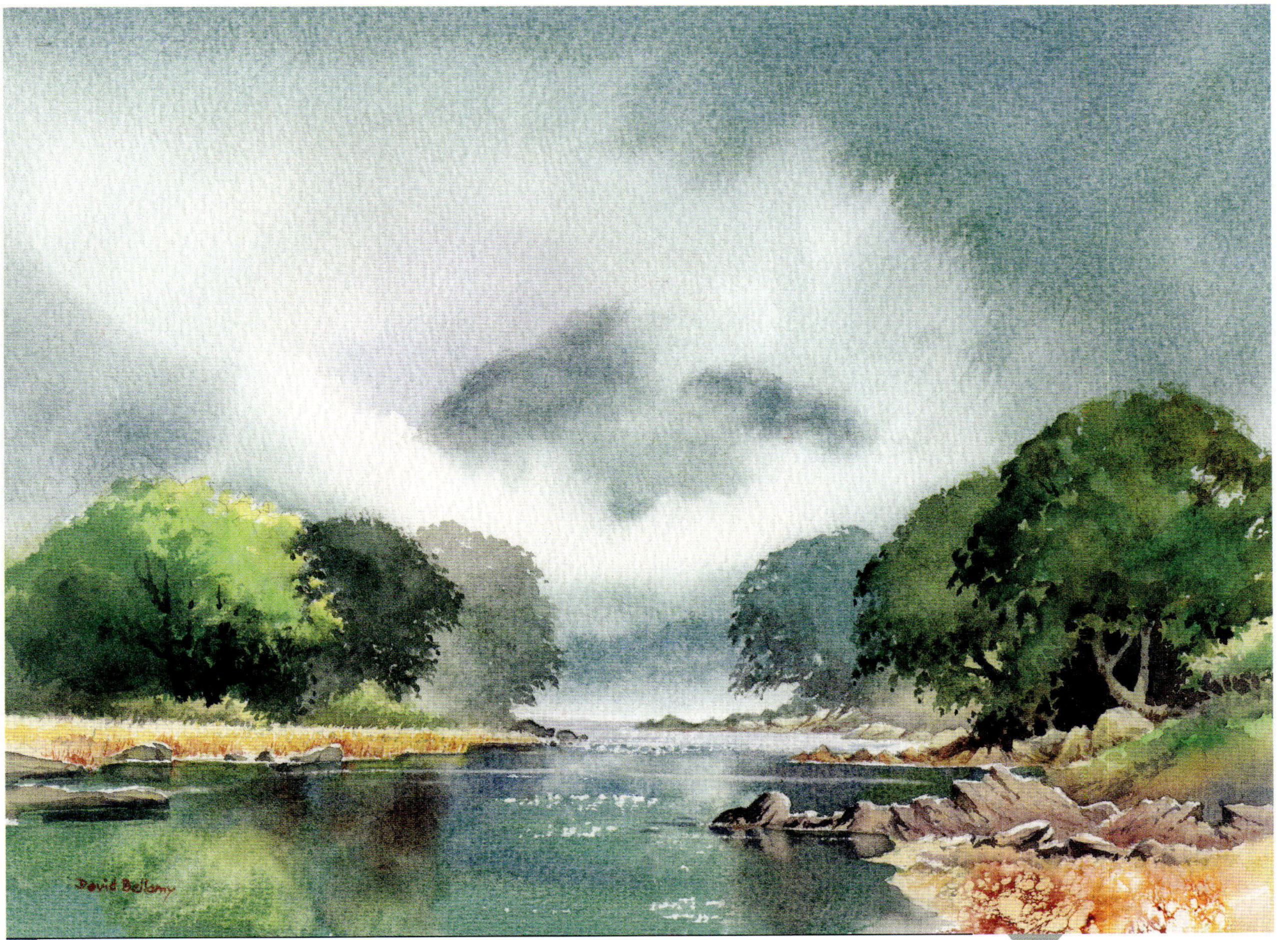

Painting *The Tranquil Wye*

One device I find extremely effective on occasions when I wish to create a strong
variation between the distance and closer features is to lay down a cool colour
for the far distance, keeping that as a separate plane of colour as in this scene.
For that I usually keep to blues or greys. This is also an effective way of managing
greens in a landscape and ensuring that they do not overwhelm the work.

- Sky, hill and cloud were all painted with lunar blue, a cool colour to suggest
  great space. The greens in the waterside trees become warmer as they
  get closer.
- The stones at the bottom right of the painting were rendered by
  dipping a cosmetic sponge into various warm colours laid out on
  the palette, and applying it to the paper.
- The warm colours of the stones counterbalance the
  predominance of blues and greens.

The Tranquil Wye
30.5 × 23cm (12 × 9in)
Saunders Waterford 300gsm
(140lb) Rough surface paper

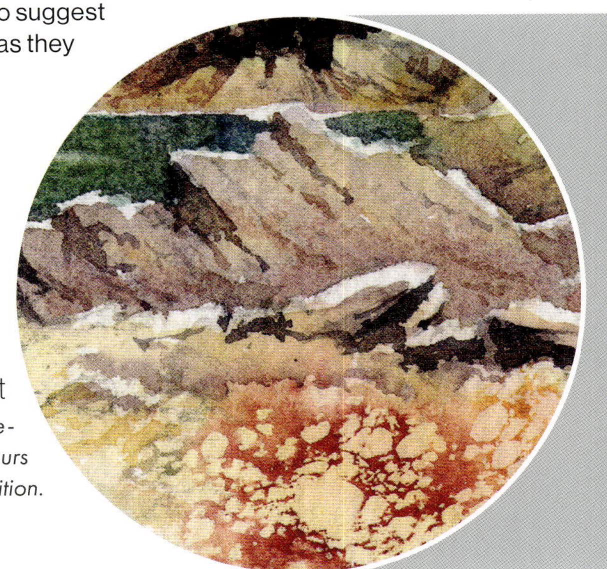

Sponging for impact
*Even this small area of sponging is arresting. The eye-
catching texture combined with the contrasting colours
makes this an important part of the composition.*

TECHNIQUE

Stamping

Applying paint with the edge of a piece of card that has been dipped in watercolour is a way to produce straight edges for masts, posts, drainpipes and similar features, and is often more effective than trying to use a brush held in a shaky hand.

  The two dark bamboo uprights on the left of the painting on the opposite page were achieved in this way.

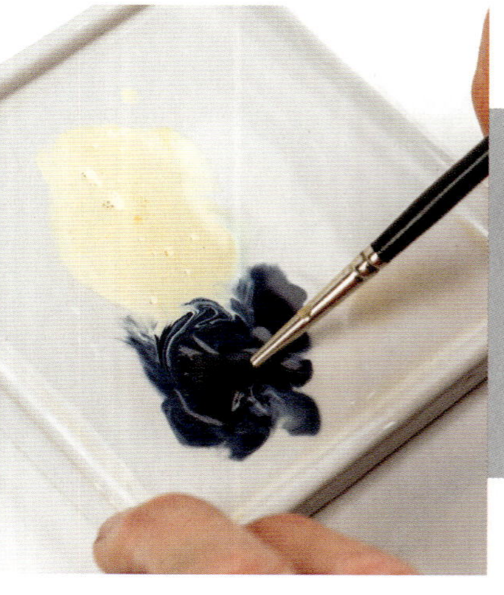

Preparing paint Prepare your paint in a flat palette to load the card. You can create a vari-coloured effect by adding one or two extra colours into the mix.

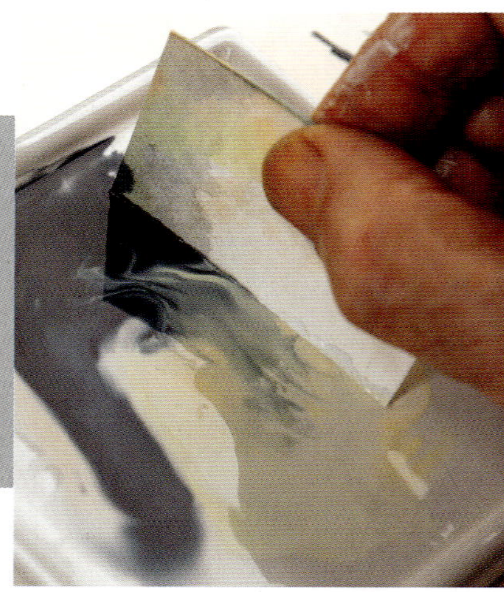

Loading Dip the card edge into watercolour on a flat palette to load the card.

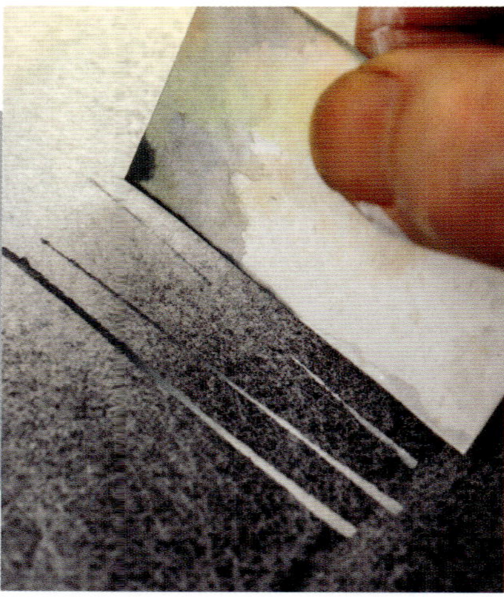

Stamping Here I have added Sodalite genuine to the top of the card edge and white gouache to the lower end. Firmly press down the card where you want to make the mark, then lift away cleanly.

The keys to stamping success

- After dipping the card, test the effect on scrap paper to ascertain whether it is the right consistency before using it on your painting.
- You can use almost any stiff paper or card – I often use offcuts of 300gsm (140lb) watercolour paper.
- Consider any tonal variation you need in the finished image and mix the colour(s) accordingly.
- Adding gouache to the mix will allow you to stamp light over dark areas.

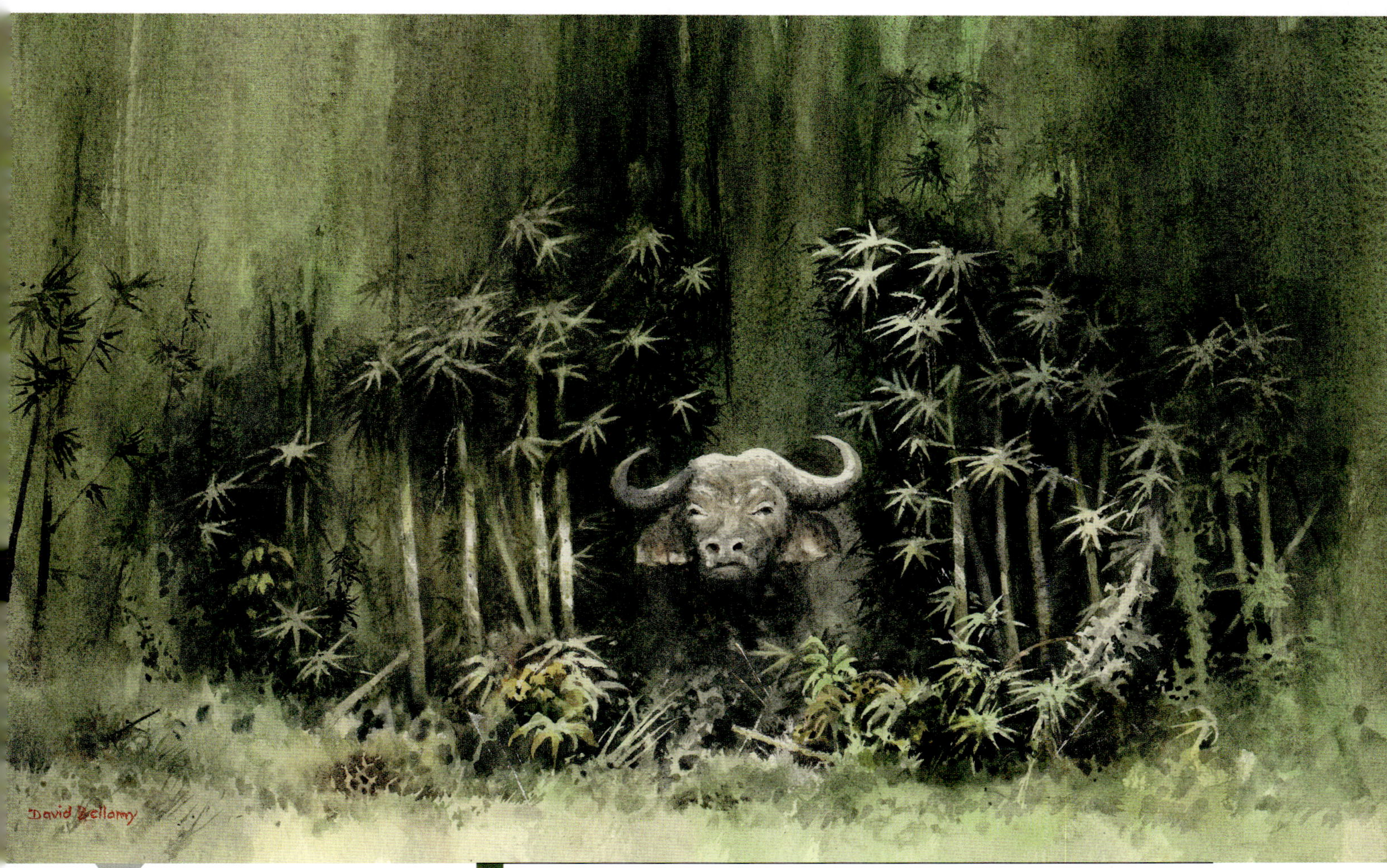

Buffalo in Bamboo Jungle

35.5 × 23cm (14 × 9in) Saunders Waterford
640gsm (300lb) Not surface paper

*This bull buffalo stood staring at me out
of the bamboo forest on the slopes of
Mount Kenya as I hiked along the trail,
my guides a long way behind. Had I time
to leap up a tree if he charged? I already
had sketches of the bamboo forest, but
I quickly got in a few photographs. Sadly
he failed to smile for the camera.*

Painting *Buffalo in Bamboo Jungle*

A work where green is the predominant colour, and green apatite
genuine is present in various degrees of strength.

- The light bamboo leaves and trunks were achieved with masking
  fluid, while the dark trunks were mainly created with the side of a card
  dipped in green apatite genuine, in places with burnt umber added.

- Near the bottom the undergrowth becomes more abstract: rather
  than describing masses of blades of grass I dabbed darker shapes
  in places, making these darker slightly higher up to suggest the mass
  receding into the depths of the forest.

- Where the overall colour and tone is a dull medium tone, bringing
  in yellows and perhaps orange to brighten part of it up can work
  well, and also some blue and perhaps burnt or raw umber to create
  dark areas.

- Light areas look brighter when juxtaposed against dark ones.

- Don't feel you have to paint every green tree green: introducing some
  dark trees using French ultramarine with raw or burnt umber can
  enhance a scene and add variety and depth.

Improving composition

There are many varied ways of enhancing a subject, some of which can be minor details, while others can have a profound effect on the scene. In this example, and the one overleaf, I aim to show you how I go about altering or adding to a composition, and to start you thinking about how you can apply these ideas to your own work.

Simple devices to enhance your compositions

The optimum time to consider the sort of enhancements described here is before you begin painting – preferably while you are creating a studio sketch to work out not just the overall structure, but also minor points which will bring your work to life.

   While neither of these examples include people, animals or birds, adding in these forms of life can also give your work added appeal. To get the most benefit out of this, take a scene and see how you can apply these devices in a composition you might like to paint.

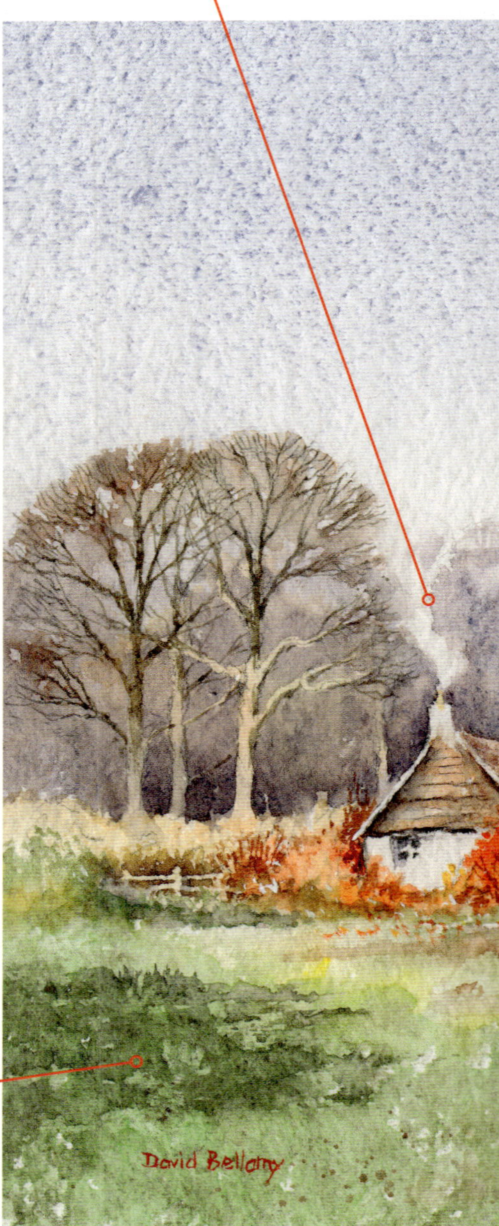

Rising smoke breaks up the line of trees in the background – it wasn't in the original scene.

Cast shadow across part of the foreground can add a feeling of depth to a painting.

Edge of the Forest
33 × 23cm (13 × 9in) Two Rivers 425gsm (200lb) Rough surface paper

The arrows indicate features of the scene that have either been added, or enhanced in some way.

This more prominent tree creates a sense of space
by pushing back the line of trees to its right.

This large tree helps to balance the composition,
otherwise most of the interest is on the left side.

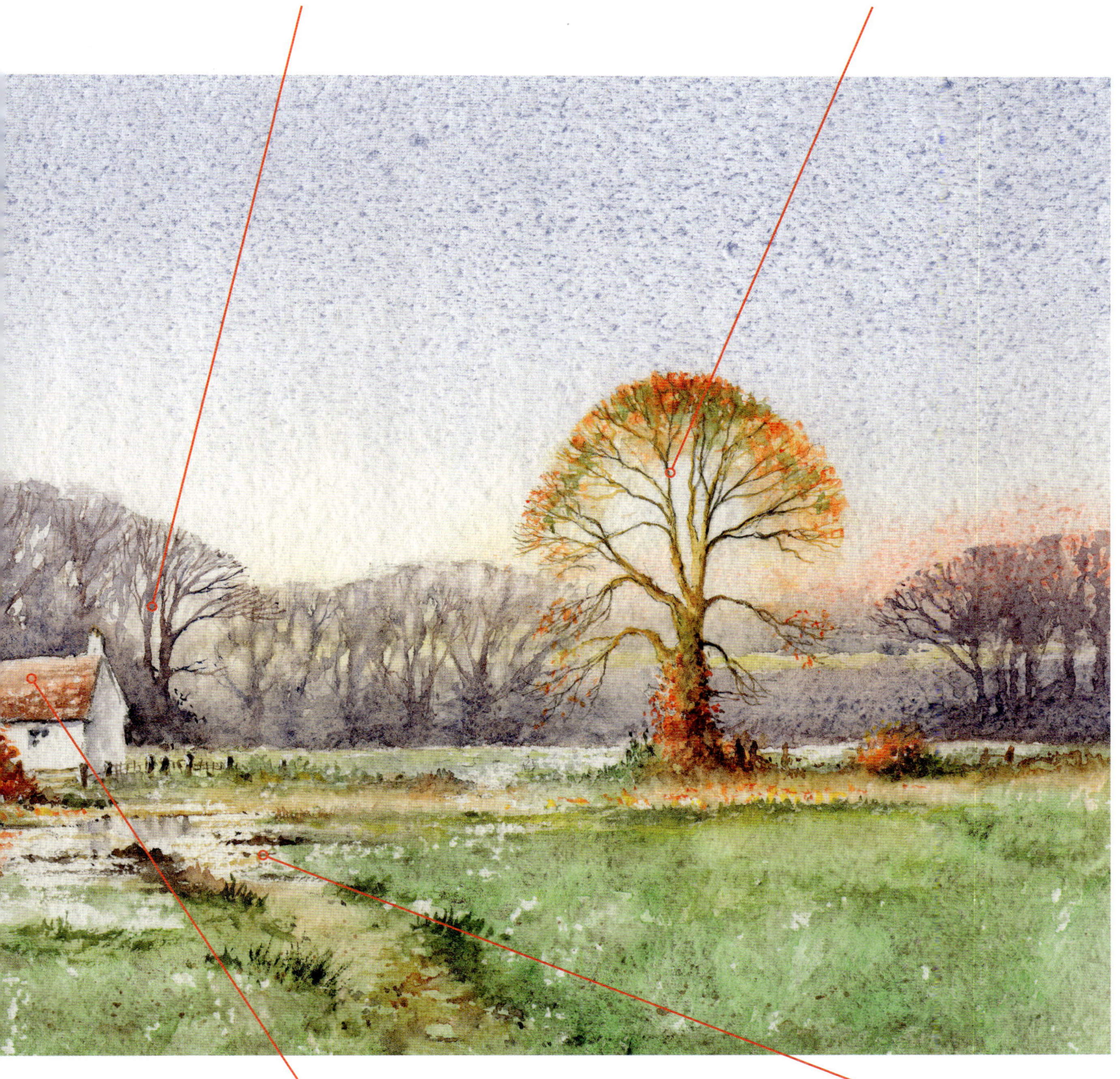

Counterchange (see page 67) on the
roof to help define the outline.

Neither the puddle nor the pathway lead-in were present
in the scene, but they add to the overall effect.

Painting *Tranquil Evening, Angle*

This composition displays a further collection of devices I use to improve a painting, and though it departs considerably from the mood and time of day at which I took the photograph, it is still a faithful rendering of the place.

When I see a good sky, I sketch and photograph it so that I can use it for compositions where something more inspiring is needed than what comes with the scene at that time. I moved the stream a little way to lead in towards the church, and placed the boats where I felt they would work best for the composition, at the same time removing the twin keels so that they each flopped to one side.

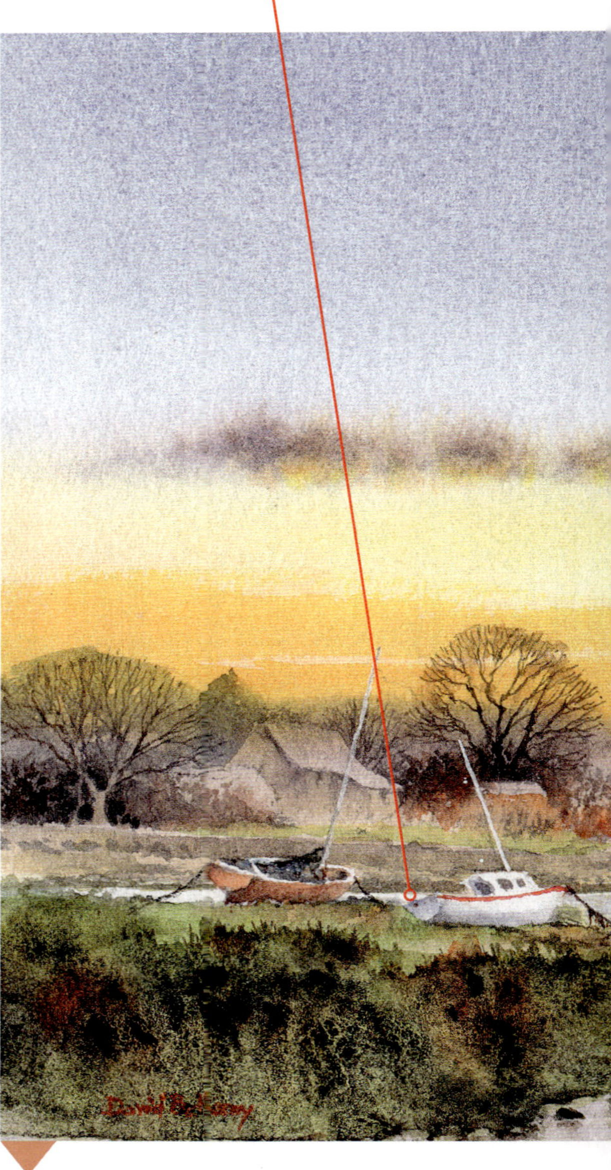

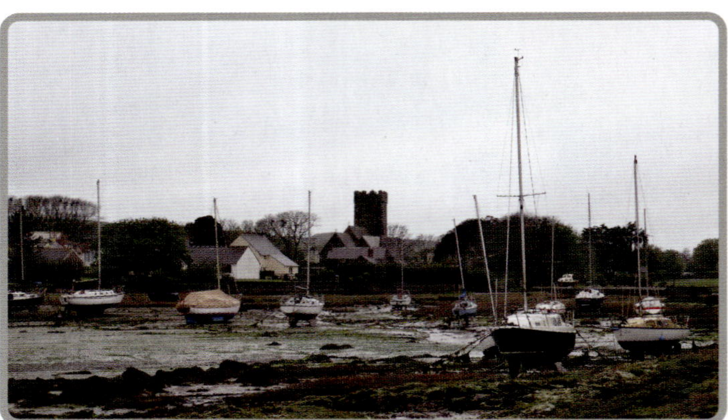

Reference photograph

I have many photographs of this subject, but this is the most useful and closest to the composition that I created from this visit to one of my favourite sketching locations. As you can see it was a dismal day, with boats lined up like soldiers on parade, a feature further emphasized by the boats having twin keels which kept them upright. I strongly felt the need to inject some magic and get rid of the regimented formation.

Tranquil Evening, Angle
35.5 × 23cm (14 × 9in) Saunders Waterford 300gsm (140lb) Not surface paper

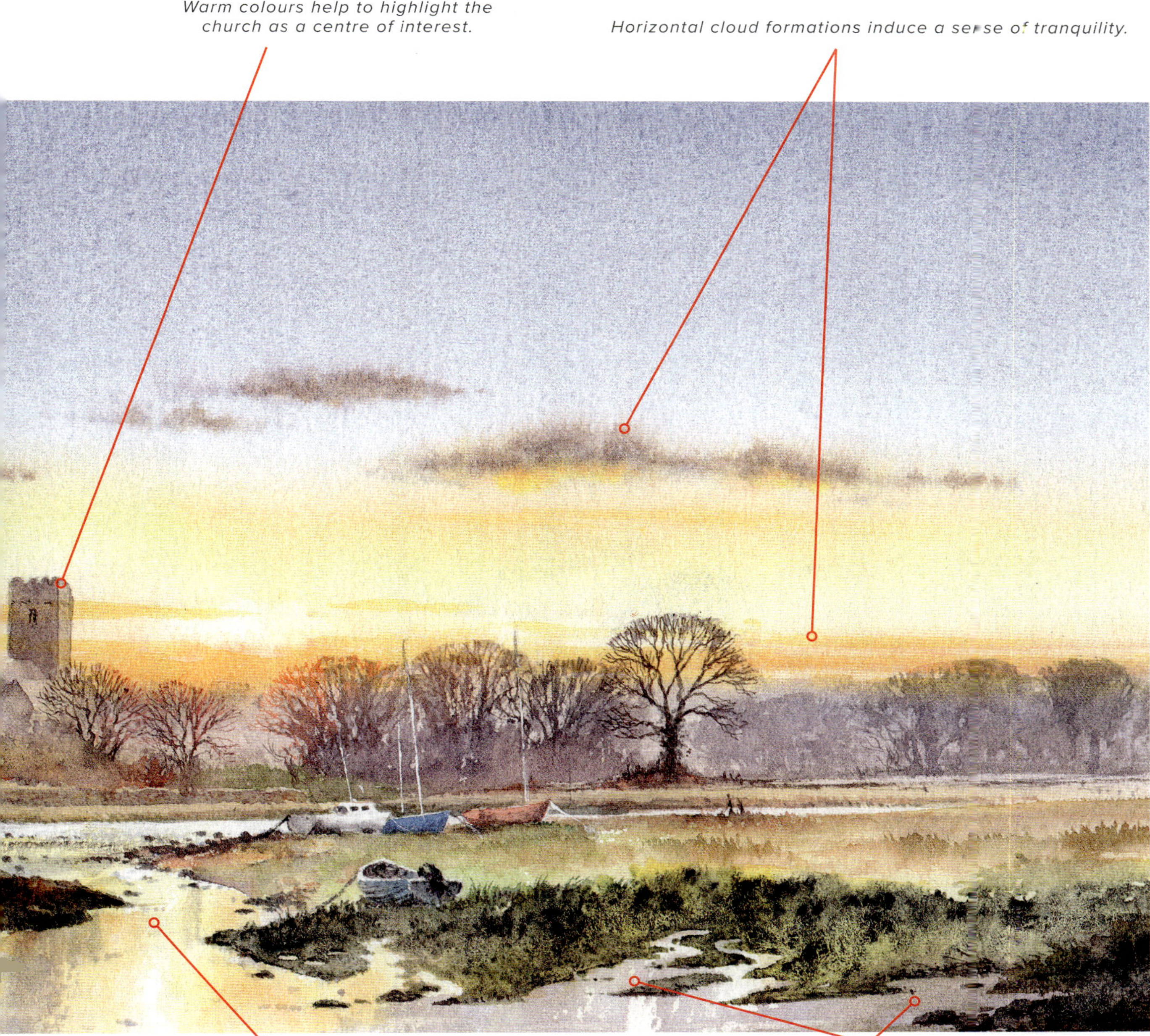

Warm colours help to highlight the
church as a centre of interest.

Horizontal cloud formations induce a sense of tranquility.

The stream is positioned to act
as a lead-in to the church.

Rivulets break up the foreground line.

Drama and energy in composition

When you are considering your composition, think about the drama and energy you may wish to include. You can achieve this in a number of ways: skies and lighting effects portrayed by vertical or diagonal washes can add a sense of energy and vigour, as can wind-lashed trees, waves, figures and so forth.

Towering cumulus cloud effects emphasize drama, as can vertical drops in cliff and rock scenery. Losing the bottom of an abyss in atmosphere increases the sublime quality of a scene to a more terrifying pitch.

Strong contrasts of lighting and colours can also add a certain tension, while dark, forbidding, storm-laden cloud masses combined with a dark landscape and perhaps with a small patch of light, will provide the ultimate drama.

An excellent combination for a fiery sky is quinacridone sienna set against a violently dark colour such as lunar black, sodalite genuine or even moonglow. Vigorous application of the paint further enhances the sense of strong energy.

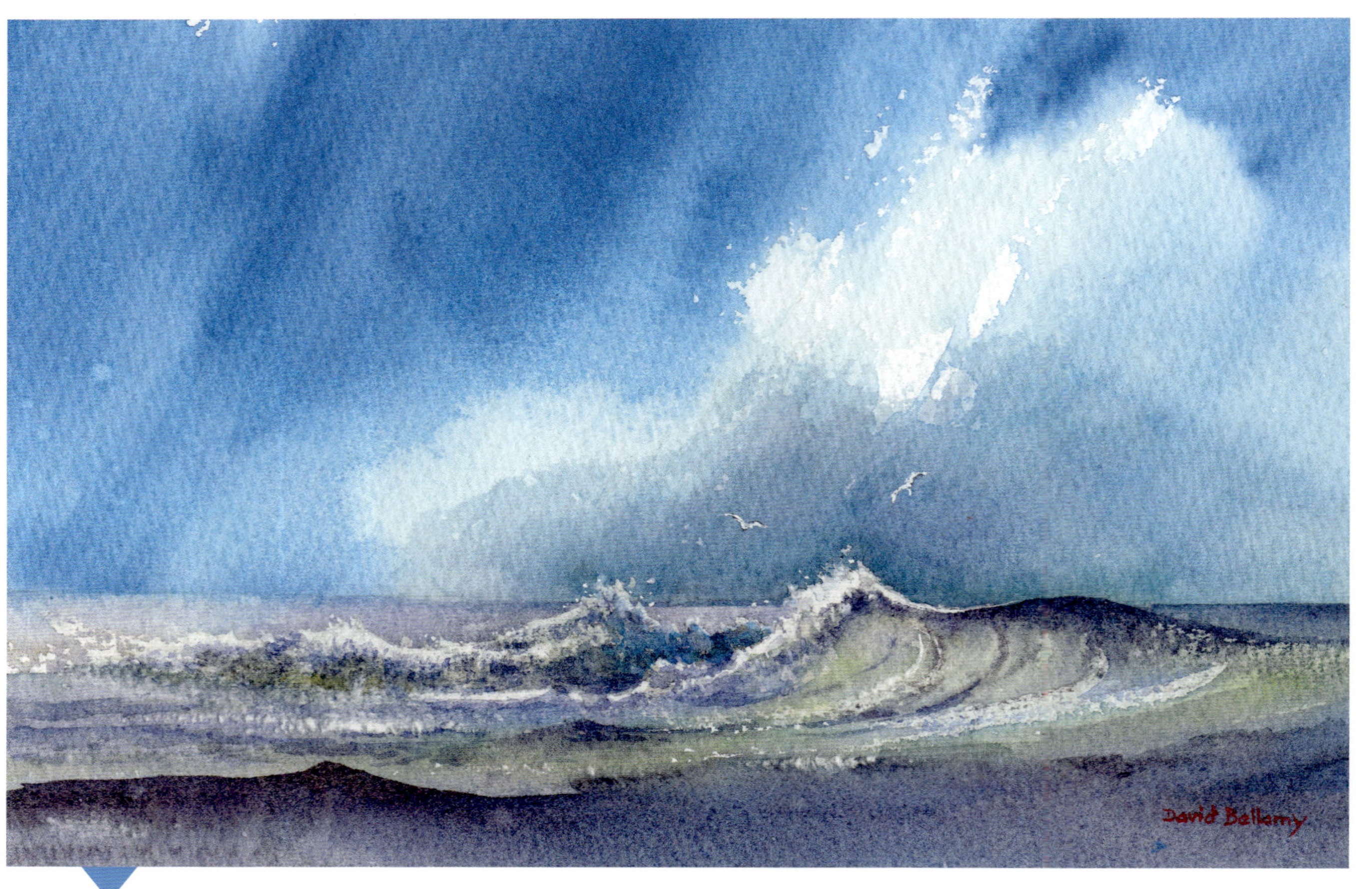

Boisterous Surf
25.5 × 15cm (10 × 6in) Saunders Waterford 300gsm (140lb) Rough surface paper

In this work the diagonal aspect of the cloud structure and front of the wave suggests restlessness and energy. Note also the counterchange (see page 67) on the sea horizon and the way the wave breaks up the horizon line to avoid a long boring line. Where you have strong, long lines across the composition like this, or perhaps with the parapet of a bridge for example, it is essential to break it up in some way.

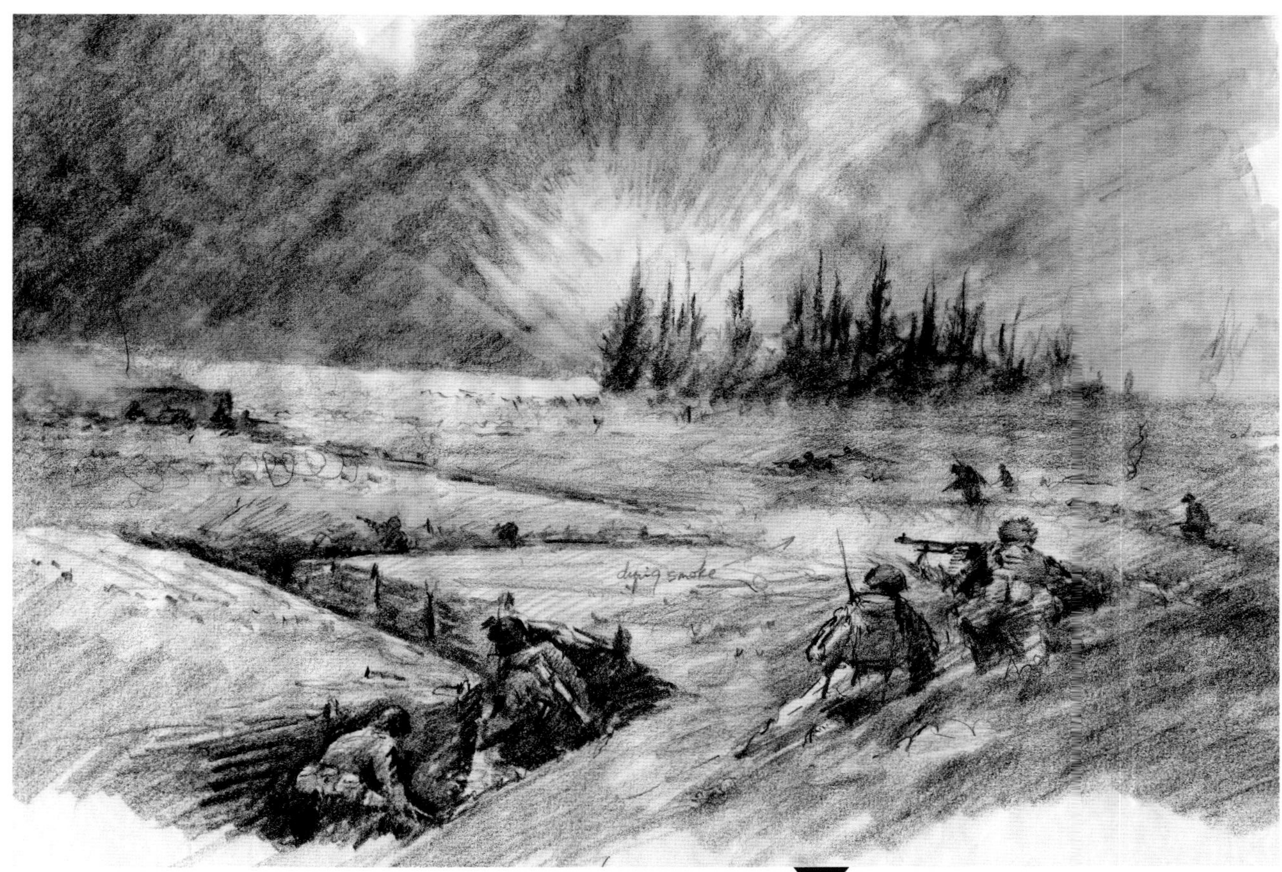

Combining reference for improved composition

This is a study for a large painting depicting a night exercise in the Epynt Mountains. I pieced together the scene from various sketches carried out on location on a wild winter night. The trenches were about three-feet deep in water, so the soldiers using them for cover were not terribly happy. Flares constantly lit up the battlefield, but even so my camera was not up to getting fleeting shots of the more distant features or the flashes of explosions, so I had to rely almost entirely on my sketches, done in near-complete darkness.

Back in the studio, I brought the sketches together on a large sheet of layout paper, measuring 56 × 42cm (22 × 16½in), using a water-soluble pencil. I annotated it in several places with points such as 'move the trench further to the left to enable me to extend the small rise and afford the machine-gunners more cover', and 'include muzzle flashes from defending Ghurkas on the left' as I couldn't easily show these on the layout sheet. The machine-gunners are the centre of interest, but defenders at the smoking bunkers provide balance on the left.

Night battle study

This is quite different to what normally work on, but it illustrates that where you have many actions taking place it is important to ensure that one of the figures, or groups of figures, is made more prominent than the others. In this case it is the machine-gunners in the bottom right who form the main centre of interest.

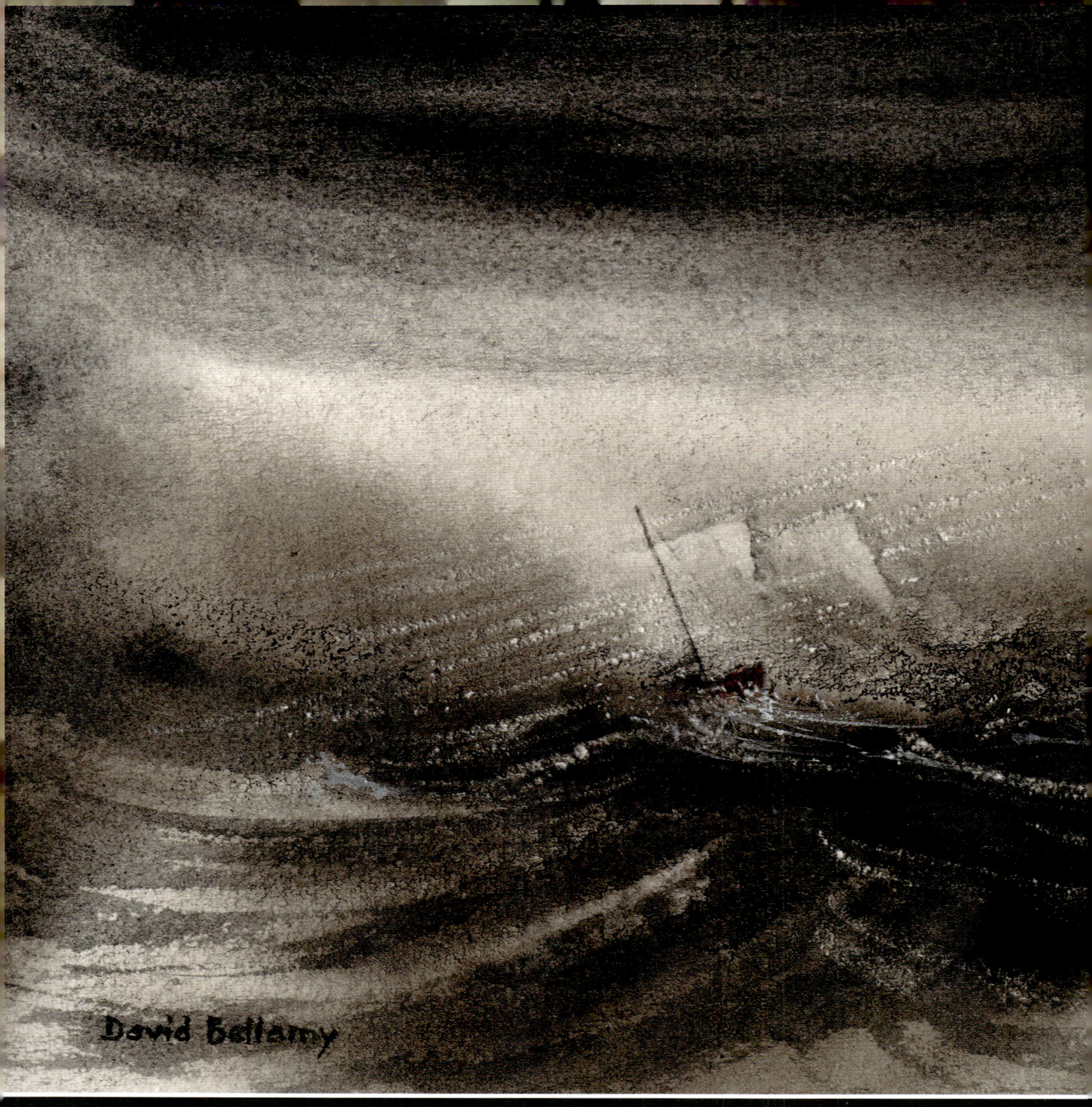

Injecting atmosphere and drama

This was almost entirely painted with lunar black, the only exception being a spot of cadmium red on the boat hull, which was touched in over the black. By only half-seeing the main features a sense of mystery is generated, and the dark night sky, created with energetic brush-strokes, adds to this feeling.

The tiny craft and glacier cliffs are only partly visible, and the surface of the paper was scratched with a scalpel wielded with ferocious effort to suggest the snow squall.

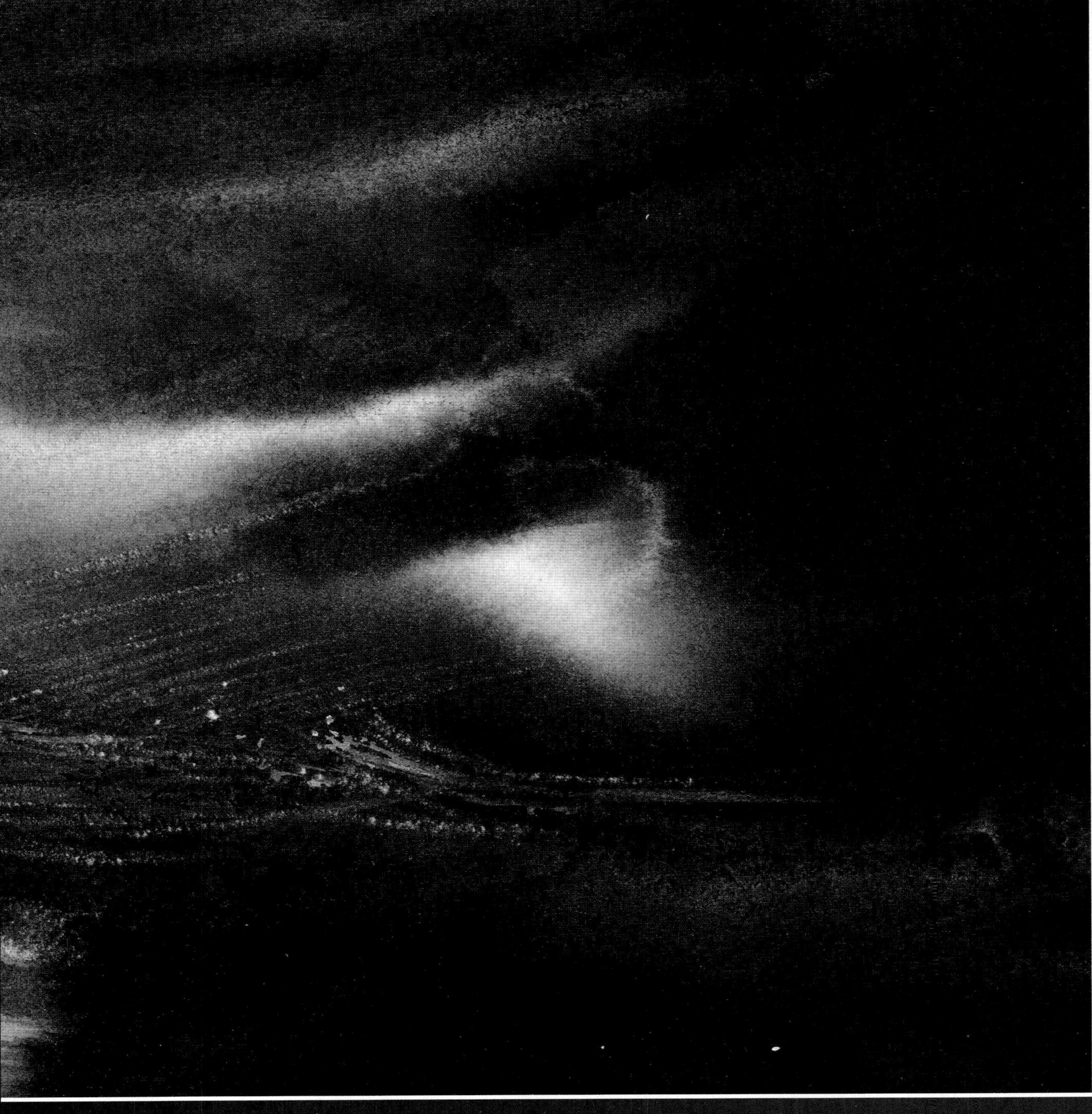

Through the Arctic Night

28 × 12.5cm (11 × 5in) Saunders Waterford 300gsm (140lb) Not surface paper

These were tense moments as we weathered the storm off north-west Spitzbergen in Svalbard, northern Norway, throughout the night. Naturally, I couldn't view the boat from this angle as I was on board, but I had sketched it many times during our expedition.

Light and space

In this section we look at ways to enhance the sense of light and space, using various techniques to highlight or subdue features, to give the impression of distance and to create light features using negative painting techniques.

TECHNIQUE
Pulling out colour

Pulling out colour is a useful method both for creating shapes and for repairing minor errors, and can be done on wet or dry surfaces. It can be used for softening edges with a damp brush or eliminating intrusive flecks of watercolour that have strayed beyond the boundaries you may have set with a pencil. In this role a small flat brush can be most effective.

Pulling out from wet paint involves using a 'thirsty' brush – that is, one with no paint, and hardly any water – to remove patches of damp or wet watercolour. Press the belly of the brush down to draw out the colour from the surface. If the paper has already dried then you need to have more water on the brush and scrub out the shape with the tip rather than the belly.

As well as allowing you to rectify errors, this technique produces a different quality to your work and can be an excellent substitute for the wet-in-wet technique.

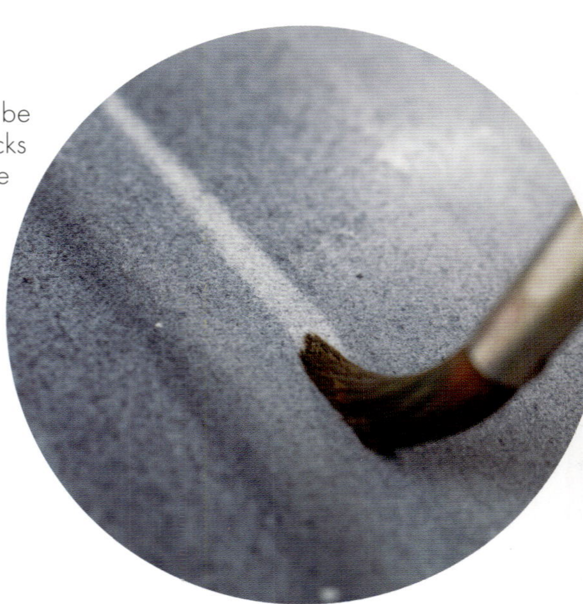

Blackbird Wood and
12.5 × 15cm (5 × 6in) Saunders Waterford 300gsm (140lb) Rough surface paper

I applied a wash of lunar blue over the background, let it start to dry, and then pulled out the light shapes of the negative spaces with a damp brush to suggest tree trunks and branches.

Pulling out is an excellent technique for creating light patches where shadows have been cast on the ground by trees, or for repairing a situation where a wet-in-wet feature might have strayed too far and changed your misty tree branch into a flying hedgehog.

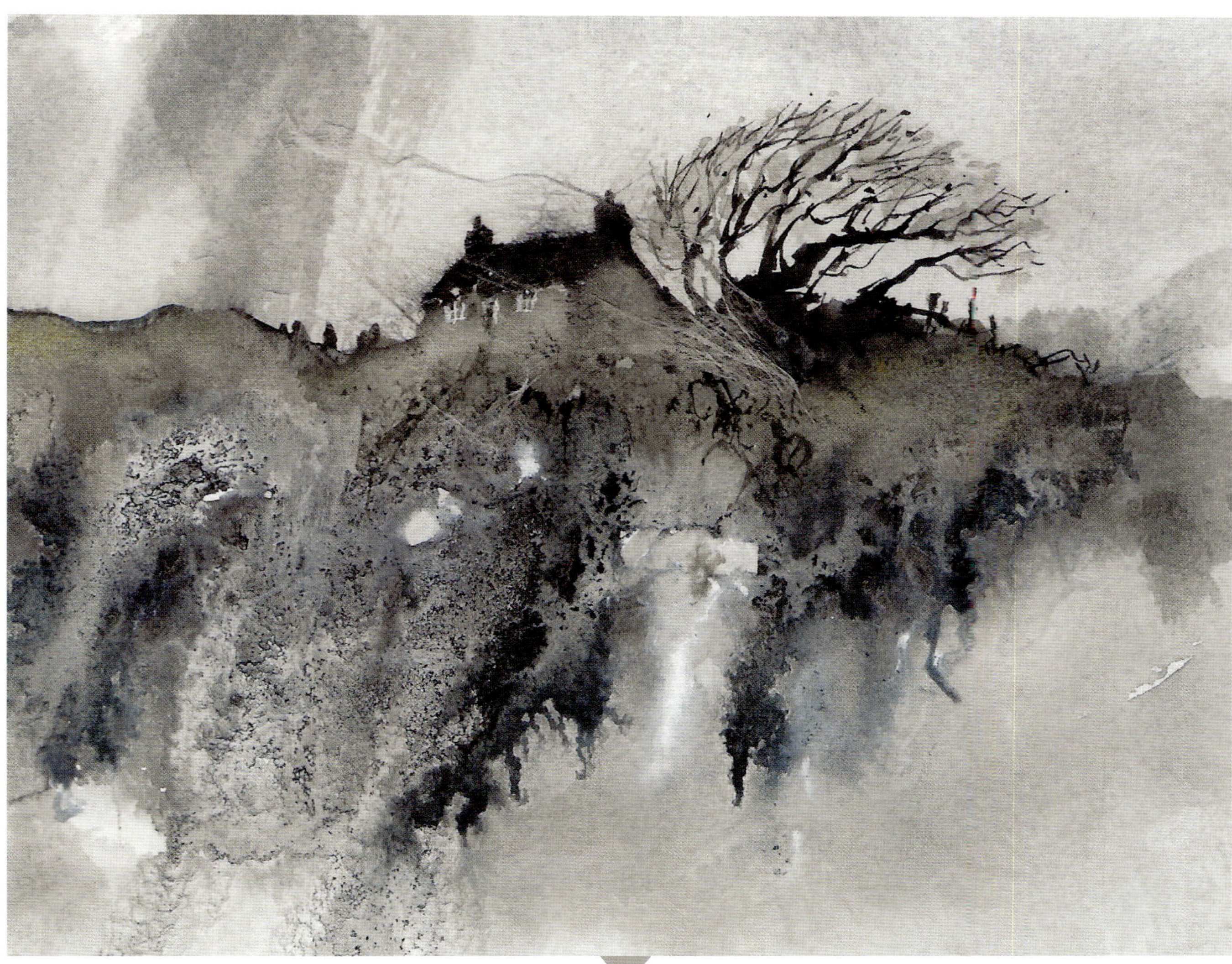

Abstract shadow

Light illuminates what it falls upon – and so we can use its absence to hide areas we do not want to include. These areas of shadow do not need to be flat and dull.
 Abstract passages can be extremely useful when you need a substitute for an ugly or intrusive part of the overall subject or a confusing mixture of objects where you might otherwise end up with an artistic rubbish tip.

Cottage on Hill
15 × 12.5cm (6 × 5in) Bockingford 300gsm (140lb) Not surface paper

For this I used Payne's gray acrylic ink, dropping in a little yellow ochre and Indian red in places. Before it dried completely, I also put in a few touches of white ink.

I felt the cottage stood out too darkly on the horizon, so decided to overlay it with a veil of oriental tissue paper to subdue it slightly. This can often be a more effective way of subduing a feature than trying to reduce the strength though sponging and creating messy edges.

See page 45 for some more examples of abstraction.

Colour, tone and space

You're probably familiar with the idea that warm colours advance and cool colours recede, but there are times when a distant feature may be lit up by strong evening light to create a warm-coloured distance. In such instances, you can emphasize the darker tones and strong detail in the foreground to evoke the feeling of space and distance, as in *Evening Light on the Roaches*, below.

Colour temperature for your main passages in a composition should be considered before applying any paint and you can see in the example of *The Tranquil Wye* on page 53 how cool blues and greens have been employed to push back the distant tree masses.

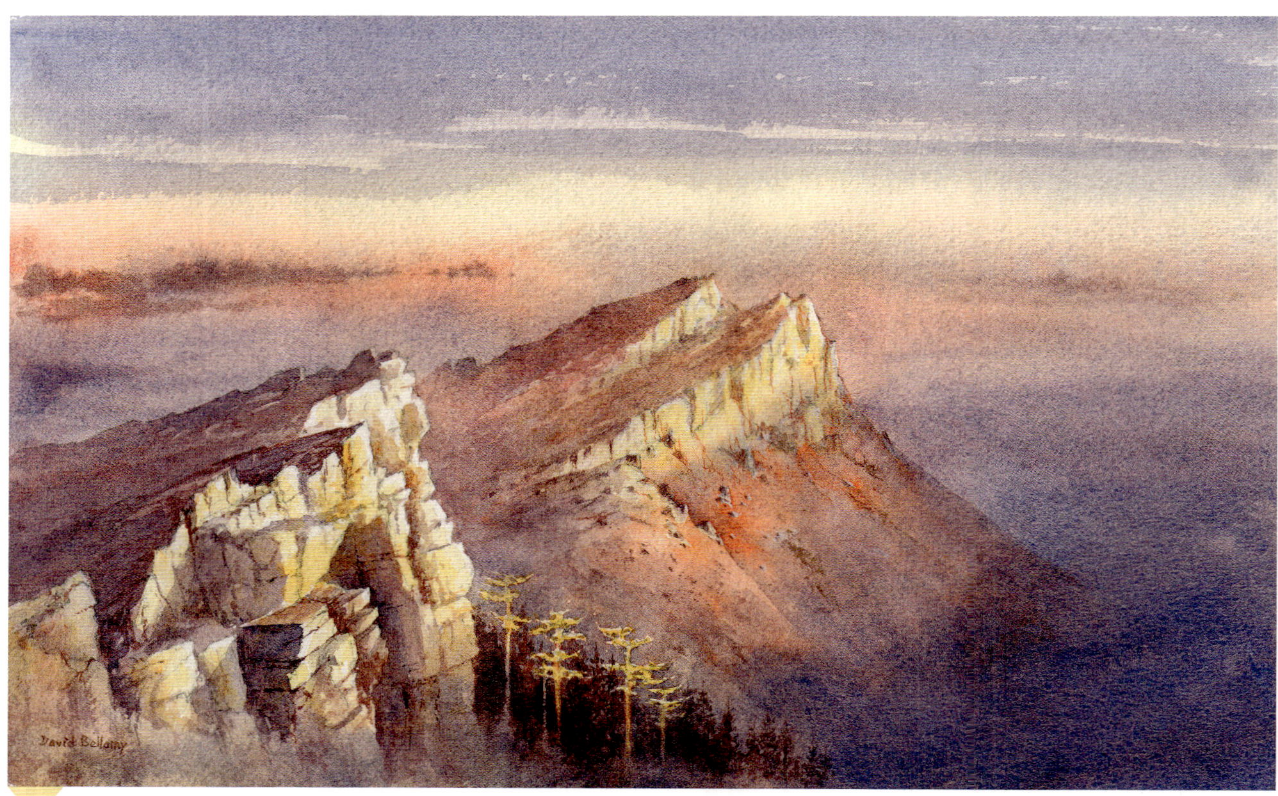

Evening Light on the Roaches
30.5 × 20.5cm (12 × 8in) Saunders Waterford 300gsm (140lb) Rough surface paper
In this work the illusion of distance is suggested by the darker tones in the foreground which override the warm colours on the more distant crag.

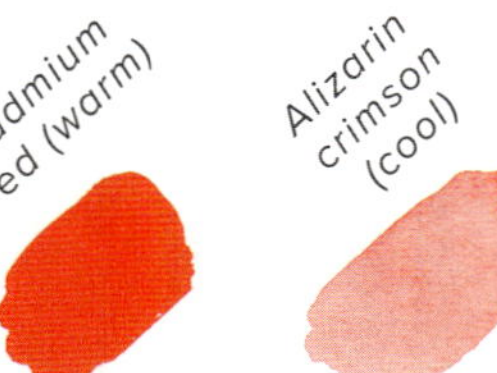

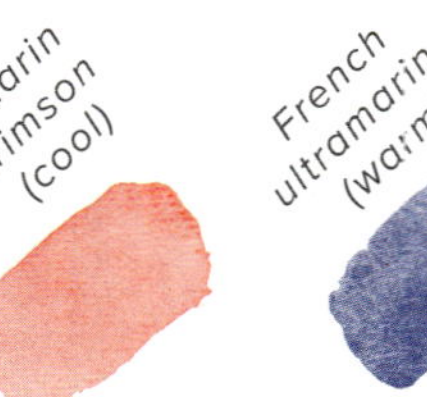

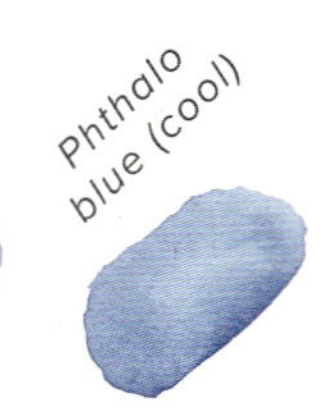

Reds, oranges and yellows are warm colours while blues, greys and greens are cool ones, but even within the reds there are warmer and cooler pigments. For example, cadmium red is warmer than alizarin crimson, as seen here. Likewise, French ultramarine is warmer than phthalo blue. This is particularly useful when determining how to emphasize a feeling of space and distance.

Counterchange

A device that adds interest to the scene, counterchange is an extremely effective way to ensure an important area or feature stands out against a background that changes considerably in tone.

It is achieved by contrasting the tone of the object with the background, as seen in the painting below – the bridge is light where the background is dark; and dark where the background is light.

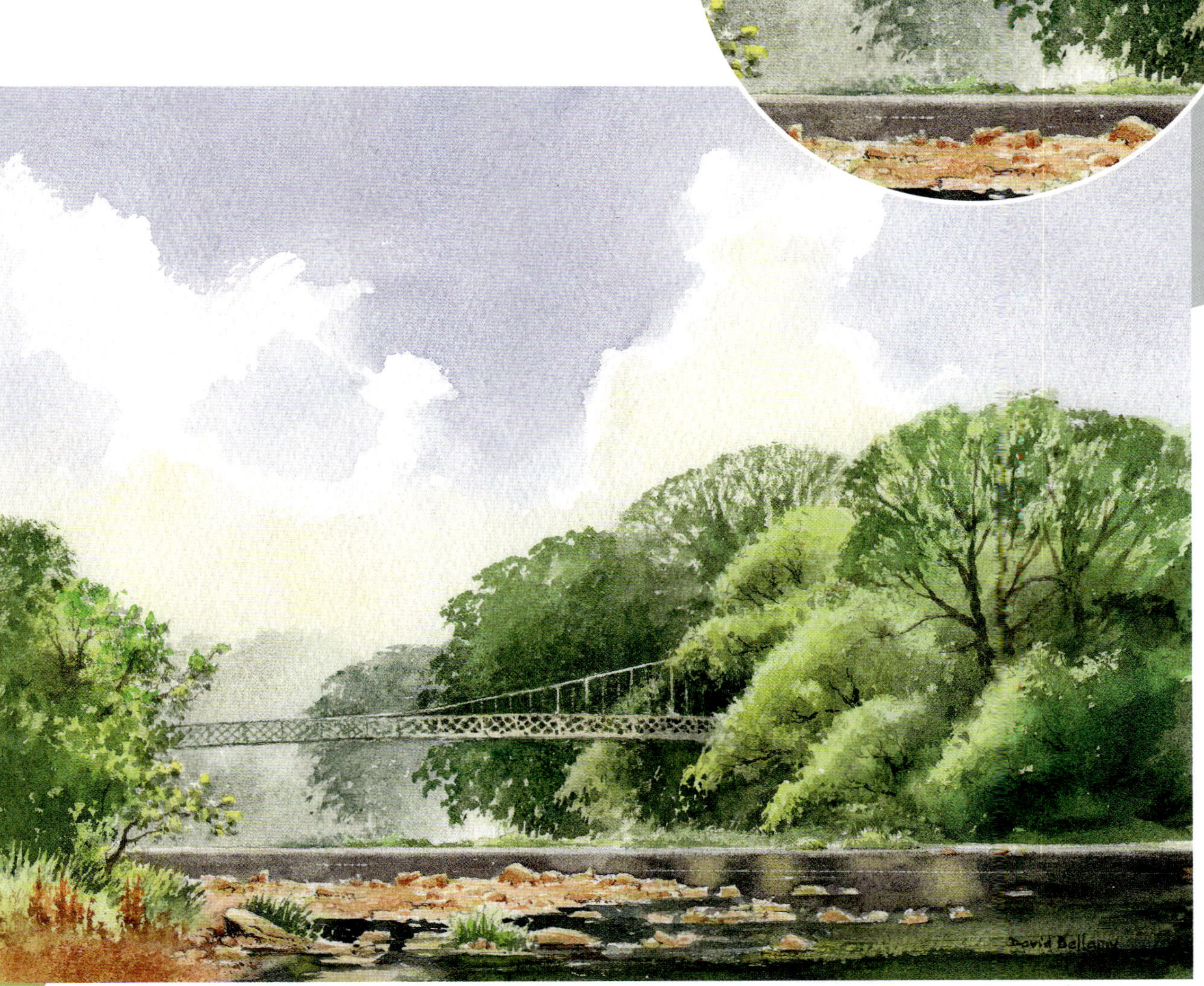

Llanstephan Bridge

28 × 20.5cm (11 × 8in) Saunders Waterford 300gsm (140lb) Not surface paper

Counterchange can be extremely effective on a bridge – the close-up detail at top right shows how the background changes from dark (on the right) to light, so that the bridge structure is painted light where it stands against a dark background, and becomes dark against a light part of the background.

Note also in this painting how the tones on the trees beyond the bridge fade into paler values of terre verte to create a powerful sense of trees receding into the distance.

Negative painting

It may be counterintuitive, but you create light in watercolour by painting shadow – it is the space that you leave, and the contrast you create which will give the sense of dazzling light.

Painting the gaps, or negative spaces, between lighter positive objects (such as chair legs, light posts, tree trunks and so forth), is a vital and extremely effective technique in watercolour painting.

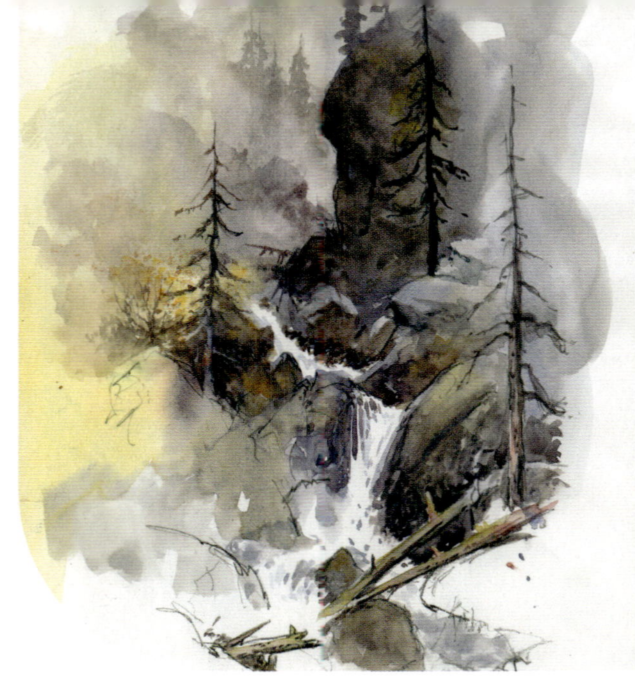

Keys to success with negative painting

- Take time to refine your areas of negative painting. Negative painting without such subtleties can appear too stark. Glazes over parts can add authenticity.

- Tumbling white-water rapids and falls are excellent subjects to begin practising negative painting, leaving the falling water as the white of the paper, including any slivers of falling water, and little 'baubles' of white splashing.

The tumbling white water here was defined by painting in the dark adjacent rocks with a fine-pointed brush. To reduce the stark contrast, touches of grey colour were brushed into some of the edges. Note that the lower trunk of the left-hand tree has been rendered by pulling out colour with a small flat brush.

This was painted while I was in grizzly bear country; in such situations I usually sing loudly – the noise is so awful that any self-respecting bear runs away. Here, however, the noise of the tumbling water drowned me out, so my concentration was not at its best!

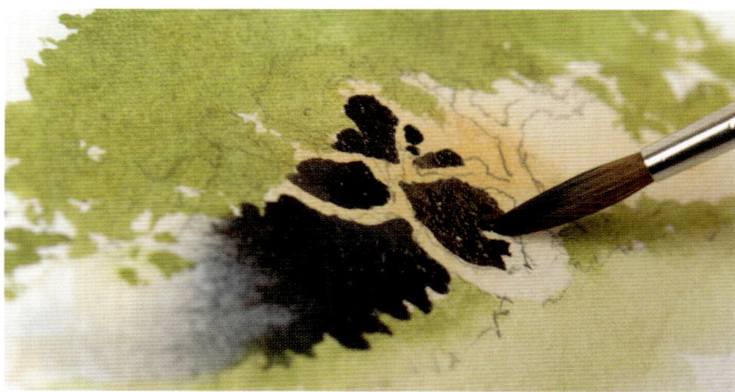

Establishing shapes wet on dry Working on a dry initial wash, define the positive features (the trunk and branches here) by painting in darker negative spaces (the gaps between them).

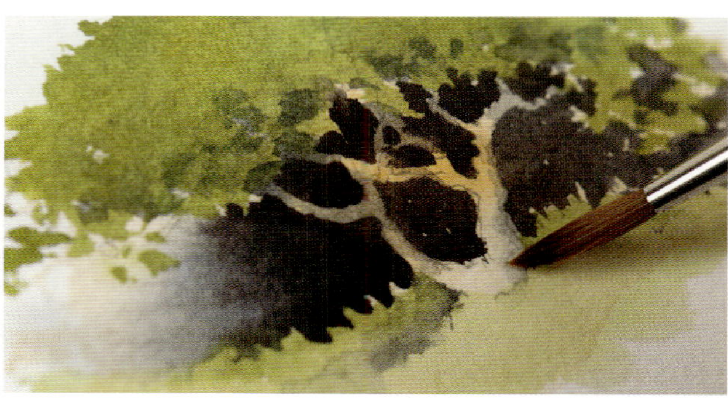

Shadow and details Once dry, apply a medium tone to part of the positive feature to suggest shadow, otherwise the effect can appear too much like a stark cut-out.

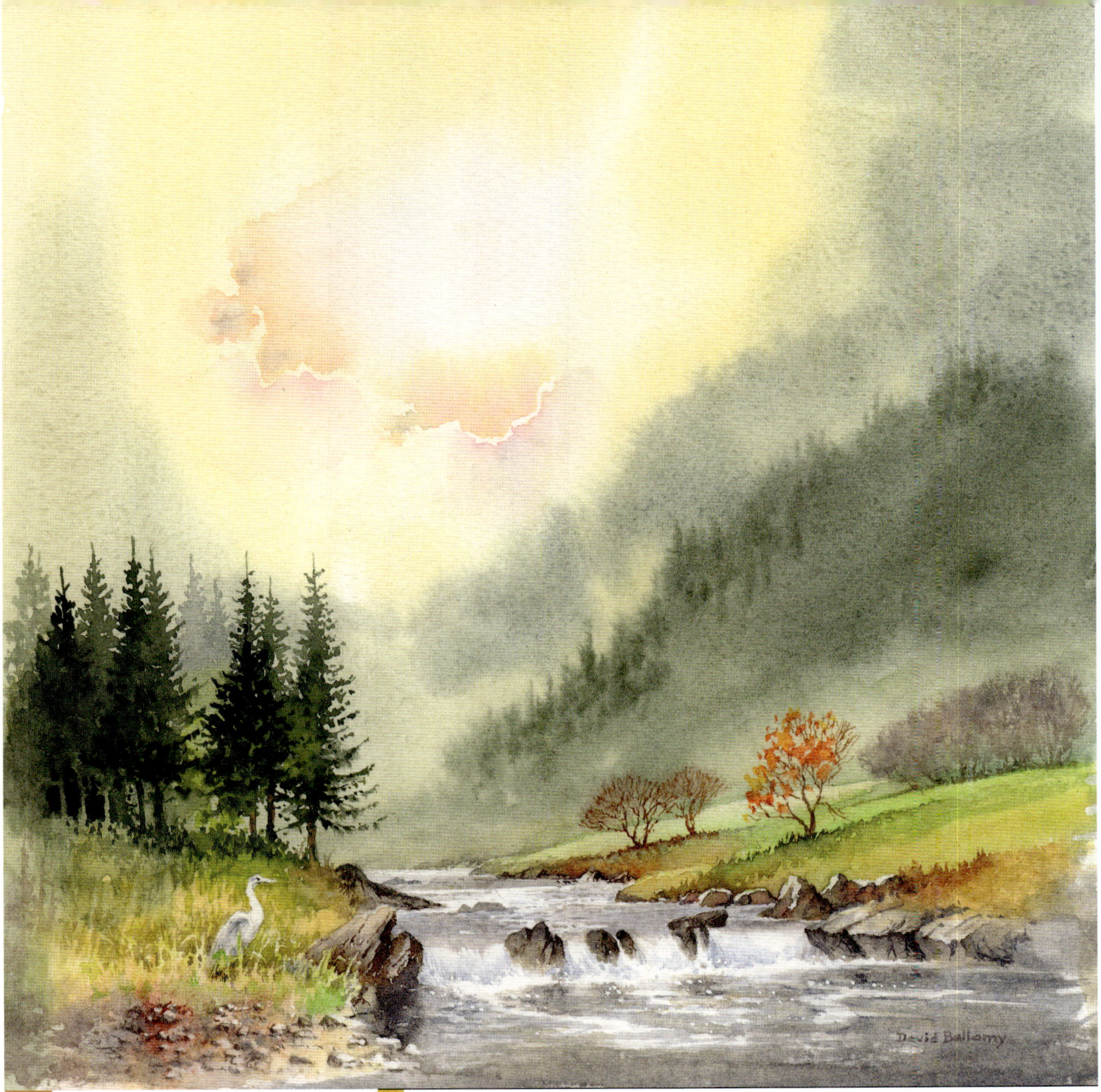

Waiting for Dinner

23 × 25.5cm (9 × 10in) Saunders Waterford
300gsm (140lb) Not surface paper

Painting *Waiting for Dinner*

- The grasses were defined with the negative technique firstly by laying a base wash of cadmium yellow and running Naples yellow into it at the bottom.
- Once the paper was dry, the grasses were described with raw umber and a touch of yellow ochre for the darker negative spaces in between.
- This mixture was also applied around the heron to make it stand out.

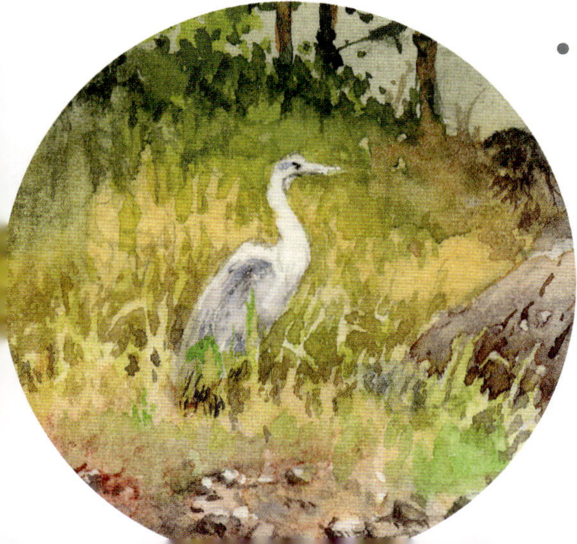

This is a close-up of the heron, so you can see how the negative painting in the surrounding grasses helps to create texture and frame it naturally.

Creating highlights in the sky

While many skies work perfectly well in a simple, uncluttered form, adding some interest into your skies can enhance a composition, especially where the landscape element is fairly simple.

Including the sun can add a real sense of mood – in particular at sunrise or sunset, or when it is shimmering through thin cloud. Interesting cloud formations, with or without silver linings, can highlight tall structures such as castles, prominent crags or striking features that rise above the main landscape, as in the painting of *Clouds Rising over Crib Goch* on page 82.

These more detailed parts of the sky can also be used to provide a counter-balance in compositions where the opposite side involves considerable detail.

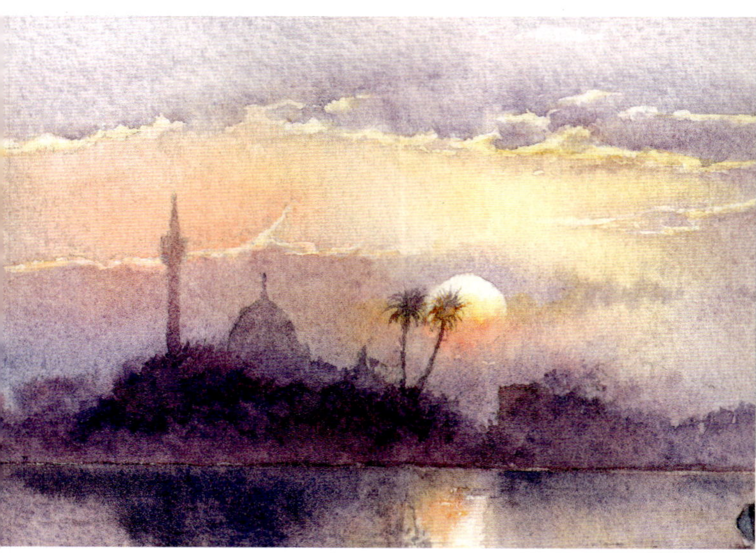

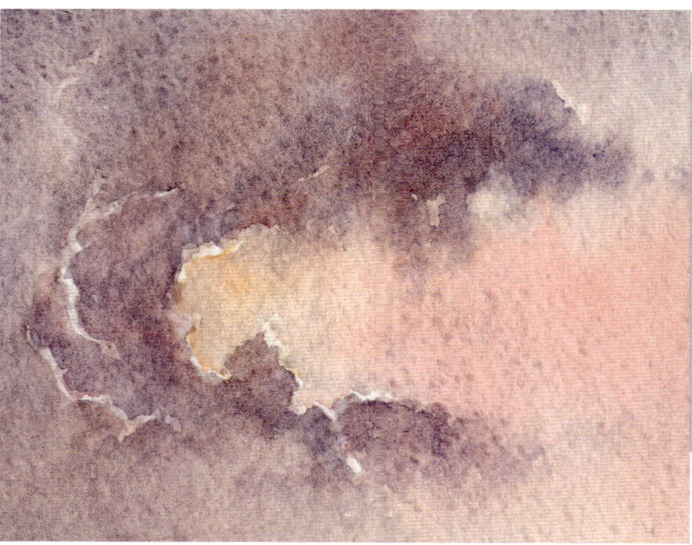

Just a half

If you wish to include the sun it is sometimes more effective to avoid making the sun a complete circle, and introduce a more moody effect while adding a sense of mystery.

Creating a silver lining on clouds

Creating a silver lining or two in the sky can greatly enhance the atmosphere, and generally it is best to make the part above the silver lining a bit lighter than the cloud below. Avoid putting too many linings in: simplicity has much greater impact.

Here I used Naples yellow and weak permanent alizarin crimson for the background sky, and French ultramarine plus cadmium red for the clouds. The white linings are untouched paper.

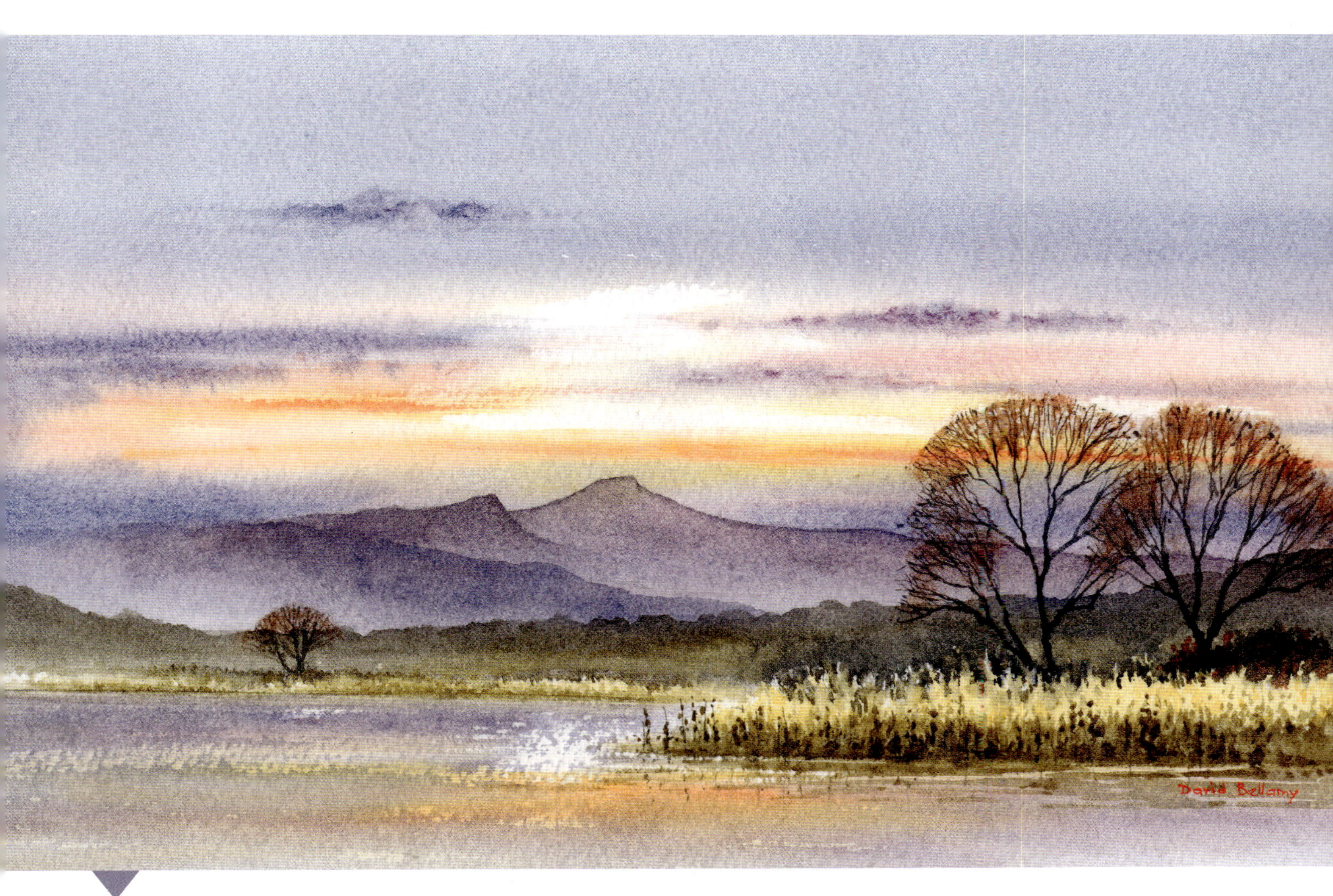

Sunset over the Beacons
28 × 15cm (11 × 6in) Saunders Waterford 300gsm (140lb) Not surface paper

Try to keep sunsets fairly simple: it is easy to get into a complicated mess. The clouds here were introduced with the wet-in-wet method, touching in a mixture of Aussie red gold and quinacridone sienna when the sky was just damp. Bringing in stronger tones with each successively closer ridge enhanced the sense of space.

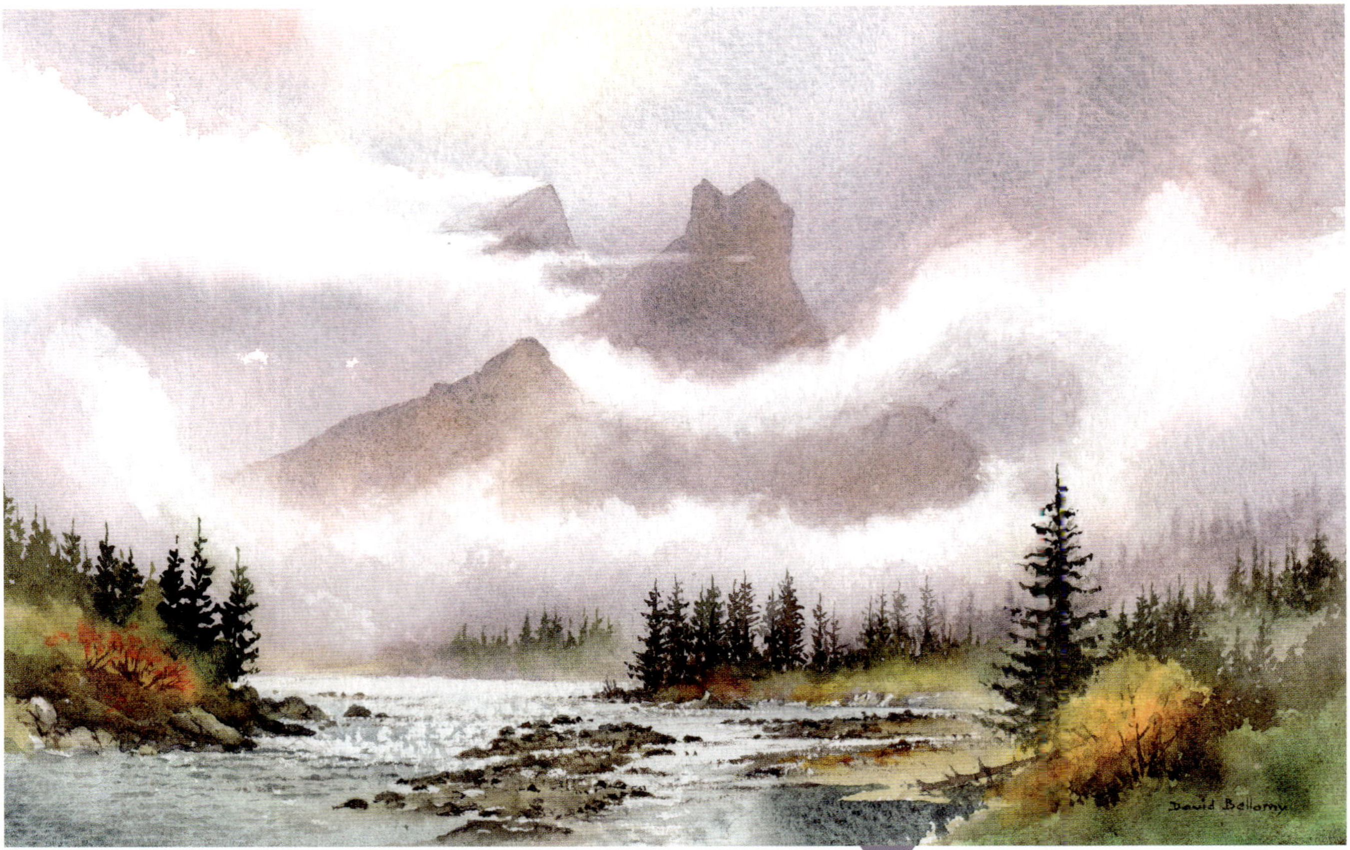

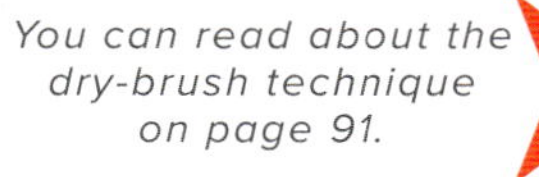

Softening edges and strong lines

Even though you may see many hard edges on features before you, it is best to subdue and soften many of these. What works well in reality or in a photograph does not always translate successfully into a painting.

For softening off and pulling-out techniques I employ a variety of brushes. In *North Saskatchewan River*, above, a thin flat brush was used to pull out the thin sliver of cloud just below the summit of the main peak, while a battered old tatty-headed flat brush was used to soften off some of the cloud edges using a swirling, circular motion; both when softening edges and improving the shape of a cloud.

You can read about the dry-brush technique on page 91.

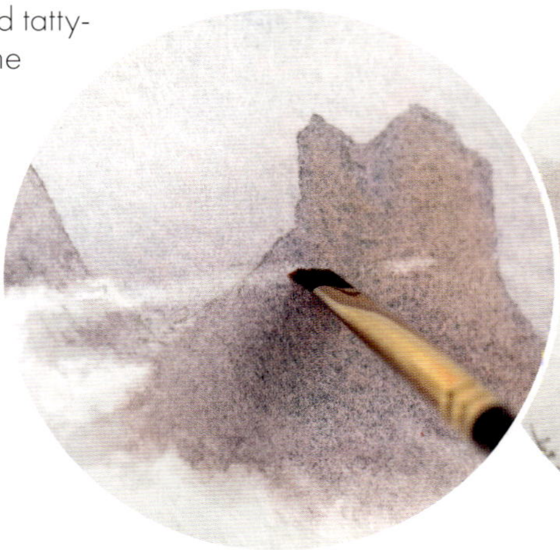

North Saskatchewan River
30.5 × 23cm (12 × 9in) Saunders Waterford 640gsm (300lb) Rough surface paper

Here I have used streams of cloud to break up the hard lines of ridges and massed trees, and softened some of those edges. The Rough paper enhances the effect of sparkle on the water achieved with a dry-brush approach.

Pulling out
Pulling out wet on dry with a thin flat brush.

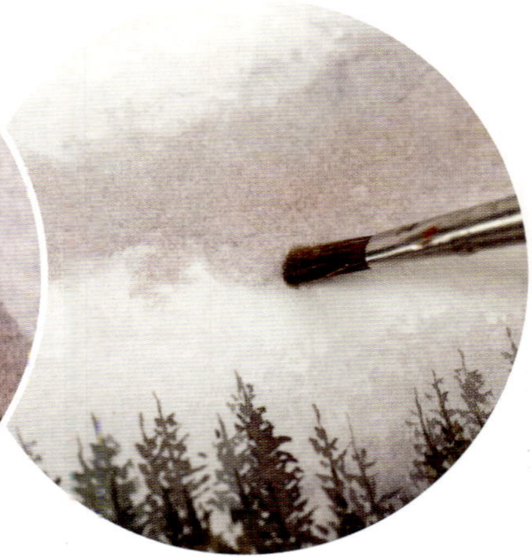

Softening
Softening edges with an old brush.

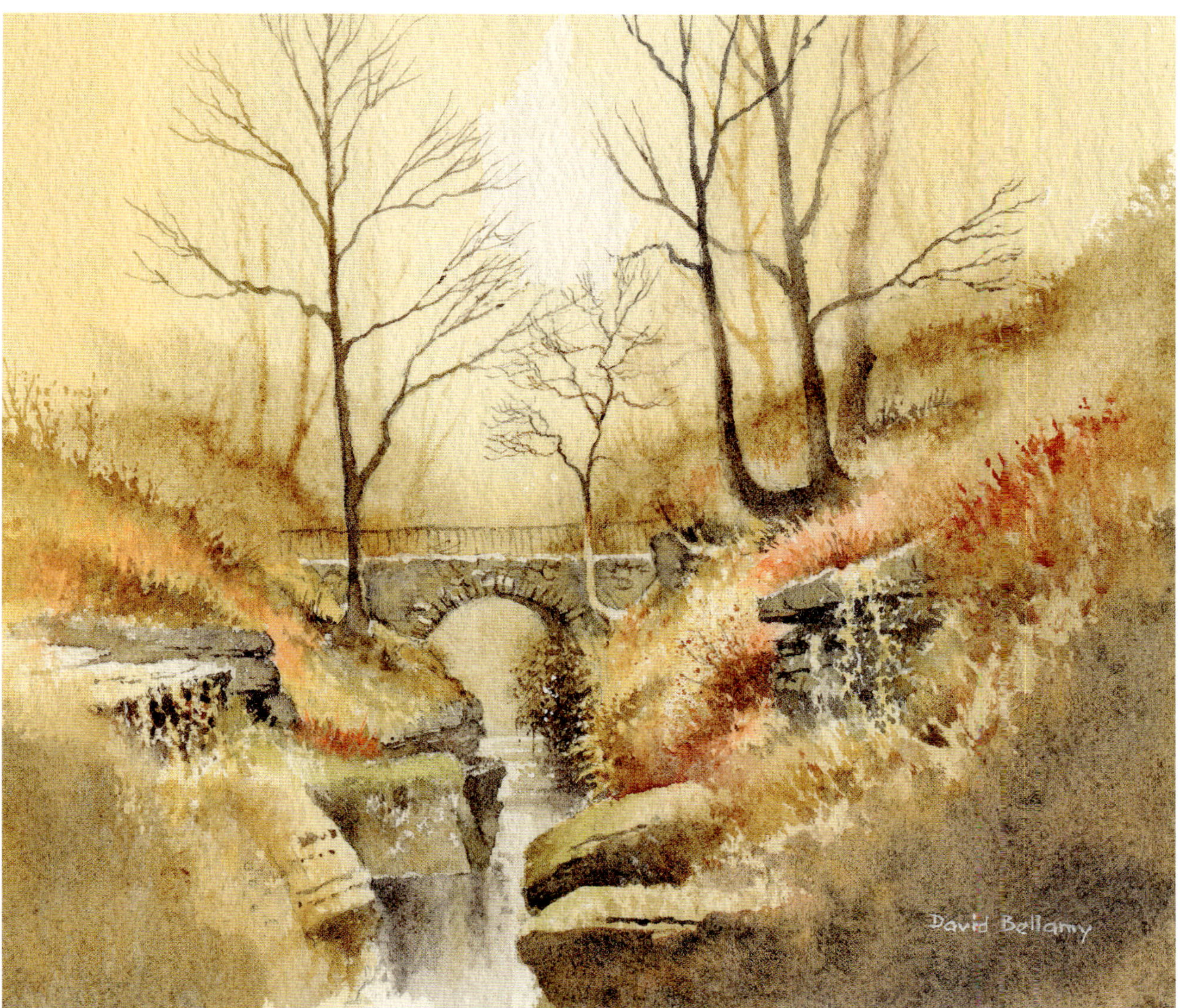

Painting *Bridge in the Cynfal Gorge*

- While the sky was still wet, I suggested the further slopes and tree trunks with burnt umber, using the fine size 6 sable to render the trunks without needing to change brushes. This produced a misty effect beyond the bridge, with the tree trunks soft-edged.

- The rest of the work was done with the same colours with the addition of French ultramarine for the darker features and touches of transparent red oxide in places.

- While you need some variation in the colours, and not just green, don't overdo this. Note that the foreground trees are rendered with dark, hard edges to bring them forward to create the sense of distance.

Bridge in the Cynfal Gorge

20.5 × 18cm (8 × 7in) Saunders Waterford 640gsm (300lb) Not surface paper

For this I kept to a warm colour temperature throughout – see pages 20–21 for more on colour harmony. I began the sky with Naples yellow, introducing some yellow ochre in the extremities.

Water

Water can be one of the trickiest subjects to paint, so here we look at a few methods on how to make this easier to tackle.

Running and still waters

Even in a short stretch, rivers can reveal several different forms of water, such as where a fast-flowing run feeds into a placid pool. Blending these forms together in a realistic manner can sometimes be tricky, but these methods are worth trying to help build up your experience.

In this composition we have three areas of concern, each of which requires a slightly different treatment.

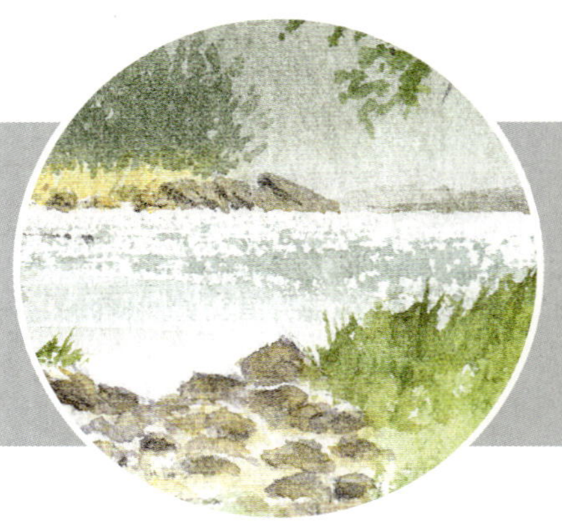

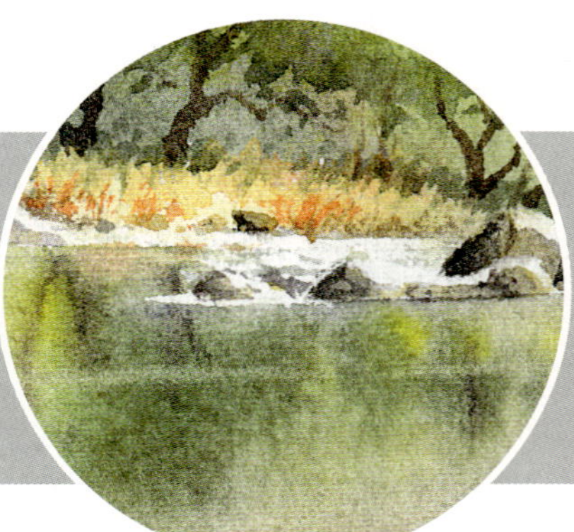

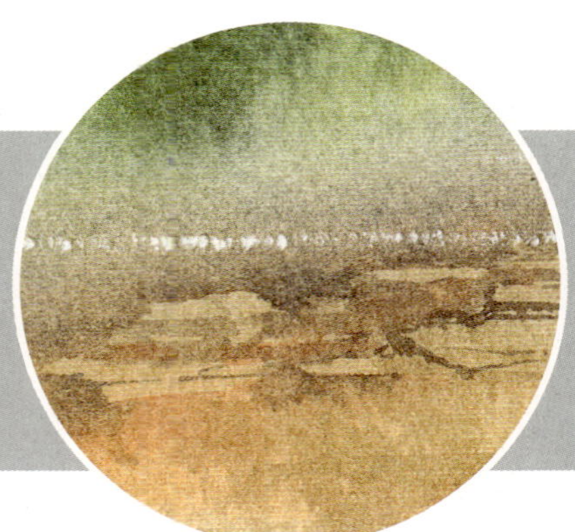

Sparkling ripples

On the extreme right the water is catching the light. In this area, use a weak mix of French ultramarine with a hint of burnt umber for a pleasant weak grey, applying the paint with the dry-brush technique.

If you find the bottom of this narrow band of sparkling water ends up with an unsightly blob, brush it away quickly with a wet brush before it has time to dry.

Calm, reflective surface

On the left and centre is placid water with reflections of the trees. Blend this into the sparkling section by wetting the whole area down to the bottom of the paper, and into the left-hand side of the sparkling water, then applying a wash to the placid section. You can instead fade it out between the two areas.

This large area of water is moving slowly so the reflections are not precise. Some have been inserted into the wet wash with the wet-in-wet method, while other reflections have been pulled out with a 5mm (¼in) flat brush.

Submerged rocks

In the foreground, rocks are visible underwater. Bringing the upper wash right down to the bottom of the paper means you are unlikely to get hard edges forming, so once all the paper is dry re-wet the whole river area and lay a weak wash of burnt umber over the lower part, then allow it to dry. With a stronger application of burnt umber you can then define the rocks, bringing in the shadow tones, and again let it dry.

Lay a weak glaze of burnt umber over the underwater rocks and, once dry, scratch a horizontal highlight over the area with a scalpel.

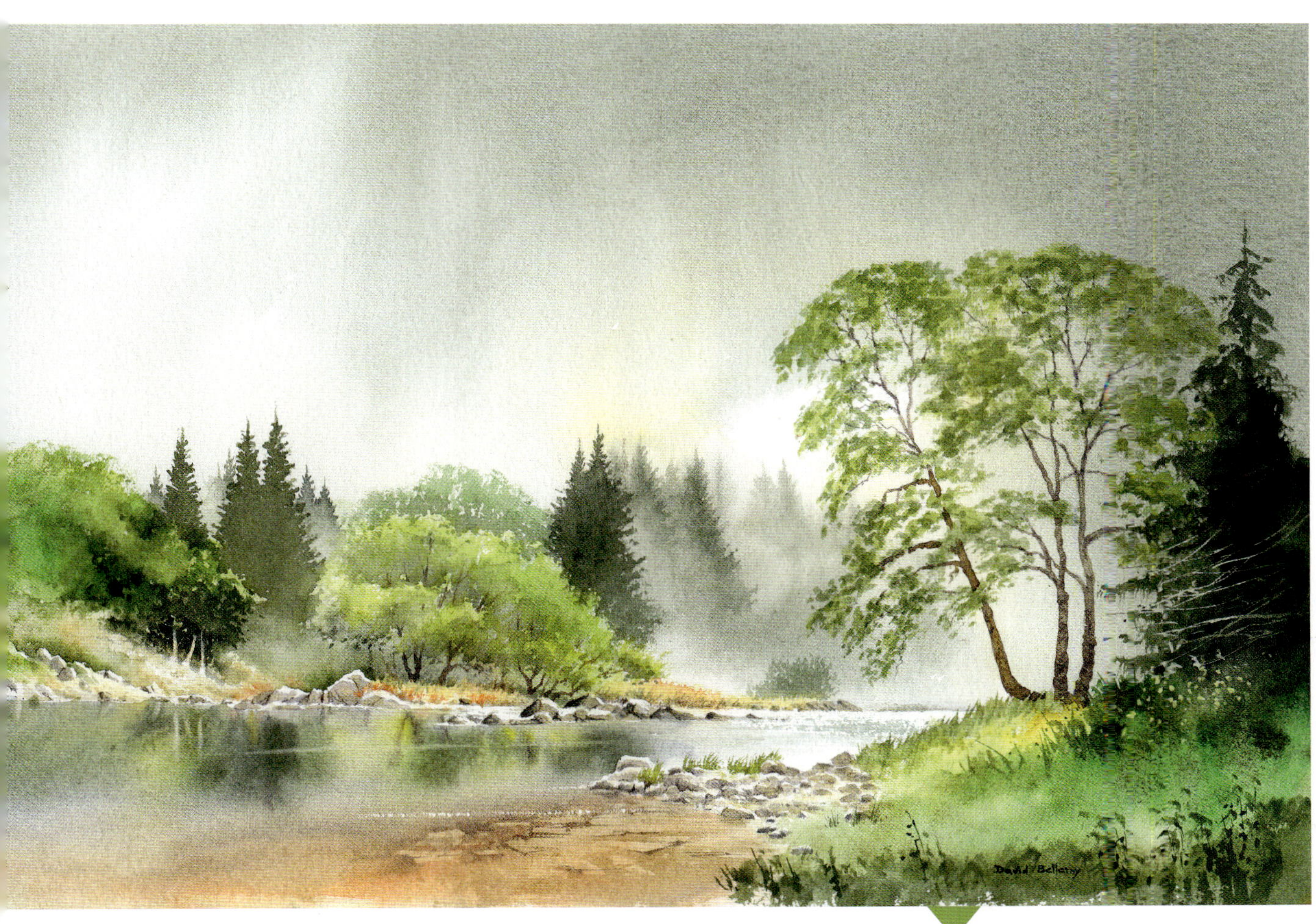

Misty Wye at the Rocks
38 × 25.5cm (15 × 10in) Saunders Waterford
300gsm (140lb) Not surface paper

Keys to success with water in watercolour

- Water is alive with reflective colour, reflective highlights, ripples, underwater features, shadows, light-coloured baubles, nuances of tones in running and tumbling water. This can be terrifying to the less experienced artist – so don't try to include it all.

- Look for the most prominent elements and simply record some of these, reducing as much detail as you can.

- Breaking up reflections in a placid surface with a horizontal scratch made with a scalpel, or using a thin flat brush, invariably works well.

- As well as the dry-brush technique, applying ripples with a small sharp-pointed brush can be effective. In such cases I usually follow up with a weak glaze of blue or grey over the ripples to soften the overall effect.

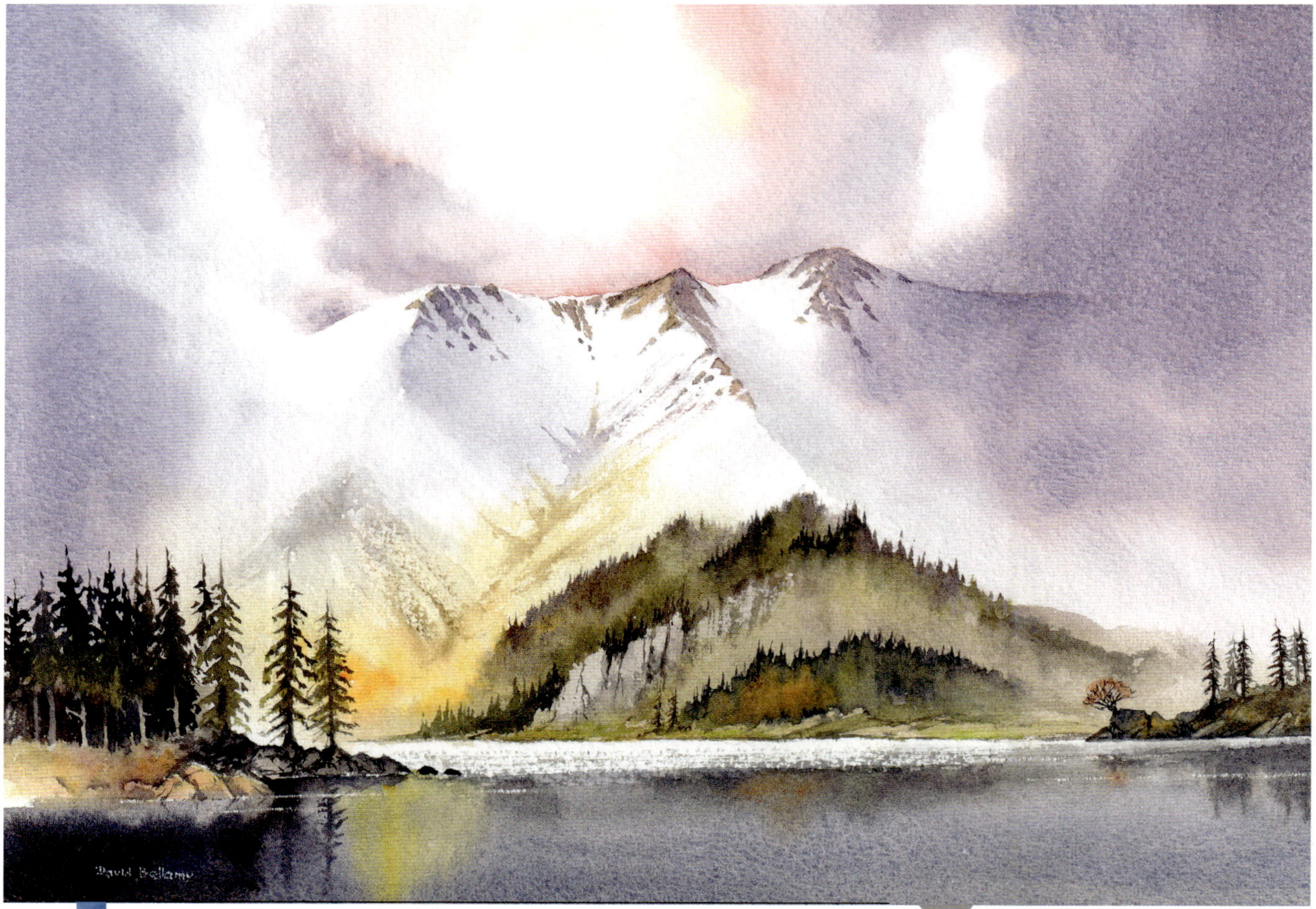

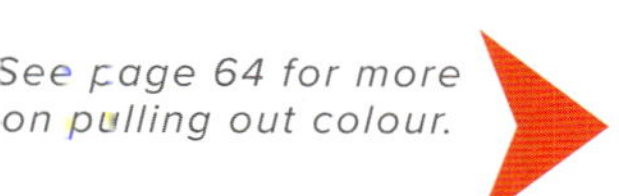

Painting *Blencathra from Thirlmere*

As is common in lakes, here is a situation where there are two types of water. Part of the surface is ruffled by wind, creating a sparkling area beyond the rocky promontory.

- For the sparkling water I used a dry-brush method to catch the texture of the paper, leaving much as the clean white surface.

- Where it is placid in the shelter of the trees, the dark reflections were painted wet in wet. After waiting a few moments the reflections of the light rocks were pulled out with a damp brush.

- Once the paper had completely dried, a scalpel was used to scratch a couple of horizontal lines through the dark water.

Blencathra from Thirlmere
30.5 × 23cm (12 × 9in) Saunders Waterford 300gsm (140 b) Rough surface paper

In the sky, note how the ridge sloping away to the left-hand edge has a wisp of cloud rising before the ridge becomes completely lost. Little devices like this help to add interest in a subtle way.

See page 64 for more on pulling out colour.

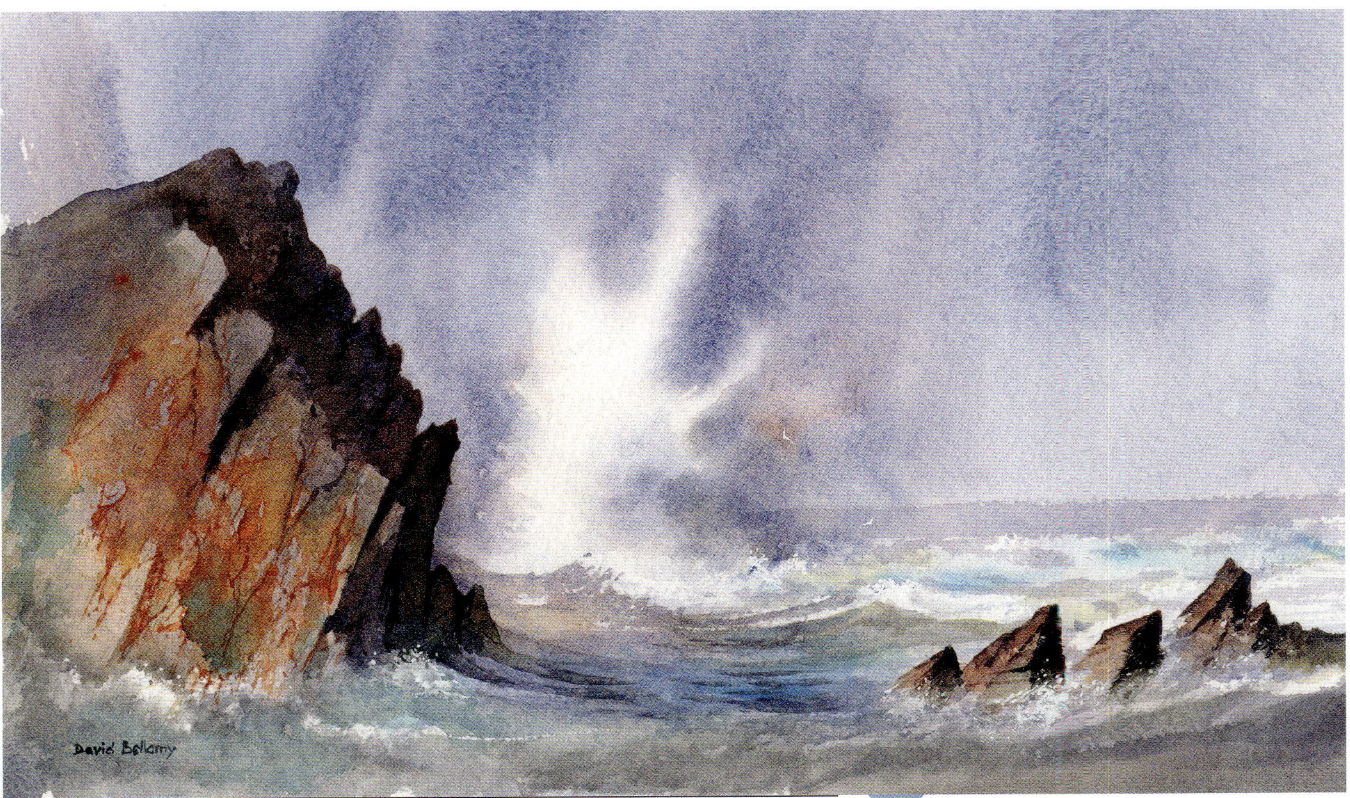

Painting *Dollar Cove, Cornwall*

A truly wild day – exciting, if challenging, with the sea in a state of constant change. Stand and watch the water for a while to work out the best moment, and fire away with the camera to obtain several configurations of the splashes and movement. Only once you have decided on the best combination of rock, surf and shadow should you start sketching and observing the nuances of colours and tones.

- I laid on the band of blue-grey to define the horizon, let the paper dry and then completely wetted the sky and down over the top of the cliff and the horizon band. A wash of French ultramarine was applied with vertical brush-strokes and worked round the white splash in a negative wet-in-wet method; then it was reinforced in places with touches of cadmium red.

- As the wash began drying, I quickly added some darker ultramarine to the right of the splash to strengthen the edges before it dried too much. If it dries too quickly and you are in danger of creating run-backs, wait until the paper has completely dried and then re-wet it. When the right moment arrives you can then introduce the stronger tones.

- I love to create texture by using the side of a brush to scumble paint over an area that has already been painted with a weak tone. You can see this effect in the red part of the cliff, where it was achieved with transparent red oxide, with yellow ochre dropped in here and there, and even phthalo blue into the top parts to create a light grey.

- Once dry, the fracture lines in the rock were painted with a rigger using burnt sienna.

Dollar Cove, Cornwall
30.5 × 20.5cm (12 × 8in) Waterford 300gsm (140lb) Not surface paper

This watercolour was done from the original sketch with help from photographs. Here and there you will see variations of blues where I brought phthalo blue into the mainly ultramarine sea. Even if the sea does not vary in this way it can still be a nice touch to add variety through reflections of colour in gently moving water.

See page 92 for more on scumbling, and page 68 for more on negative painting.

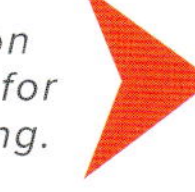

Gouache

Gouache is an opaque water-based paint with a strong covering power which enables it to cover even dark colours on your paper.

MIXING MEDIA
Using gouache

Normally I only use gouache to add in seagulls, white masts, small flowers and other minor features, but some of the paintings that follow illustrate how much further you can take the medium.

It is best not to mix it with watercolour, although I have included a rare example of a work where this has been done – don't forget, rules are there to be broken at times, especially when experimenting.

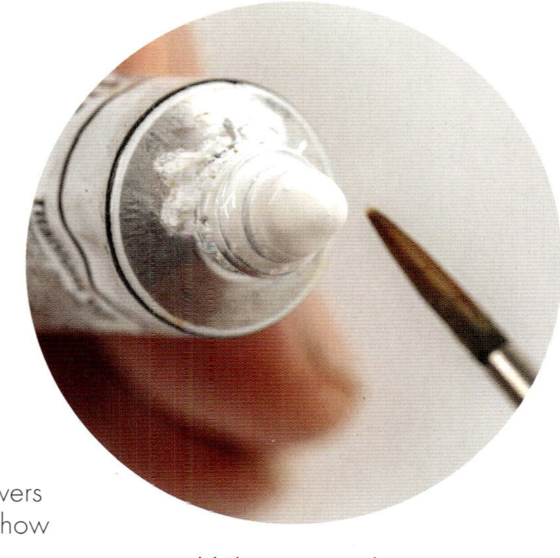

Using gouache
Gouache can be used neat. Squeeze the tube gently and load the brush directly, as shown.

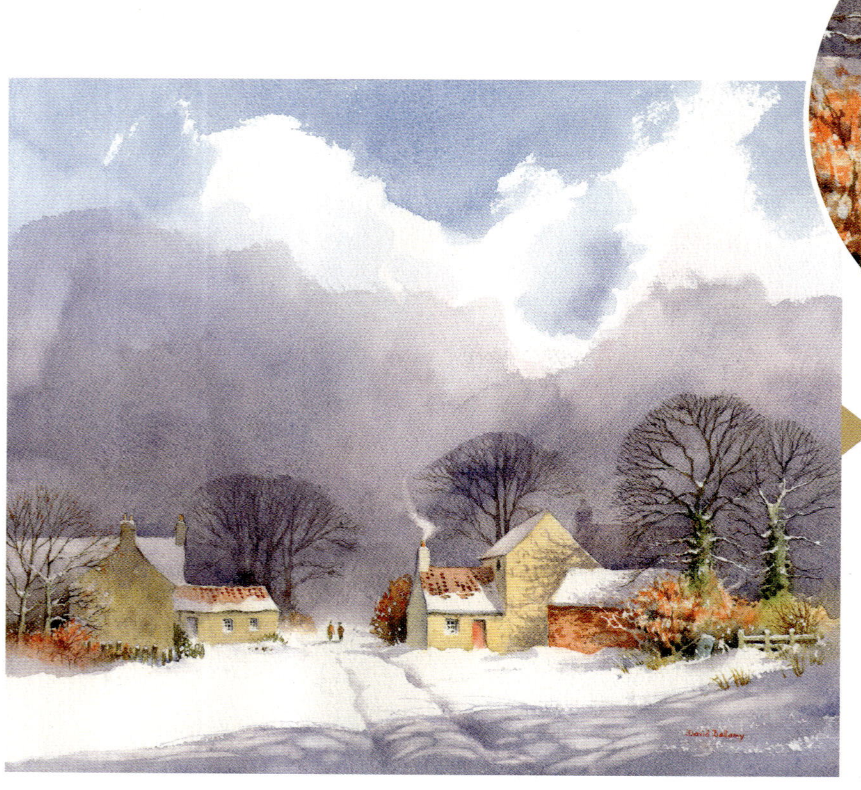

▶ Exton Village under Snow
33 × 28cm (13 × 11in) Saunders Waterford 300gsm (140lb) Not surface paper

Most of the white in this painting is the pure white of the untouched paper, but features like snow resting on branches and fenceposts are a little trickier to achieve, so in most cases I use white gouache to show these. There's no need to cover every branch with gouache, simply apply it to a select few of the larger branches.

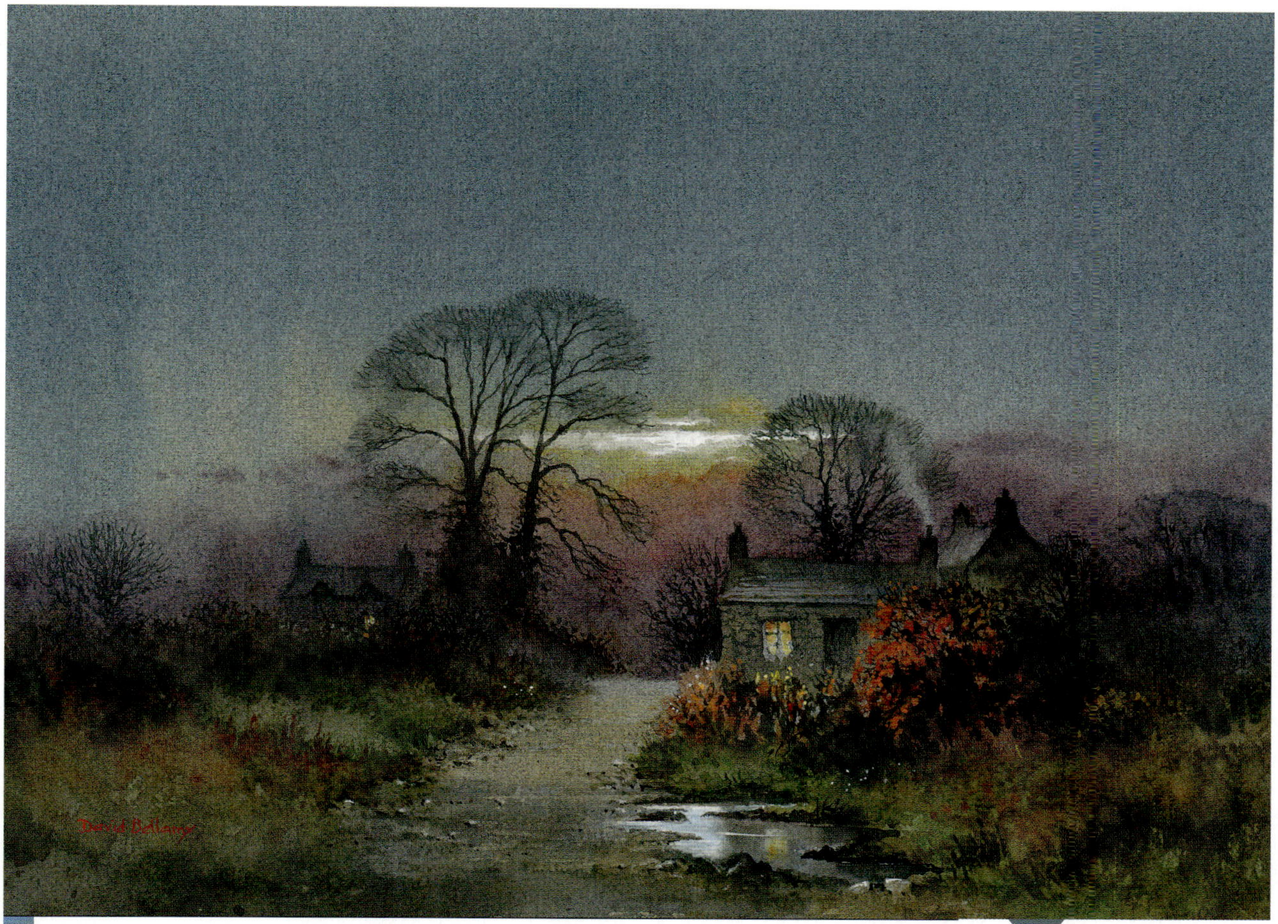

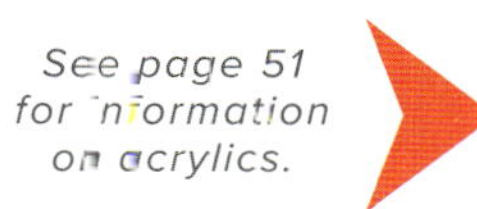

Painting *Still Evening, Felindre*

Working on tinted papers can release the pent-up creative blocks that artists encounter from time to time. To obtain any highlights on tinted papers, gouache is almost essential to avoid the result being rather dull. Acrylic paints or light-coloured pastel pencils can also be effective.

- I kept the evening sky plain with just a wash of phthalo blue. At the bottom a mixture of permanent alizarin crimson and moonglow was applied.

- Most of the tree and building detail was carried out with burnt umber and French ultramarine, and once all the watercolour elements had been completed I resorted to gouache, which is vital for creating highlights on tinted papers.

- White gouache was used for the sliver of light in the sky, the associated reflection in the puddle, and also in the windows, though the latter was eventually overlaid with Naples yellow and a touch of Aussie red gold watercolours.

- Pyrrol red gouache warmed up the bushes, the colour slightly muddied in places with yellow ochre.

Still Evening, Felindre
28 × 20.5cm (11 × 8in)
300gsm (140lb) Turner
Grey paper

See page 51 for information on acrylics.

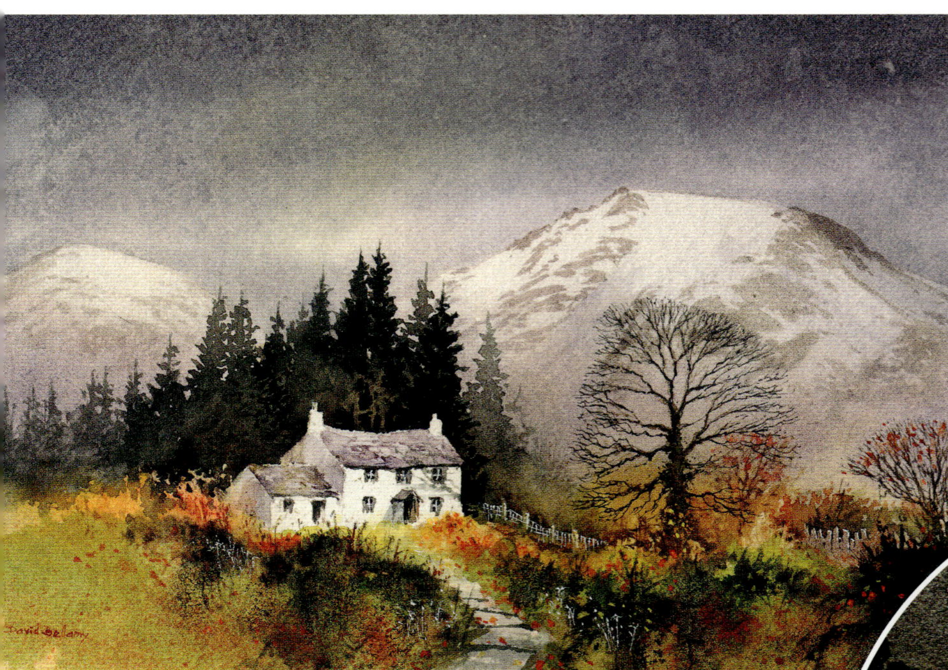

Snowdonia Cottage

25.5 × 18cm (10 × 7 n) Saunders Waterford 425gsm (200lb) Rough surface paper

This was painted in the usual way, except that a pen loaded with a mixture of burnt umber and French ultramarine was used for the fine branches on the main tree, and one with white gouache used for the fences and cow parsley.

These small touches of gouache can greatly enhance a watercolour without appearing intrusive when carried out in a subtle way.

Keys to success with gouache

- Subtle touches of white gouache can add a lively quality to a watercolour when used to depict seagulls, masts, fenceposts, plants or highlights of frothing water.
- Care is needed when introducing larger passages of gouache as this can intrude on the more transparent watercolour areas, and you need to blend these in if possible.
- Alternatively, bold application of gouache with a brush or painting knife can also work, especially on tinted papers, as in the following pages.
- Red, yellow and orange gouache is also effective for flowers and plants, for example, and sometimes it is worth applying white gouache first and then these colours once the white has dried. I often use this method of working for foreground flowers.

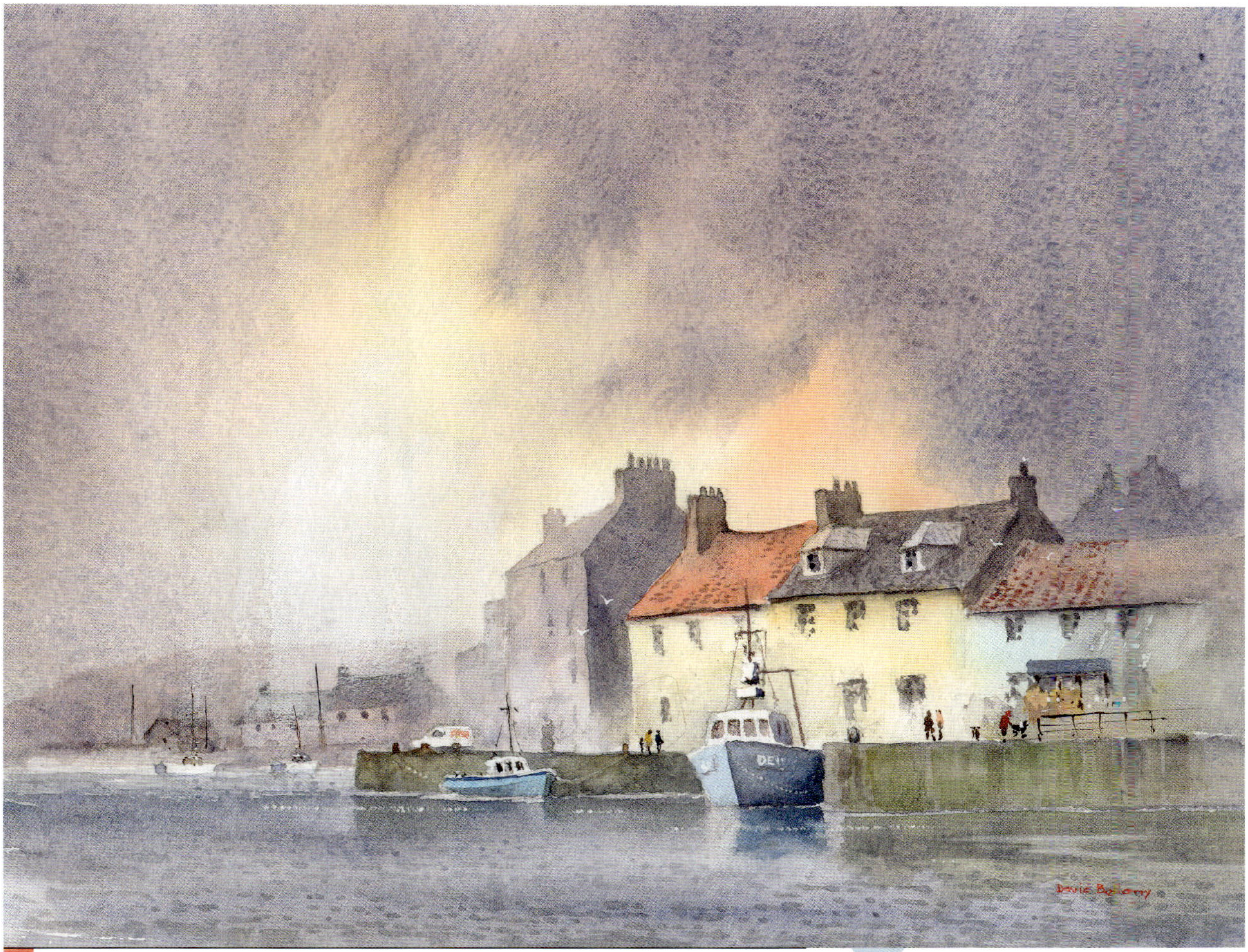

Painting *Wintry Squall, Pittenweem*

To give the impression of a sleet squall coming in from the left and blotting out the far buildings, we would normally lay a glaze with a transparent colour; washing it down over a passage already painted. Here, I instead opted to use white gouache, quite the opposite to the accepted method.

- The sky, distant ridge and buildings were painted first, and the paper left to dry completely.
- I then wetted the sky above the buildings with clean water and blobbed some white gouache into the centre of the wet area, then immediately brought it down over the buildings with a 12mm (½in) flat brush.
- I swept the brush down rapidly with the dry-brush method (that is, without much water on the brush). As it was Rough paper the gouache did not stick to every part of the area covered, thus creating a squall-like texture, and allowing parts of the buildings to remain visible.
- At the bottom of each stroke I lifted the brush up so that the boats and harbour wall would not be affected.

Wintry Squall, Pittenweem
28 × 23cm (11 × 9in) Saunders Waterford 425gsm (200lb) Rough surface paper

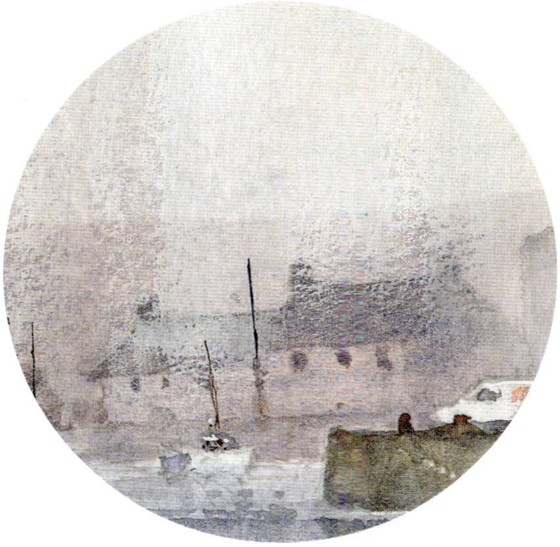

Using gouache with watercolour

It can be liberating to throw caution to the wind and enjoy experimenting with new approaches.
The method of mixing gouache with watercolour in the Crib Goch painting (see below)
is not normally recommended, but as you can see, here it has created a dramatic effect.
Likewise *Crashing Surf* is vastly different in terms of style from my usual way of working, but the
resulting painting has a powerful sense of movement and drama. It pays to ignore the rules of
watercolour occasionally, and see what happens.

Clouds Rising over Crib Goch

25.5 × 20.5cm (10 × 8in) Saunders Waterford 640gsm
(300lb) Not surface paper

*Here I decided to have a little fun by laying white
gouache cumulus clouds over the sky of indigo
and lunar black while the wash was still wet.*

*I swirled phthalo blue into parts of the wet
gouache to create shadows in the clouds, and
also dropped in a little cadmium yellow pale to
add variety. I especially enjoyed working on the
straggly bits of light clouds.*

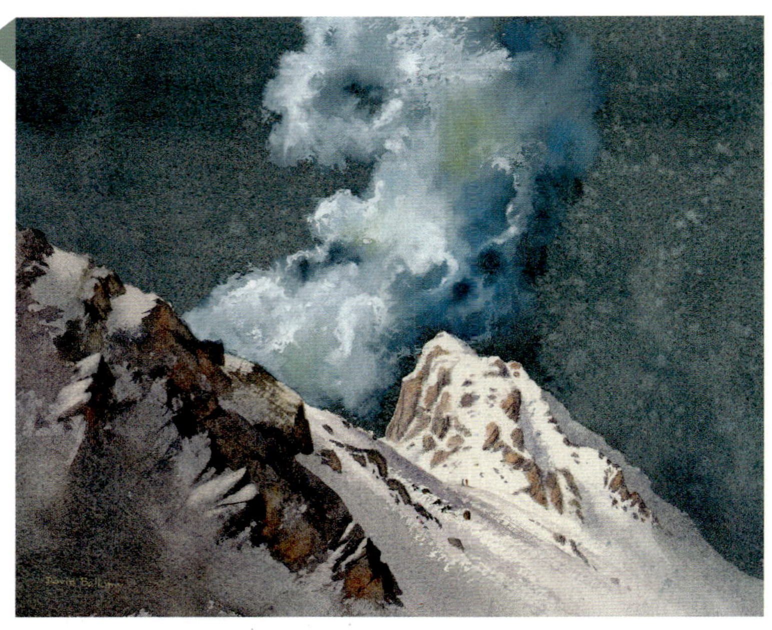

Crashing Surf

38 × 23cm (15 × 9in) Bockingford 300gsm (140lb)
grey Not surface paper

*After wetting the whole paper, I applied an
energetic wash of lunar black, bringing in cobalt
blue lower down. I then added blobs of black
across the horizon and up into the cliff – some of
this delightfully disappearing under the deluge.*

*Once dry I used a painting knife to apply large
blobs of white gouache straight from the tube.
Some of this was strung horizontally as surf, and
some as splashes rising above the rocks, much of
it as a heavy impasto. The large black rock and
white gulls were painted in to finish.*

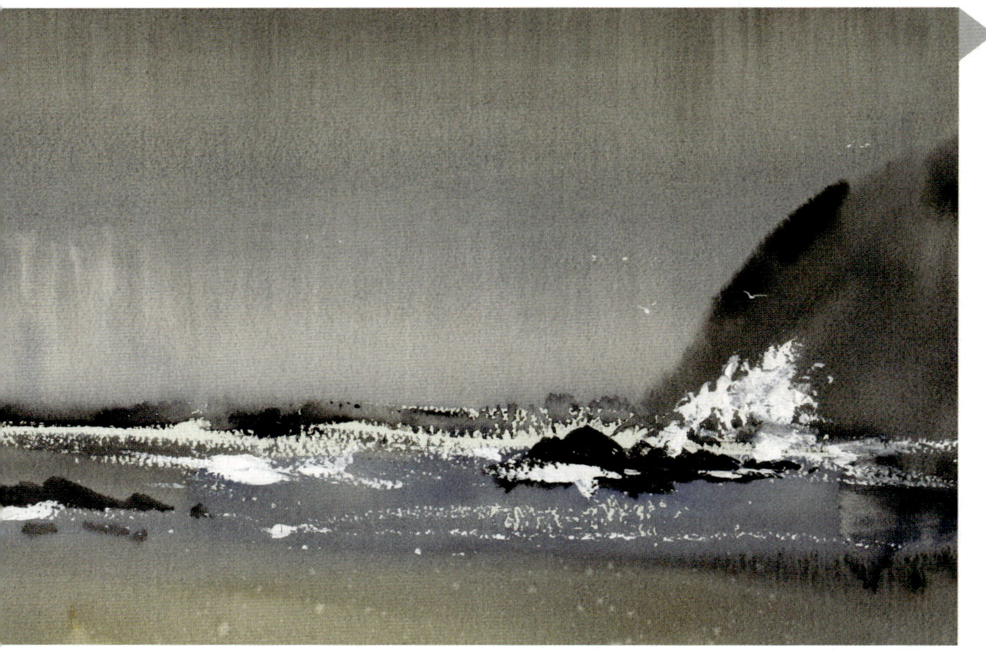

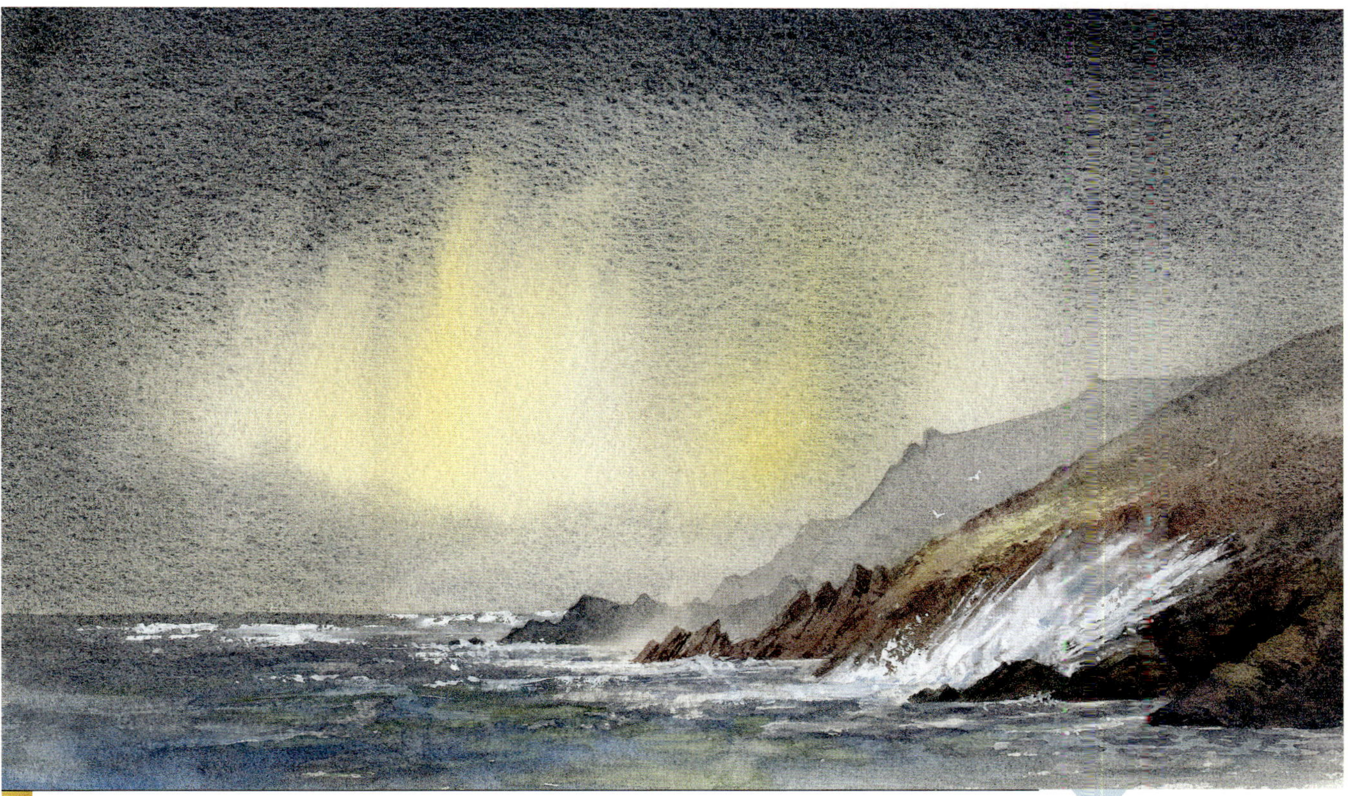

Painting *Wild Coast*

All of the white elements within this painting were done with white gouache, but it is the large splash at the bottom right which holds the attention of the viewer, and was created with a combination of techniques. Sometimes you may wish to add more power and movement to your splashes of surf, and in this example are several techniques with which to achieve this.

- Starting on the left of the splash, white gouache was applied to the paper in the general angle of the splash using the flat of the blade of a painting knife.
- Slightly to the right of this, gouache was stroked vigorously with the knife, creating a more linear form at the same angle.
- In the middle right of the splash, the paper was wetted with a brush that was loaded with a little French ultramarine before the gouache was swept into that part of the splash. This produced a wet-in-wet effect with the ultramarine suggesting a shadow area within the splash.
- Finally, on the right-hand edge of the splash white gouache was again introduced with the knife on dry paper, using the same vigorous action. A few tiny spots of white gouache were dabbed into the edges of the splash to complete the effect.

Wild Coast
28 × 13cm (11 × 7in)
Saunders Waterford
300gsm (140lb) Not
surface paper

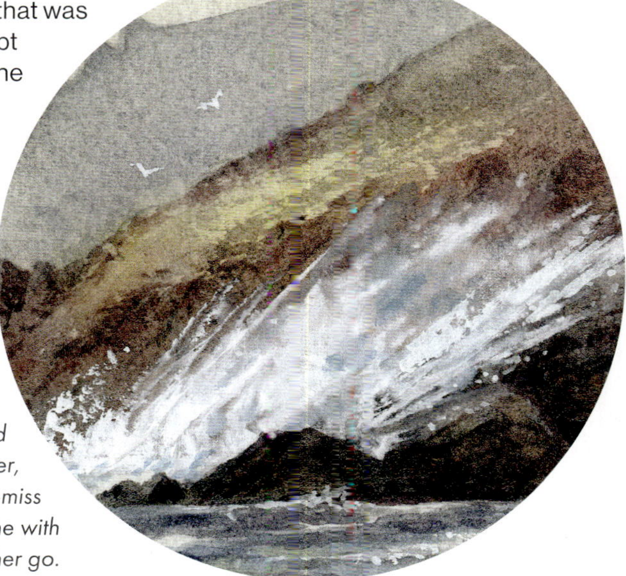

Detail of the splash

Of course, you don't have to include all these methods within one splash, but it does help to have part of the splash hard-edged and part soft-edged by the method of sweeping the gouache into water, or softening the edge off later with a damp brush. It can be a hit-or-miss technique, but if it ends up looking wrong then wash out the gouache with a brush, dab it with a tissue and leave it to dry. Then have another go.

Figures

Figures add a sense of life into any landscape. They instantly become the focal point in a composition, which is a very useful advantage in subjects where there may not be an obvious centre of interest.

Character

I do like to make my figures individual and full of character, rather than create a battalion of stylized one-and-a-half-legged carrots marching along some high street (see right).

There are numerous examples of figures scattered throughout the book, and you may like to check out the farmer in *Windy Day in the Pennines* on page 21: although he is extremely tiny the bow-legged stance implies that he is holding himself against the wind as he walks across the farmyard. In *Robin Hood's Bay*, on page 110, the left-hand figure was meant to be leaning on her stick, but it looks as though she is adjusting her thigh-garter – and in public! My sense of humour made me leave it as it was, but it's easy enough to wash out the lower part of the body with a small brush and try again if you are unhappy with a stance.

Basic figures

The commonly taught approach of basing your figures on carrot shapes is a good starting point. Just a few details can turn an abstract carrot shape into a more sophisticated carrot man or woman – but this approach has limits, and will soon start to look monotonous. Once you become adept, try to make your people look as though they belong to the place.

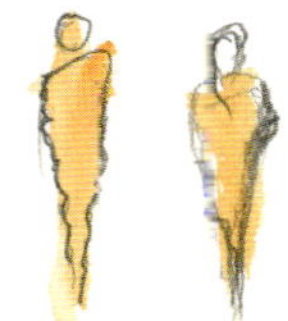

Carrot man and woman

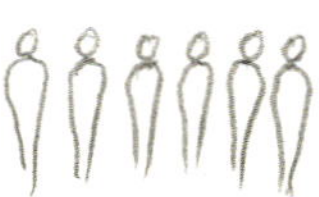

Avoid carrot regiments!

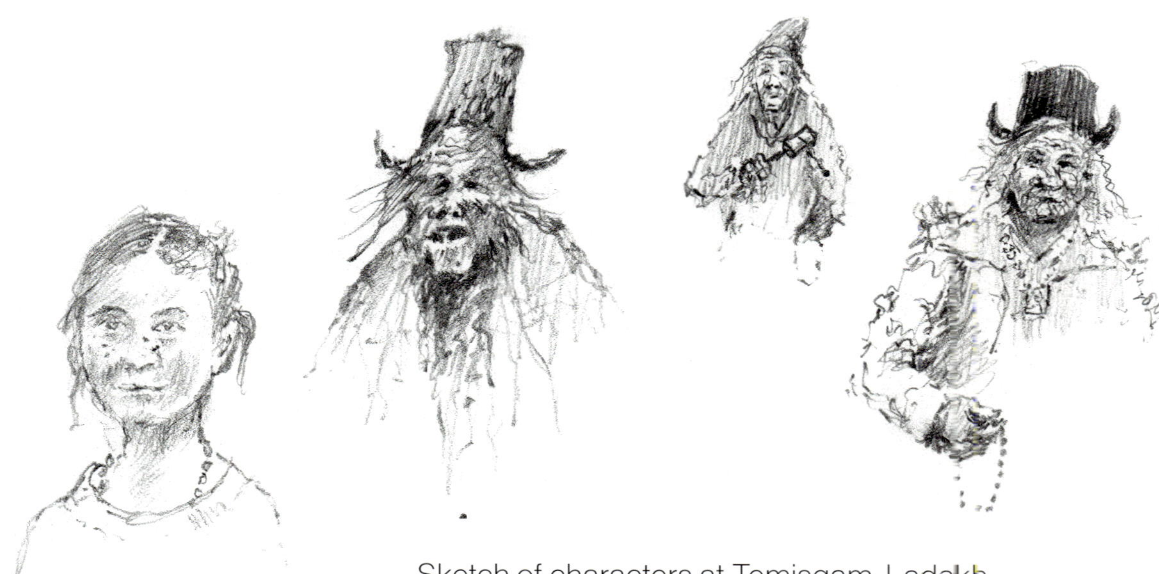

Sketch of characters at Temisgam, Ladakh

I love to engage with local people wherever I am and try to encourage them to stand still for a while as I sketch them. If you have a partner with you then it's great if they can engage people while you sketch them. Trying to draw moving people is not easy, though the young girl stood quite still while I sketched. She spoke excellent English and wrote her name on my sketchbook, as you can see to the left.

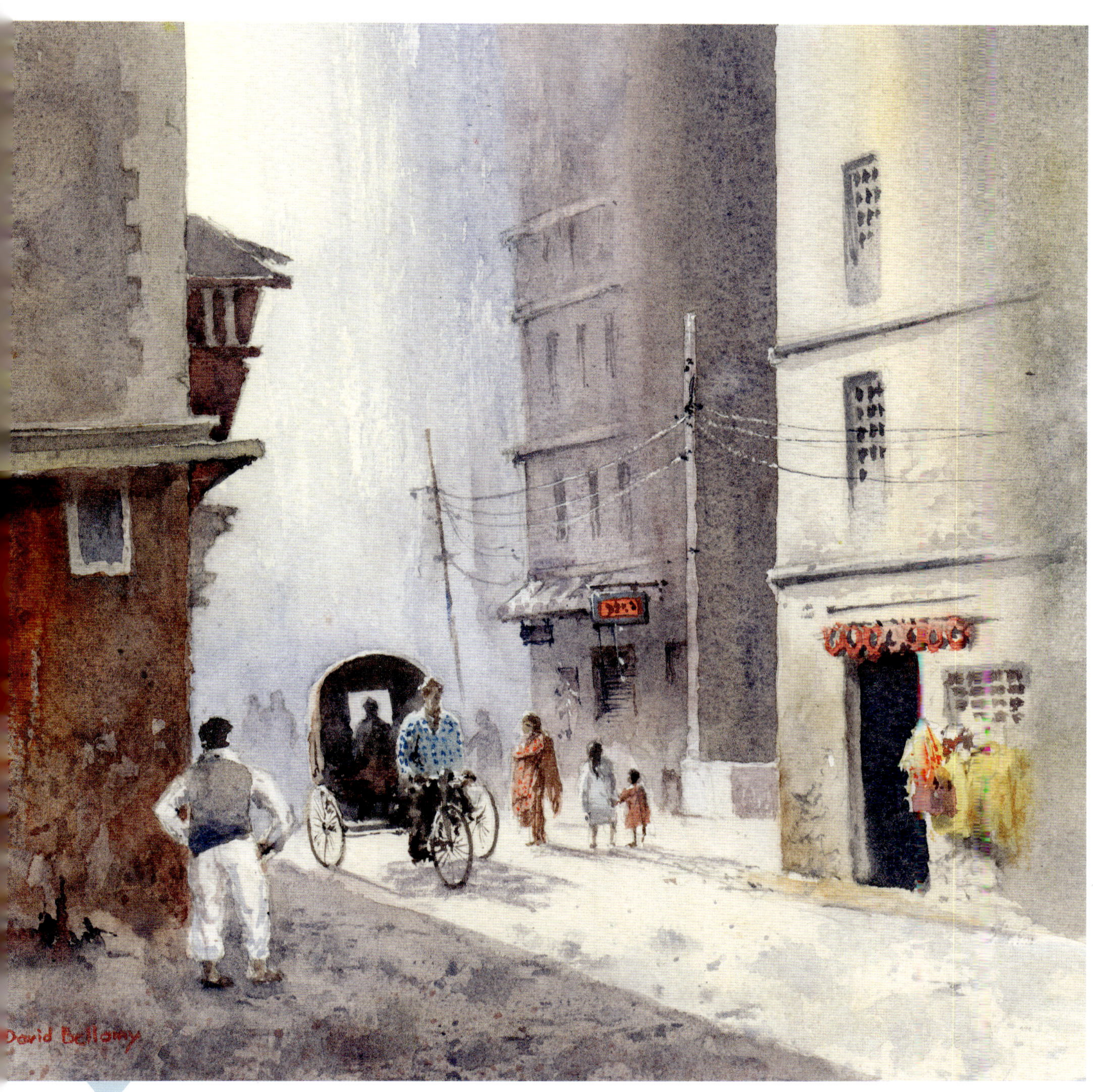

Morning Light, Kathmandu

23 × 23cm (9 × 9in) Saunders Waterford 425gsm (200lb) Hot-Pressed surface paper

I often add a little humour into my figures, although I subdued the urge in this work.
With the rickshaw cyclist I painted the blue pattern on his shirt first, then let it dry
before applying the grey shadow over his front, leaving his shoulders as white paper.
This method reduces the starkness of the blue and white pattern.

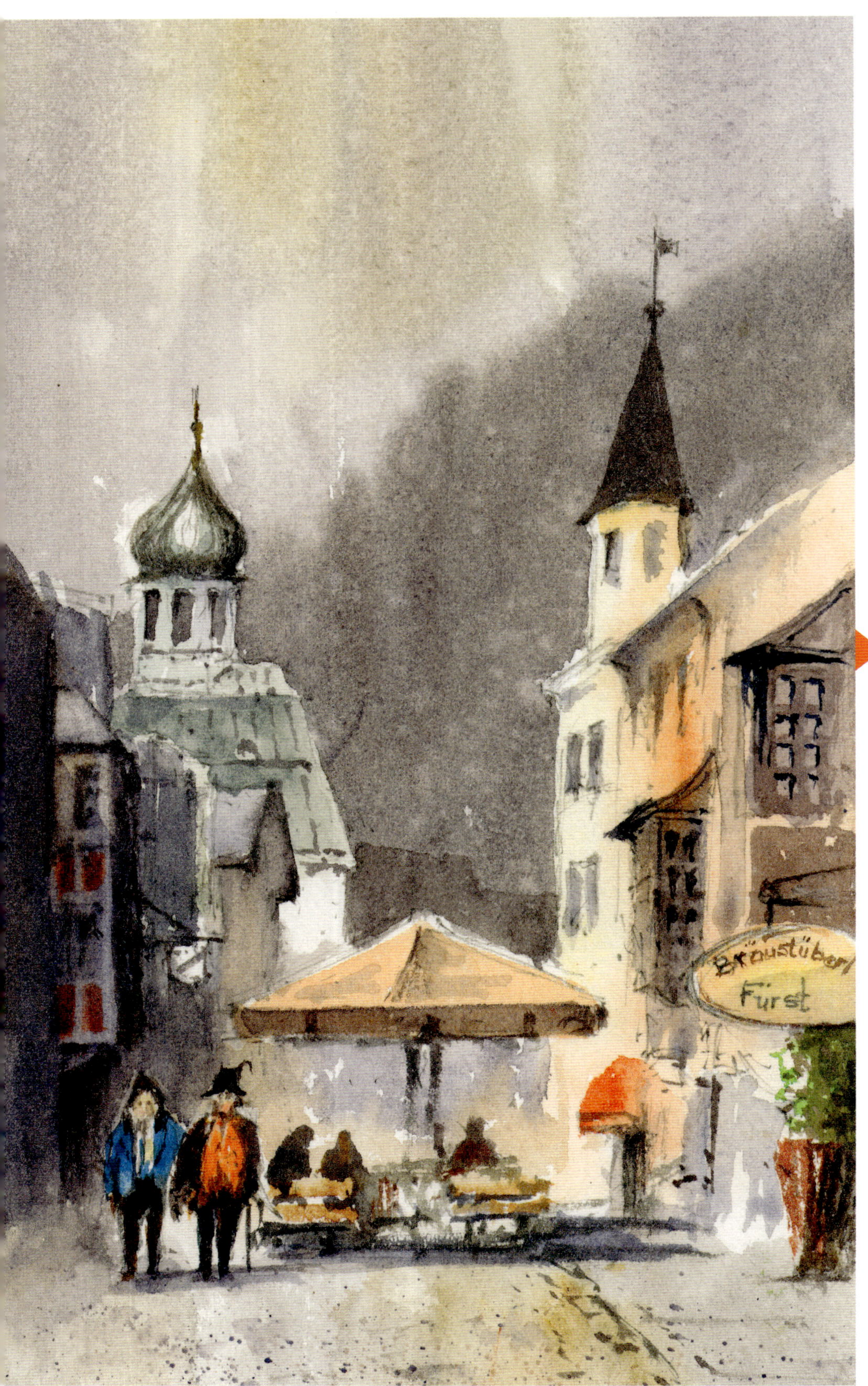

Figures in context

Certain subjects, such as towns, harbours and villages call out for figures. Towns and cities are not easy places to set up and carry out a full painting, but you can often find some corner where you are less likely to be disturbed.

Note how the architectural detail of the buildings behind the figures here has been lost so that they stand out as focal points.

▶ Rattenberg, Austria
14 × 23cm (5½ × 9in) Saunders Waterford 300gsm (140lb) Hot-Pressed surface paper

With this alfresco painting it began raining as I started with the sky, the rain spatters clear in places, but it soon stopped. My idea was to get a fairly rapid impression of the scene, with some features suggested rather than delineated in detail. I wanted the elderly couple on the left to appear as though they were strolling along stiffly and unhurriedly, their legs straight and the right-hand figure holding a stick.

As with most cases of painting outside, I finished it off in the studio later, having ensured that I already had all the most important aspects of the scene completed before I left. Your work will improve immensely when you master this method of working.

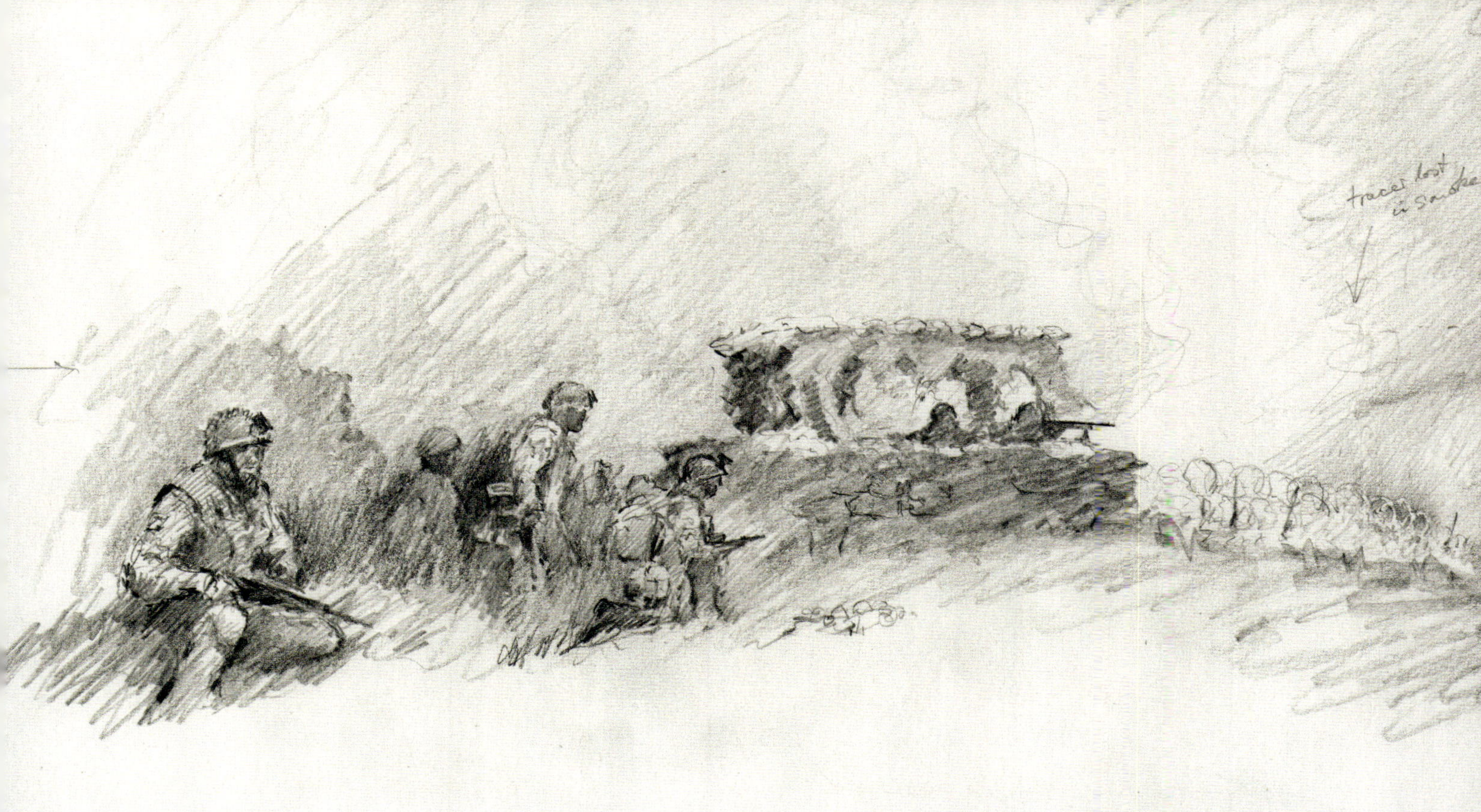

Relationships

With groups it's important to ensure that all the figures relate well not only to their environment, but to each other. This sketch was carried out during an army battle exercise in the Epynt Mountains.

Preparing to counter-attack

It's not often I get the opportunity to sketch a group in a leisurely way, but during a lull in the mayhem and chaos of battle I was able to carry out a pretty well complete drawing of these troops as they prepared to counter-attack.

The sangar – a temporary defensive position – has taken on an extremely tatty appearance, and the pale light catches the coiled barbed wire in places. Shortly afterwards, replenished with ammunition, the squad moved off into action to continue the exercise.

Keys to success with painting figures

- Try to ensure that the figures you introduce are actually doing something as this gives the work much more authenticity.

- One danger which you should always be aware of and check before painting, is that of making the figures out of scale with their surroundings and each other: is that dear old lady far too big to get through the shop door? Is that policeman really supposed to look like a midget? It's something we all do at times.

- More distant figures can be left simply as monochrome shapes – treat them like any other part of the painting.

Masking

Apart from the standard way of applying masking fluid which we looked at on pages 40–41, it can be used in many creative ways which we explore here.

Knifework

Masking fluid can be applied with a painting knife to create extra-fine lines, something which is extremely difficult with a brush. Test it on scrap paper first.

 If you get a thick line or an unsightly blob of masking fluid after reloading the knife, let it dry completely then simply rub off the offending bit and try again – or adapt and turn the mark into a fallen branch.

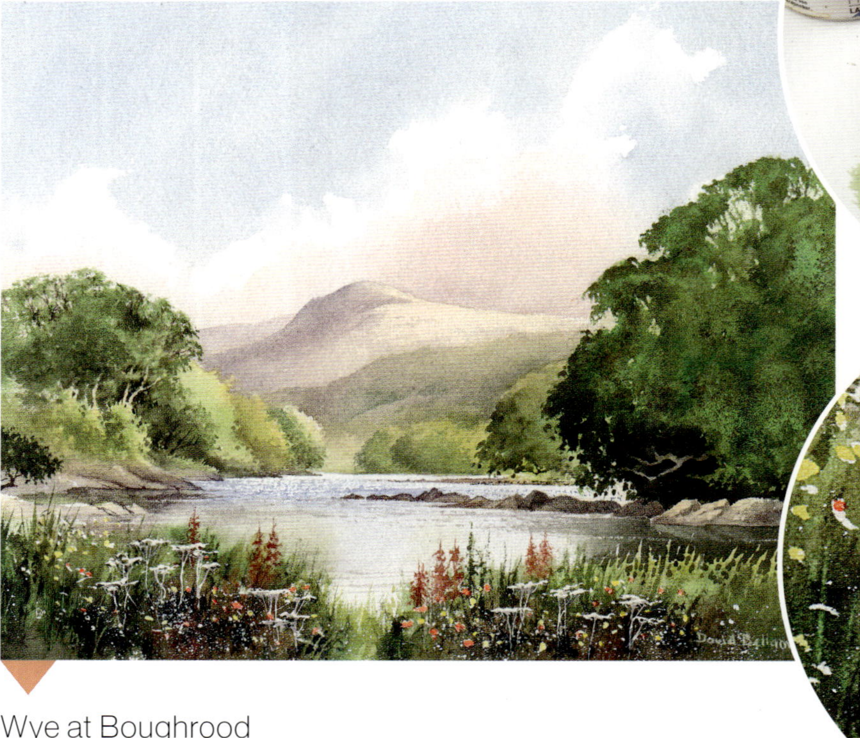

Wye at Boughrood
25.5 × 20.5cm (10 × 8in) Saunders Waterford 300gsm (140lb) Not surface paper

I have deliberately included a lot of detail in the foreground to illustrate how useful masking fluid is for retaining light in fine detail. The tops of the cow parsley were also blobbed in with masking fluid on a knife. Superimposing a dark area of vegetation over the masking fluid ensures the result really stands out.

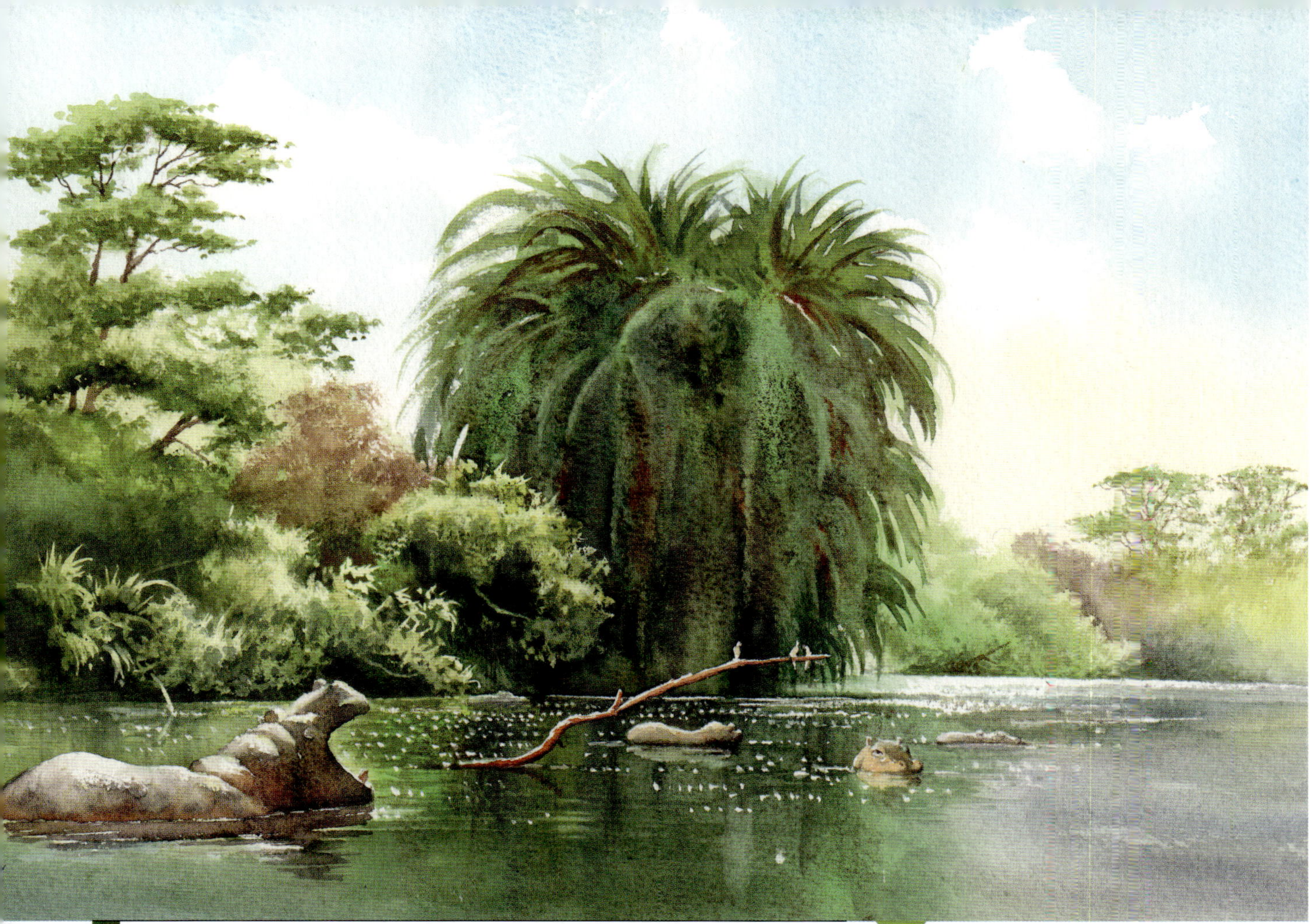

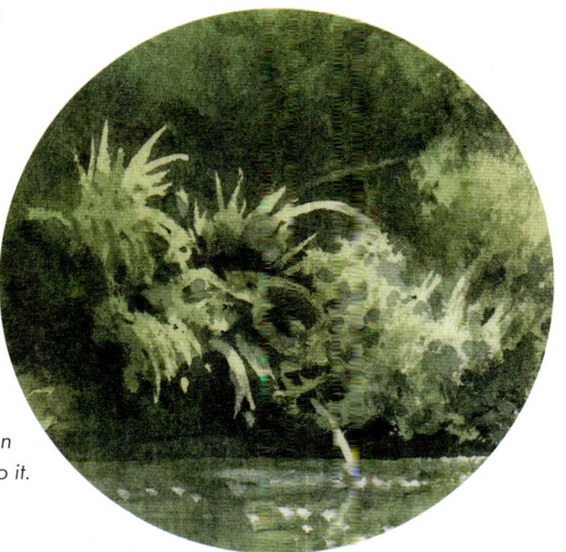

Painting *Hippo Pool*

- I used a lot of masking fluid on this painting: it was used on the foliage on the left-hand side of the composition, for the white baubles of froth in the dark water, on the sunlit backs of the hippos, and for the tree-trunk sticking out of the water, on which the egrets are perched.

- When it was dry I slightly rubbed the lower edge of the masking fluid on the back of the closest hippo to create a ragged edge.

- I have used green apatite genuine over much of the work, and quite strongly over the mass of palms in the centre, where I pulled out some colour with a size 8 round brush to suggest the lighter fronds. Some granulation medium added a little texture here and there.

- Hippos are dangerous animals and I was quite close, but the thing that made me finish the original sketch prematurely was the appalling smell.

Hippo Pool
35.5 × 25.5cm (14 × 10in) Saunders
Waterford 300gsm (140lb) Rough
surface paper

Sunlight

*The masking fluid on the lower bushes set
against the palms has worked well in defining
a sunny edge to the foliage, and this can be an
effective method so long as you don't overdo it.*

Depicting scree

Scree, the loose rock lying down the slopes of craggy mountains is useful in suggesting rough, steep slopes, and can be depicted quickly with a few dry-brush strokes. I often exaggerate the amount of scree because it is so effective.

Scree with masking fluid and dry brush

The dry-brush technique is simply dragging any brush loaded with very little water – a 'thirsty brush' – across the paper. Because the paint barely flows, it catches only the upper parts of the paper texture, and leaves small irregular gaps; great for texture.

   I normally rely on the dry-brush method alone to depict scree on a mountainside, but masking fluid can also be used, and is especially effective to create light rocks amidst the scree when laying on a fairly dark colour.

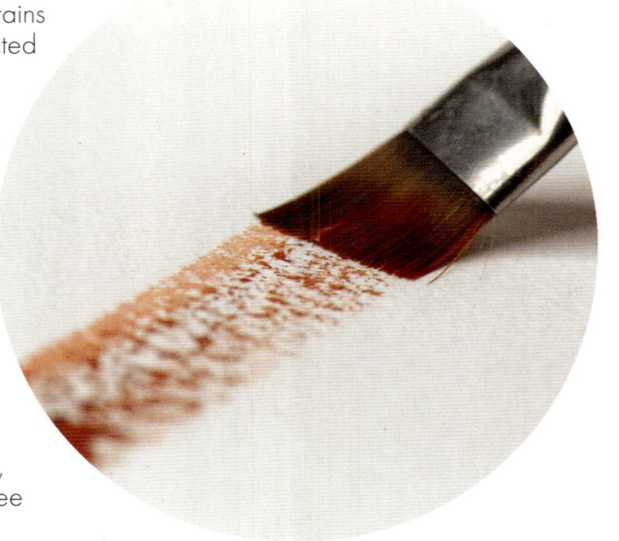

Dry brush

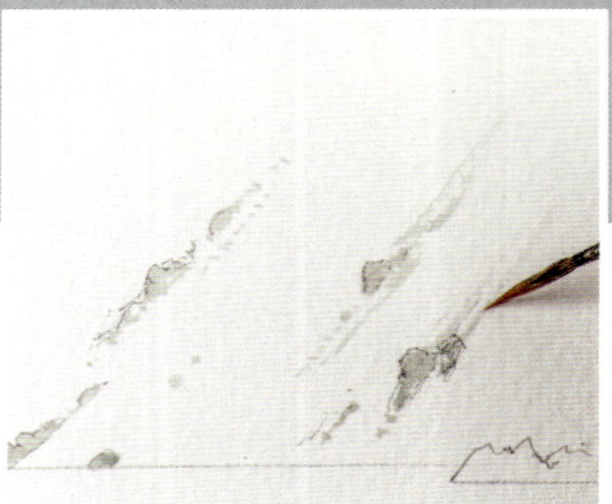

Larger rocks Working on rough paper, dot in some masking fluid with a small brush. Work at an angle that suggests the diagonal slope.

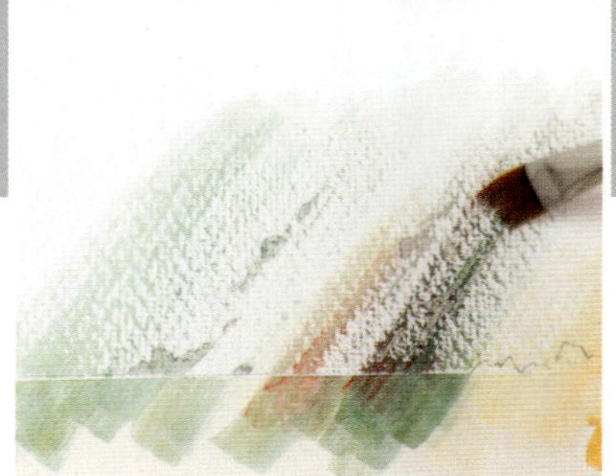

Dry brush Once dry, hold a sheet of paper to protect the edge of the water, then lay on various colours diagonally over the slope with an angled 12mm (½in) flat brush, using the dry-brush method.

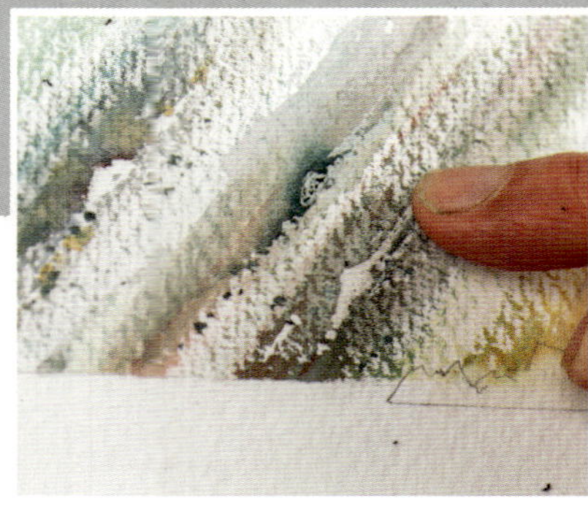

Adjusting Removing the masking fluid will reveal how this approach allows the larger blobs to complement the dry brush effect.

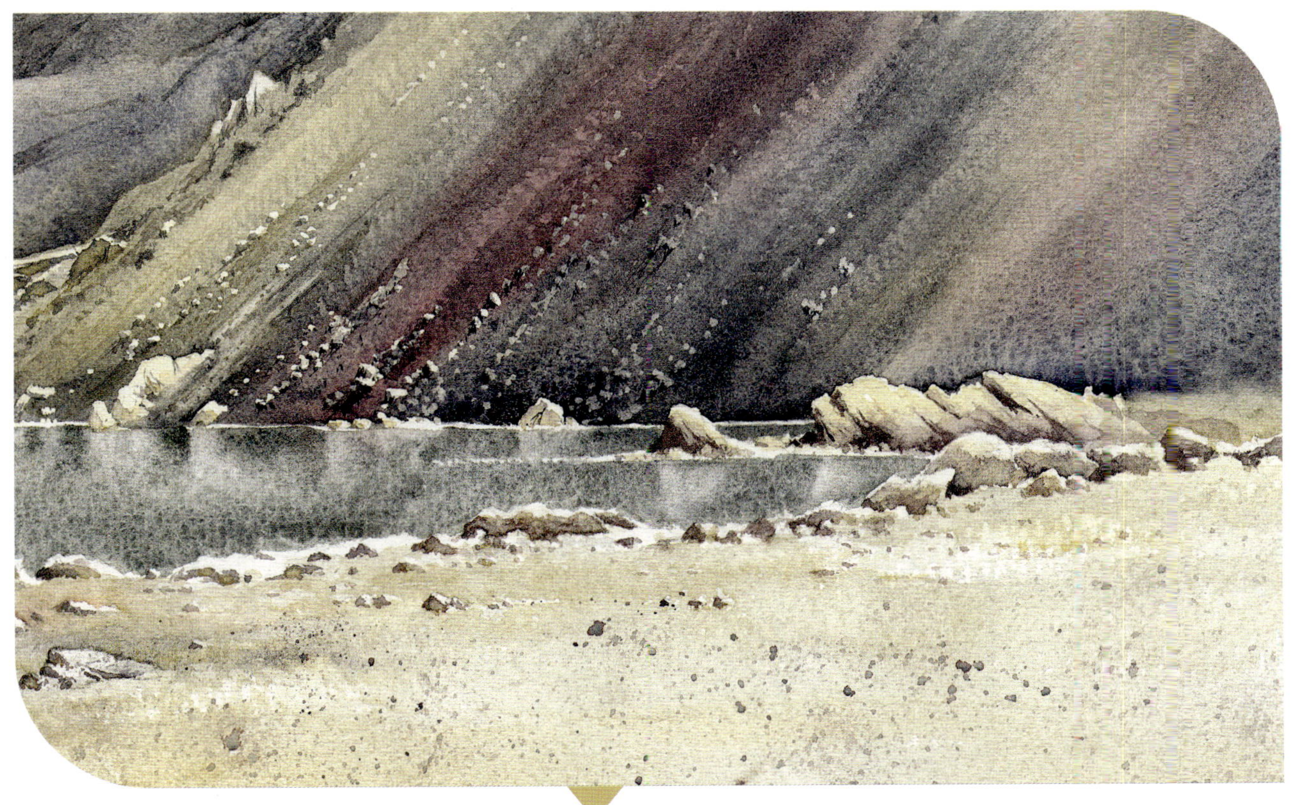

Detail from *Streaming Clouds over Sermitsiaq Glacier*

This is a detail from a full painting which appears in my Arctic Light book. It was painted using the technique described opposite. After removing the masking fluid, I glazed weak indigo over some of the white spots left by the masking fluid. This still allowed them to be seen, but they were less prominent, which gives a more varied and realistic result. I chose Saunders Waterford Rough paper to enhance the effect of the dry-brush work. The reflections of the rocks in the placid lake were achieved by swiping downwards from the rocks with a small, damp brush.

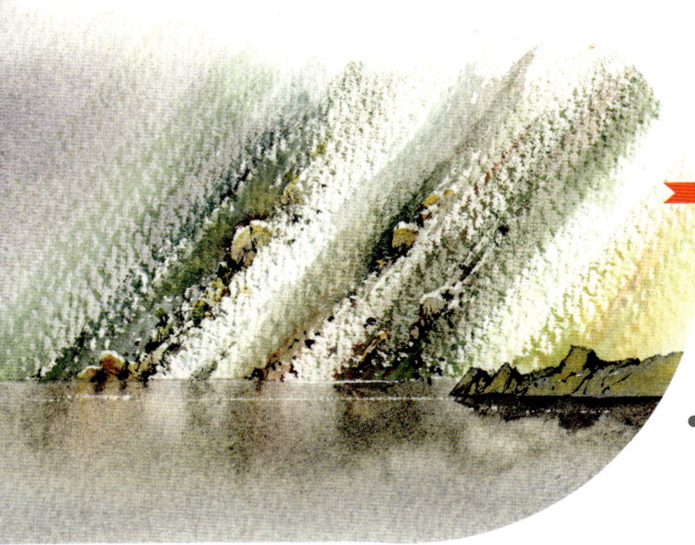

Keys to success with dry brush

- The rougher the paper, the more broken and obvious the effect.
- Test it first on similar paper to ensure that the paint on the brush is not too dry or too wet.
- Vary the colours, if you wish, to add more interest.

TECHNIQUE

Scumbling

I use this technique to create visual texture, almost always with a Rough surface for best results. This involves generously loading a brush with paint and swirling it across the paper while keeping it at a low angle to allow as much of the belly of the brush to ride across the surface. In this way the action generates ragged edges to the wash, with gaps here and there, as shown to the right. A good example of this is on page *77* on the cliffs of *Dollar Cove, Cornwall*. While this is wet, I often drop other colours in for variation.

Scumbling masking fluid for rocks

The scumbling technique can also be used with masking fluid, but be sure to remember to use an old brush and not your best sable, as masking fluid left on a brush will damage it. I find a size 2 or 3 rigger can work well for this, and again Rough paper encourages best results.

   This method can work well for textures on rocks, walls and so forth, and also for creating clouds. For natural features you will need to lay a wash of lightish colour before applying the masking fluid.

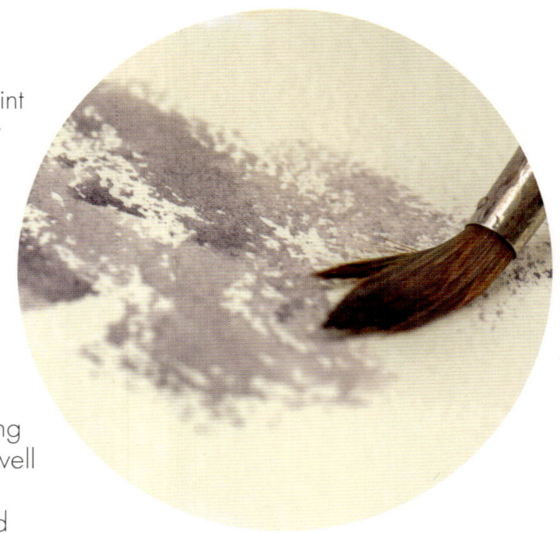

Scumbling

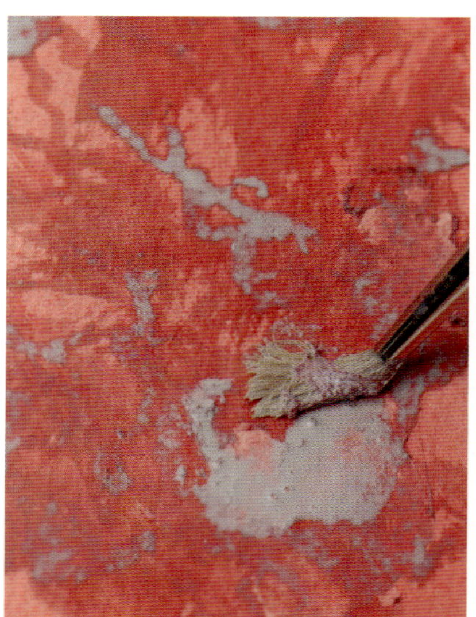

Scumbling Begin with a pink wash over the paper. Once dry, scumble on masking fluid using an old brush. Trail the tip of the brush to add some fine lines, too.

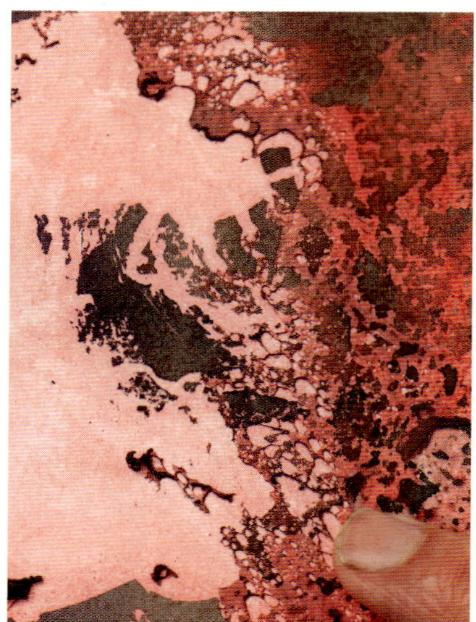

Darks Once dry, examine the masking fluid, mainly for the quality of the edges – you don't want hard, definite edges all round. If necessary, rub some edges with a finger to increase the raggedness. Next, apply a dark burnt umber wash and allow to dry.

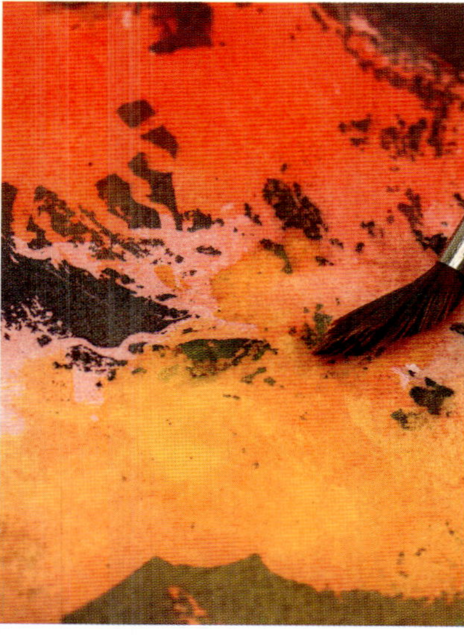

Warmth Remove the masking fluid, then lay some warm colour over areas of the composition. If you are not entirely happy with the result when you remove the masking fluid you can always apply a further layer and repeat the action.

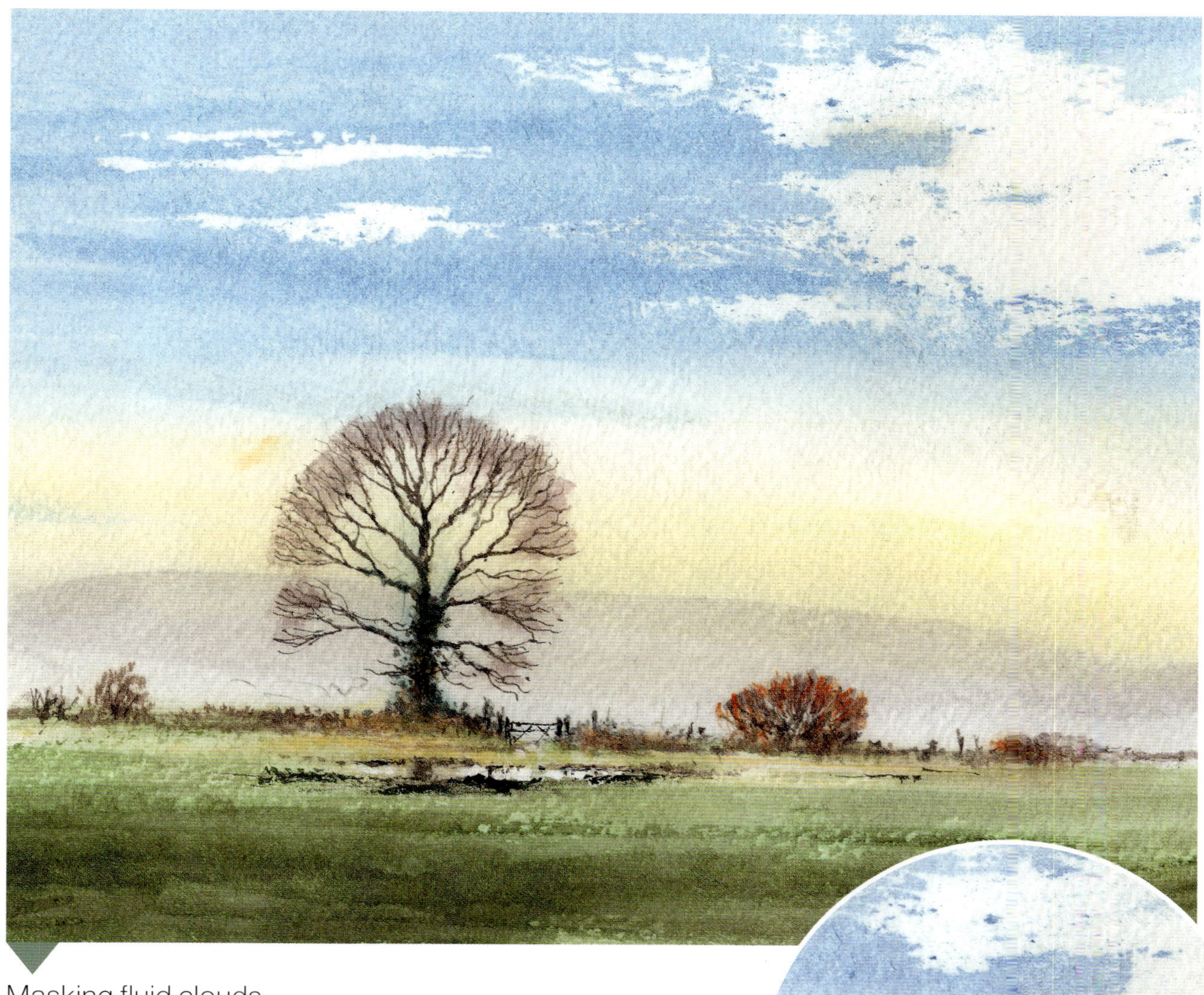

Masking fluid clouds

Scumbling can also be used to produce cloud effects. When using the technique opposite, you can leave the paper clean, resulting in white clouds as shown here – or you can apply an initial wash before applying the masking fluid, to produce coloured clouds.

Keys to success with scumbling

- Have a clear idea of the effect you are aiming at before you start.
- If in doubt outline your boundaries with a soft pencil.
- Rubbing off some of the dried masking fluid can produce interesting edges and gaps.
- If you are not satisfied with the shapes, you can add more masking fluid if you wish.

Visual texture

Creating texture in a landscape painting will add considerably to the overall effect. We can do this visually by suggesting an impression of roughness – either in the manner in which we apply the brush-strokes, or we can stick various materials to the paper to create physical texture. This latter method is described later in the book.

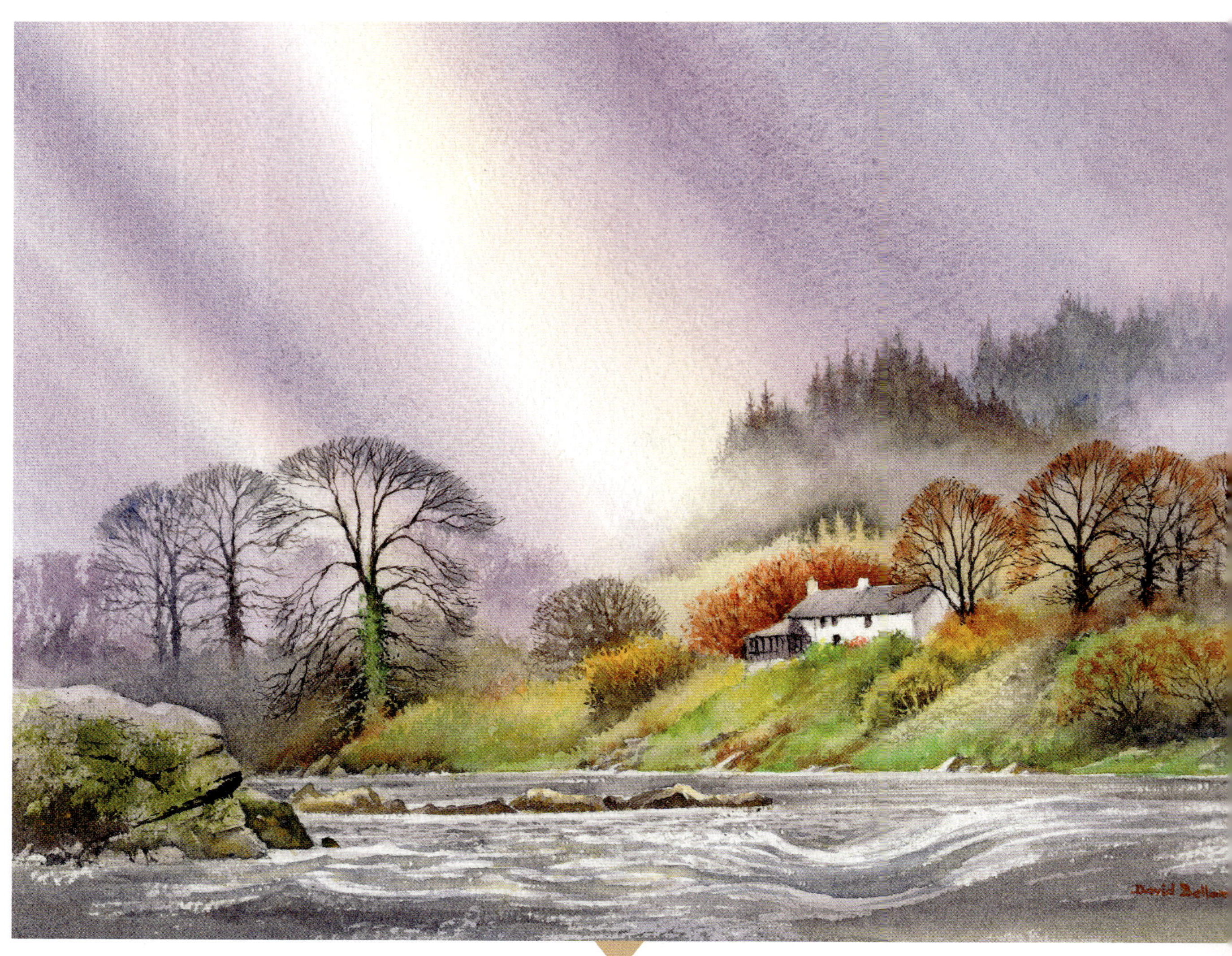

Sunshine & Mist on the Wye
33 × 25.5cm (13 × 10in) Saunders Waterford 300gsm (140lb) Rough surface paper

The lower parts of most of the trees here are lost in atmosphere. The original sketch was carried out in a most uncomfortable position, propped against a tree over the water's edge while peering through the bushes like some lurking bandit.

Contrast in visual texture

This composition, *Sunshine & Mist on the Wye*, is a good example of highly contrasting textures achieved with paint alone. I was keen to achieve the interesting texture on the large rock at the bottom left-hand corner.

The sky was painted with the board at quite an angle so that all the washes ran straight down. I began with weak Naples yellow and some quinacridone gold for the shaft of light, then brought down a mixture of French ultramarine and permanent alizarin crimson. This was painted over the right-hand conifer masses to suggest more atmosphere.

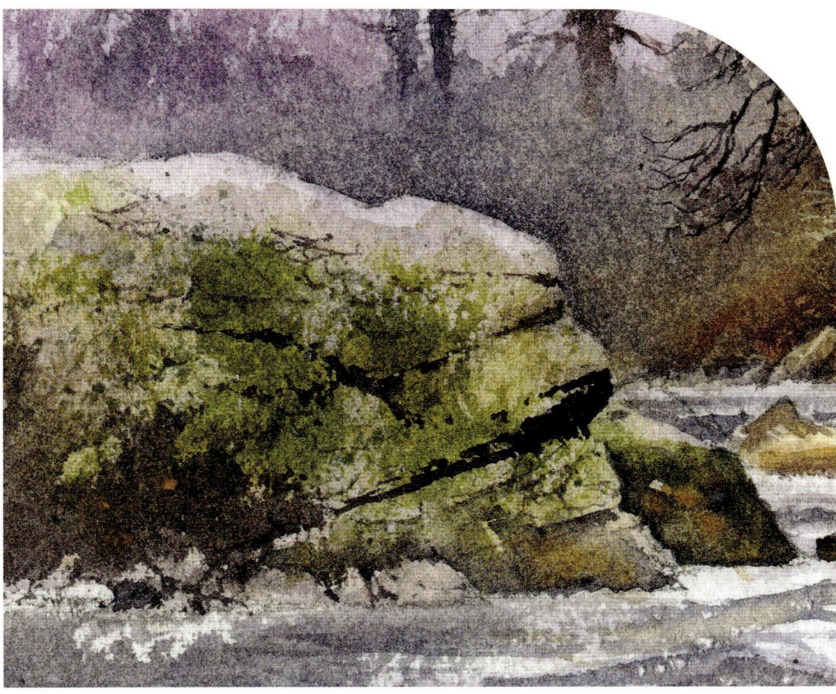

Key area: the rock

- I brought the sky wash right down over the rock, weakly at this point. Once dry I smothered much of the rock, apart from where the light was catching the top, with strong yellow ochre, using the side of a size 10 round sable to create a broken wash, rather like the way the rigger was used in the painting of *Dollar Cove, Cornwall* on page 77.

- I let this dry and then introduced the green parts to suggest moss. For this I used a mixture of green apatite genuine and yellow ochre, again spreading it with the side of the brush.

- Finally, once that had dried, I took a fine-pointed size 6 sable and drew in the crevices with a mixture of burnt umber and French ultramarine.

Texture with watercolour pencil

I mainly use watercolour pencils for sketching rather than painting, especially during misty and wet weather or when it is snowing, as they allow me to continue sketching despite the conditions. However, there is no reason why they can't be used to enhance a watercolour. The Derwent Inktense pencils with their stronger and more intense colours are particularly useful in this respect.

Dropping in scrapings

To sketch the tens of thousands of starlings that appear in their gatherings – called murmurations – can be quite a challenge, but the truly uplifting sight of so many birds performing their swirling formations at dusk is so inspiring. To create thousands of tiny marks, we can use watercolour pencils in a creative way.

  Coarse sandpaper is much better than the finer versions for this purpose.

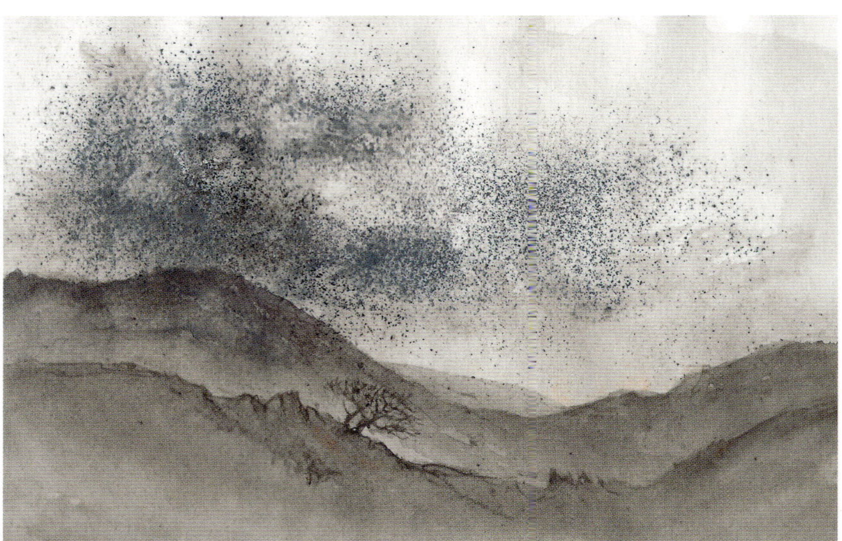

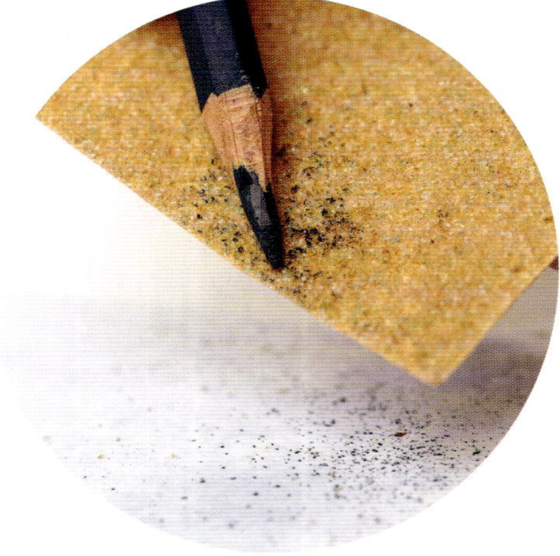

A prepared pencil being drawn over coarse sandpaper; note the length of the pencil lead.

Prepare the sky Use watercolour washes to create the sky before the birds arrive.

Re-wet the area for the birds As the birds begin their ritual, use clean water to re-wet the area where you want the starlings to appear.

Prepare the pencil Sharpen a blue-grey watercolour pencil to reveal a larger than usual area of the pencil pigment (see left).

Scrape the pencil Holding the pencil above the paper, rub the exposed pigment with coarse sandpaper, dropping the tiny speckles onto the wet paper where you want the birds to appear.

Vary the application Vary the amount of rubbing to suggest fewer birds at the extremities of the formations and introduce a little ivory black from another watercolour pencil for the darkest mass of birds.

Pencil into wet watercolour

As we saw on page 15, drawing into a wet surface with Inktense or watercolour pencils is an extremely effective way of suggesting detail. In these scenes I have used a black Inktense pencil, but you can use a variety of colours as you wish, though the lighter grades won't show up so well. They are also a powerful way of rescuing a painting that hasn't quite worked.

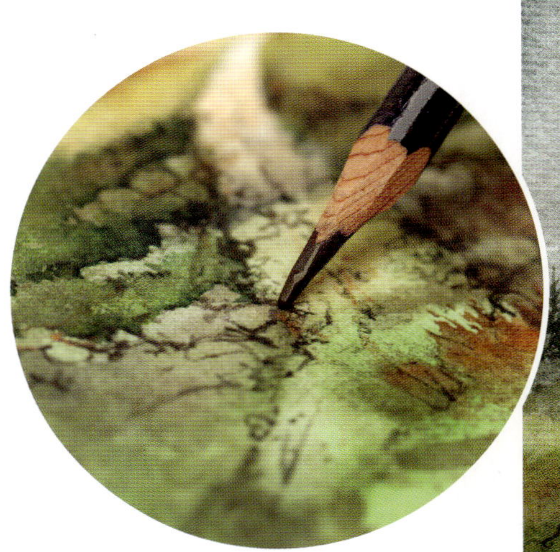

Inktense pencil used for detail on a damp surface will soften in slightly but retain clear marks.

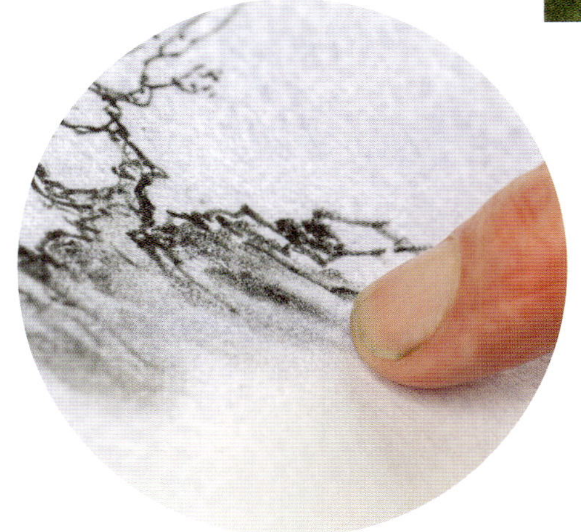

Used on a wet surface, Inktense pencil can be gently smeared with a clean finger.

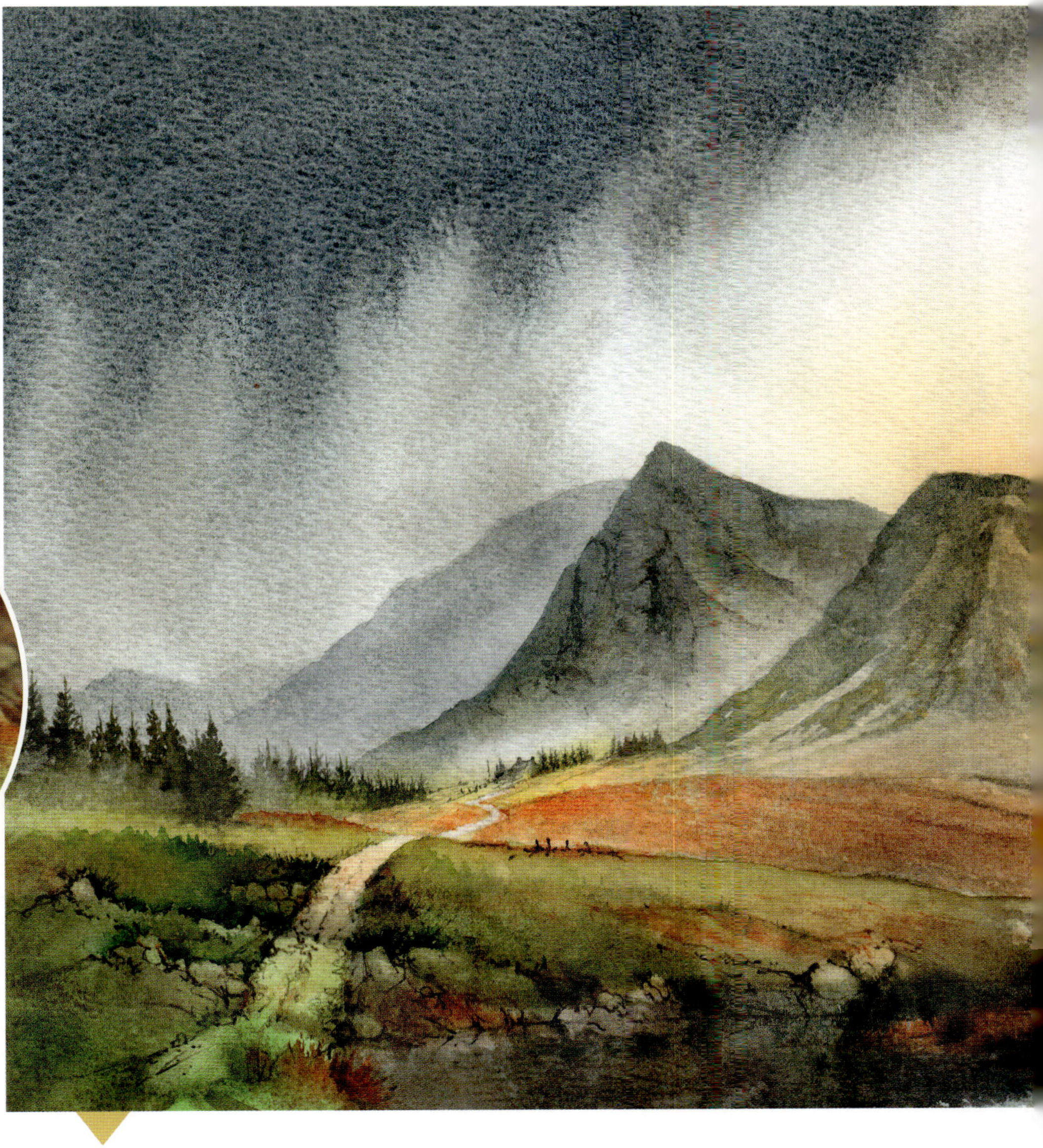

Mountain Track

25.5 × 23cm (10 × 9in) Saunders Waterford 640gsm (300lb) Rough surface paper

The foreground highlights were pulled out with a tissue and damp brush while the wash was still wet, and the foreground detail was drawn with a black Derwent Inktense pencil. A watercolour pencil, though not so intense, would produce a similar effect, and these pencils can be used to rescue a painting that has perhaps lost its way, usually because the tonal values don't work to best effect. Note that to obtain the maximum benefit you need to re-wet the paper before carrying out the drawing.

MIXING MEDIA

Plastic food wrap

Laying plastic food wrap over a wet wash can create some interesting effects, especially when you introduce more than one colour, and while this can be effective for plant and undergrowth subjects, I find it particularly exciting for ice.

Another excellent effect you can achieve with plastic food wrap is that of striations across open landscapes such as mountains and moorlands.

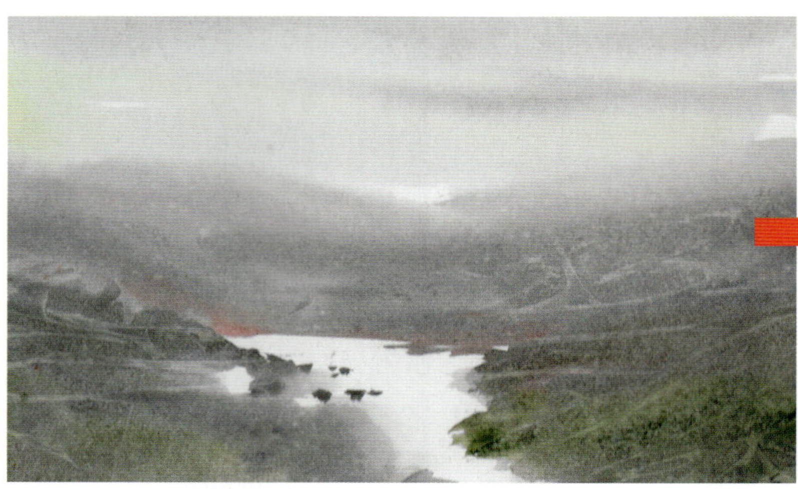

Detail of an early stage of the painting opposite, immediately after the food wrap had been lifted away.

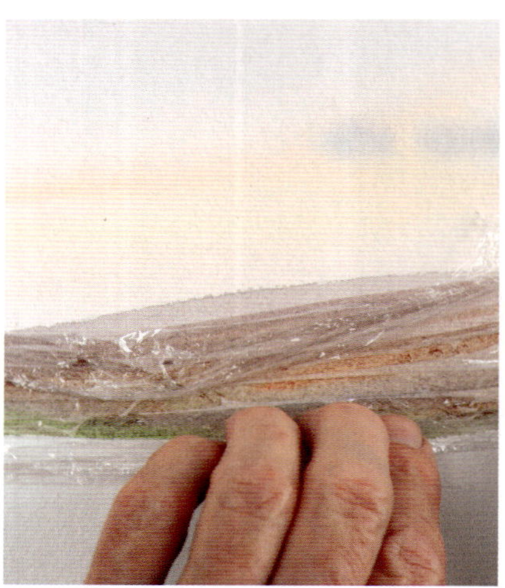

Place the wrap Lay the plastic food wrap onto the wet surface and gently pull it to form creases in the direction you want.

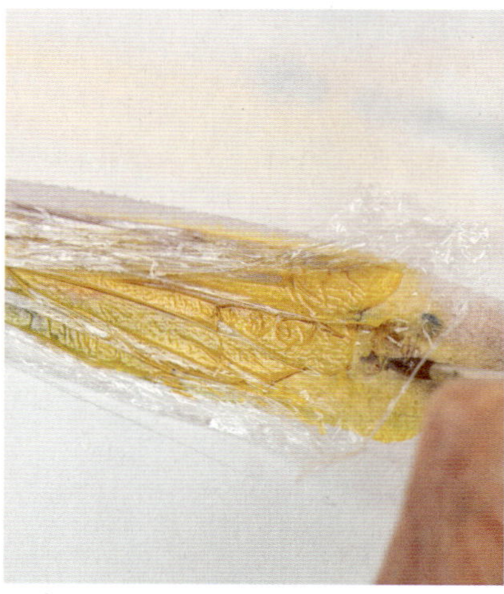

Add more colour You can add more paint – in the same or different colours by lifting the wrap and sliding a brush or pipette in, then replacing the wrap.

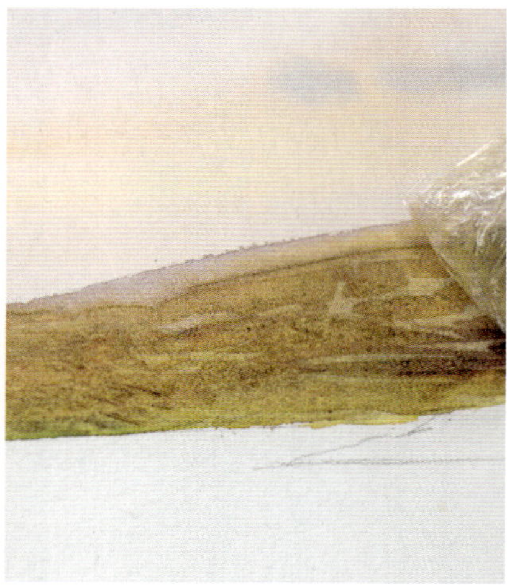

Reveal This technique may take a while to dry, so make sure it is perfectly dry before lifting the wrap if you wish to have hard edges. It's a good idea to try a number of experiments before employing the method on a finished painting.

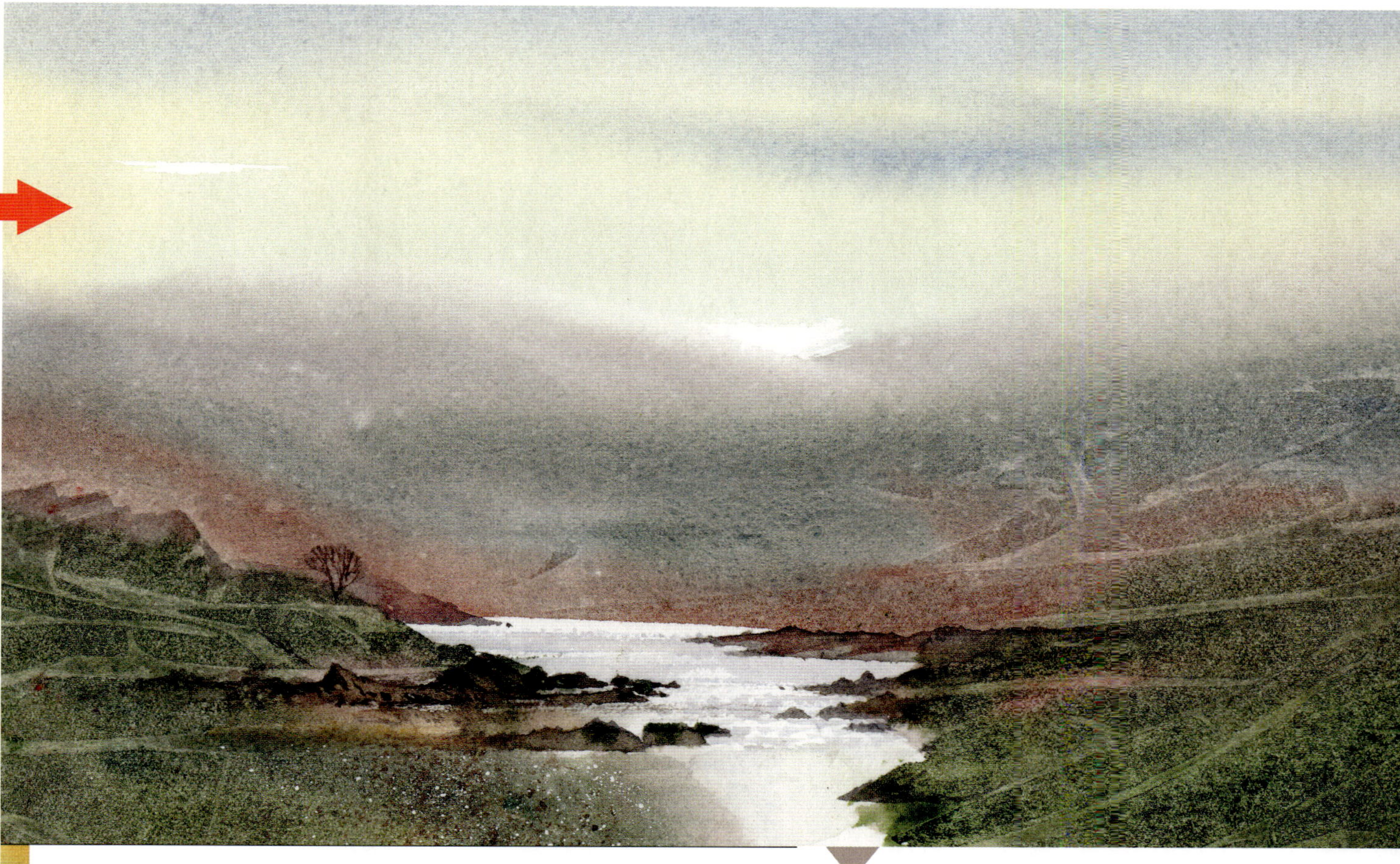

Painting *Highland Mist*

Here I have suggested a misty day by laying washes of various colours across the smooth surface, while avoiding the area of the lochan. The lower half of the composition was covered with plastic food wrap and allowed to dry (see detail opposite).

- The rocky shorelines were painted in with a mixture of French ultramarine and burnt umber, which was also used for the small tree to the left.

- A little spattering with a toothbrush added some interest in the foreground.

- There was no need to soften any edges off in this instance, but it is worth remembering that if you use staining colours with food wrap, it is almost impossible to soften the edges.

Highland Mist
23 × 12.5cm (9 × 5in) Saunders Waterford
400gsm (140lb) Hot-Pressed paper

Spattering is explained on page 12.

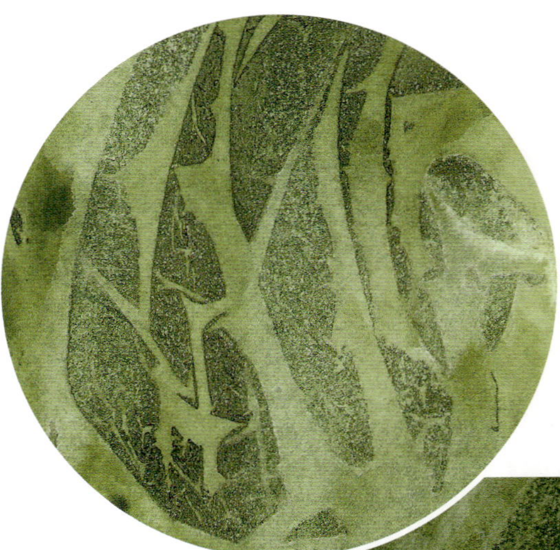

Woodland and vegetation

Plastic food wrap can also be convincing in depicting plants and vegetation, though the result usually needs further work with the brush, and often some softening of some of the hard edges.

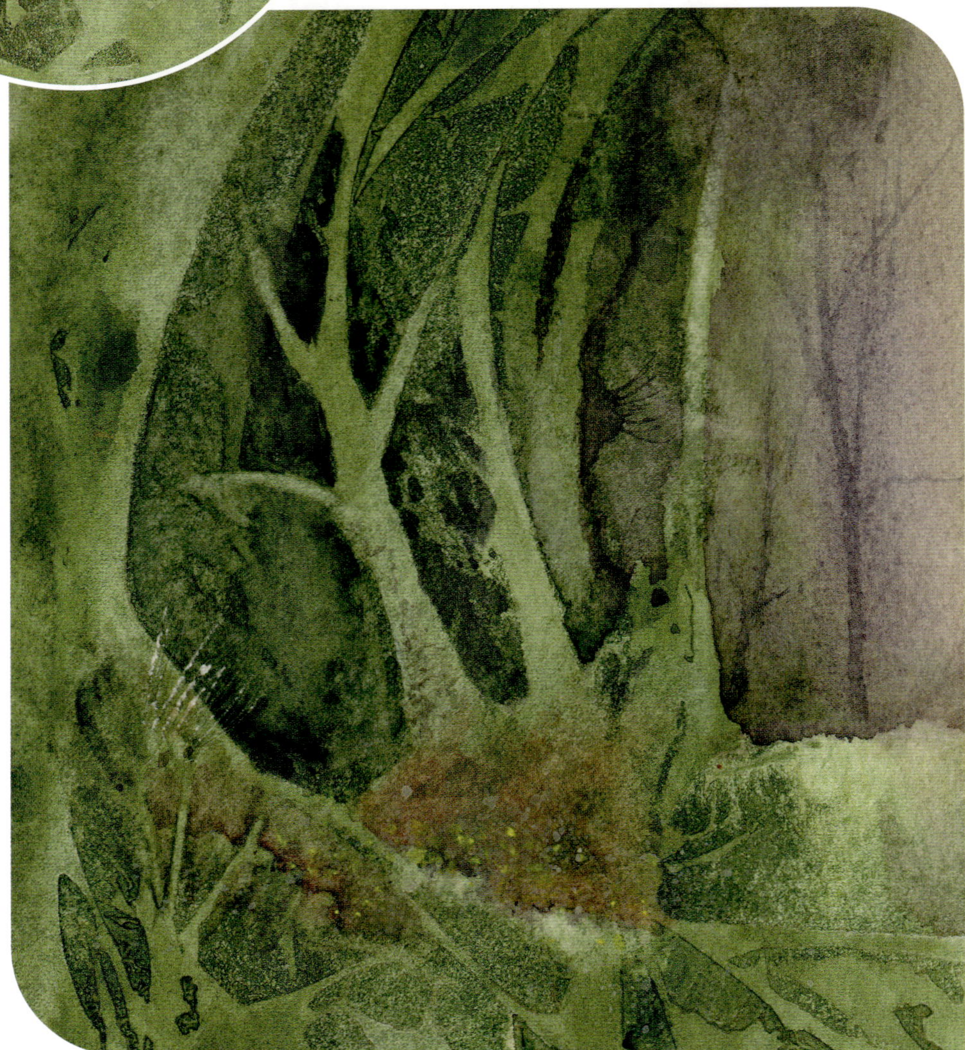

The tree trunks were created by pulling the plastic food wrap vertically once it was laid over the wet wash. The inset shows how it appeared when revealed, and this was enhanced by some negative painting to emphasize the trunks.

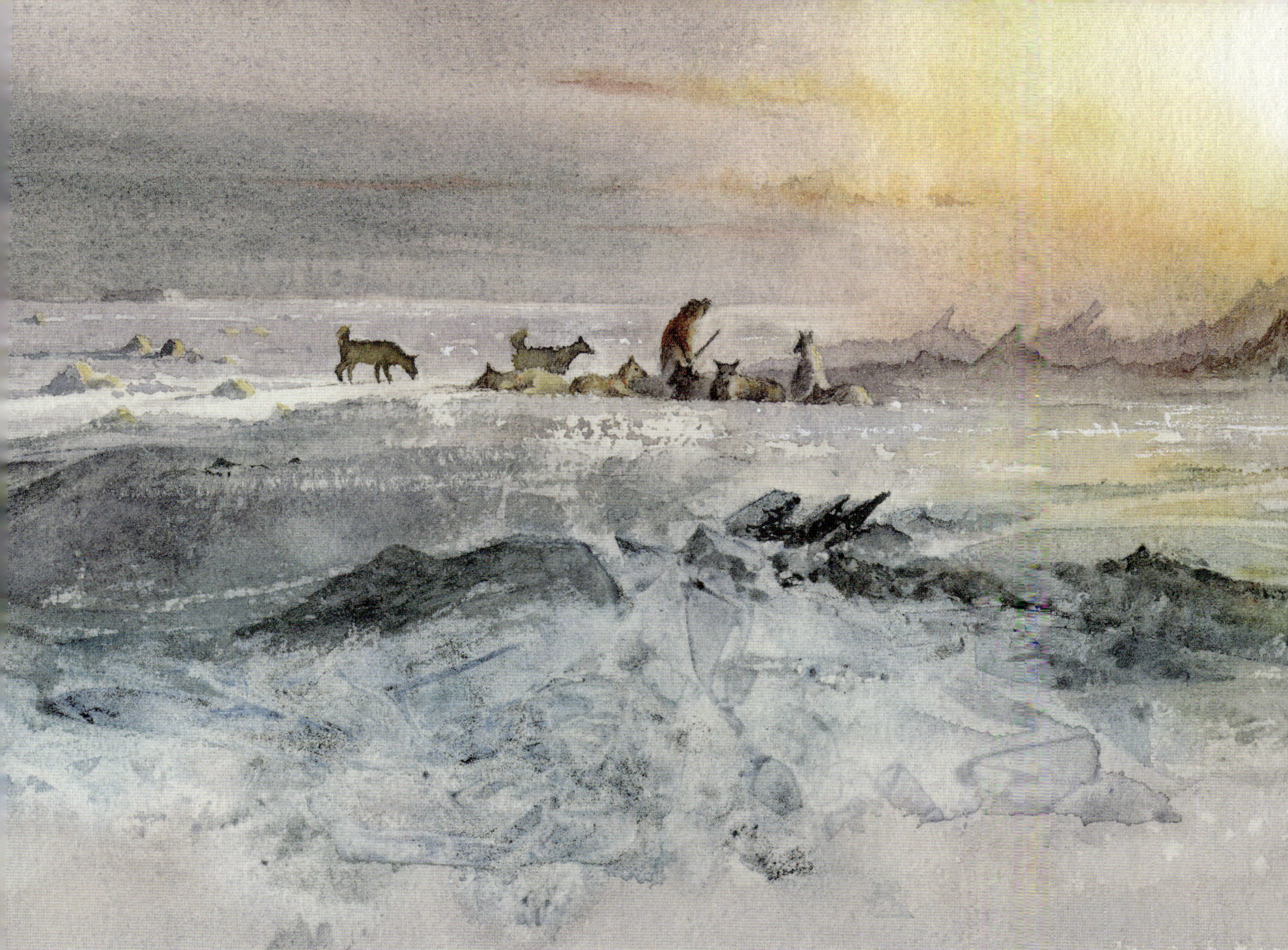

Painting *Arctic Sunrise*

This is part of a painting from my *Arctic Light* book, which is not a how-to-paint guide, but contains many inspirational paintings and sketches. This detail shows how effective it can be to use plastic food wrap to create exciting ice patterns.

- In the foreground I laid a mixture of French ultramarine and burnt umber, the strength of the burnt umber input varying, and I then dropped in phthalo blue in places.
- I covered the wet wash with plastic food wrap and dragged it slightly to the right before allowing it to dry completely and removing the film. The colours are given greater force by juxtaposing the icy foreground with the warm sky.

Detail from *Arctic Sunrise*
45.5 × 28cm (18 × 11in) Saunders Waterford
640gsm (300lb) Not surface paper
(full painting)

The original sketch was done in East Greenland while Isak, our guide, was feeding his huskies, but you don't need to travel all the way to the Arctic to find ice. The effect of the plastic food wrap is excellent for suggesting the sharp edges that often occur in ice patterns.

TECHNIQUE

Super-granulations with granulation medium

The tendency of some pigments to granulate (see page 18) can be further exploited by using granulation medium and papers with a Rough surface.

Adding granulation medium to a wash will increase the granulations of many pigments, although not all will respond to this. Squirting the medium into a wash of granulating colours, however, will produce exciting results, usually in the form of speckles of colour running down the paper, as can be seen in the dramatic examples on pages 106 and 107.

The effects created can suggest quite powerful textures; useful for large passages of quiet areas such as sky, large fields or rough ground, beaches, mountainsides and the like. This can simplify the scene by obviating the need to introduce more definite detail or textures with a brush.

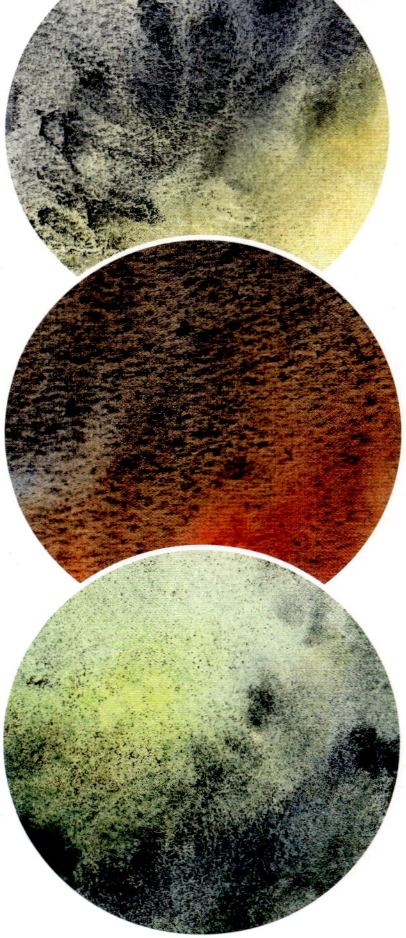

Examples of dry washes treated with granulation medium added when wet.

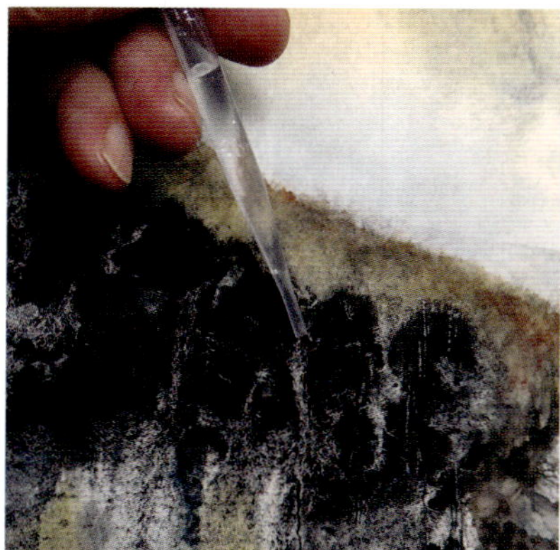

Add neat Use a pipette to add granulation medium directly to a wet wash. This gives you control.

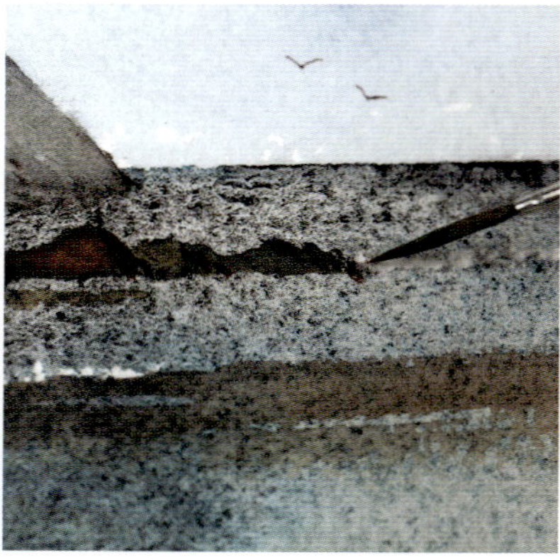

Pull out details Once the wash is dry, you will be left with highly textured areas to develop and incorporate into your painting.

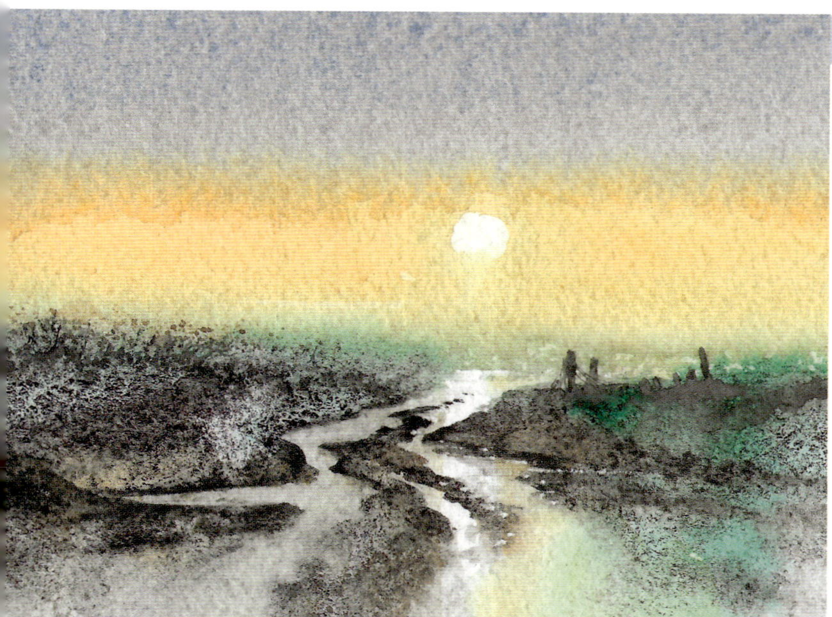

Estuary Sunrise

20.5 × 12.5cm (8 × 5in) Saunders Waterford 300gsm (140lb) Rough surface paper

Sparkling sunlight can turn even mud into jewels: this simple marshy track with a low sun is an ideal composition for you to experiment with watercolour washes and introduce granulations.

I laid jadeite genuine green with burnt umber mixed in some places, and lower down lunar black, then quickly dropped in some Winsor & Newton granulation medium to suggest the organic structure of massed roots.

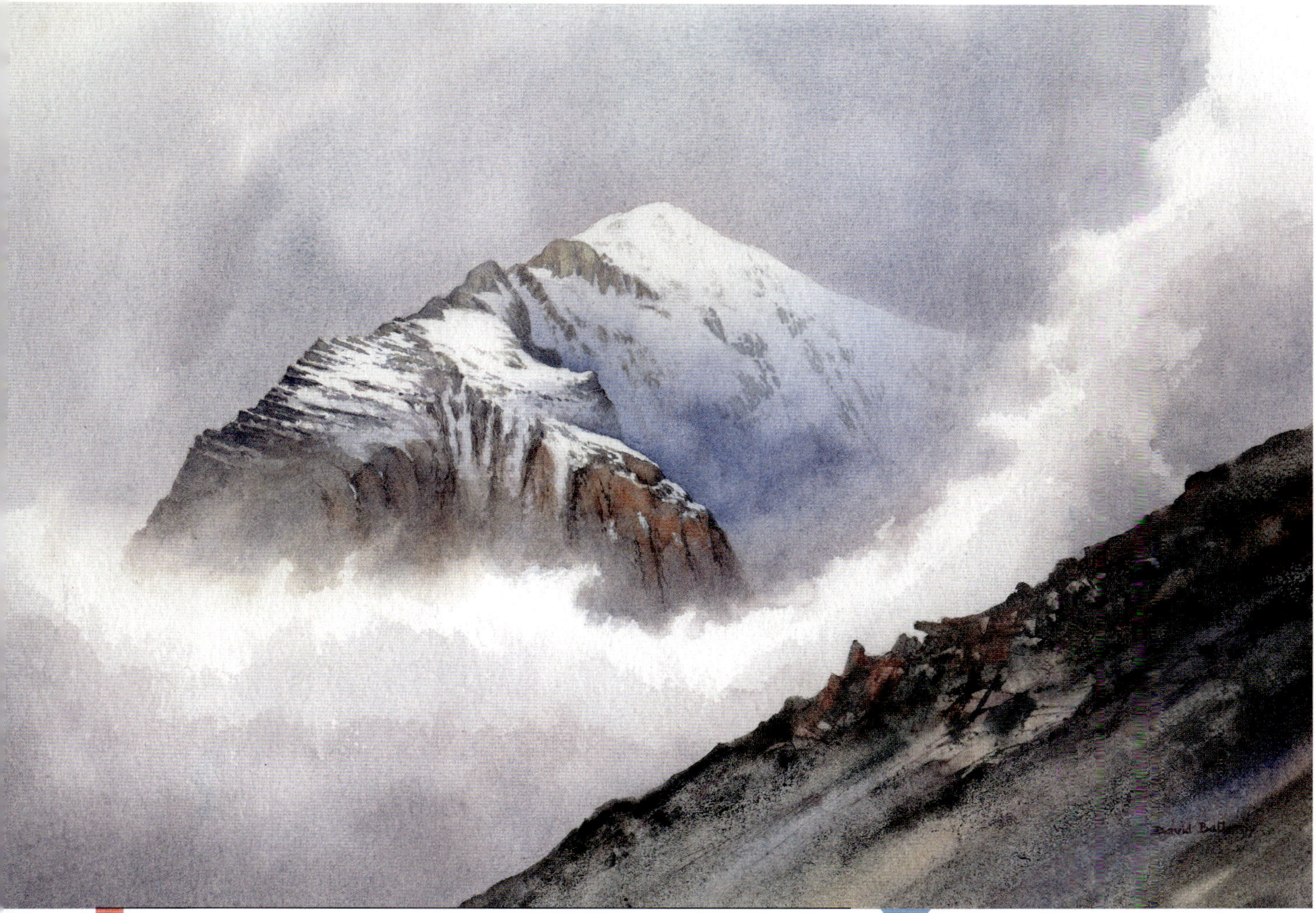

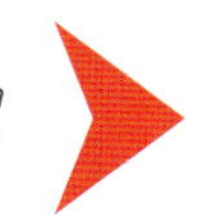

Painting *Crib y Ddysgl, Snowdonia*

Most of the time to suggest scree and stones on a mountainside I use the dry-brush technique, but here I have tried a different method using granulations.

- I applied a strong mixture of lunar black and bloodstone genuine at the top of the diagonal slope on the right, then holding the board at an angle I squirted granulation medium from a pipette to direct the granulations to follow the slope downwards.
- The light rocks at the upper edge of the slope were dug out with a broad-shaped painting knife using a stabbing motion while the paint remained damp.

Crib y Ddysgl, Snowdonia
40.5 × 28cm (16 × 11in) Saunders Waterford 640gsm (300lb) Rough surface paper

You can see how the dry-brush technique can be used to depict scree on pages 90–91.

Keys to success with granulation medium

- You need to keep the wash very fluid to attain the best results with granulation medium. Using plenty of water allows the medium to flow well and create the speckles of granulation.
- While wet, you can hold the board at different angles to influence the flow, add more colour and granulation medium, or just sit and watch the paint perform its magic.
- Different pigments generate varying results – lunar black, lunar blue and sodalite genuine are some of the most powerfully granulating colours. Hematite violet genuine and green apatite genuine are also good candidates.
- Experiment with different papers and paint consistencies. You can introduce granulation medium with brush or pipette.

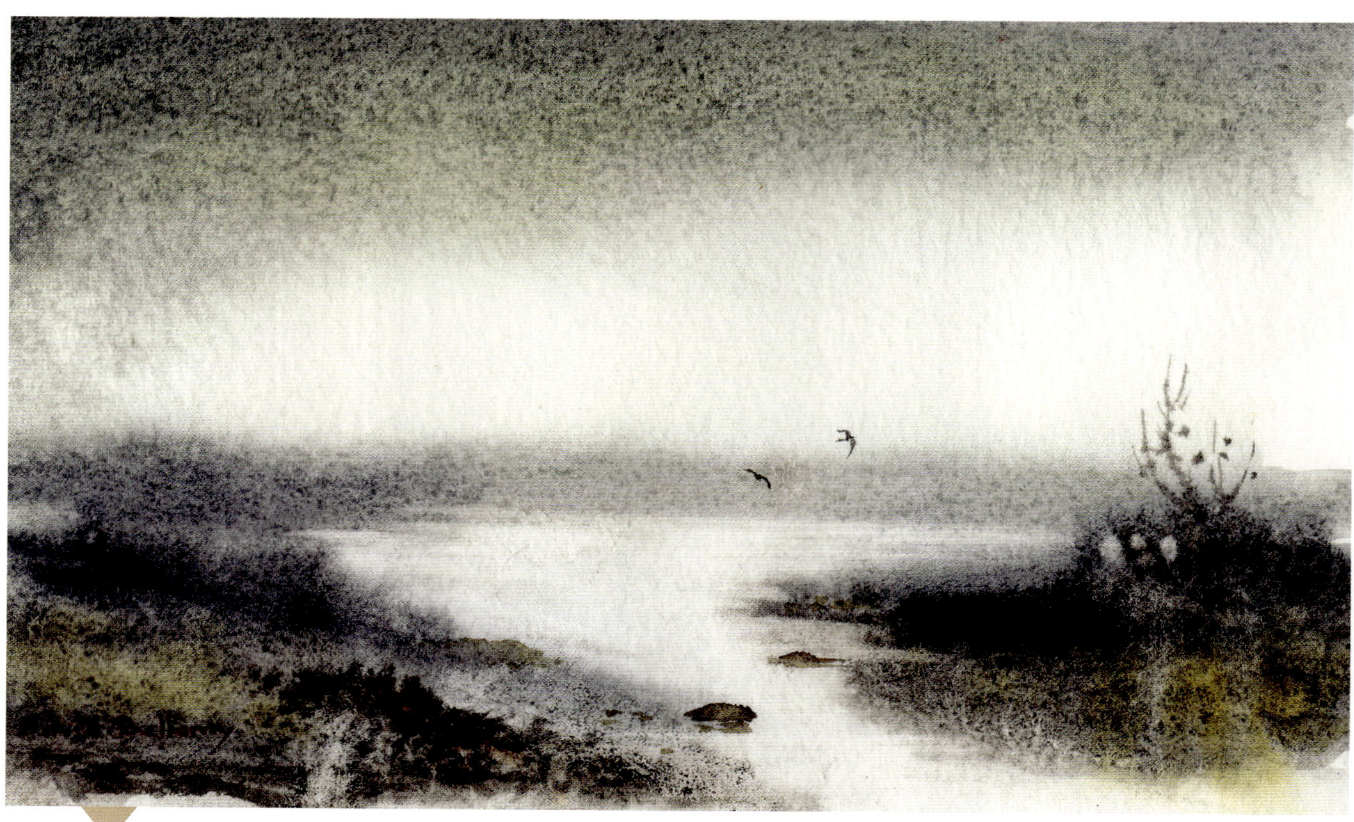

Estuary Scene with Birds
18 × 10cm (7 × 4in) Saunders Waterford 300gsm (140lb) Hot-Pressed surface paper

A scrappy exercise that I liked so much I turned it into a small painting, mainly painted with lunar black with some cadmium yellow pale and yellow ochre in places. The soft, ethereal mood and granulations combined to produce a haunting image. As with many paintings in this book, I wished I'd worked on a larger sheet, but I was simply playing around.

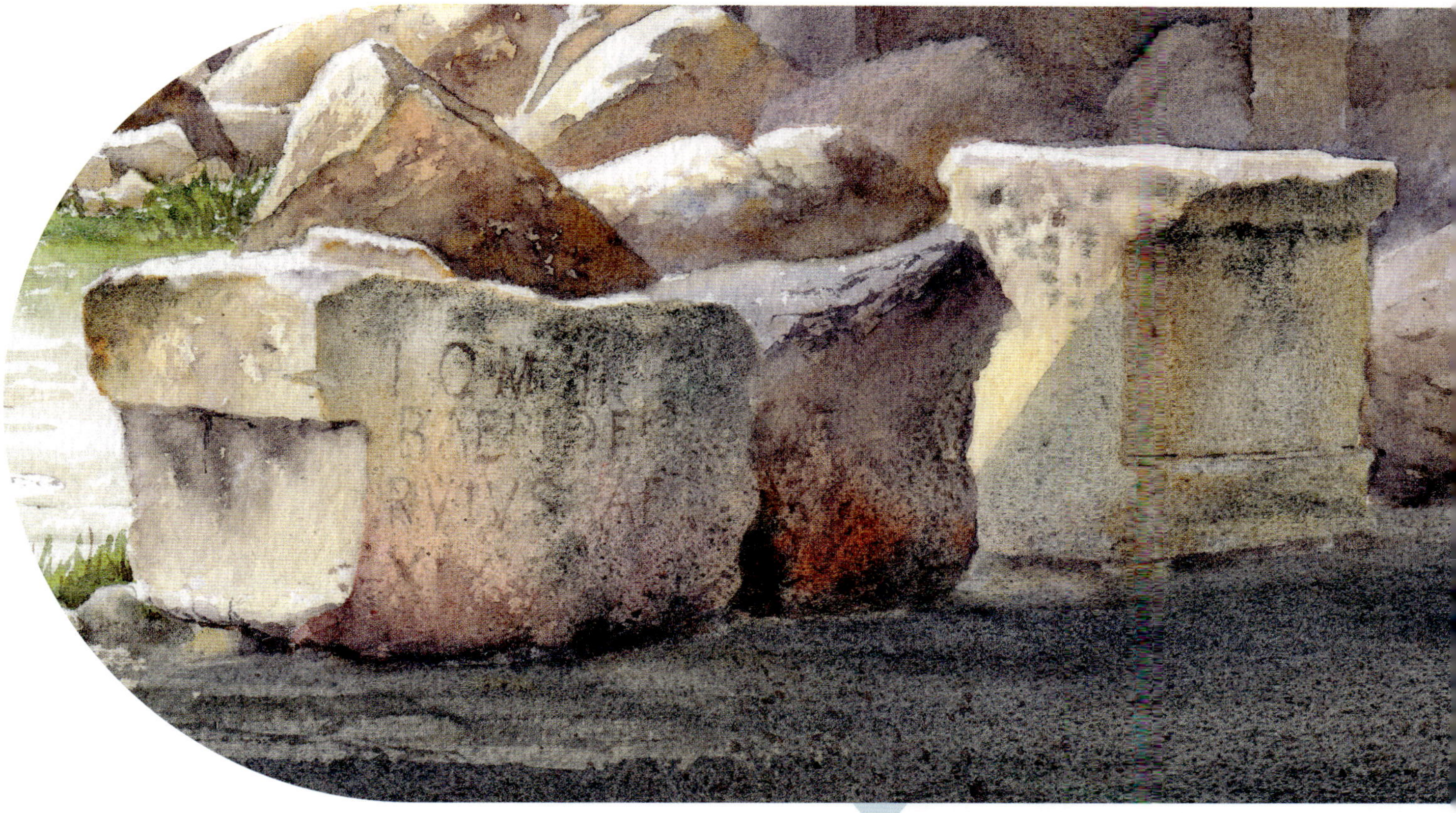

Achieving an ancient look

This small piece is part of a full imperial painting of the Roman ruins at Baalbek in Lebanon. Some of the stone blocks fascinated me, especially those with inscriptions, and this one had a lovely worn texture I just had to re-create. Here's an insight into the process:

Establish the base Lay a weak wash over the stone with yellow ochre and some permanent alizarin crimson.

Pick out letters unevenly Once dry, describe the faint lettering using a size 1 rigger brush with lunar blue and burnt umber, leaving some letters incomplete.

Granulating wash To render the textural element lay on a wash of lunar black. The granulations make the whole thing appear quite ancient.

Detail of Roman lettering on stone
66 × 48cm (26 × 19in) Saunders Waterford 640gsm (300lb) Not surface paper

The complete painting can be seen in my book Arabian Light, which includes many architectural subjects.

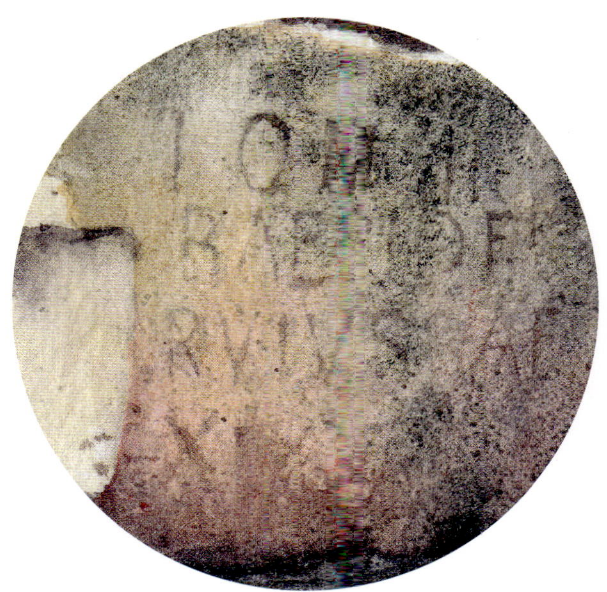

Creative granulating

The granulating process can form a minor part of a composition, but it can also become a major element of a painting. The examples here took the latter approach; the process of deciding on a specific subject abandoned in favour of throwing caution to the wind and laying a wash of a strongly granulating colour (see page 104 for some ideas) and then dropping in some granulation medium.

At some stage in this process you can usually work out some image emerging from the paper – rock structures, falling water, grainy sand or even a bad-tempered troll! While this can be great fun, you are also learning, gaining valuable experience of what can be achieved by this imaginative approach. You will note how in certain ways you can create awesome cascades or textural effects on cliffs that look otherwise impossible to achieve.

This approach can produce some exciting results – and sometimes exciting rubbish – but it is certainly worth a try. You may begin with some idea of the subject, or just splash on the colours and let it happen.

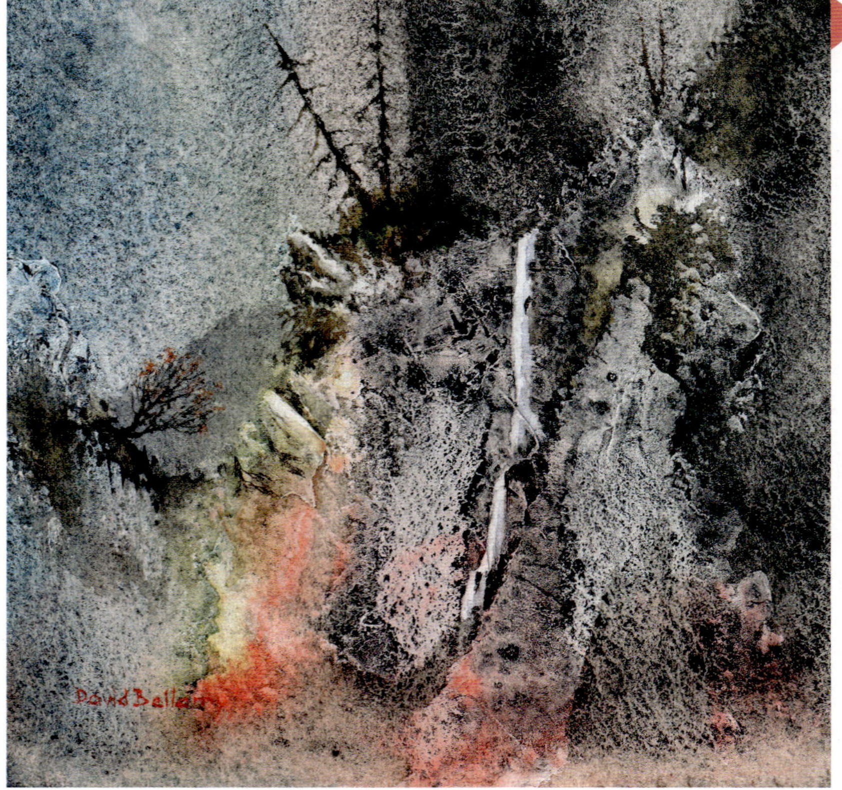

Waterfall
12.5 × 12.5cm (5 × 5in) Saunders Waterford 640gsm (300lb) Rough surface paper

This was a fun experiment on a scrap of paper, the frustration coming at the end when I saw the fascinating result and heartily wished I had used a much bigger piece of paper!

Initially I had no idea of what subject would be depicted, and began by smudging in some gesso with a knife, mainly in the central area. Once thoroughly dry, I swamped the paper with lunar blue and lunar black, along with spots of pyrrol red and nickel titanate yellow in places. I then immediately dropped in granulation medium using a pipette, letting it flow downwards, and ended up with an amorphous mess of delightful textures with absolutely no sense of what they actually described.

At this point the cascade effect gave me an idea. It's easy to rub colour off the gesso, so I highlighted some rocks and described the trees with a small sable, then added white gouache for the falling water. Suddenly it made sense and I had my subject.

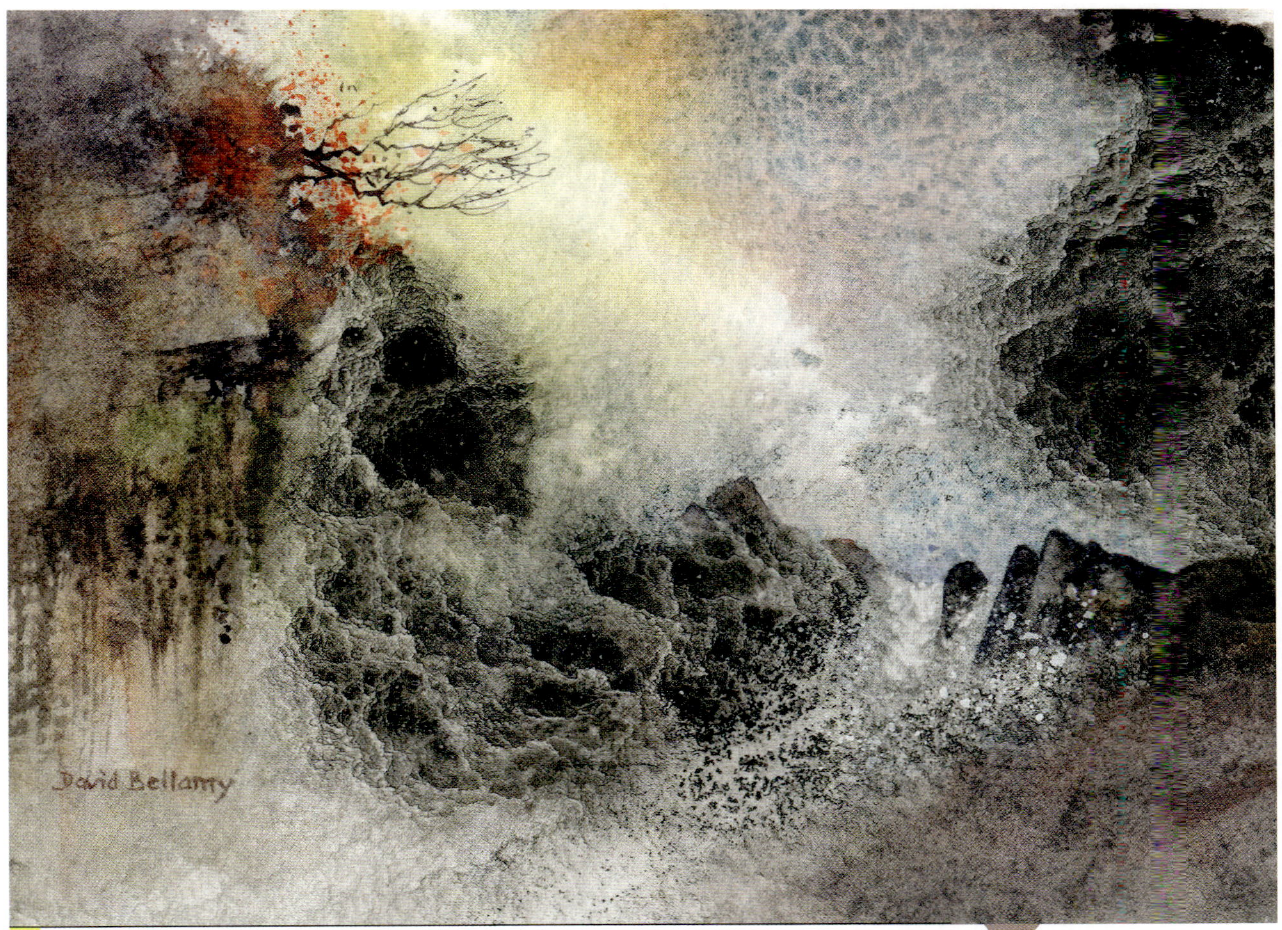

Painting *Cascade of Light*

I enjoyed painting this watercolour immensely as it was done with gay abandon, mainly with lunar black, which is a super-granulating colour, along with some lunar blue and nickel titanate yellow.

- After laying in the lunar black I used a large pipette to squirt in copious amounts of granulation medium over the black; varying the angle in places.
- Some of the rocks were suggested as it was still wet, but the more prominent ones were painted when the paper had dried.
- The protruding bush was achieved by loading a dip pen with watercolour from a brush, hence the very fine branches.
- I also spattered a little white gouache over the rocks on the bottom right to suggest spray.

Cascade of light
15 × 11.5cm (6 × 4½in)
Bockingford 425gsm (200lb)
Rough surface paper

Physical texture

The counterpart to the illusion of visual texture is, of course, physical texture: a raised or uneven surface created through different means.

MIXING MEDIA

Aquapasto

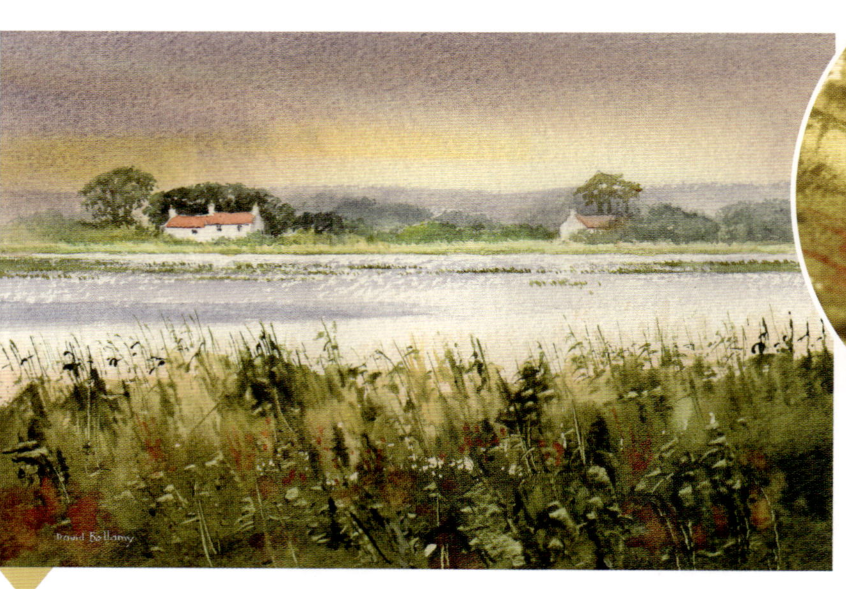

Aquapasto is a medium that is mixed with the watercolour in roughly even proportions. It creates a subtle impasto effect and decreases the flow of the paint. It can be very effective where you may wish to scrape out highlights in a passage; the results normally being more pronounced than if you tried it on watercolour alone. You can use it for light reeds, grasses, tree branches, masts, light marks across the landscape, and so many features.

To get the best out of Aquapasto, use very little water in the mixture.

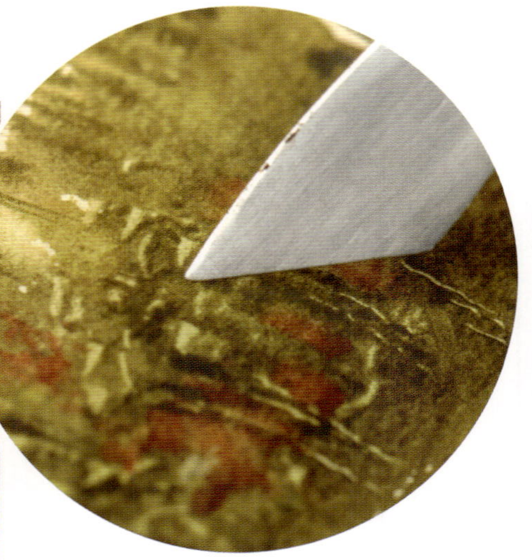

Scraping out
A painting knife is useful for gently moving paint on the surface.

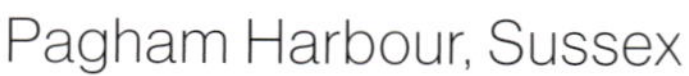

Pagham Harbour, Sussex
25.5 × 18cm (10 × 7in) Waterford 300gsm (140lb) Rough surface paper

Aquapasto with green apatite genuine was used in the foreground, the colour tinged with yellow ochre and cadmium red in places. While damp, I drew in the thin reeds with the green and then scraped out light stalks and leaves with the knife. The addition of Aquapasto strengthens the effectiveness of the scraping technique.

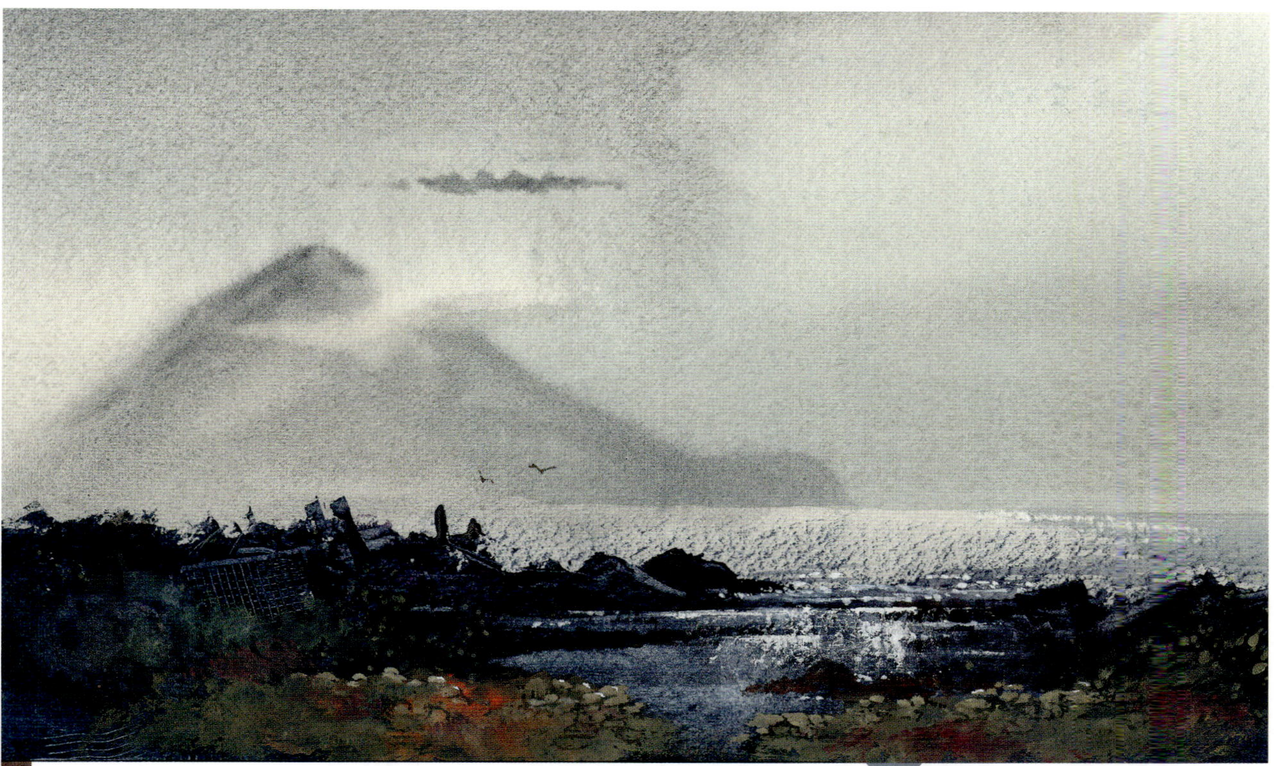

Painting *Damp Morning*

- The foreground wash comprised indigo mixed with an equal amount of Winsor & Newton Aquapasto, plus a little water, thus creating a thick, dark mixture that was applied with a size 10 sable brush.

- The net-like pattern on the left was rendered while the wash was still wet. I drew down through the paint with a small novelty comb that came out of a Christmas cracker; then repeated the action horizontally. The wider top line was achieved by scraping with a painting knife, and then the bottom parts of the mesh were brushed over to hide the area and make it look more natural.

- The posts were painted with a small piece of 425gsm (200lb) paper loaded with indigo, which creates a slightly different feel to that made when applying the paint with a brush.

- The warmer colours at the bottom were painted with gouache; and cadmium orange and yellow ochre (in places mixed with white gouache) were dropped in on the surface once it was dry.

- I pulled out some colour in places to suggest highlights on rocks and the foreground pool using a 12mm (½in) flat brush.

Damp Morning
28 × 18cm (11 × 7in) Saunders Waterford
420gsm (200lb) Not surface paper

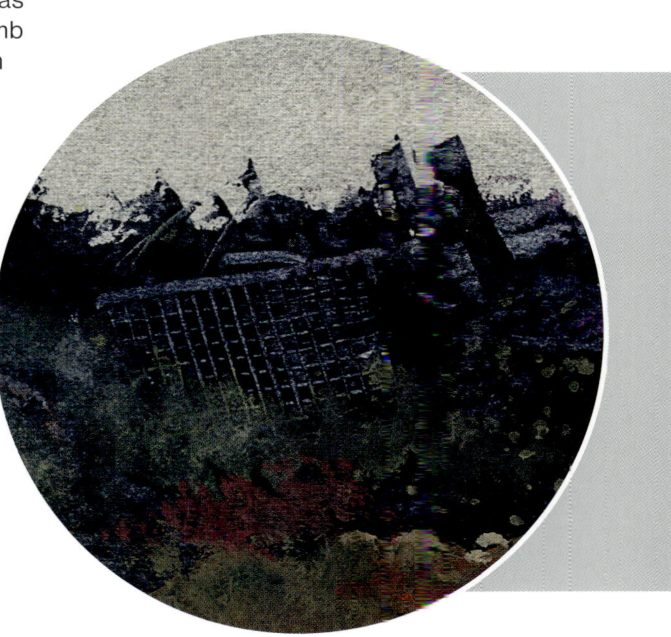

The techniques for stamping with a card and pulling out paint can be found on pages 54 and 64 respectively.

Detail of the net-like pattern
By including the Aquapasto, the resulting netting is much more effective.

MIXING MEDIA

Gesso

Gesso is a primer, normally used for acrylic and oil paintings, and can be applied with a roller, brush, spatula or painting knife. It is often used with watercolour, mainly to create textures, although watercolour does not always adhere well to it. This, however, can be used to advantage by rubbing off colour if so desired.

To size (or prime) mountboard, ready to accept the watercolour paint, the gesso is usually applied thinly with a brush. Once dry, it creates a beautiful texture to work upon.

Gesso can also be applied using a painting knife. When applied with a knife, the thick, heavy, textural qualities of a surface prepared with gesso complement watercolour beautifully; lending what can be an ethereal medium some real muscle for rugged landscapes.

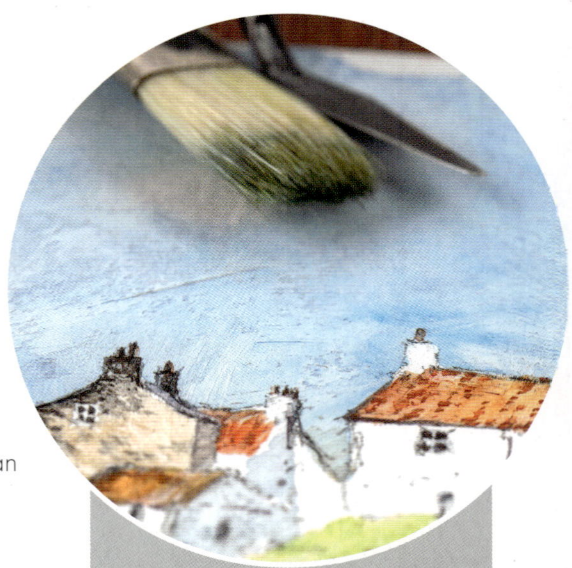

Applying gesso
Gesso can be applied using either a brush or a knife for different effects.

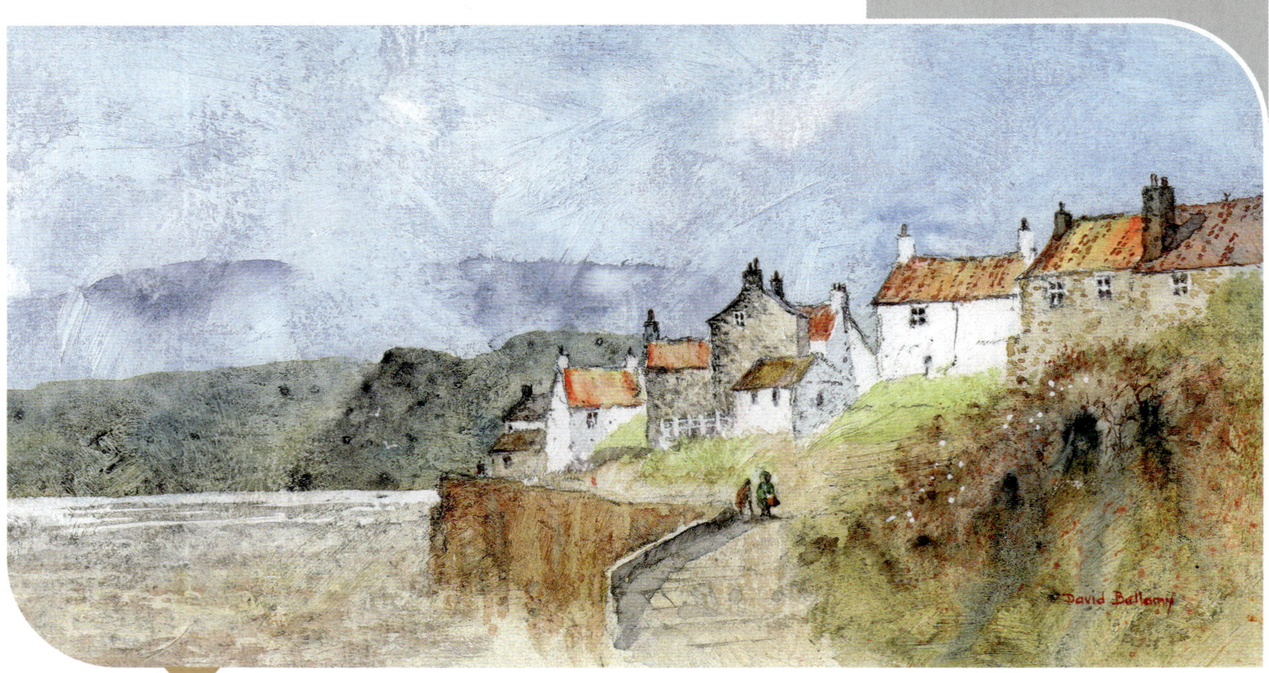

Robin Hood's Bay
23 × 12.5cm (9 × 5in) gesso-sized mountboard

Here the gesso was applied roughly with a bristle brush, leaving some strong brushmarks. I broke up the distant whaleback ridge with a suggestion of mist and allowed it to fade out as it approached the houses. Many of the houses have simply been left white with the untouched gesso. Added interest was created by rendering vari-coloured roofs. I deliberately left the foreground devoid of any detail.

Big Pit, Blaenavon

20.5 × 15cm (8 × 6in) mountboard covered with gesso

In contrast to the light sizing used opposite, here I applied gesso to the mountboard with a painting knife, using vigorous sweeps in places to induce textural patterns, and left it for a few days.

I drew the mine, keeping it in the distance to suggest its bleak surroundings. The rudely handled gesso helped suggest the rough foreground.

Some cadmium red was spattered over the Naples yellow passage to give it a lift.

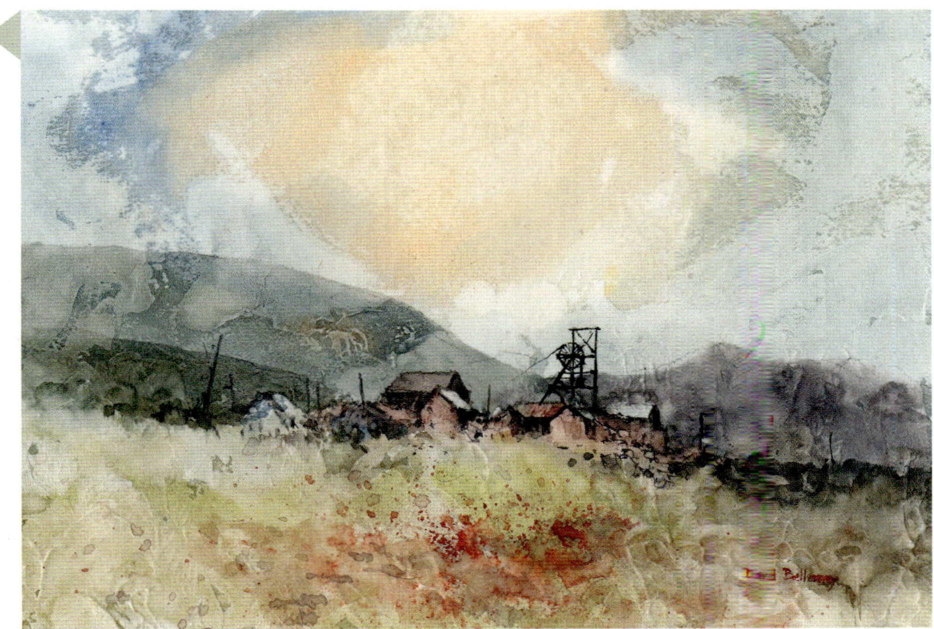

The Boathouse

23 × 12.5cm (9 × 5in) mountboard covered with gesso

The entire surface was covered with gesso, mainly brushed on thinly with a bristle brush, which in places has left some prominent brushmarks. In places the gesso was applied more thickly using a painting knife. Where the left-hand tree stands, the flat blade of the knife was lifted off the gesso vertically to create a stronger textural effect.

Covering all the sky with gesso may seem excessive, and it is better to have some quieter passages in a composition, so you may prefer to simply cover the sky with transparent watercolour ground brushed on smoothly to create a suitable surface to accept the watercolour washes.

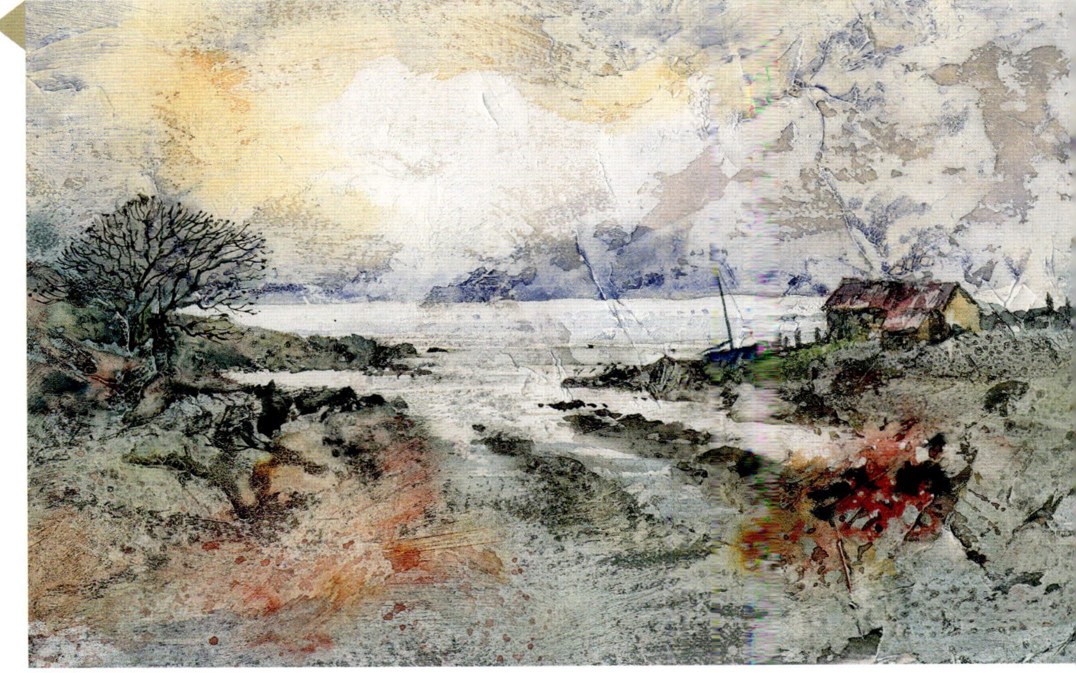

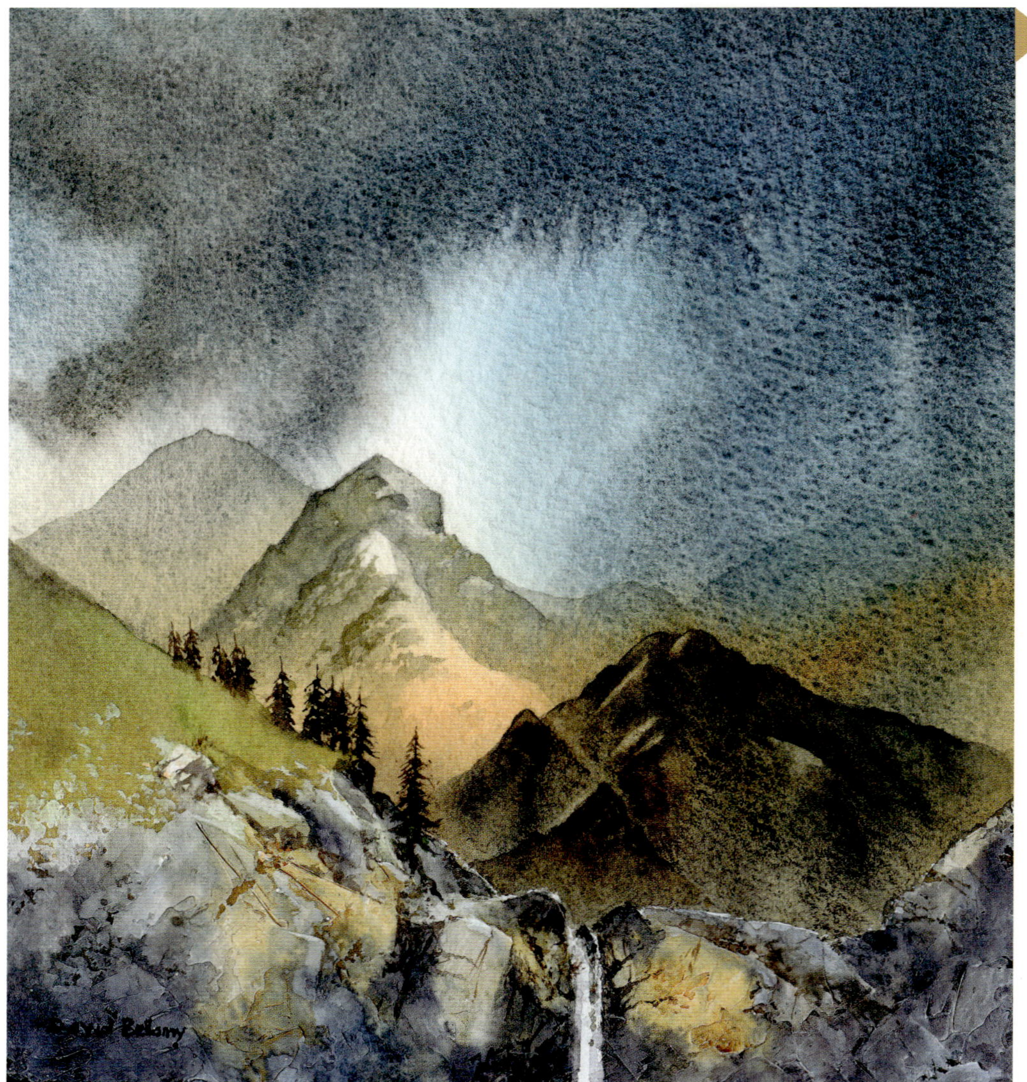

Approaching
Alpine Storm
17.5 × 20.5cm (7 × 8in)
Saunders Waterford
640gsm (300lb) Rough
surface paper

Painting *Approaching Alpine Storm*

- I plastered gesso over the foreground with a painting knife and scored lines into it on the left, then left the painting for a couple of days to dry out.

- With lunar blue and a touch of burnt umber I laid on the half-seen distant ridge on the right horizon. Once dry I wet the whole surface and laid Naples yellow over the left-hand peaks, and immediately brought weak lunar blue over the upper sky to run into the Naples yellow. Without pausing I applied a much stronger wash of lunar blue over the top part of the sky and held the board at an angle so the wash flowed down over the right-hand ridge.

- The rest of the painting was carried out in the usual manner. I varied the foreground crags with Naples yellow, yellow ochre and lunar blue, which brought out the strong textures of the gesso.

- The waterfall was done with white gouache. While gesso can create similar effects as the Daniel Smith watercolour ground, the watercolour does not stick so well, but colours can be pulled out easily to create highlights.

There's more about gouache on pages 78–83.

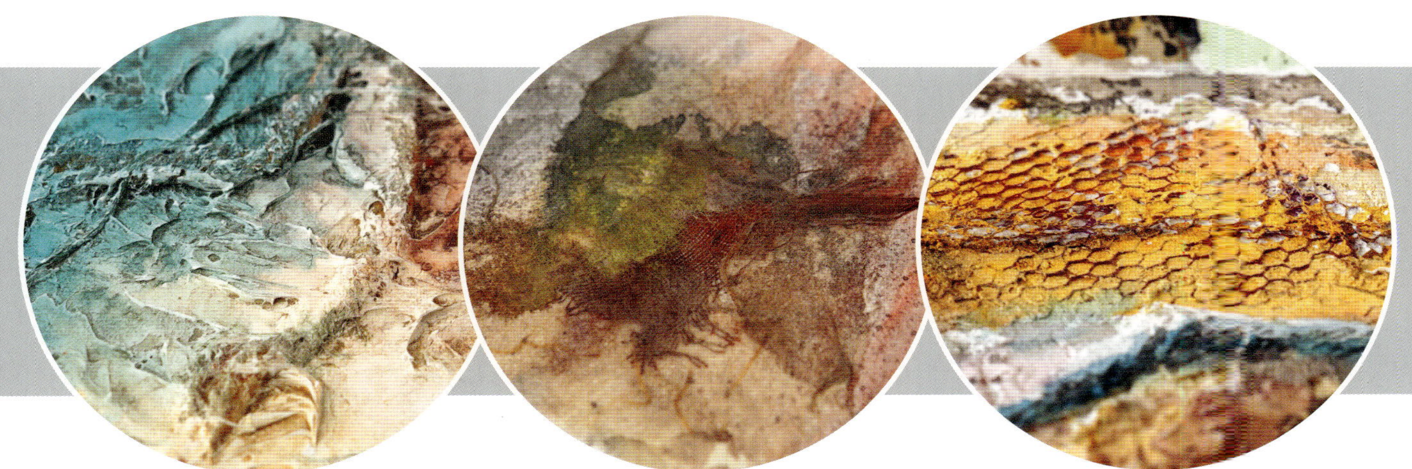

Gesso, texture paste and found materials

Found materials can be embedded within your artwork using gesso or texture paste. You can use almost anything, from the small netting bags that come with household washing products to bits of cotton or thin cord, strips of bandage, cut paper shapes and limitless other items.

It is worth carrying out small experiments to see what can be achieved with various combinations of mediums and found materials.

Above left to right: Gesso applied over cotton thread; cotton bandage secured with texture paste; and part of a net bag for laundry tablets secured with gesso.

See page 118 for more on found materials.

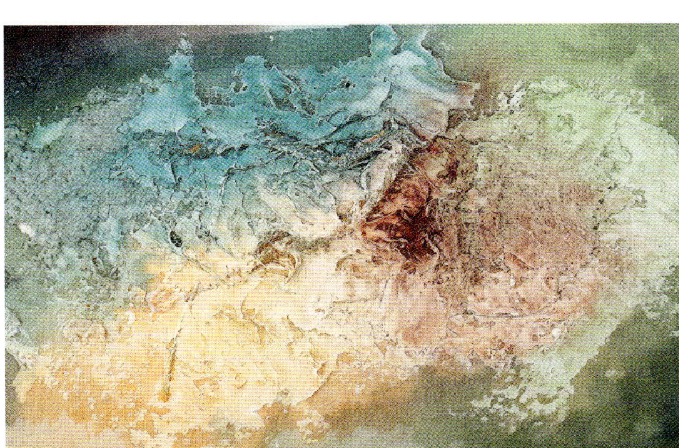

Texture paste and gesso

Here some Schmincke coarse paste was applied with a knife on both left and right sides, then gesso was laid on the paper and two short lengths of string stuck into it, before more gesso was applied over the string. Once dry I painted over it – you can see a close-up detail at the top left of the page, too.

I especially like the combination of phthalo blue running into the Naples yellow. This treatment can be highly effective for abstract passages, but also when you want to combine it with a realistic subject.

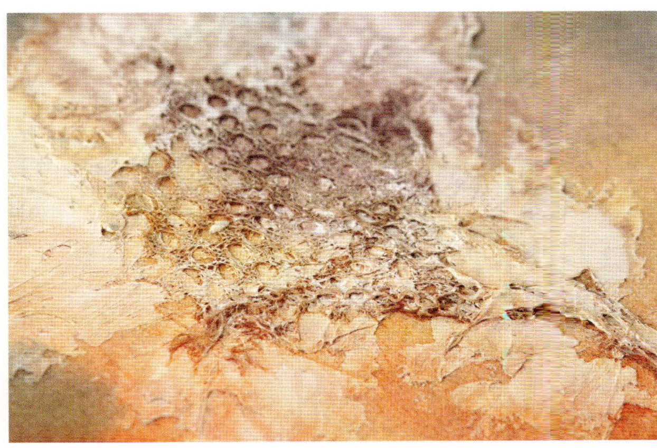

Gesso with fabric

This is another example of using gesso as a base to secure the small piece of fabric, and then plastering more over the edges. The hole pattern in the fabric is partly filled with gesso, varying the pattern. This technique is particularly useful for creating abstract or semi-abstract areas in a painting, or for creating a suggestion of detritus in a foreground, for example.

MIXING MEDIA

Watercolour ground

While gesso can work well with watercolours, it is a little unpredictable as watercolour does not always adhere well to it. Watercolour ground is a medium designed specifically to prepare any surface for watercolour paint, and so works very well.

  In addition to being brilliant for creating striking and dramatic textures, it can also be used in a more subtle manner.

Working with watercolour ground

Watercolour ground comes in two forms. The Schmincke version is transparent and liquid and can be brushed onto a surface to prepare it to take watercolours or seal a surface (see page 122), while the Daniel Smith version is more like gesso. This is a paste that comes in several colours, including white, black, buff and transparent. It is the Daniel Smith watercolour ground that I use for texture as it is unparalleled for creating fabulous physical textures and can secure small objects such as netting, shells, bits of string and so forth to the paper, and this is what we concentrate on here.

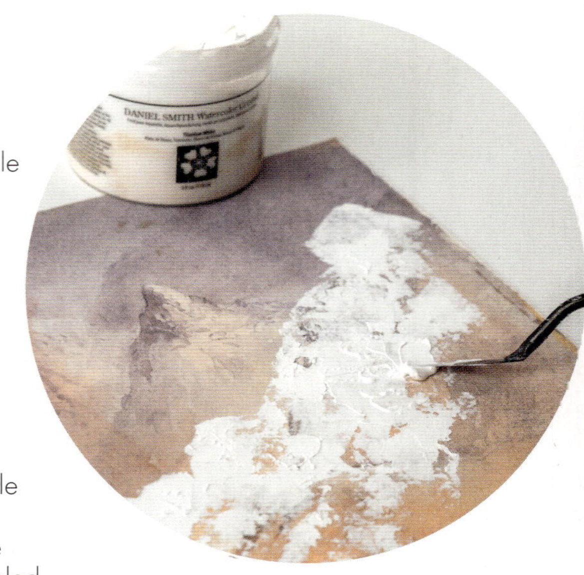

Applying watercolour ground

Watercolour ground can be applied just like gesso (see page 110), using either a brush or a knife.

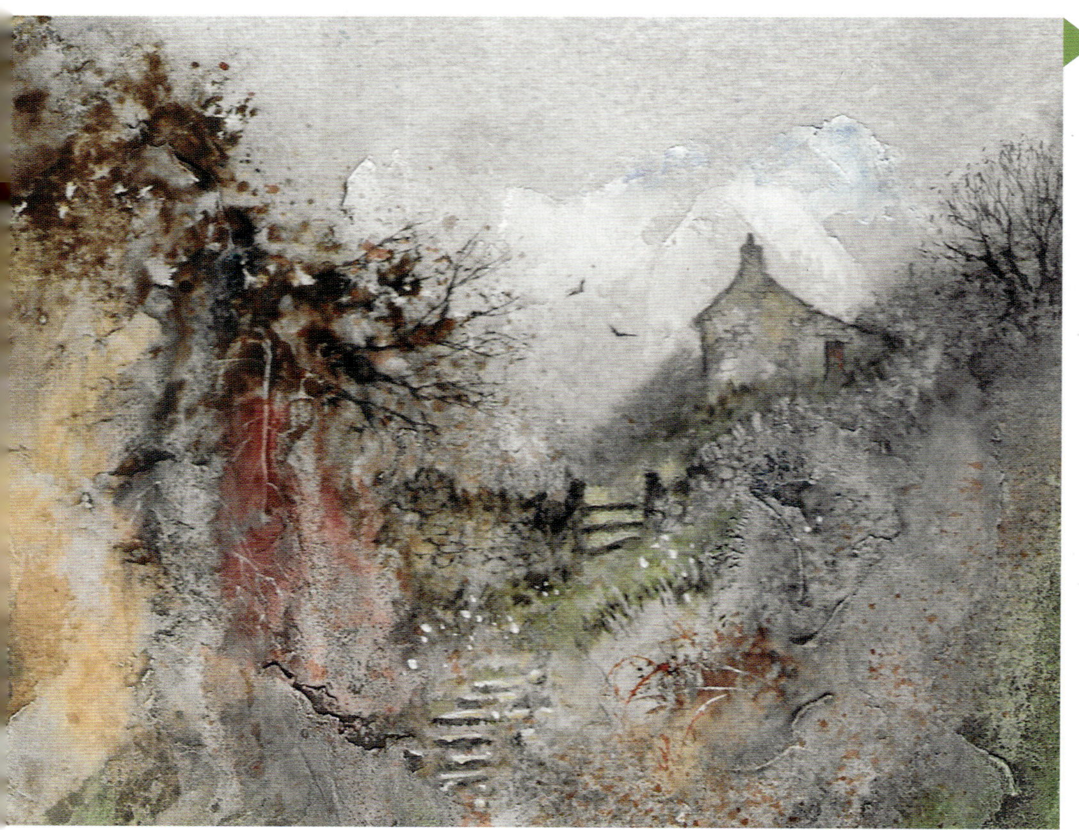

▶ The Stile

17.5 × 15cm (7 × 6in) Saunders Waterford 640gsm (300lb) Rough surface paper

After painting the sky, watercolour ground was spread over the lower part of the sky by the cottage, and then over the foreground.

Once it had dried, the rest of the painting was completed, leaving the bare watercolour ground for the white clouds. The ground works well for this, and is an excellent way of covering up any problem you may encounter in the sky or elsewhere.

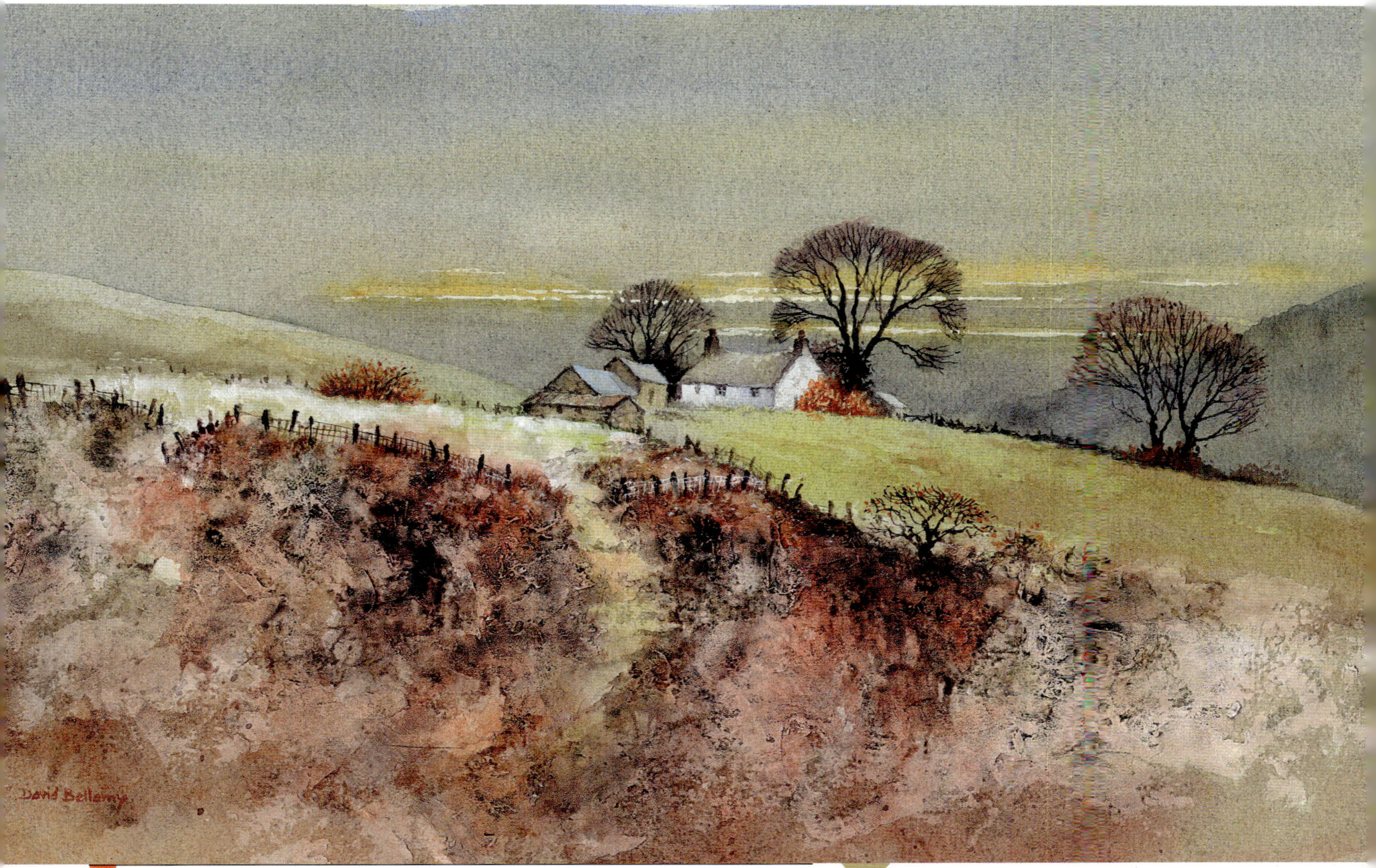

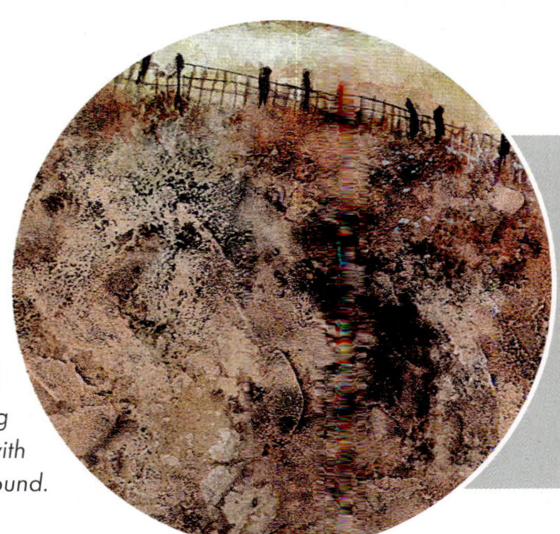

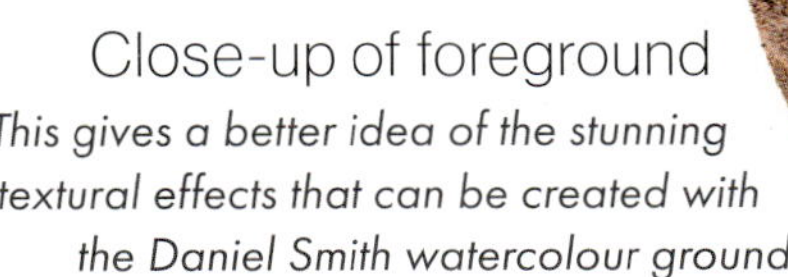 Painting *Farm near Ffestiniog*

- The light horizontal streaks in the sky were achieved with a mixture of white and cadmium lemon gouache, and the walls of the farmhouse with white gouache.
- Daniel Smith watercolour ground was applied all the way across the foreground with a painting knife, sometimes thinly and in other parts with a heavy impasto for variation.
- Once the surface was completely dry, I dropped in a variety of colours within the warm spectrum of the colour wheel, imparting an abstract quality to the rough ground.

Farm near Ffestiniog
33 × 20.5cm (13 × 8in) Blue Lake grey tinted paper

Close-up of foreground
This gives a better idea of the stunning textural effects that can be created with the Daniel Smith watercolour ground.

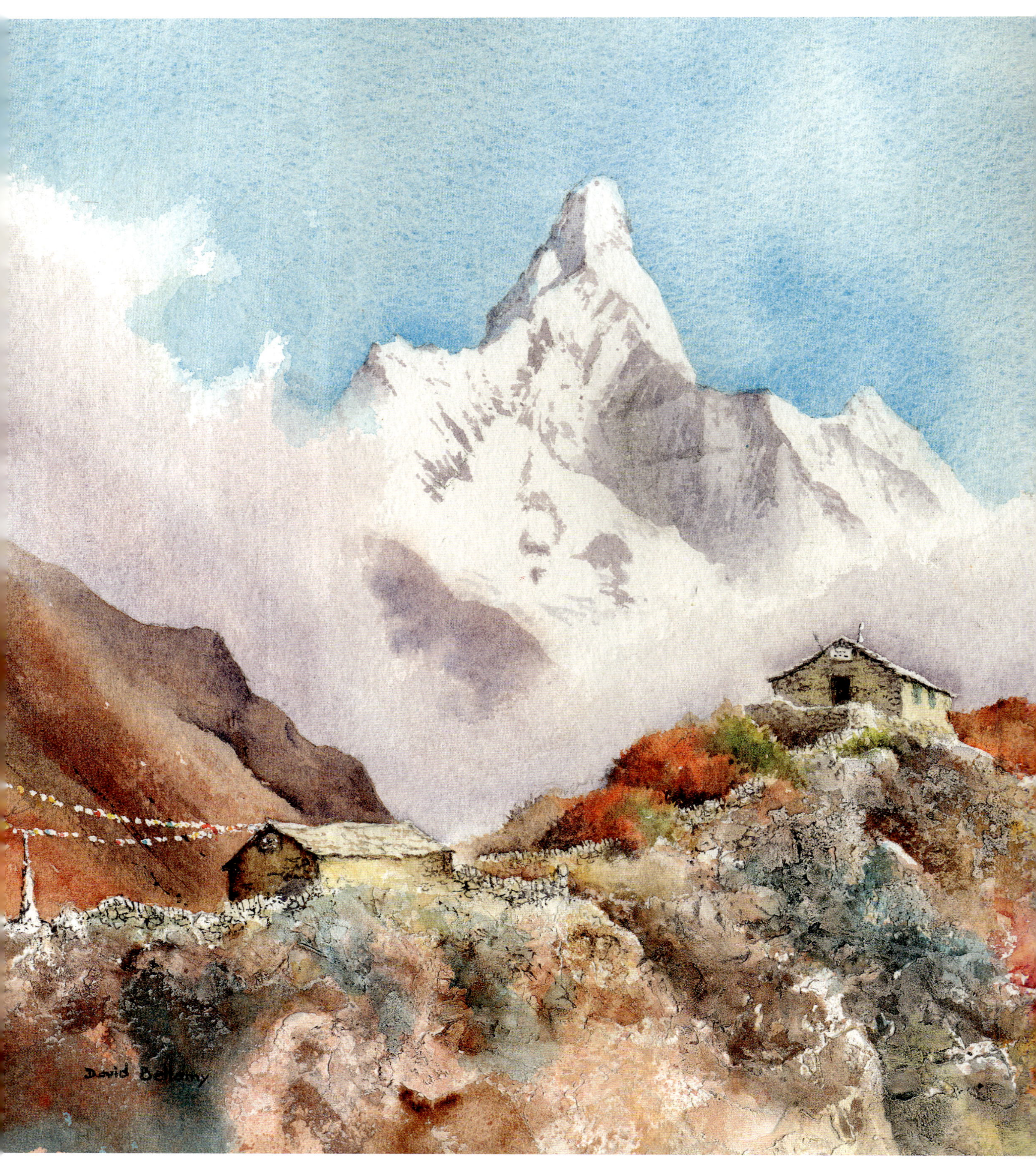

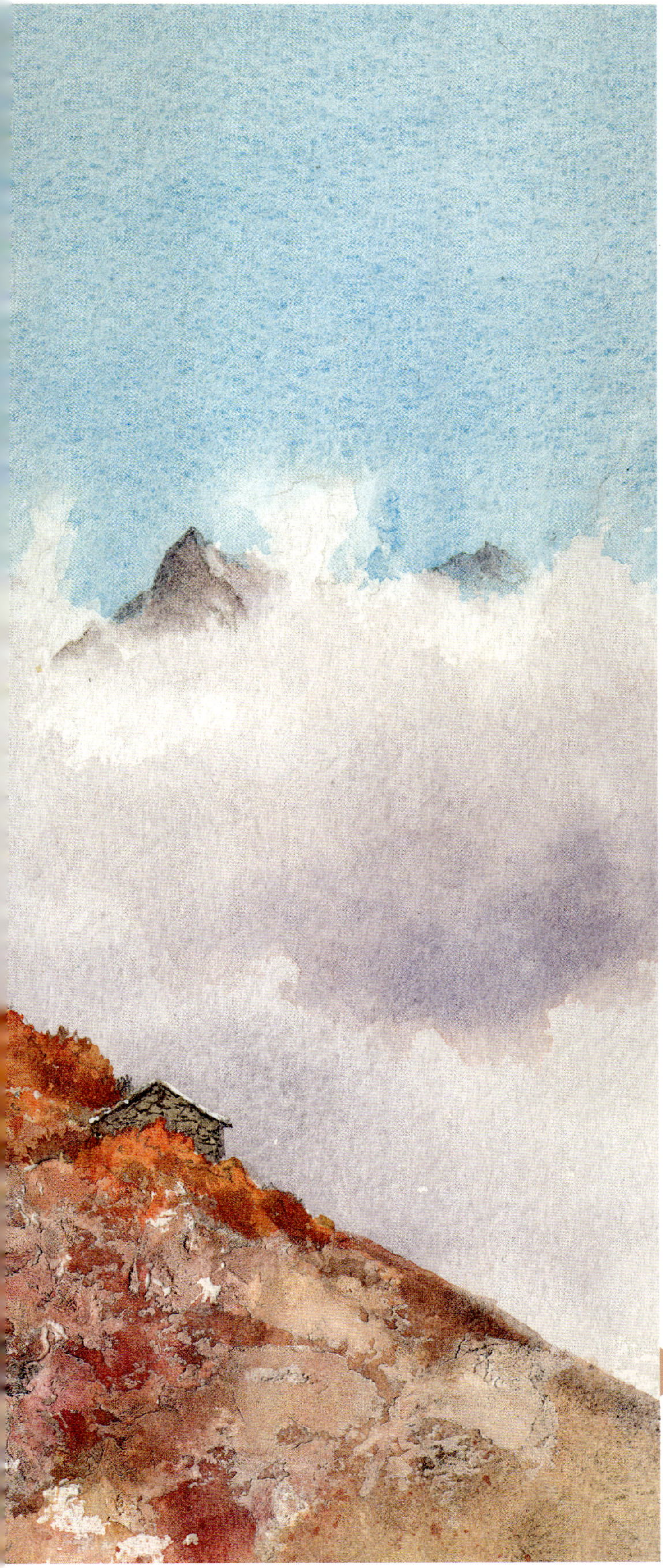

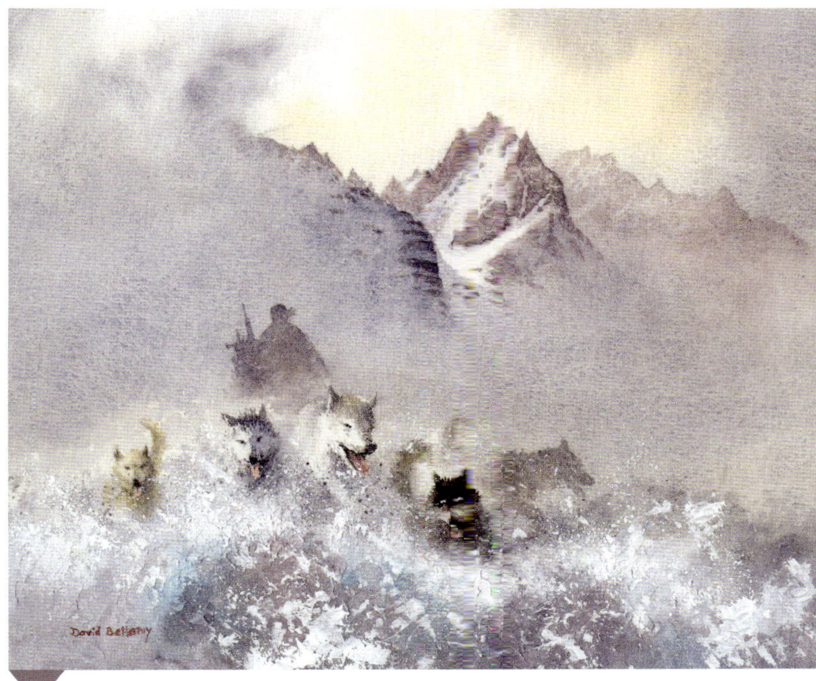

Huskies in Snow Flurries

28 × 23cm (11 × 9in) Saunders Waterford 640gsm (300lb) Hot-Pressed surface paper

This painting appeared in my Arctic Light book. The original sketch was done while hurtling down a steep snow-slope, swaying from side to side. In the flurries of snow I could see only the heads of the huskies emerging from the whiteness and the vague silhouette of Jens the sledge-driver. The East Greenland peaks rose high to the rear, but as I could easily sketch them when we paused further along, I concentrated on the action.

After laying on all the watercolour and details of the dogs I plastered on Daniel Smith watercolour ground to suggest the snow flurries, and when it had all dried, I spattered white gouache over the foreground.

Ama Dablam from Mong La

40.5 × 30.5cm (16 × 12in) Saunders Waterford 640gsm (300lb) Rough surface paper

The clouds boiling up around this Himalayan giant add to the sense of drama. The foreground was a mixed terrain of rocks and bushes, but I decided to create a more abstract area here with Daniel Smith watercolour ground plus a few patches of Schmincke coarse paste.

Watercolour ground with added objects

Found materials (see page 113) can be stuck into the Daniel Smith watercolour ground with a painting knife, and plastered over with more ground to create physical textures. This needs to be left to dry for a few days before applying any paint. The two paintings on the opposite page embody these additions in their foregrounds to create fascinating effects.

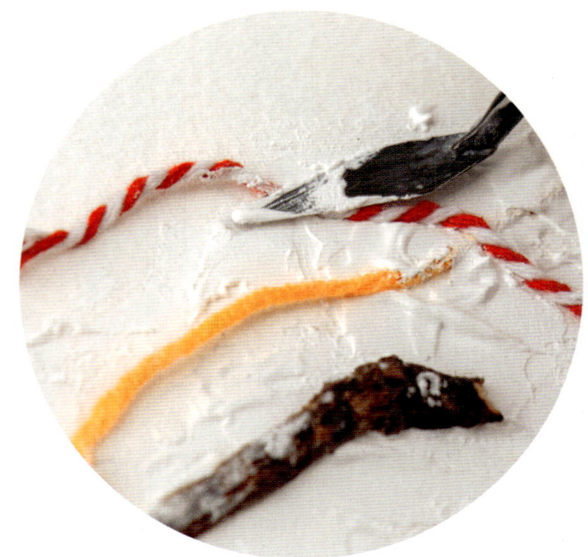

Attaching found materials
Found materials being embedded with Daniel Smith watercolour ground.

Keys to success with watercolour ground

- It is best to keep some of the area covered by the watercolour ground smoother and less rugged so that there is variation in its appearance.
- Allow a few days to pass in between applying the ground and painting over it.
- While found material can be positioned to suggest features like fences, fallen trunks, ruts in a cart-track and so on, it can also be used in a more abstract way to produce interesting shapes.

Opposite, above:
Cottage above Rhosgadfan
30.5 × 23cm (12 × 9in) Saunders Waterford 640gsm (300lb) Rough surface paper

I glued a couple of cut strips of bandage to the paper to suggest fencing, and laid some lengths of cotton along the track, before covering the cotton and bottom edges of the bandage with Daniel Smith watercolour ground. In places I plastered on Schmincke coarse paste to add to the roughness. Once all this had dried, I painted over it with a variety of colours, and included a little spatter above the fence.

Opposite, below:
Moorland Cottage
23 × 17.5cm (9 × 7in) Waterford 640gsm (300lb) Rough surface paper, mixed media

The sky, hills and cottage were painted in watercolour in the usual way, and then I spread Daniel Smith watercolour ground over the foreground with a painting knife. Short strips of cord were then stuck into the watercolour ground and plastered over with more ground.

Once completely dry, I painted over the foreground with Naples yellow, Potter's pink and phthalo blue. This sort of treatment is excellent for depicting rough ground, as shown in the detail to the left.

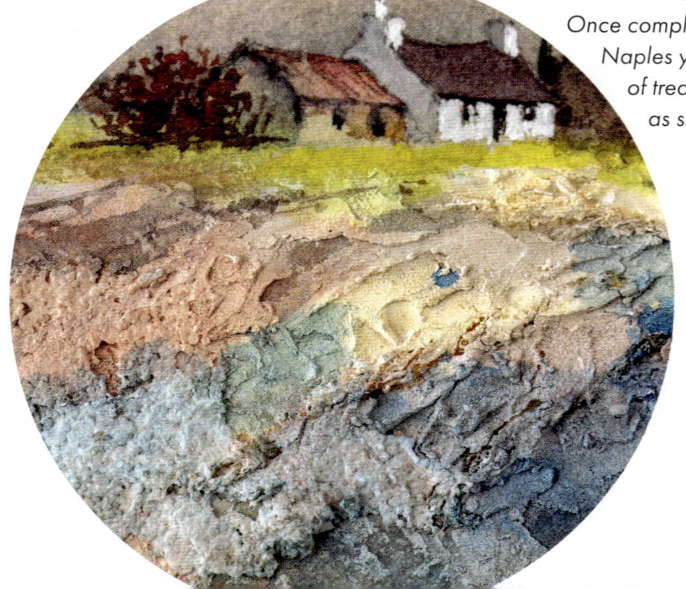

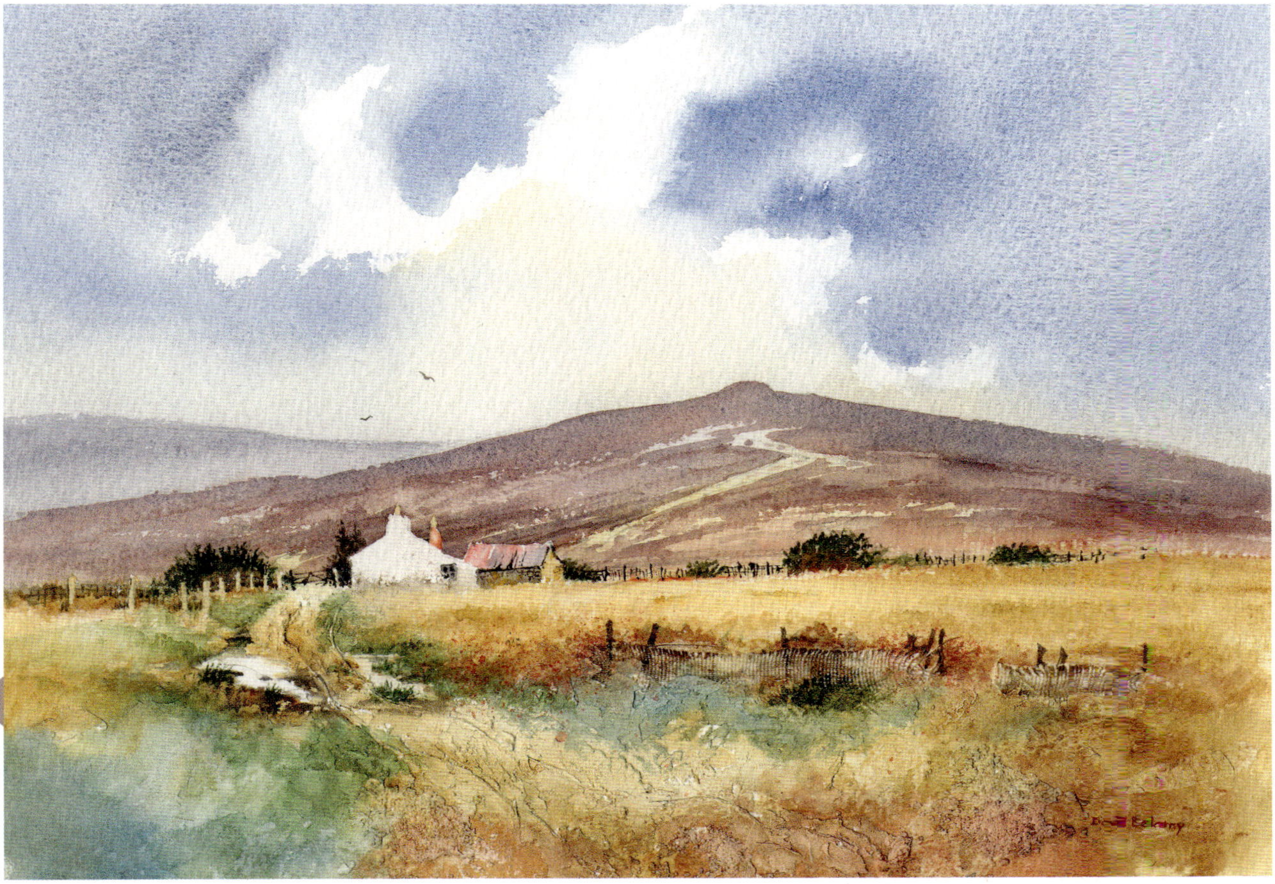

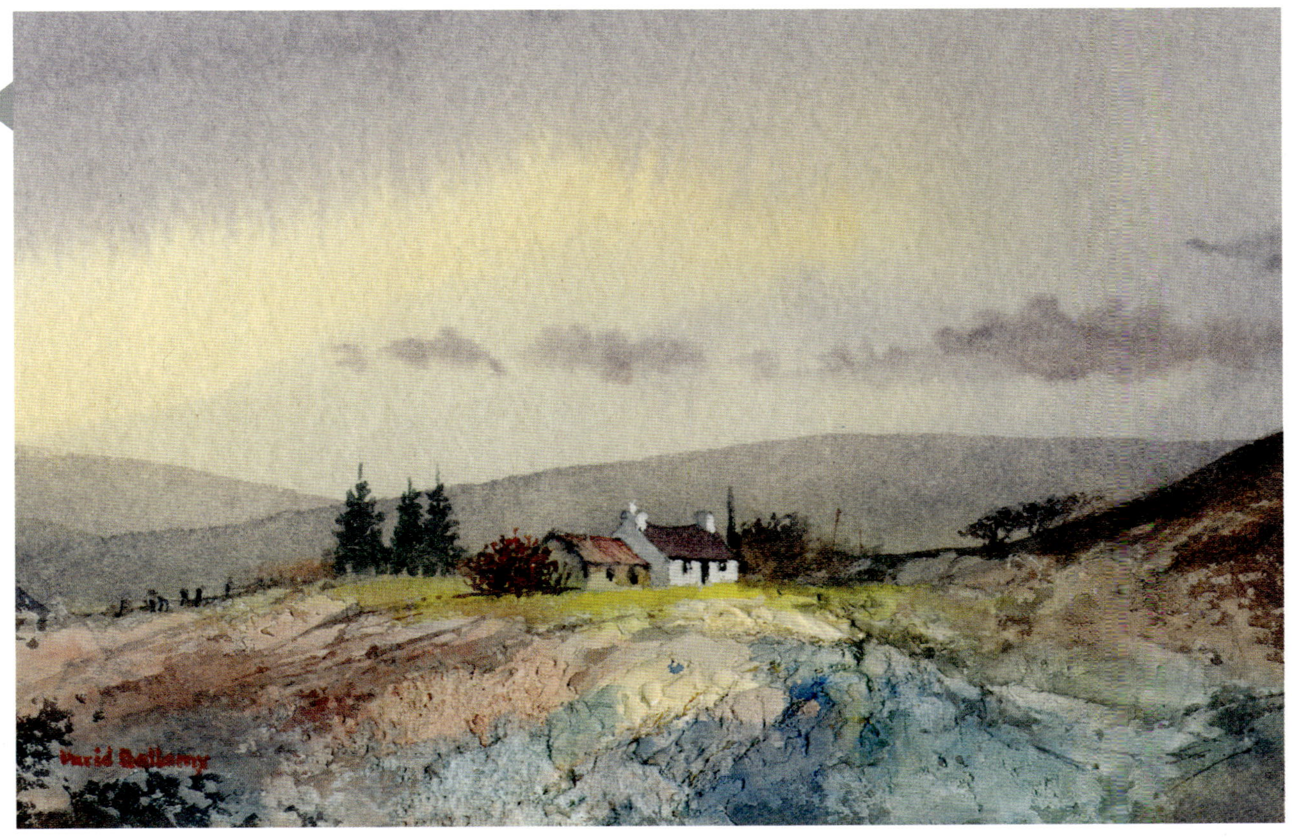

Collage

Collage can take many forms, from subtle scraps of oriental tissue paper to bolder coloured papers, or cut-out images of figures, signs, labels, and so on. The challenge is usually where to put such elements in a composition and how to blend them in.

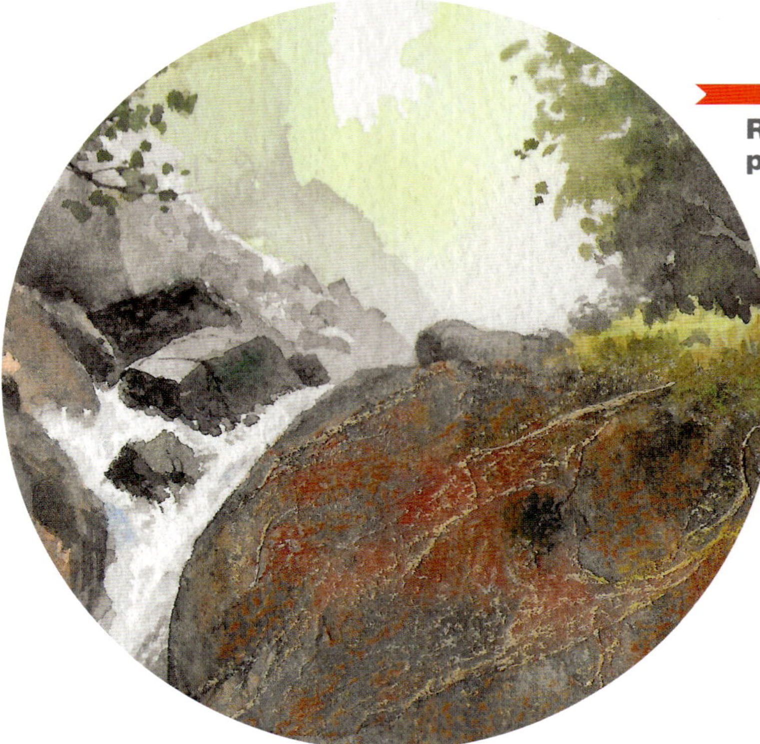

Rock texture with oil pastels and collage

- Oriental tissue paper with long fibres was glued to the right-hand rock face, and when dry the watercolour was carried out in the usual manner.

- Once the paper was completely dry, an oil pastel of Naples yellow was rubbed along the lines of the upstanding fibres of the Oriental paper while trying to avoid touching the actual paper surface, to create the linear effects. This method can be used for tree rcots, twigs, and a host of other items.

Rock texture with tissue paper

- I glued flimsy oriental tissue paper to some of the rocks to suggest texture, and this is another alternative if you find painting rocks difficult, or indeed if you have messed them up and wish to repair the problem.

- These were overpainted variously with yellow ochre, raw umber and burnt sienna. The collage edges can stick out like a sore thumb in places, so in the bottom left I have drawn lines to help disguise that effect. You could instead spread thin watercolour ground or gesso over the edges.

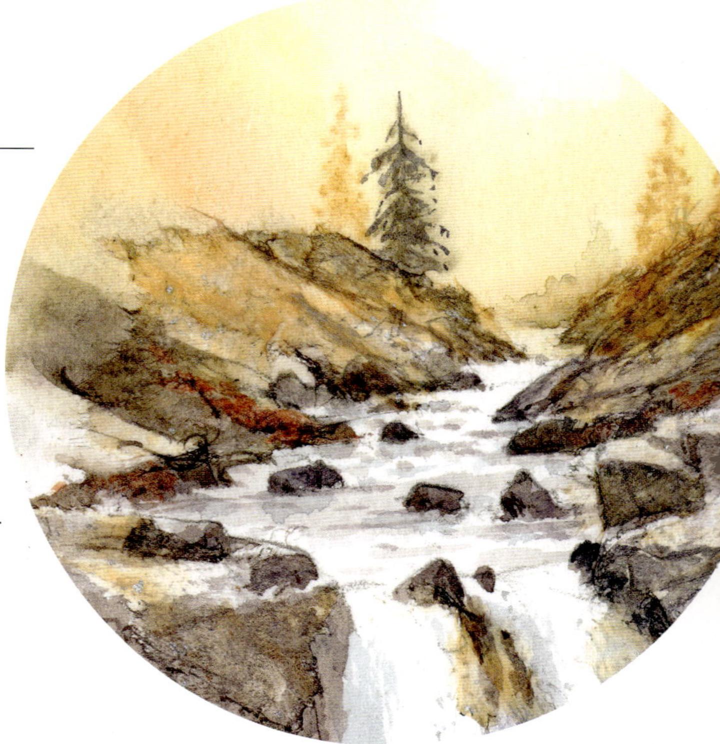

Kap Hoegh

20.5 × 17.5cm (8 × 7in) Saunders Waterford 425gsm
(200lb) Rough surface paper

*This image appears in my Arctic Light book;
Kap Hoegh is where we spent a few days during an
East Greenland expedition. I painted the polar bear
head at the top, with a warm grey sky, and stuck an
appropriate collage piece on Greenland aviation
just below, then plastered on some Daniel Smith
watercolour ground with a painting knife and left it
for a few days to dry – this early stage is shown in
the detail.*

*Drawing in a map of Kap Hoegh on the right of the
painting, I then printed some
map names and stuck those on.
The coastline was accentuated
with white gouache which I dry-
brushed diagonally lower down,
and spattered over the red-brown
wash applied earlier.*

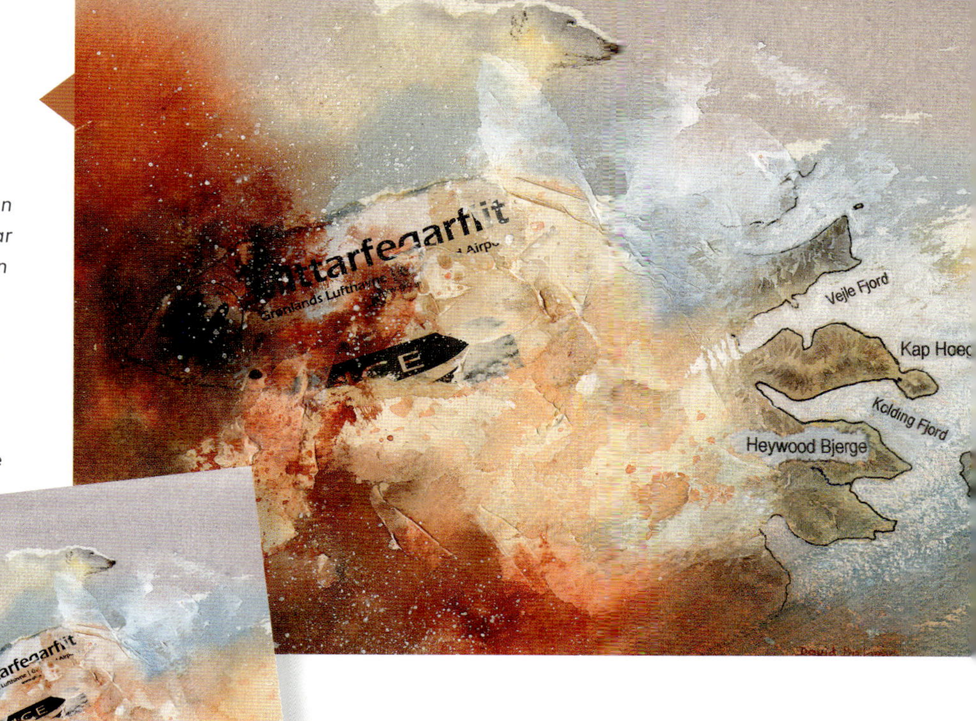

Casa Mauricio

20.5 × 16.5cm (8 × 6½in) Saunders Waterford
425gsm (200lb) Hot-Pressed surface paper

*It wasn't raining, there were many cars
around and the street sloped away
from the viewing point, but I decided to
change things. I spattered water from a
toothbrush into the grey sky and added
the neon café sign from a photograph,
with another piece of collage on the
right. The café background is bleached
out by the strong lighting, an effective
way of losing unnecessary detail.*

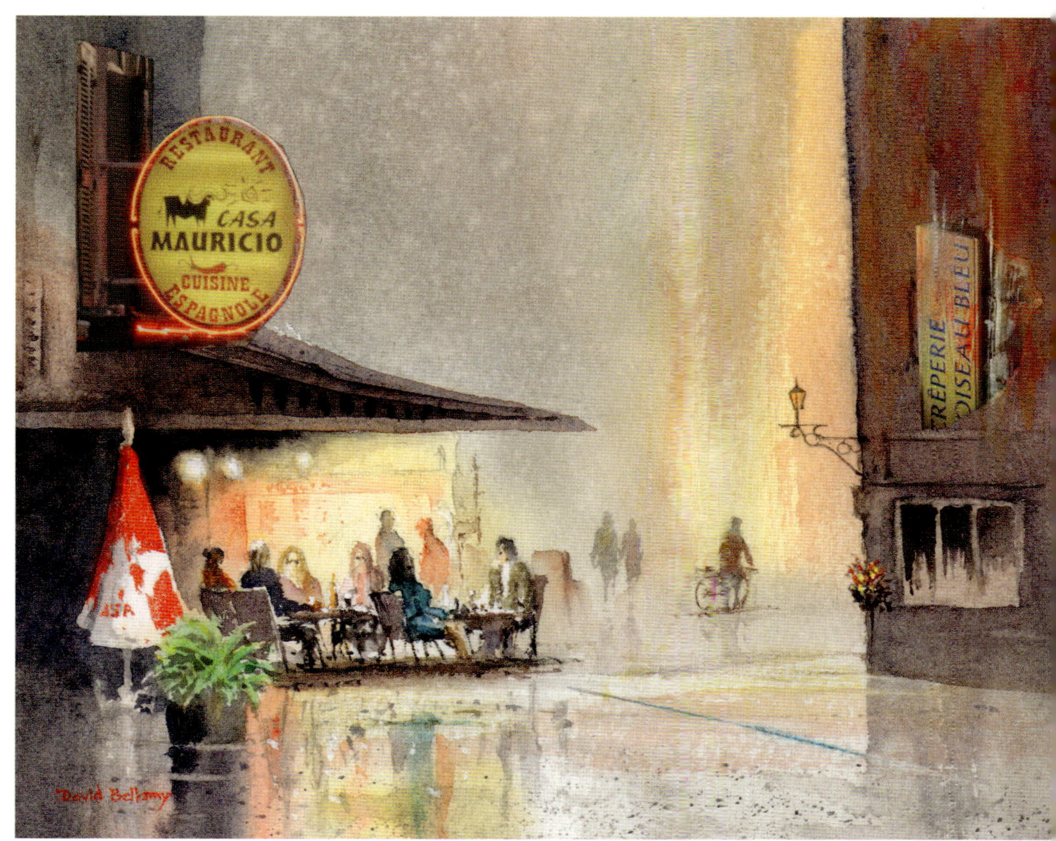

Tissue paper as a base

Tissue paper is not something I normally use, but it creates interesting effects. It can be very useful if you are uncertain about your foregrounds, as you can keep things simple, letting the paper provide textural detail instead of having to apply it with a brush.

The technique is simple, and involves nothing more than watercolour ground, tissue paper and time:

Apply the base Crinkled-up tissue paper is spread out and stuck down with Schmincke transparent watercolour ground over the rocky foreground area.

Lay down the ground On the following day, apply another layer of transparent ground over the tissue paper.

Dry thoroughly Leave the surface to dry completely – ideally overnight. After this, you can begin painting as usual, benefitting from the additional texture.

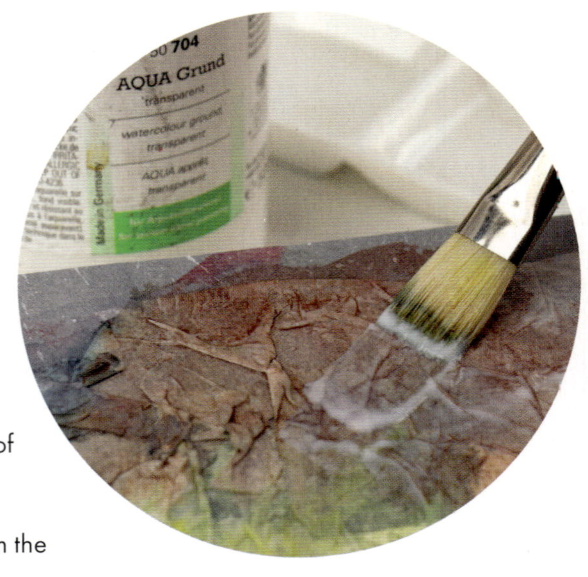

Sealing the tissue paper
*Applying Schmincke watercolour
ground over a tissue paper base to seal
the result.*

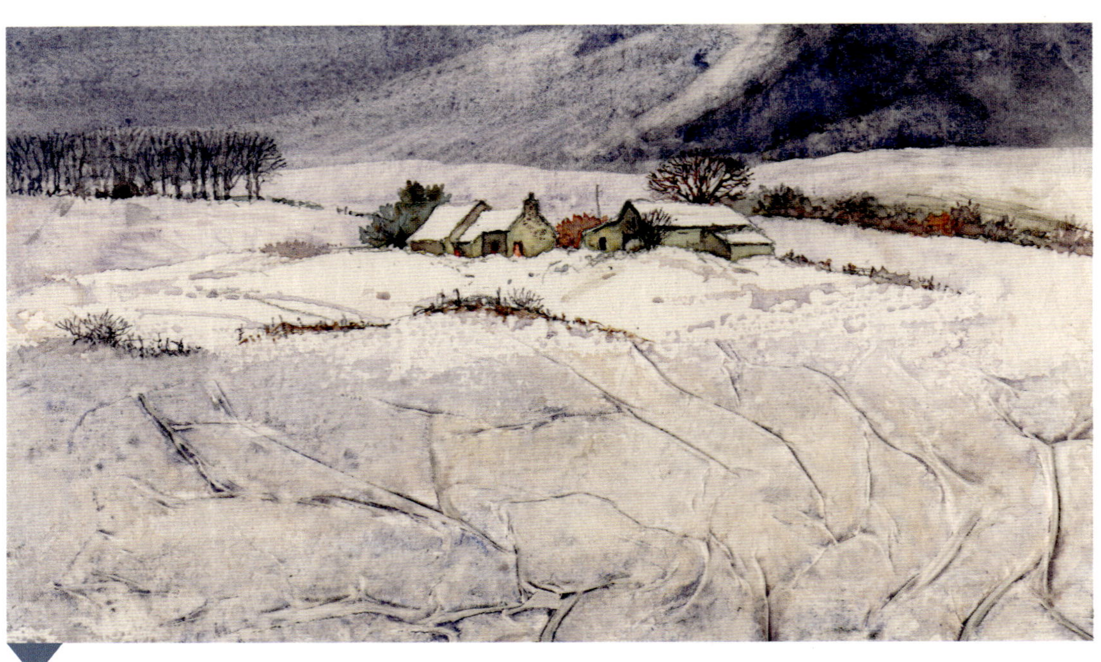

Farm at Llanfilo
20.5 × 14cm (8 × 5½in) mountboard with tissue paper and transparent watercolour ground

Tissue paper, glued in place with Schmincke transparent watercolour ground, covers the lower half of the composition here. I left this to dry thoroughly for a few days, then brushed a coat of the same watercolour ground over the whole composition. This can leave quite prominent and sometimes awkward marks over the paper when washed over with watercolour, so try not to spread it beyond the limits of the tissue paper. I mainly used indigo to paint this, touching in some light red and yellow ochre in places.

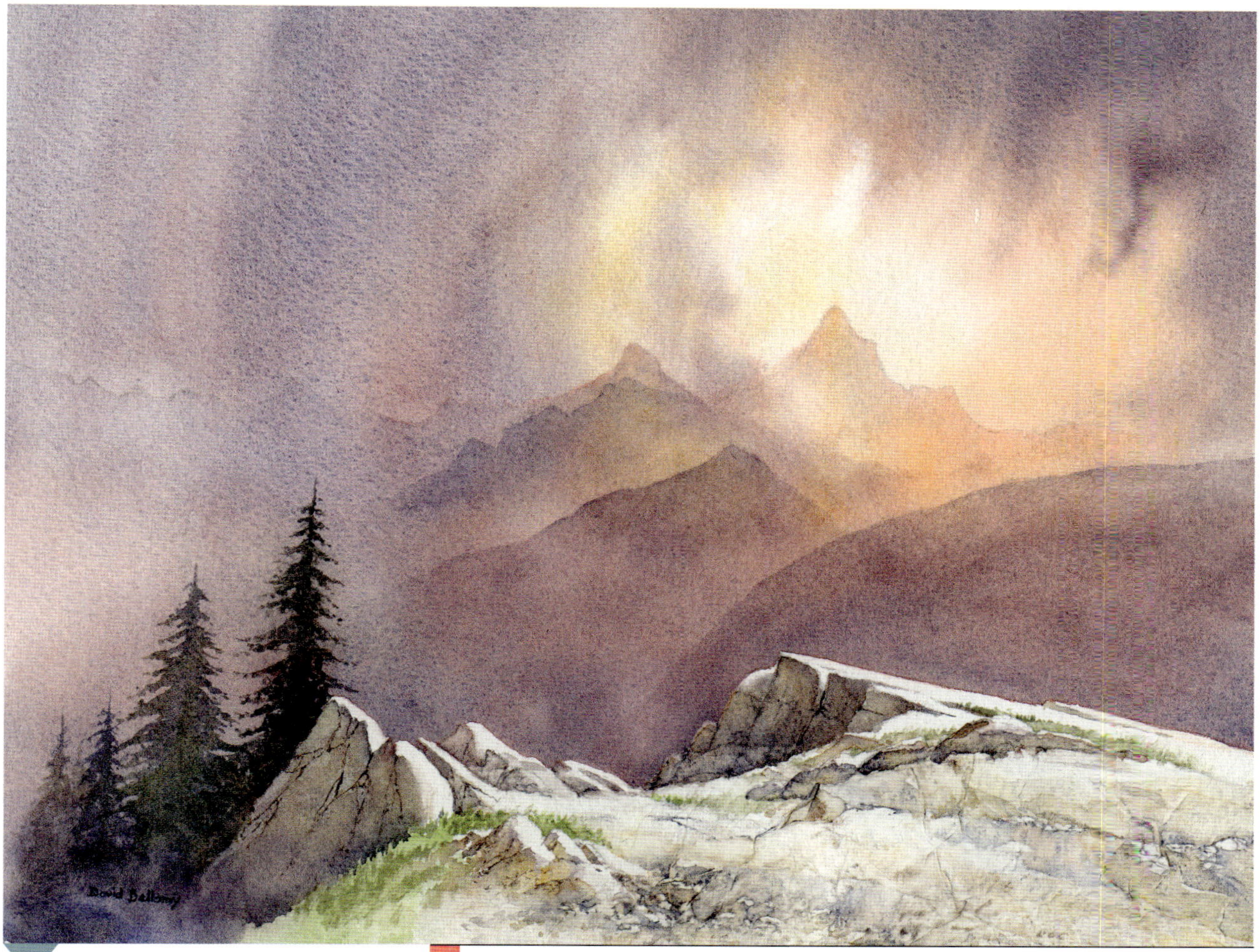

In the High Rockies

35.5 × 30.5cm (14 × 12in) Saunders
Waterford 425gsm (200lb) Rough
surface paper

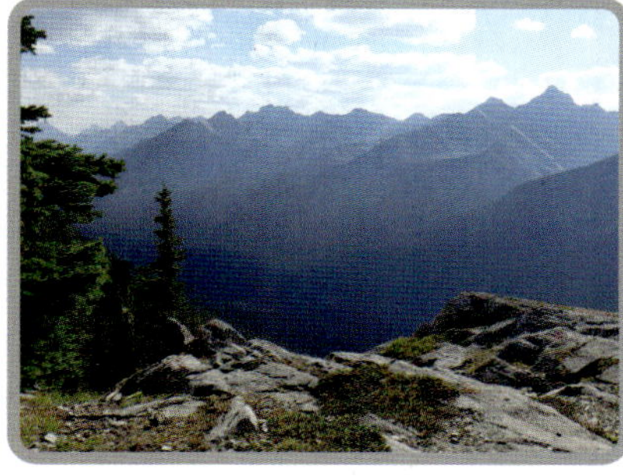

Reference photograph.

Painting *In the High Rockies*

Painting on tissue paper creates a different effect from ordinary washes, especially plainer ones. For those who find rough and rocky ground difficult to paint this can be an effective alternative.

- The crinkle ridges in the tissue paper introduce a new element and here they work well in suggesting rock fissures and features. Bear these rock structures in mind when you are scrunching up the tissue paper before gluing it down. It can rarely be perfect, but try folding and crinkling the tissue paper beforehand in a way that echoes the character of that part of the composition on which it will appear.

- As you can see, the atmosphere and time of day has been drastically altered from the original scene as portrayed in the photograph, and the highest peaks moved more towards the centre of the composition. At the same time I have lost many of the distant peaks in the atmospheric haze.

FRESH DIRECTIONS:
Interpretation and alteration

People are led to believe that you cannot change or rescue a watercolour if you make a gross mistake, but this is not necessarily so: you can enjoy the prospect of putting things right.

This chapter includes information on re-interpreting and altering subjects, whether you want to make changes to the landscape in front of you when painting from life, or later, when you take out an old painting you considered unsuccessful and decide to have a go at improving it.

We look at how to pick the right media, techniques and approach to interpret and alter a scene for our own satisfaction, change parts of the composition to eliminate unsightly or unwanted features, and also to change a completed painting that maybe didn't work out as we intended. How often have you completed a painting of which you are rightly proud... except perhaps for that small glaring error that will always nag you when you look at the work? Here I shall give you a few ideas on how to resolve these problems – often, but not always, straying away from pure watercolour.

Carn Meini, Pembrokeshire
25.5 × 23cm (10 × 9in) Saunders Waterford 300gsm (140lb) Not surface paper
Unhappy with the original foreground, I decided to overpaint it with soft pastels to illustrate how you can improve or rescue a composition in this way – but there's no reason why you shouldn't include pastels as part of the planned strategy. Even small flecks of bright pastel can enhance a scene, a particularly useful method for plants and undergrowth.

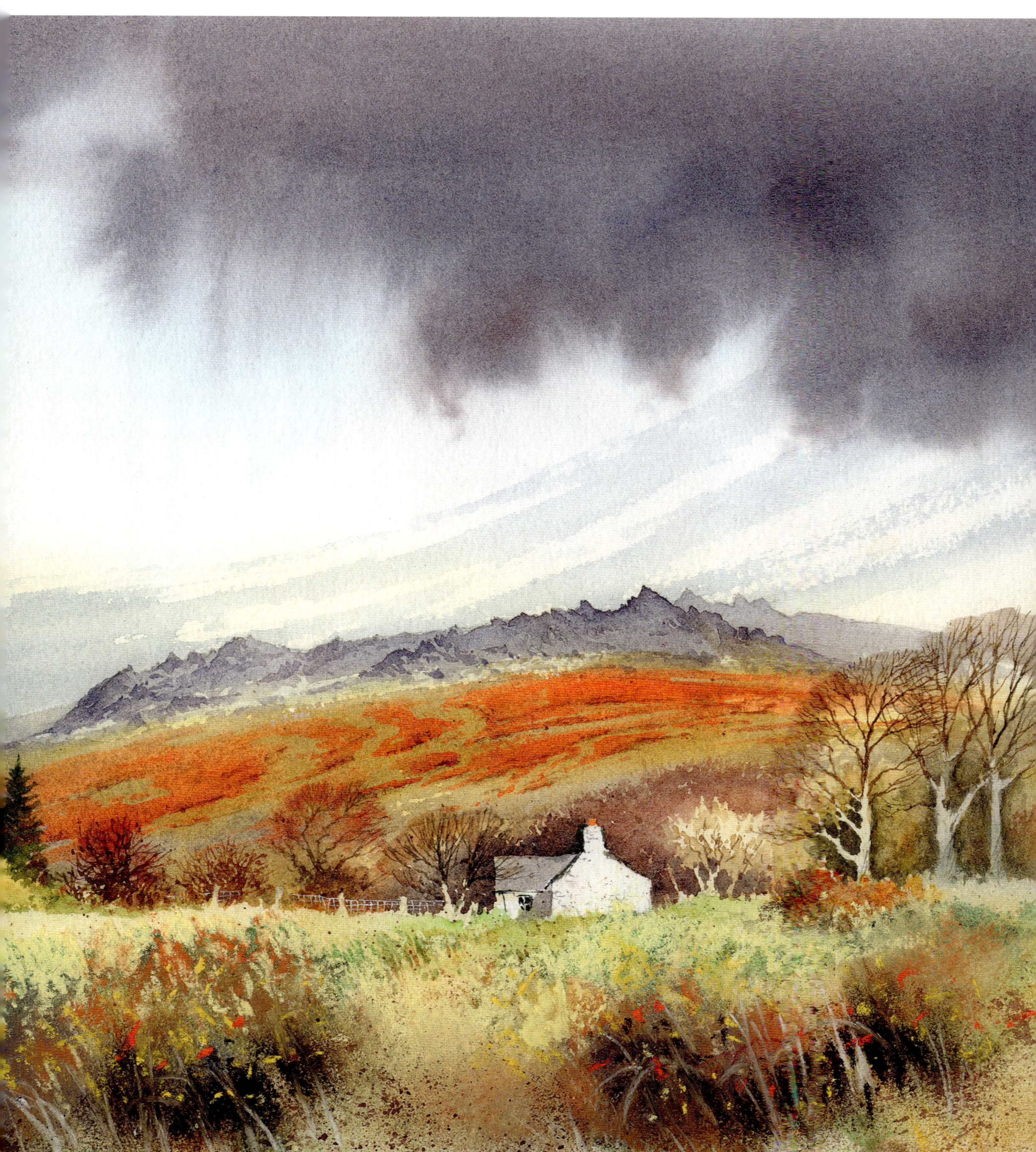

Creative interpretation

Few scenes enjoy a perfect composition in every way, and it's important to be able to stamp your own ideas on your artwork. Before we look at methods to improve or rescue a watercolour that has been finished, let's look at how taking the time to interpret and adapt the landscape before us in new ways will help us put our signature on a painting. These pages show how I approach things, and offer some key points for you to focus upon.

Pushing gouache to the fore

I noted earlier that it's usually not a good idea to mix watercolour with gouache – but sometimes only pushing the boundaries will produce the results I want. In this painting the approach is fairly traditional – except that here the emphasis is firmly on the use of gouache rather than watercolours, a decision that ensures the resulting white snow on dark background has huge impact.

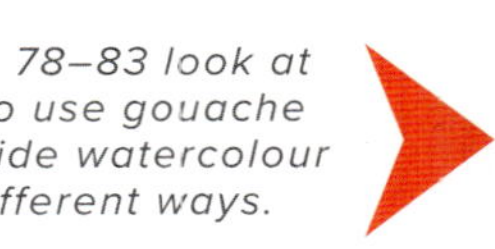

Pages 78–83 look at how to use gouache alongside watercolour in different ways.

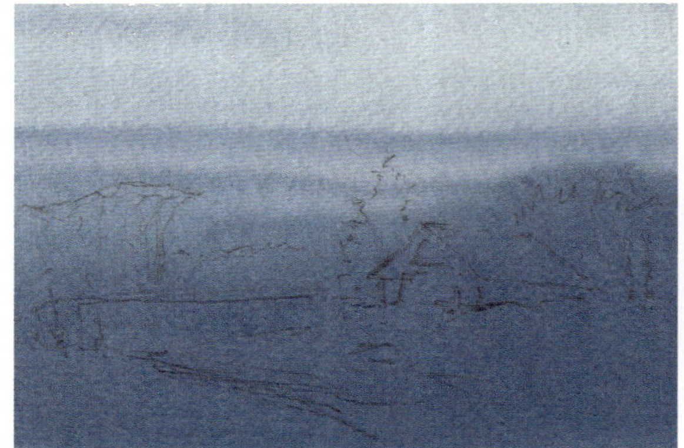

First dark wash Normally I would leave the paper a blank white for the absolutely pure white areas, but I want to illustrate how gouache can work effectively over even the darkest of colours. Here I drew in the barn and trees on an old piece of rough watercolour paper covered with an indigo watercolour wash.

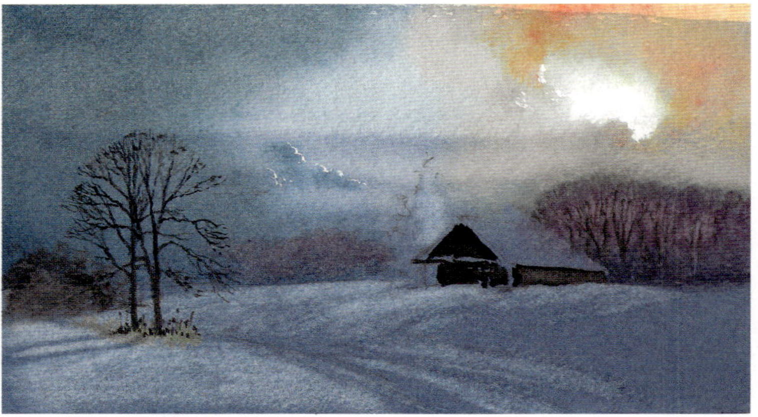

Working over the top I began by covering the left-hand sky with more indigo and a touch of phthalo blue watercolours, then the right-hand sky with hansa yellow gouache and pyrrol red touches plus titanium white for the highlights. Avoid mixing the gouache with watercolour paints: simply paint the gouache over dry watercolour.

Over the dark mass of distant trees I laid some alizarin crimson watercolour, then pulled out some of the indigo in the centre with a flat brush. This would suggest a field of snow. The left-hand tall trees were created with indigo plus burnt umber, while underneath these a further light sliver was pulled out, leaving two cast shadows of untouched paper. The dark areas on the barn were rendered with burnt umber mixed with indigo, both in watercolour.

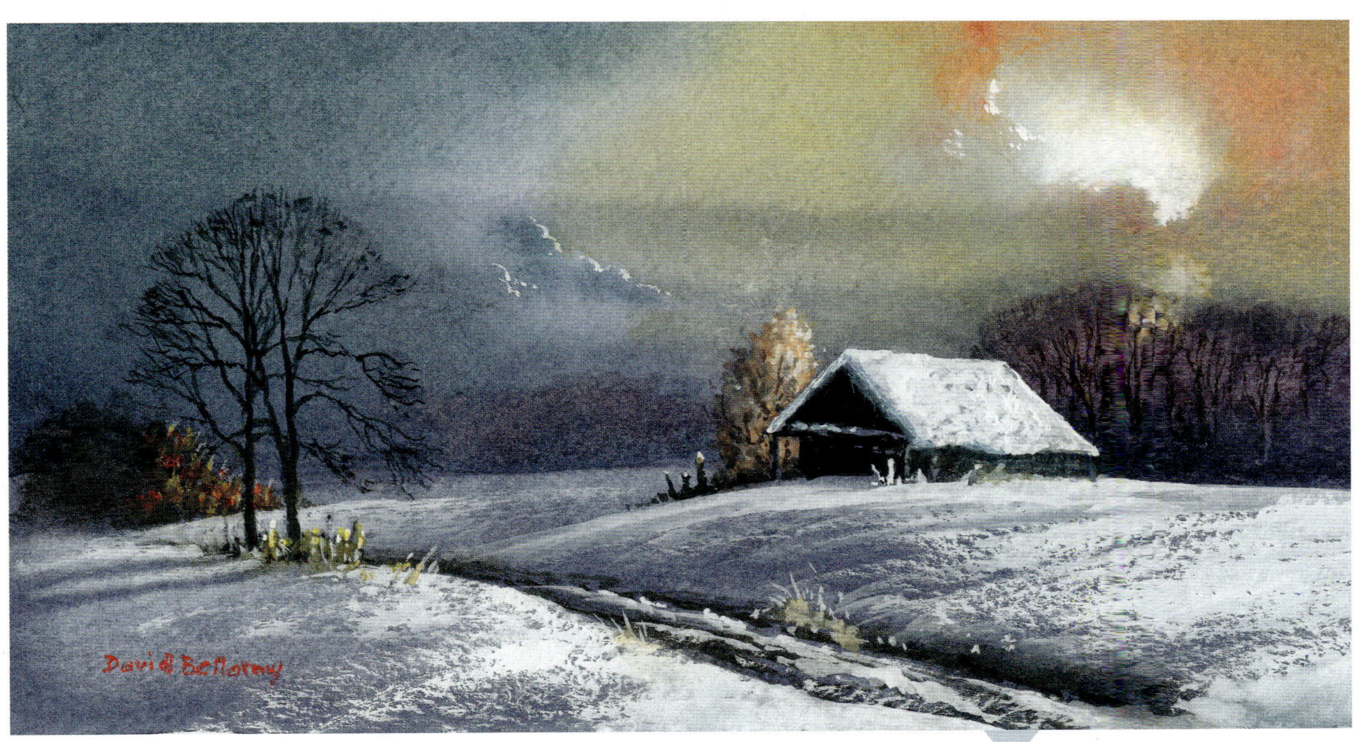

Finishing touches I heightened the whiteness of the ground by the left-hand trees using white gouache. A mixture of gouache colours – hansa yellow and pyrrol red – was used to warm up the bushes at the rear of these trees. Some light was introduced at the top of the right-hand tree mass with a mix of white and hansa yellow gouache, and the small tree beside the barn emphasized with hansa yellow and pyrrol red. Using a wedge-shaped painting knife, white gouache was applied across the roof, and finally the same colour was brushed across the foreground field, creating delightful textures.

Winter Barn
20.5 × 11.5cm (8 × 4½ in)
Saunders Waterford 300gsm
(140lb) Rough surface paper

Ghosting background features

Creating background or distant mountains or crags in a shimmering, ghostly fashion can imbue a scene with powerful atmosphere, and in this work I illustrate how to use a large sponge to achieve this effect. The actual foreground of this scene was a mass of trees, through which I could barely see the farm, but I loved the scene and decided to get rid of most of the trees and substitute rampant undergrowth.

I employed a variety of methods to create convincing undergrowth: stamping various colours on with a cosmetic sponge that had many holes like a holey cheese; white gouache spatter, sometimes with a touch of cadmium yellow pale added; negative painting to define the fenceposts; and scratches with a scalpel.

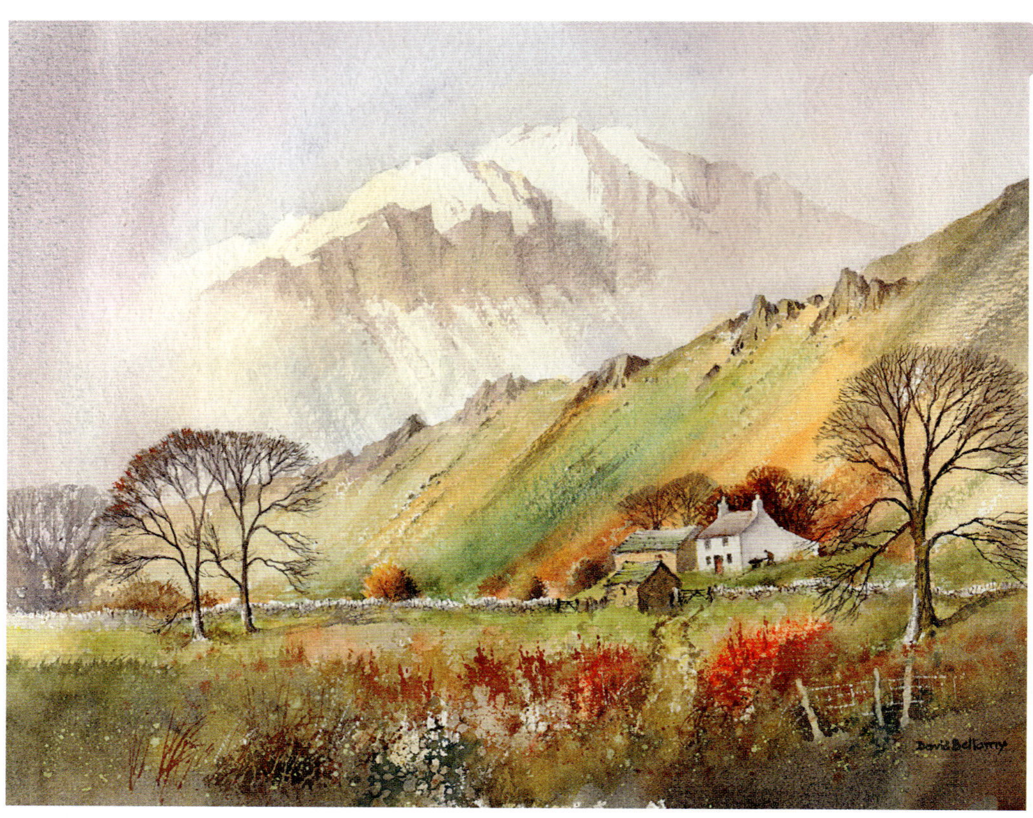

Farm below
Blake Rigg
33 × 25.5cm
(13 × 10in) Saunders
Waterford 640gsm
(300lb) Rough
surface paper

Ghostly ridge I wanted Blake Rigg to appear ghostly through a veil of mist, so I painted it with a weak wash in the sky, defining the ridge as a white top, apart from the top right end where it goes into shadow until it is lost.

Sponging Once dry I painted in the crags with a mixture of cobalt blue and cadmium red, dropping in yellow ochre in places. Again I allowed this to dry and then with a large natural sponge I swept over the whole of the sky and mountain to leave it shimmering in a ghostly fashion.

Dynamic ridge When I painted the closer ridge this created a strong sense of distance in front of the mountain, with the diagonal dry-brush strokes showing the angle of slope on the side of the ridge.

Figures The chap with the wheelbarrow was introduced to give the composition a sense of life. I keep sketches and photograph of figures – and also animals, chickens, geese, pheasants and the like – as references for this purpose.

See pages 52 for sponging and 84–87 for more on figures

Creating a slightly looser approach

I have painted Carn Llidi scores of times from various angles, and wanted to try a new, looser approach.

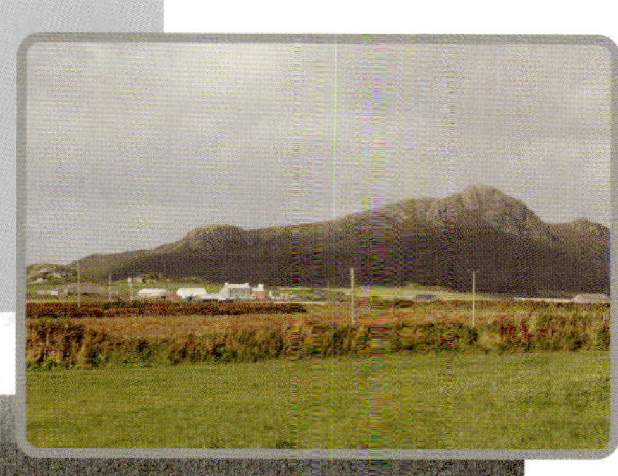

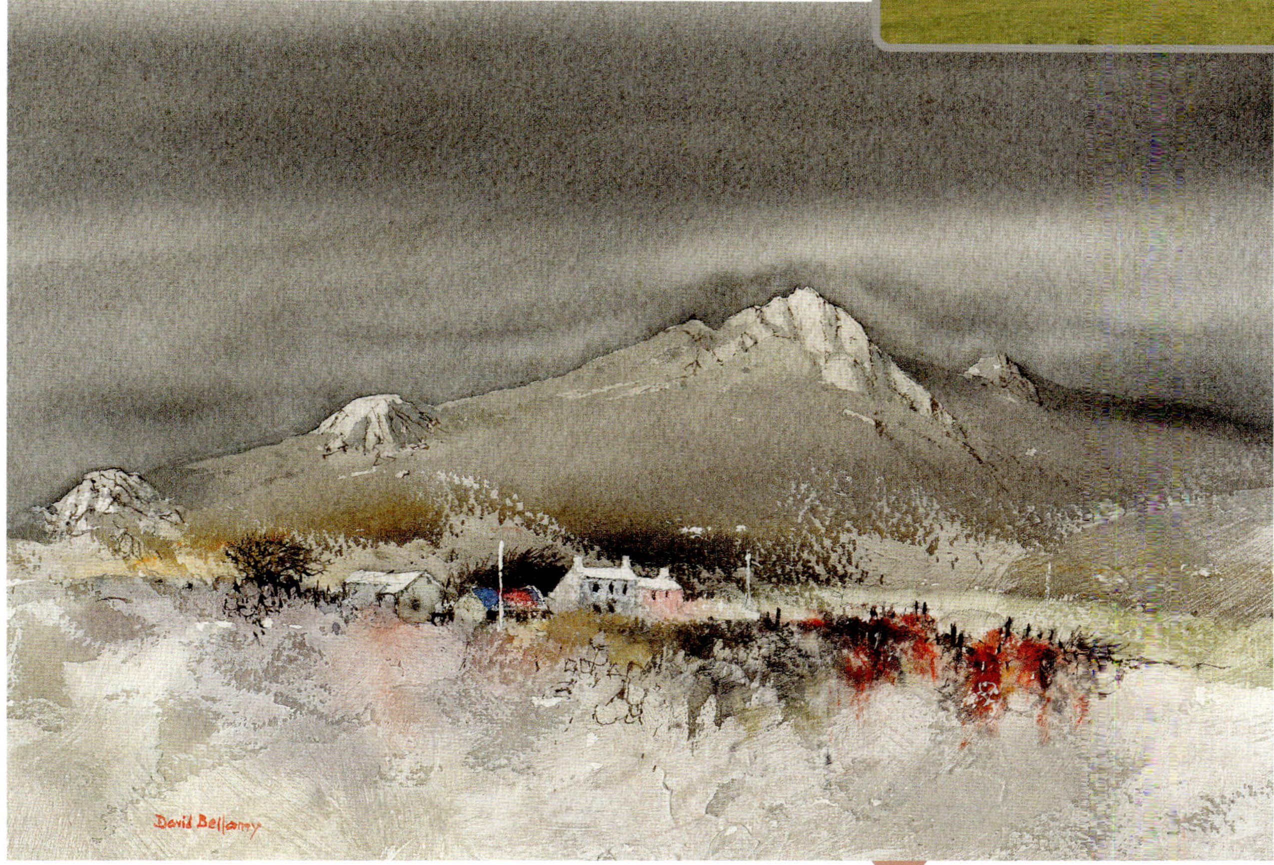

Carn Llidi, Pembrokeshire
25.5 × 18cm (10 × 7in) Waterford 540gsm
(300lb) Not surface paper

Minimal foreground Foreground detail has only been lightly suggested, and I moved the buildings a little to the right to provide better balance.

Spots of colour contrast The overall grey scheme lent a sense of unity, but I introduced bright spot colours in places to liven it up.

Knifework Daniel Smith watercolour ground was applied recklessly with a painting knife to achieve a looser effect, and in places this has been washed over with watercolour.

Counterchange I decided to reverse the tones of the crags against the sky, a method I use regularly where I feel it will improve the tonal balance.

Creating patterns with found materials

All manner of materials, such as card, bandages, patterned plastic sheets, netting, neoprene material and so much more can be covered in paint and stamped onto the paper to produce patterns in a realistic or abstract way. It's great fun to try out various items and introduce a different note in your work.

Here I use some corrugated card to suggest a corrugated iron roof, and illustrate methods of blending it into the composition.

This scene was a delightful jumble, the sort of subject that you feel you can take liberties with. While working on the studio sketch I decided to change the proportions of the barn, lighten it a bit more, make more of the trees and push the gate further to the left. As I don't like metal farm gates I turned it into a wooden one. I also decided to add some chickens.

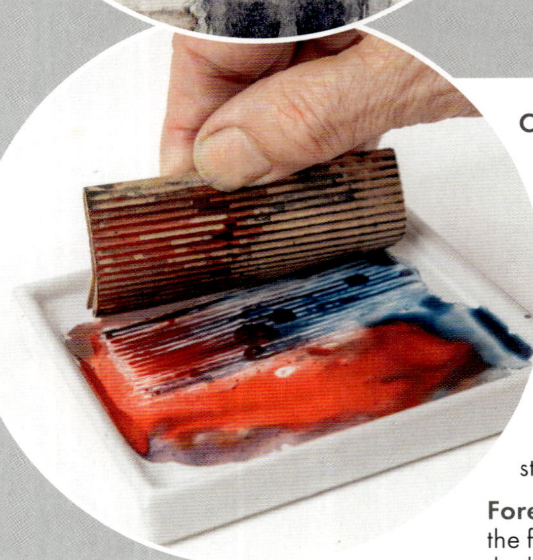

Corrugated card roof In the sky, Naples yellow formed the lower section and I then washed down shadow violet, stronger at the top, and let it flow down into the yellow. This was allowed to dry and then pieces of low-tack tape were stuck above and below the roof to prevent paint going beyond the confines of the corrugated iron roof.

I then took a piece of fine corrugated card and poked it into a flattish mass of light red on the palette, tested it on Rough paper several times until the excess liquid had been removed, and then applied it to the roof. It needed two applications on the right-hand roof, each at a slightly different angle. The roof was then allowed to dry before I laid a weak wash of light red across both sides, with some weak indigo in places on the right-hand part. This slightly softened the stark corrugations.

Foreground texture Green apatite genuine was laid over two-thirds of the foreground, and granulation medium dropped in on the right. Holding the board to slope to the left while this was wet helped an organic series of granulations to develop across the foreground. I applied yellow ochre to the area between the green and the foot of the barn, including over the gate.

Finishing Once the paper had dried, I drew in long bending grasses with masking fluid on a painting knife on either side of the barn openings, then once more allowed it to dry. The trees were painted in burnt sienna and French ultramarine, with a much darker version for the insides of the barn. Some transparent red oxide was laid over parts of the yellow ochre below the building and gate and also spattered from a toothbrush by the window. Finally I removed the masking fluid and added the cockerel and chickens.

Top: Detail of the print made with corrugated card.

Above: Loading the card for stamping

There's more about stamping on pages 54–55.

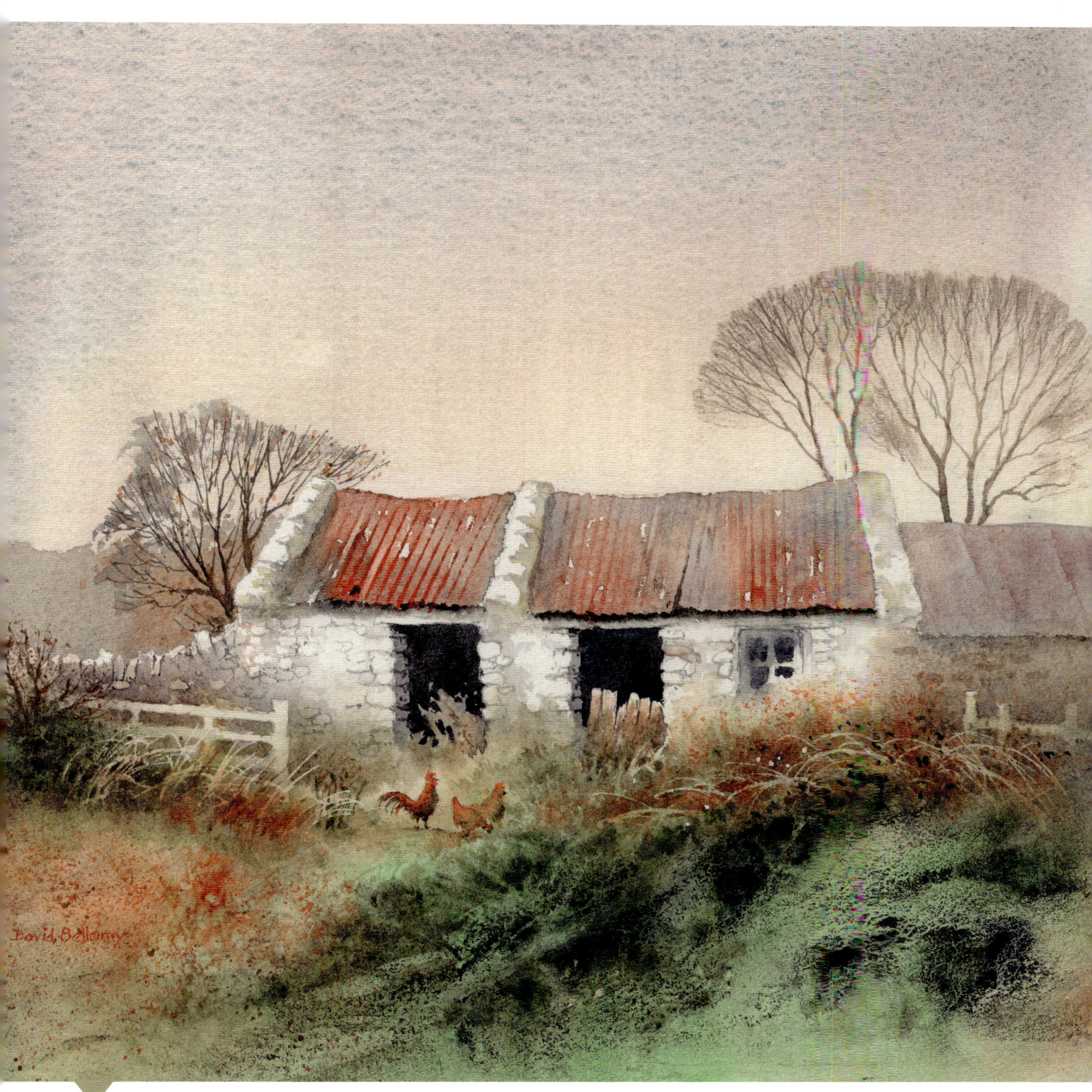

Old Barn at Trelerw
25.5 × 20.5cm (10 × 8in) Saunders Waterford 640gsm (300lb) Not surface paper

Realistic features with watercolour ground

While Daniel Smith watercolour ground is excellent for creating textures and abstract passages, it can also be employed in a more realistic manner. In this composition the found objects that I have included suggest real objects, such as plastic netting that is used to represent real fishing nets and lengths of cotton and thin cord for ropes, all held together by the watercolour ground in a way that gives an illusion of the real thing.

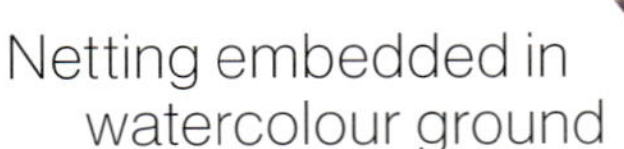

Netting embedded in watercolour ground

When adding additional objects, use heavyweight watercolour paper – such as 640gsm (300lb) – to provide a sturdy surface base.

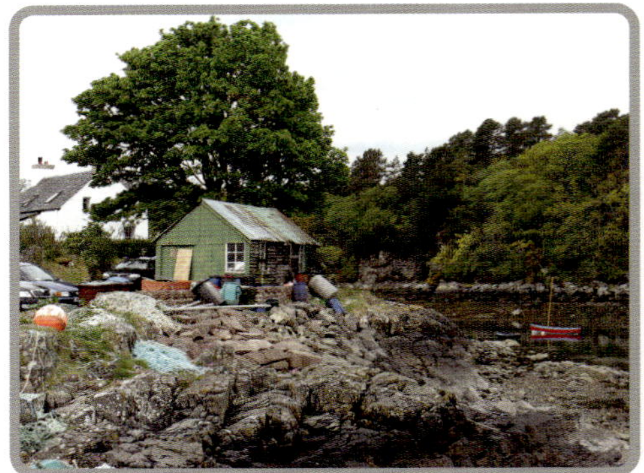

Photograph of the scene.

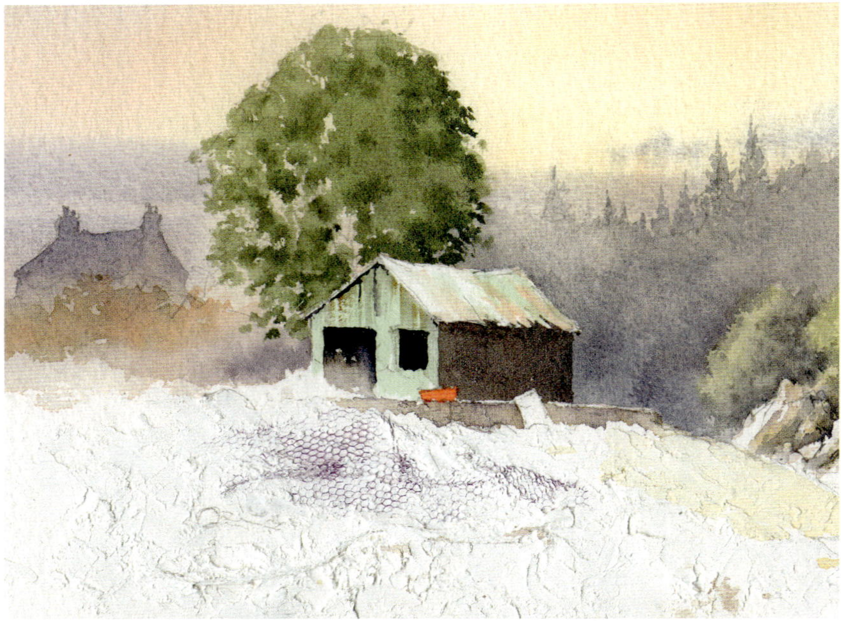

Embedding the material At this point I have painted most of the scene, apart from the foreground area where I had laid some Daniel Smith watercolour ground. I stuck some fine plastic netting into it, then a short length of cotton under the netting and a longer length of thin cord at the bottom. Over this I applied thicker watercolour ground with a painting knife, taking this further out over the rocks to each side. I then left it for a couple of days before starting the painting, so that it was completely dry.

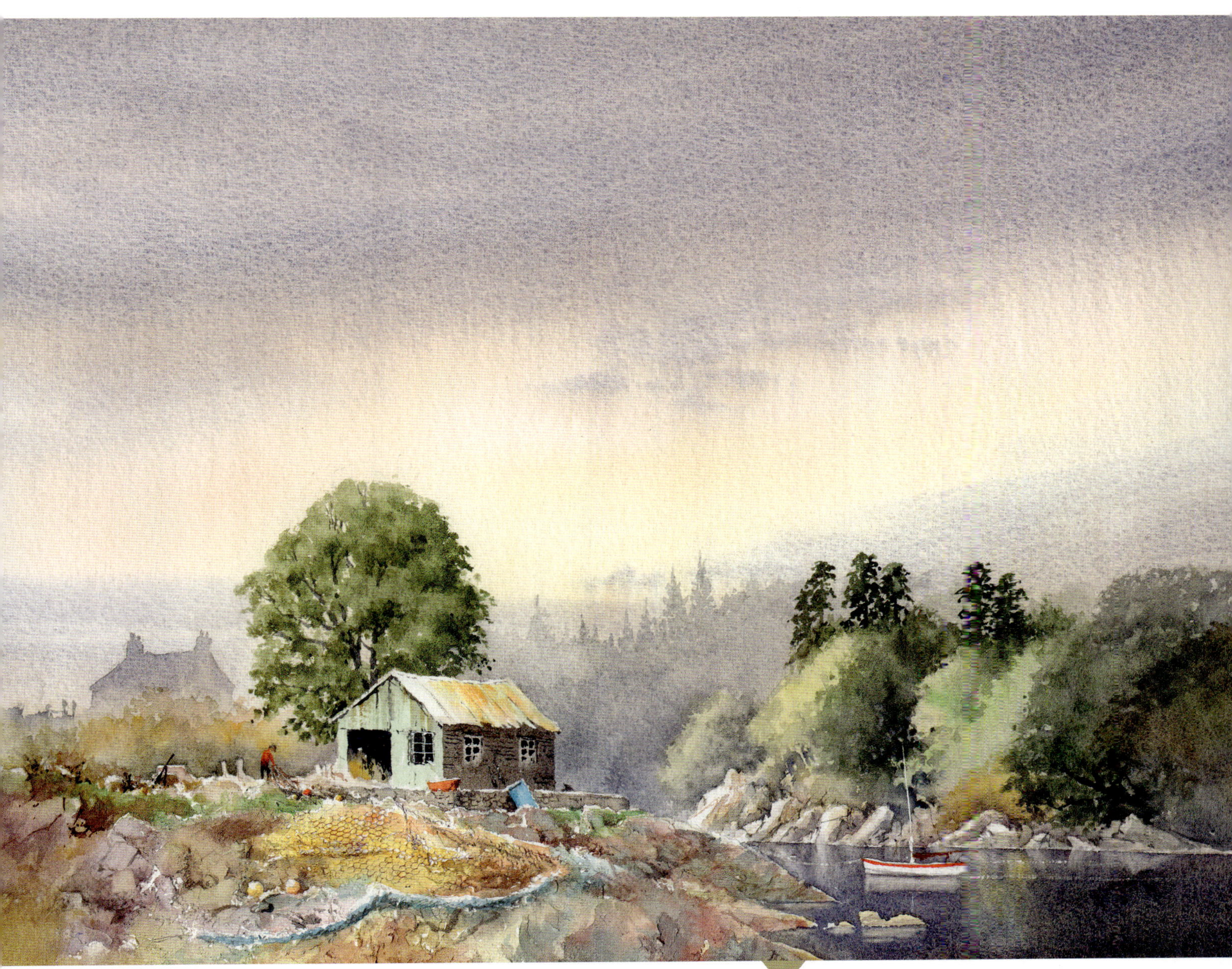

Painting the material I painted yellow ochre over the net and dabbed in raw umber in places, French ultramarine with quinacridone magenta over the rocks and phthalo blue over the cord line. When this had dried, I applied some French ultramarine and quinacridone magenta over parts of the net, using the brush on its side so that the paint did not touch the yellow ochre underneath. To complete the painting I added some detail to the rocks.

Fisherman's Shack Plockton
38 × 25.5cm (15 × 10in) Saunders Waterford
640gsm (300lb) Rough surface paper

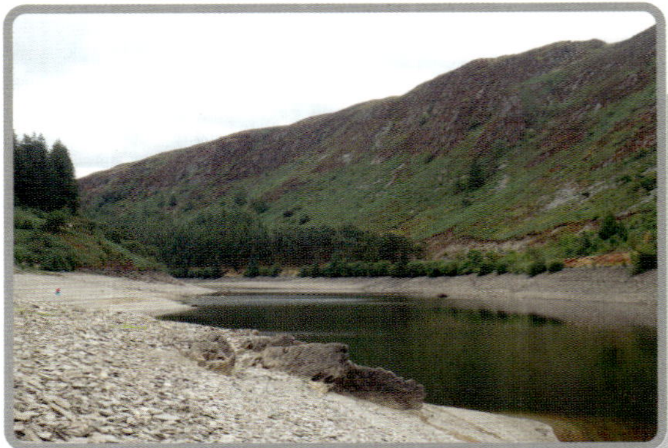
Reference photograph.

Altering the lighting

Often with a composition only the light needs changing to vastly improve the scene. The scene below is a fabulous subject, but the light on the day I visited was desperately dull – just look at the reference photograph to the left. As with a great many of my landscapes I decided to completely change the lighting and bring out the best in the scene.

The same is true of *Urn Tomb, Petra*, opposite – a little inventiveness in lighting gives the scene its due.

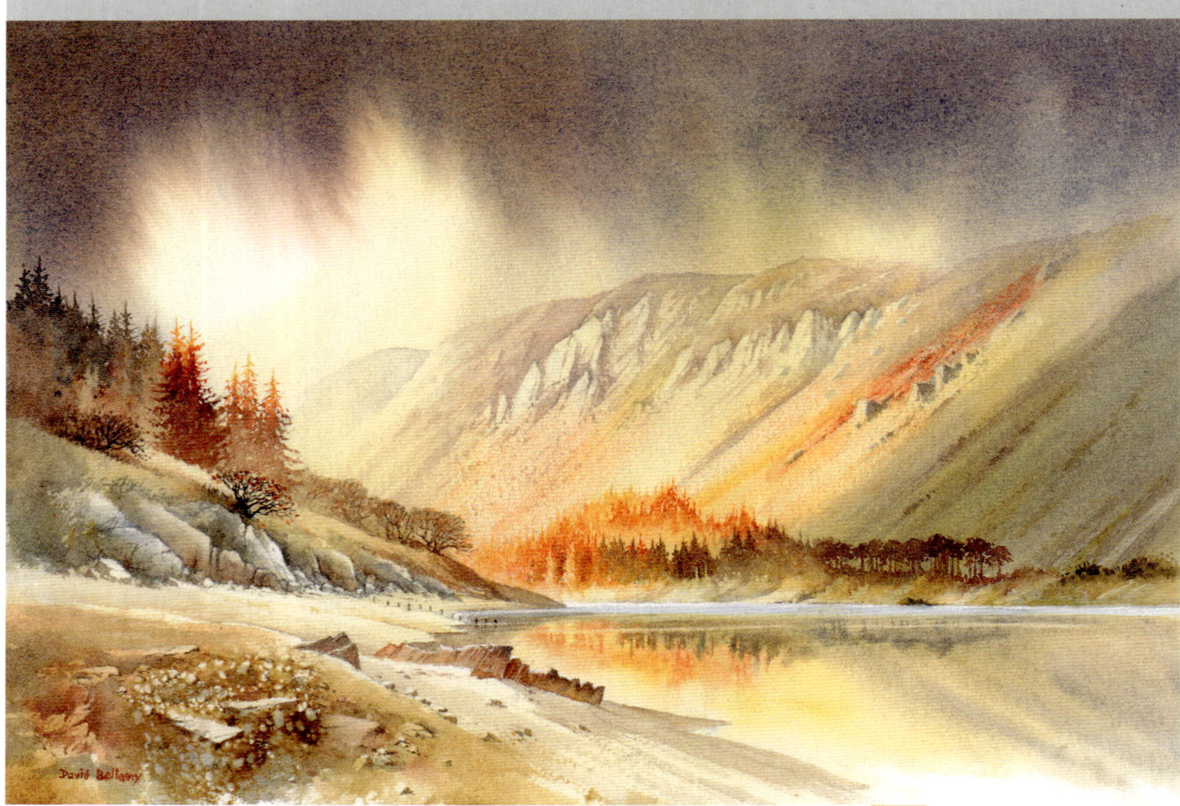

Garreg-ddu Reservoir in Golden Light
33 × 23cm (13 × 9in) Waterford 640gsm (300lb) Rough surface paper

Seize the moment The water level was incredibly low – most of the time this viewpoint is well under water, including an old fence that existed before the dam was built. Returning at another time, when the light was better, would have meant that I lost the opportunity to paint it, so improving the lighting was necessary.

Rely on your knowledge Experience in working outdoors is of enormous benefit when trying to envisage the sort of sky, lighting and atmosphere you would like to inject into a painting.

Choose the right colours The scene is brought to life with strong evening light created by quinacridone gold, transparent red oxide and Aussie red gold on the far cliffs and shore.

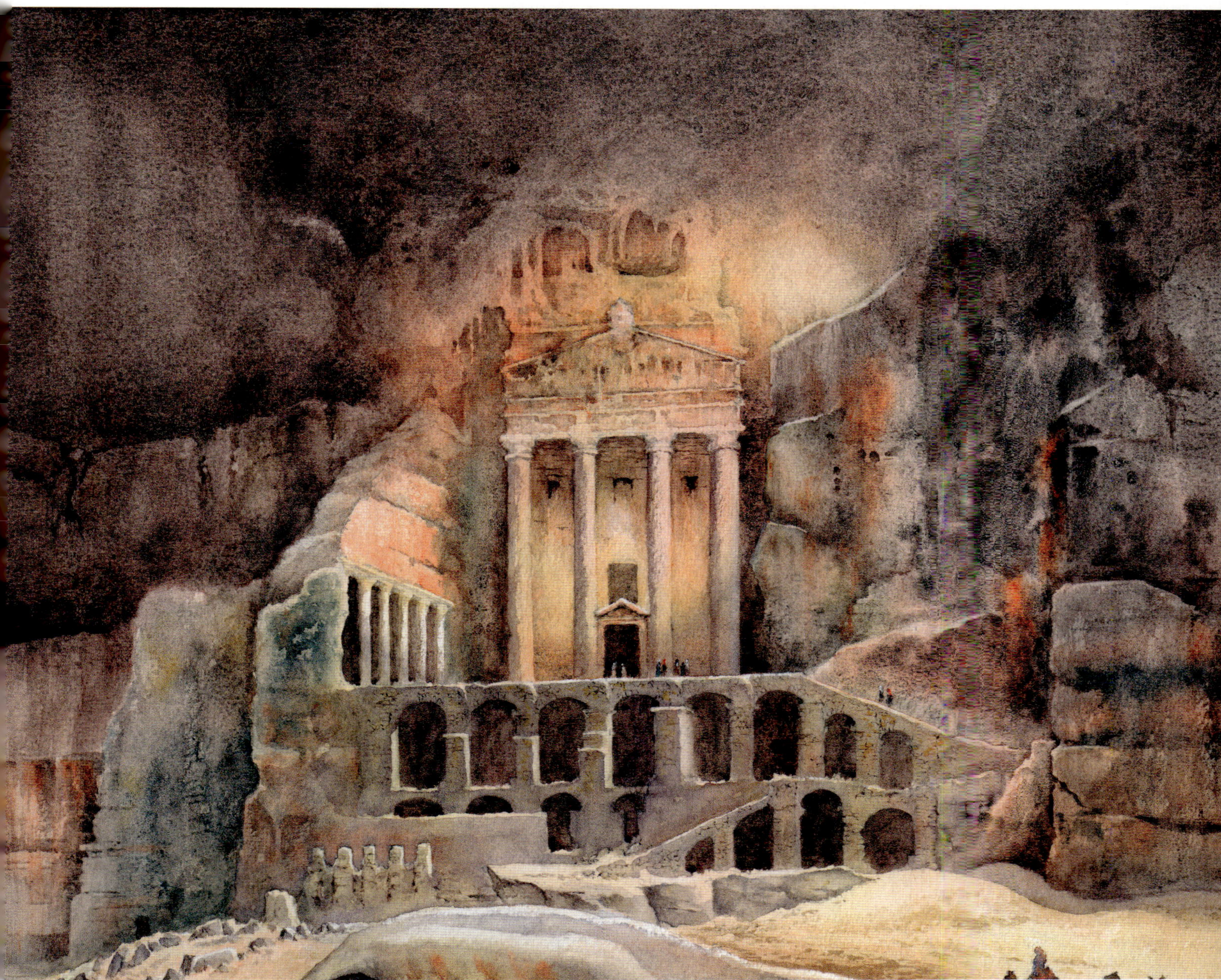

Urn Tomb, Petra

51 × 35.5cm (20 × 14in) Saunders Waterford
640gsm (300lb) Not surface paper

*At Petra the wind has turned much of the
stonework detail into an abstract form.*

*I wanted to capture the sensation of
strong architectural detail mingled with
an abstract variation, and so used
hematite violet genuine, a warm, heavily
granulating pigment.*

Invent Make up the lighting to suit your compositional ideas – here this
gave me freedom of choice to which parts to highlight.

Contrast Include dark passages to throw the emphasis onto lighter areas
and make the light seem more intense.

Figures for scale Including figures helps to give a sense of scale to
extraordinary places like this.

Be bold In this example, I laid the hematite violet genuine on quite thickly in
places and dropped in granulation medium here and there.

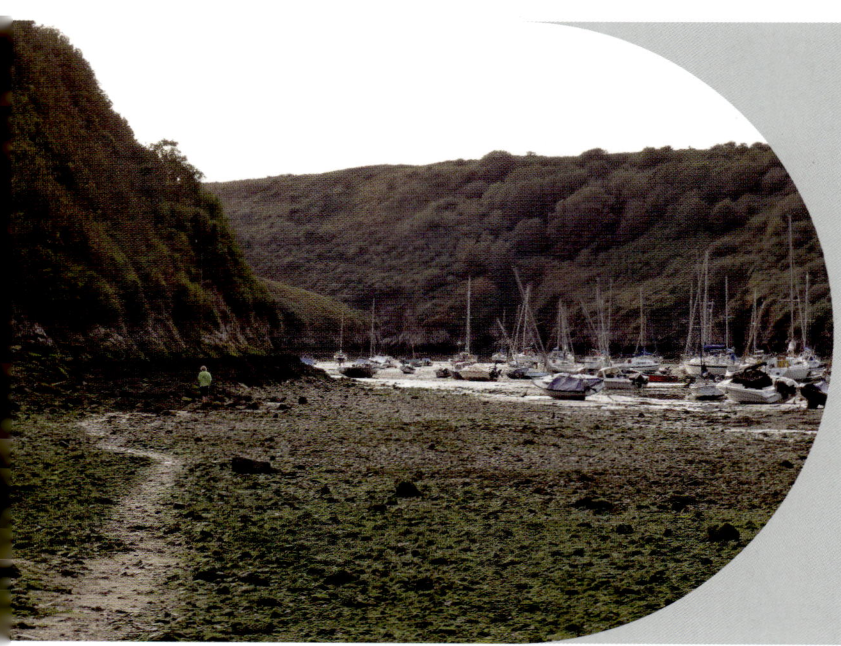

Shafts of sunlight and texture

In a landscape painting, it is vital to take time before beginning the actual painting to consider the sky, light and atmosphere. As you can see from the associated photograph, the mood of the day was dull and uninteresting, so I decided to introduce shafts of sunlight. This would determine where the highlights in the composition would occur. I also would sprinkle on sea salt to roughen up the foreground a bit to suggest texture.

What's wrong? As this photograph demonstrates, the lighting in any given scene is often not at its best. I needed to improve the composition with better lighting, losing much detail and introducing some interesting texture.

In order to increase the feeling of space I decided to warm up the foreground colour and make the left-hand cliffs much stronger in tone than the background cliffs.

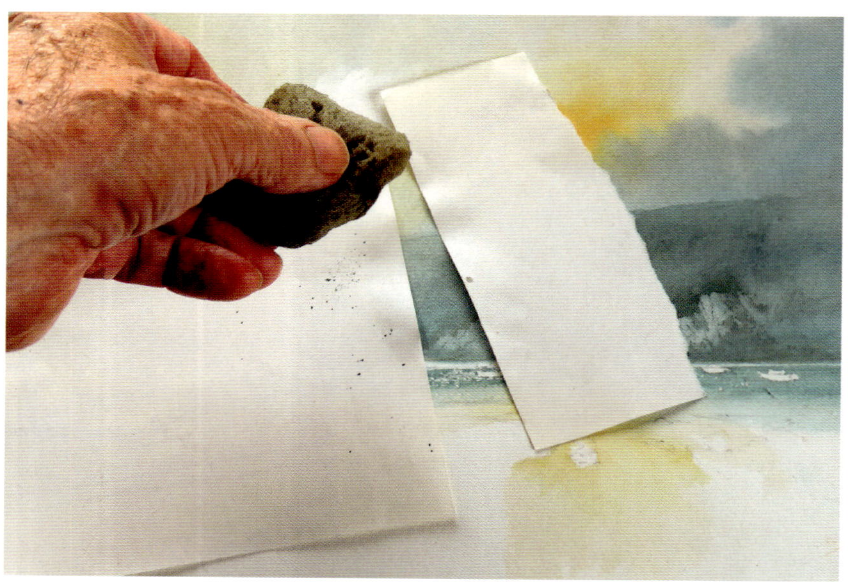

Introducing shafts of sunlight

One way, and to my mind usually the most effective, of creating shafts of sunlight over the landscape is to sponge them out between two pieces of thin card held diagonally across the area as shown here. Once the surface is protected, use a clean, damp sponge to lift out some of the paint.

You can create softer edges to the shafts by slightly varying the position of the pieces of card after two or three swipes of the sponge. The sparkle on the water should be positioned where the shafts of light hit the water.

See pages 52–53 for information on sponges, and 146–147 for sponging out colour.

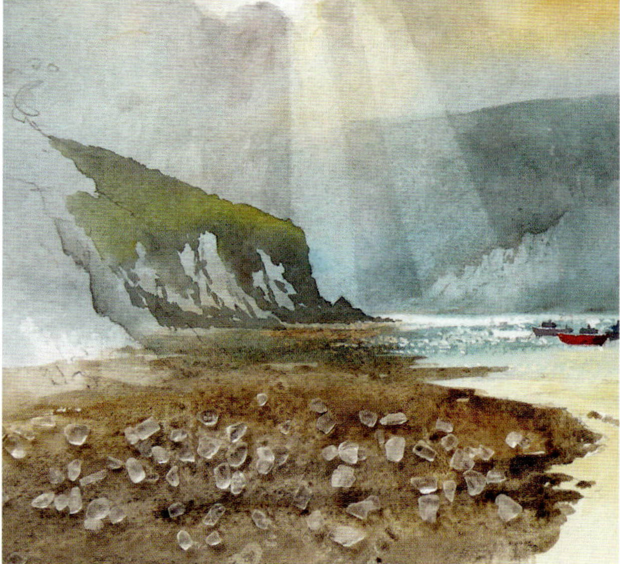

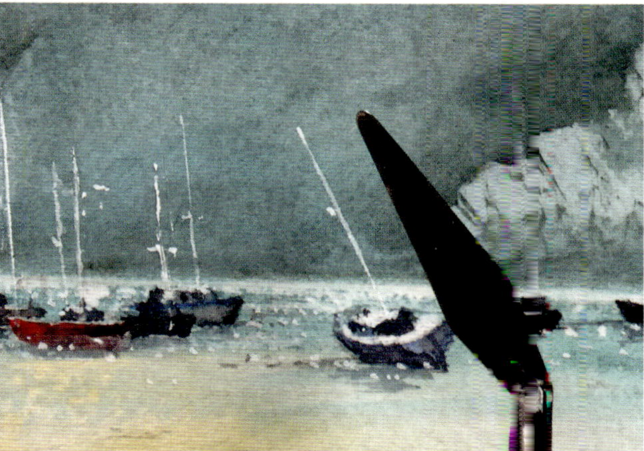

Creating texture with sea salt Before the foreground washes began to dry, I laid sea salt over parts in order to create the suggestion of texture – the salt absorbs the water, resulting in areas of dappled pigment once dry.

Describing the masts For the masts I applied white gouache to the edge of a painting knife and pressed it onto dry paper. Any unsightly blobs of gouache can be quickly brushed away with clean water, the area dabbed dry with a tissue, and the application of the gouache repeated.

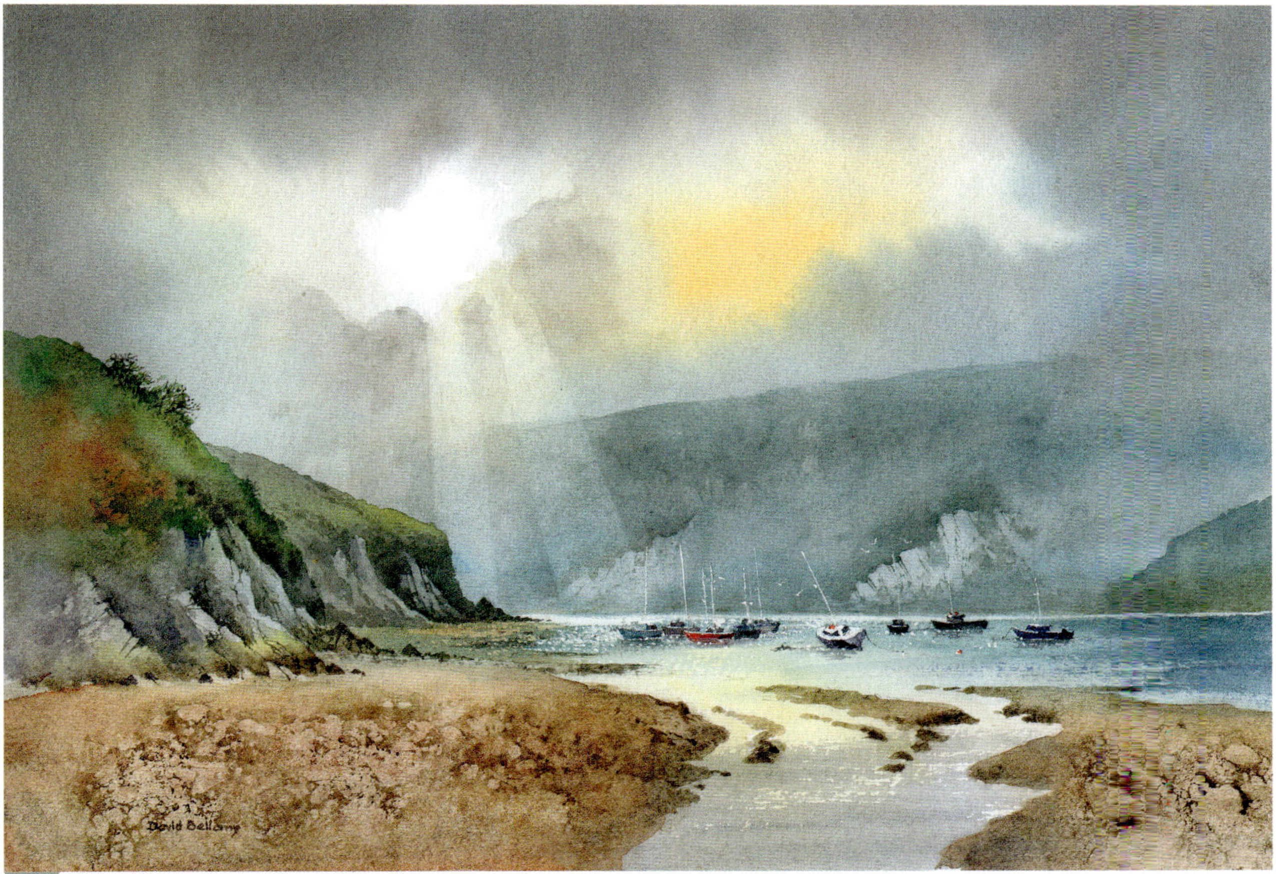

Solva Moorings

30.5 × 21.5cm (12 × 8½in) Saunders Waterford 300gsm (140lb) Not surface paper

With a cosmetics sponge I dabbed on detail in the foreground with raw umber to suggest a delicious mix of mud and stones to complete the painting.

Bringing techniques together

This painting brings together a lot of the techniques from across the book to do justice to this lovely lake scene – but we should always keep learning and bringing in new ideas. Here we also use wax resist to help capture the sparkle of light on water.

Dragging a candle across the paper to form a wax resist is a useful technique, but if you need a straight line it needs controlling. Also, being white on white it can be rather difficult to work out where the area actually starts and ends!

Before I began, I applied Schmincke coarse paste in horizontal strings over part of the foreground to represent stones on the shore.

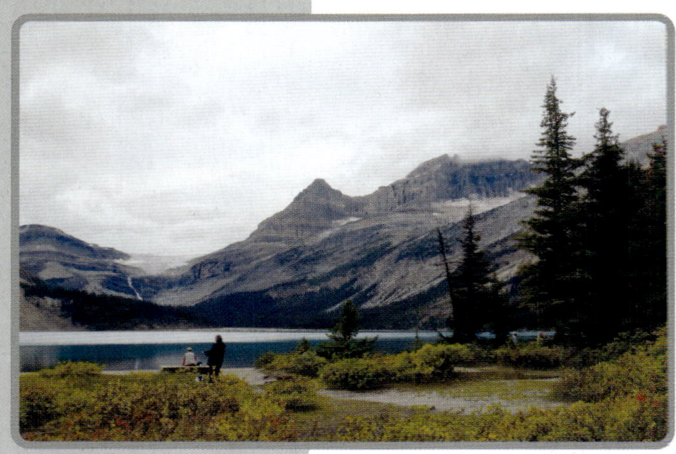

Reference photograph.

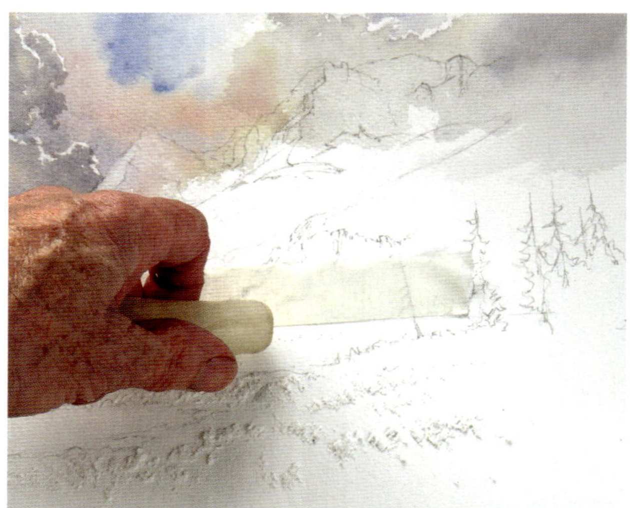

Applying wax resist After the sky was painted in, a strip of low-tack tape was applied to shield the area immediately above the far shore of the lake. I then made two horizontal strokes with a candle over the centre of the lake where sparkling light area needed. The tape prevents any wax being deposited above the waterline where it might interfere with a wash of colour.

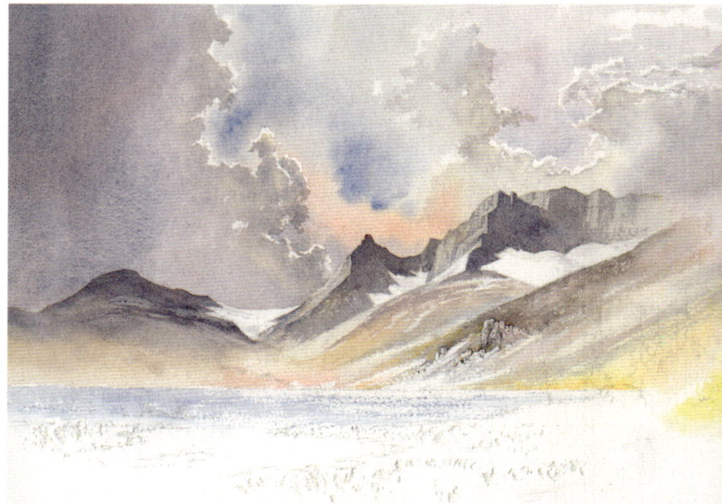

Wash and dry brush I washed French ultramarine and yellow ochre over the peaks, leaving white paper for the snowfields. The same mix was also dry-brushed onto the slopes, with in a little cadmium red for variation. The lake was painted with French ultramarine, and the left-hand mountain created with French ultramarine and light red, with some yellow ochre introduced lower down.

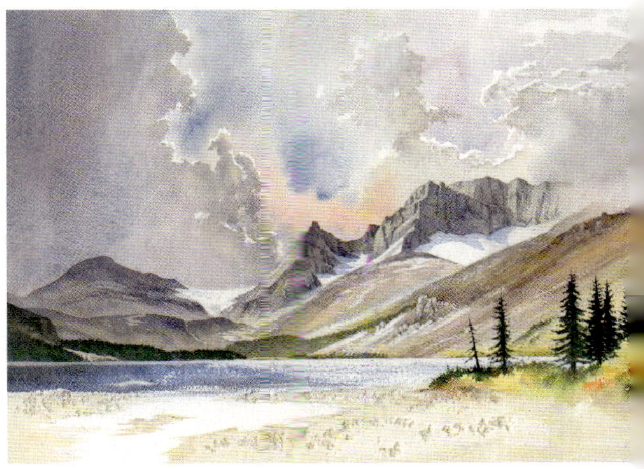

Wet on dry and dropping in I detailed the cliffs with French ultramarine and burnt umber, adding more French ultramarine wet in wet for deeper shadows. The left-hand mass of conifers above the shore were created with French ultramarine and raw umber, plus a touch of green apatite genuine. Cadmium yellow pale and a little quinacridone gold highlighted the right-hand vegetation. For the left-hand water I used French ultramarine and cadmium red, introducing a little raw umber into the wet wash on the far left to suggest this part is reflecting the dark slope. The foreground shore was painted with titanium buff, and the right-hand pine trees with French ultramarine and burnt umber, dropping in some green apatite genuine while these were still wet. The high ridge with the small knob above the right-hand pines was sharpened.

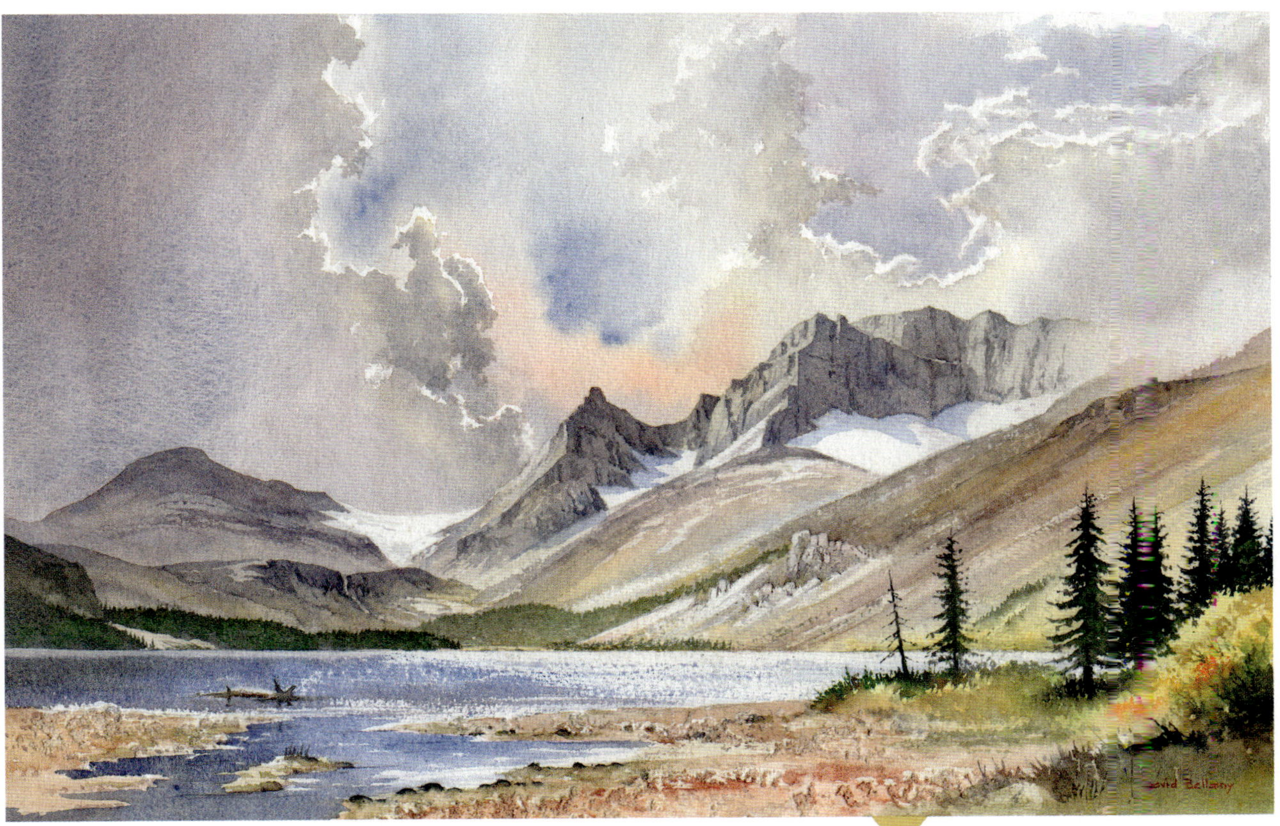

Refining I reinforced the sky with French ultramarine to enhance the cloud structures, and delineated the log in the left-hand water with French ultramarine, burnt umber and touches of yellow ochre. Although the original scene did not show any branches in the right-hand vegetation, this appeared shapeless, so I added a few thin branches, then applied some rough detail around the waterfall area below the glacier, all with burnt umber and French ultramarine. Finally, the foreground water was painted with French ultramarine, blending in some burnt umber towards the left side.

Bow Lake, Canadian Rockies

40.5 × 28cm (16 × 11in) Waterford 640gsm (300lb) Rough surface paper

For the foreground rocks I stroked a mix of quinacridone magenta and burnt umber across the paste with the side of a size 10 brush, and added a little yellow ochre in places.

Grand Canyon of Yellowstone

28 × 23cm (11 × 9in) Saunders Waterford 300gsm (140lb) Rough surface paper

I've used mist and shadow to reduce some of the considerable amount of detail in this dramatic scene, which has so many exciting ingredients. The cool colours of the moody distance enhance the warmth of the rock structures by the falls, and emphasize the sense of distance. The original sketch was carried out on a day of moving clouds, so the light falling on the vast scene was forever changing – challenging, but providing constant variety. At times like that I tend to sit back and watch for a while to work out the optimum combinations of light and shadow striking the main features, while taking photographs before I begin sketching. Sometimes it necessitates several sketches of the same subject. Here quinacridone gold and Aussie red gold bring the cliffs to brilliant life when viewed against the dark shadowy pinnacles. The conifers are predominantly a mixture of raw umber and French ultramarine.

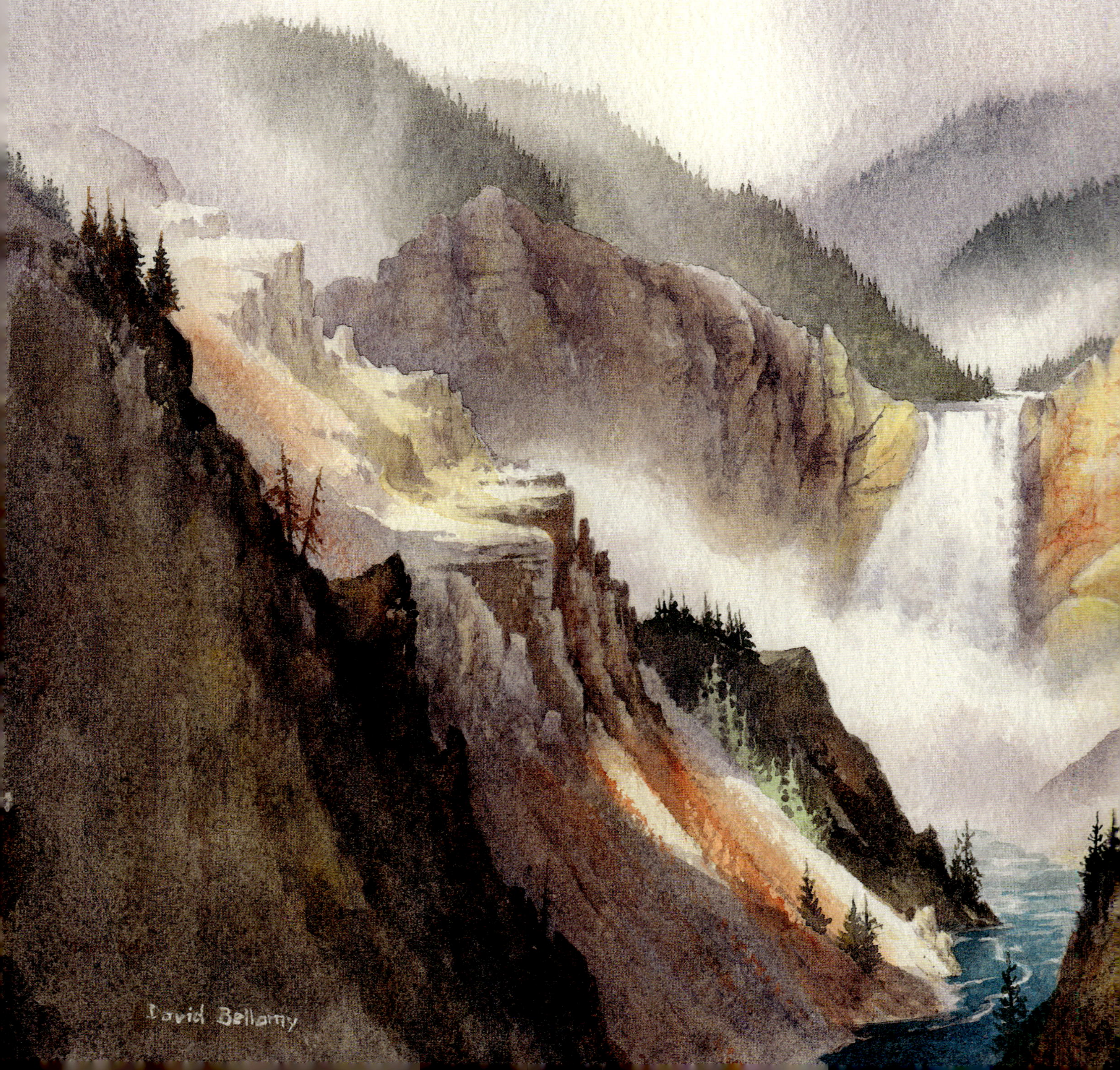

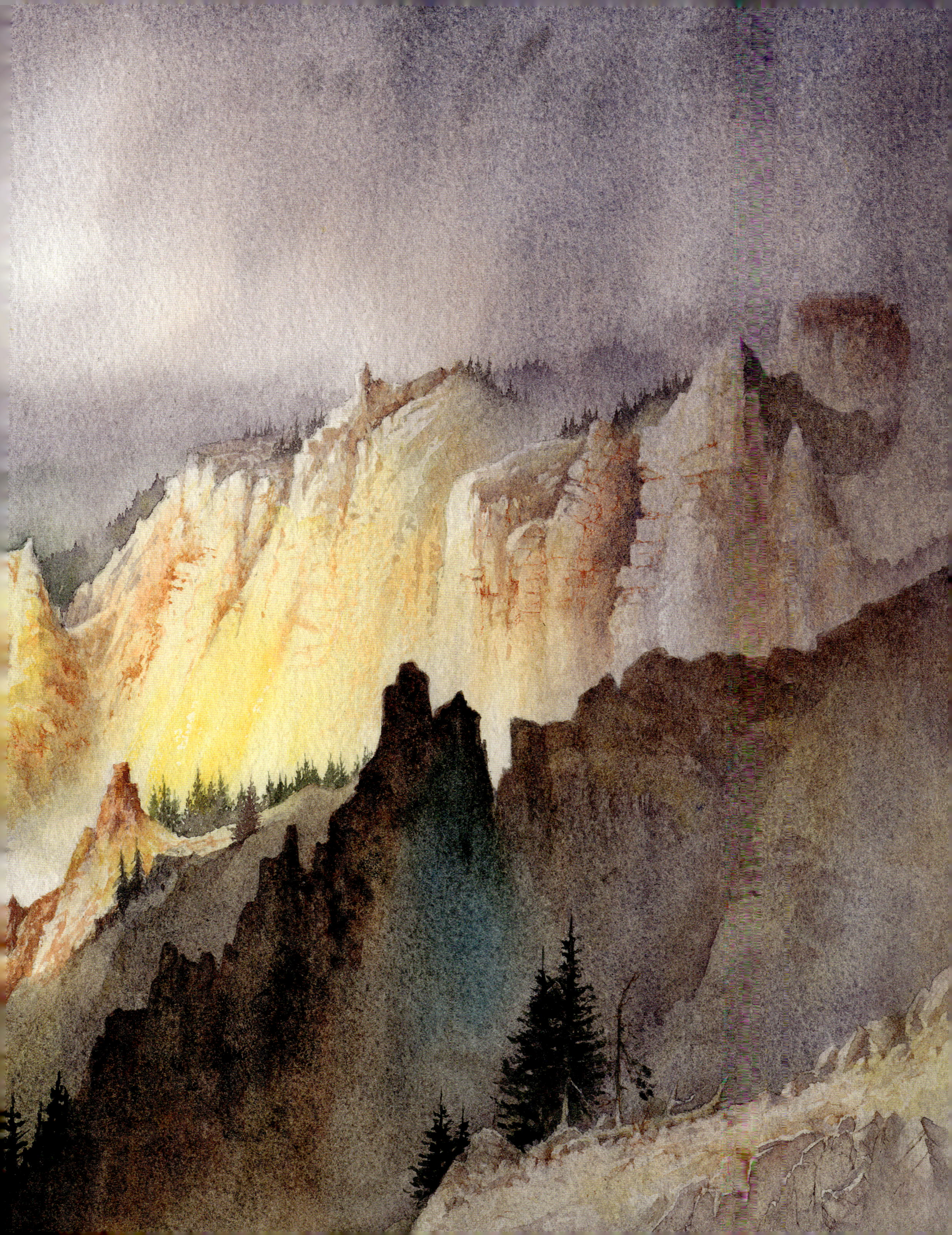

Alteration and rescue

We turn now to repairing watercolours that have some irritating but crucial flaw. You have seen how I change what I observe before me to suit my needs, and many of those methods can also help in deciding how to improve those flaws once a painting is complete – sometimes a simple glaze or an additional feature is enough to cover up an unsightly mistake, but the following techniques will help to give you ways to manage some more difficult problems.

Create a completely new foreground

Foregrounds can be notoriously difficult at times and I would have happily torn up this painting, as it would probably have been easier to start afresh. Happily it has given me the opportunity to show you a way to rescue a landscape that you feel really proud of, but where the foreground has let you down.

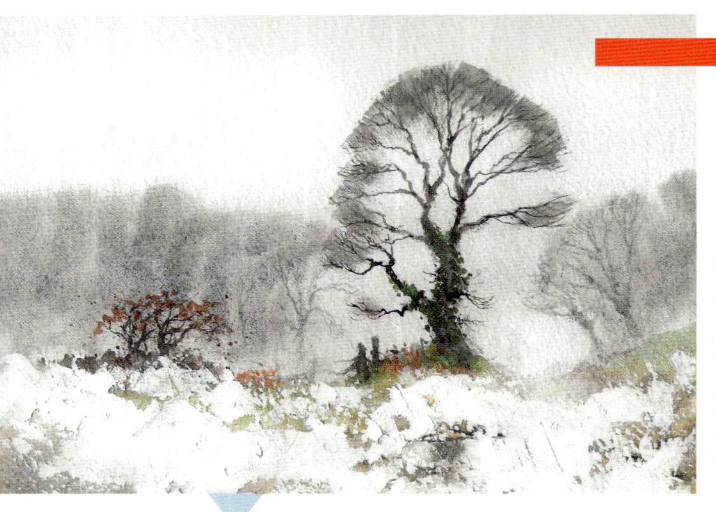

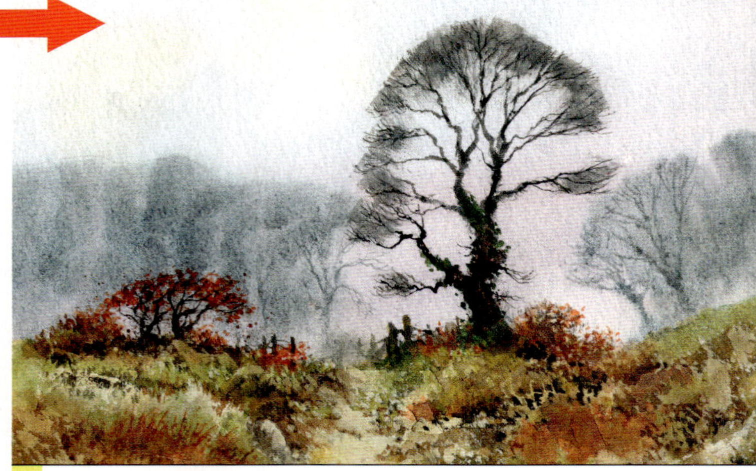

Misty Track – early stage of improvement

20.5 × 18cm (8 × 7in) Saunders Waterford 640gsm (300lb) Rough surface paper

At this stage I have simply plastered over the offending foreground and track with Daniel Smith watercolour ground, using a painting knife.

While I have altered it to a realistic foreground you may prefer to create a more abstract one, and the Daniel Smith watercolour ground with its ability to construct strong textures is ideal for this.

Improving *Misty Track*

- Before making any changes, consider carefully what you wish to achieve. It can be useful to draw a rough sketch of your proposed changes.

- I painted over the watercolour ground, which also produces fascinating textures when it is applied in varied thicknesses.

- This allowed me to create a path that leads into the centre of the composition. Try this out on some of those paintings that have not worked very well, where you have a passage that you would like to change completely.

Change the perspective

When I did the original sketch, I was looking down on the farm from a hillside, but this aspect of the finished painting did not appeal. I decided to change the perspective. In cases like this it's sometimes better to discard the painting and create a new one, but I rather enjoyed the challenge of altering the scene.

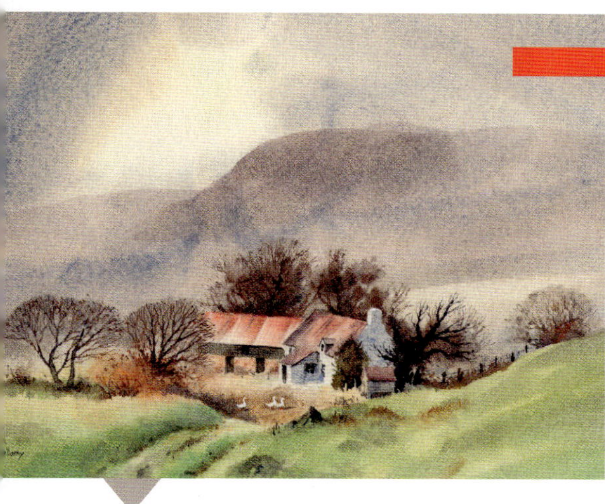

Llandegley Farm – initial
completed painting
28 × 20.5cm (11 × 8in) Saunders Waterford 300gsm
(140lb) Not surface paper

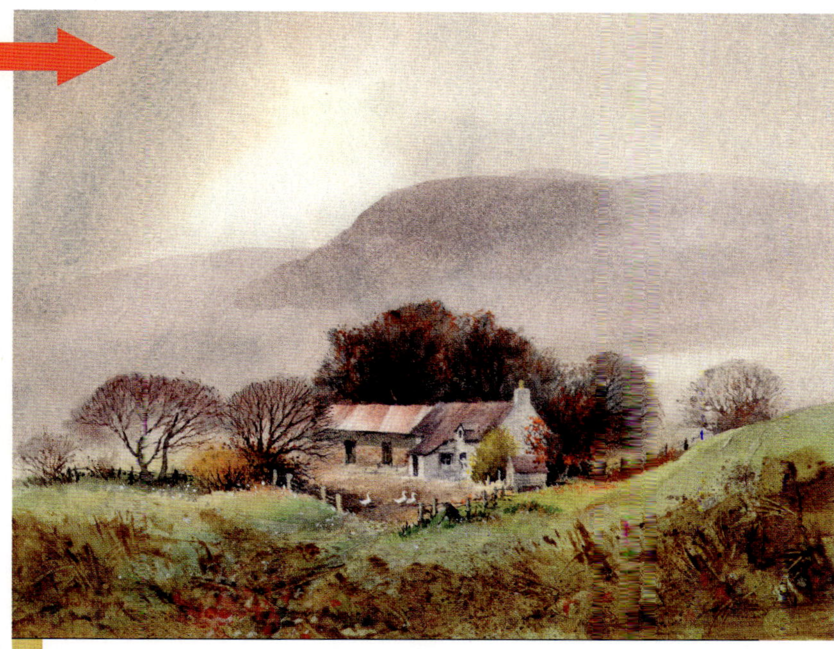

Improving *Llandegley Farm*

- By sponging out (see page 146) some of the architectural features and re-aligning the building with careful brush-work I managed to straighten it out by darkening the background trees. I then strengthened some of the colours.

- Pieces of oriental tissue paper were added into the foreground, over which I applied a strong mixture of raw umber. I should also point out that the geese were not present in the original scene, but I felt it needed some life added to it.

Fix problems caused by wax resist

Nearing completion of this painting, I was unhappy with the middle distance moorland where I had earlier laid wax resist using a candle (see page 138). I wanted to cover the area with a darker tone to give it more strength, but of course watercolour will not adhere to a wax surface.

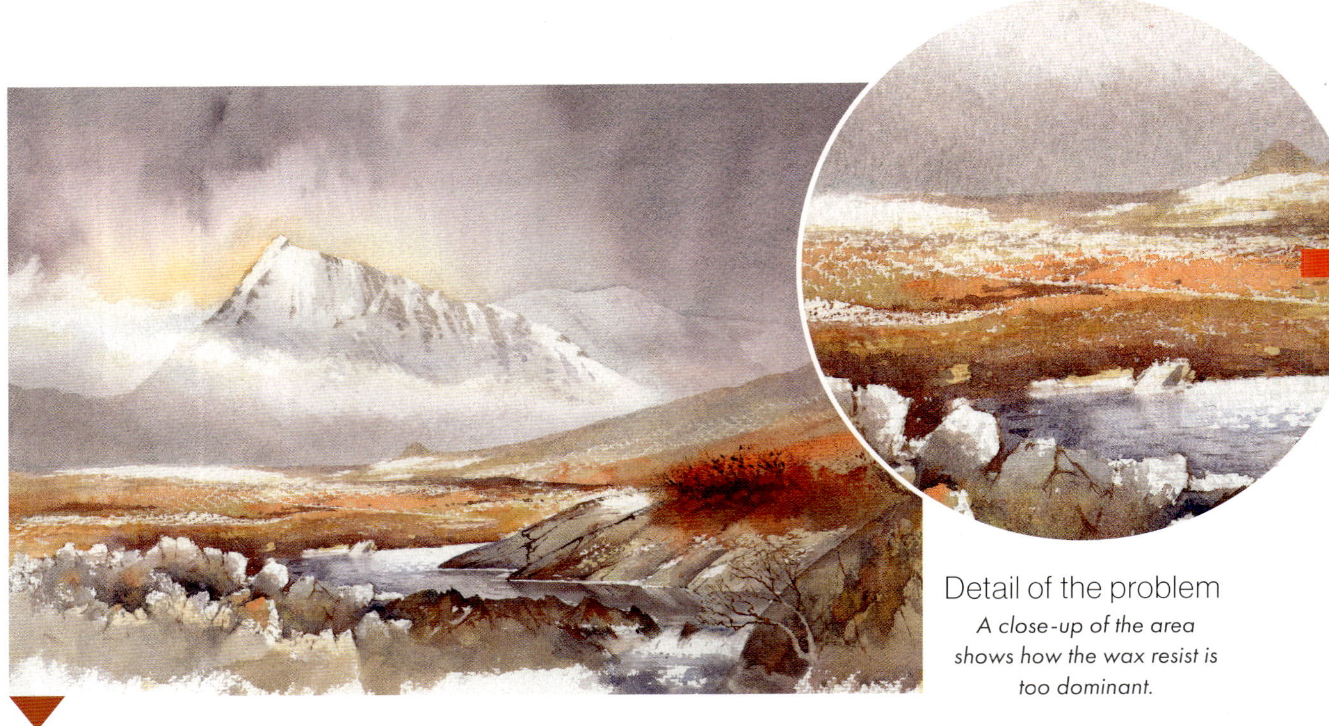

Detail of the problem
A close-up of the area shows how the wax resist is too dominant.

Crib Goch & Nant y Gwryd – initial completed painting
40.5 × 28cm (16 × 11in) Saunders Waterford 640gsm (300lb) Rough surface paper
This is the incomplete version which lacked strength and needed pulling together.

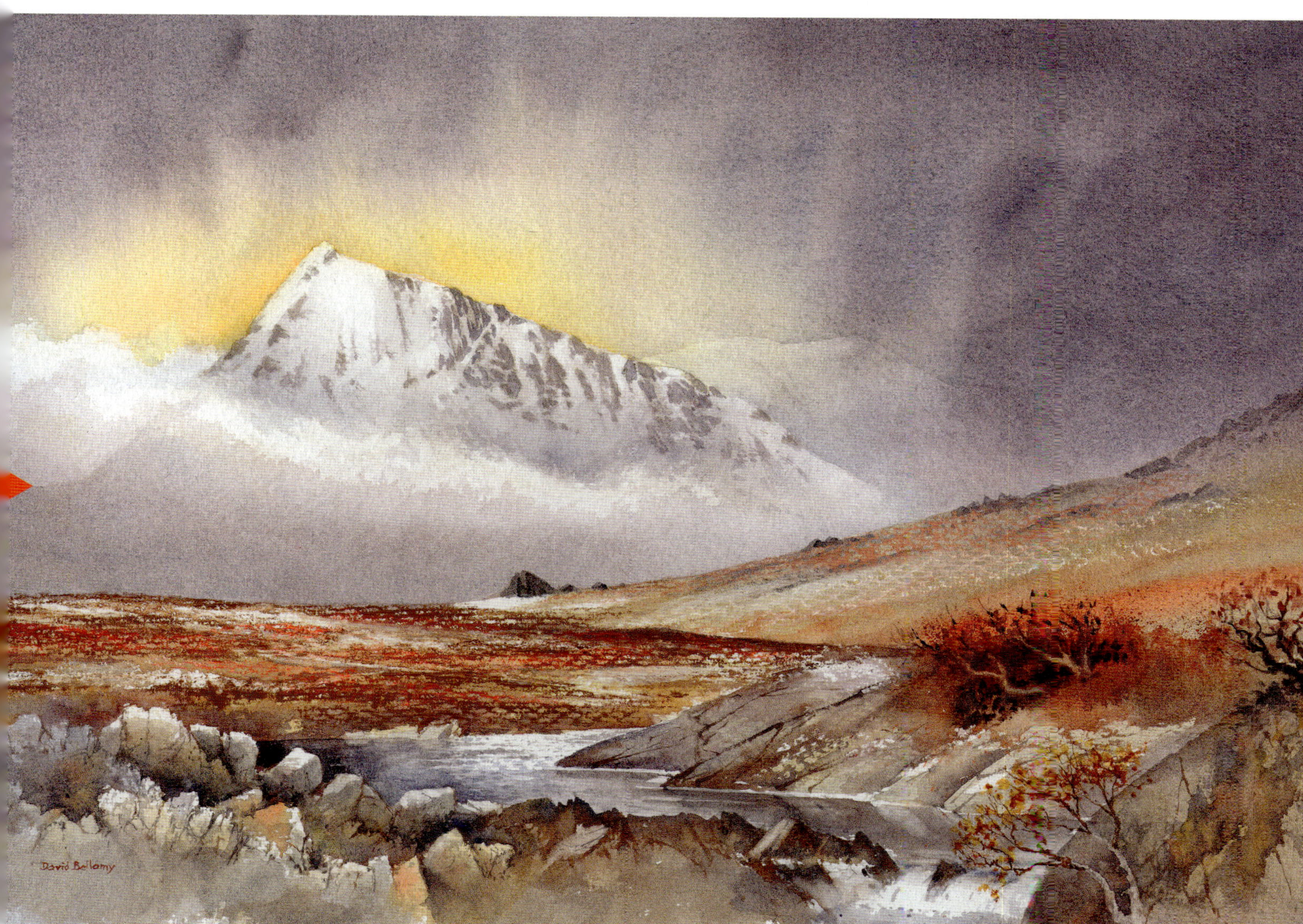

Improving *Crib Goch & Nant y Gwryd*

Because I had already laid some candle wax over parts of the moorland, attempting to overlay it with watercolour would prove impossible. Another approach was necessary.

- I began by strengthening the mountain and atmosphere.
- I used wax crayons on the middle rough band of moorland. The red and brown wax crayons laid over the candle wax and nearby parts improved the area considerably, removing its stark whiteness.
- Once the midground area was repaired, I then completed the foreground to ensure a coherent balance of tone.

Get rid of a prominent eyesore

Even with excellent planning, it's not uncommon for a finished painting to have an element in it that you want to remove. Watercolour will reactivate when wetted, at which point it can be lifted out (unless you have used staining colours). You can sponge out areas simply by gently agitating the surface with a damp sponge, then using a paper tissue to lift the reactivated paint away.

   With care, this process can be adapted to apply to most watercolours. I have rescued many watercolours from oblivion with this method, and most look as fresh as if the rescue procedures had not taken place.

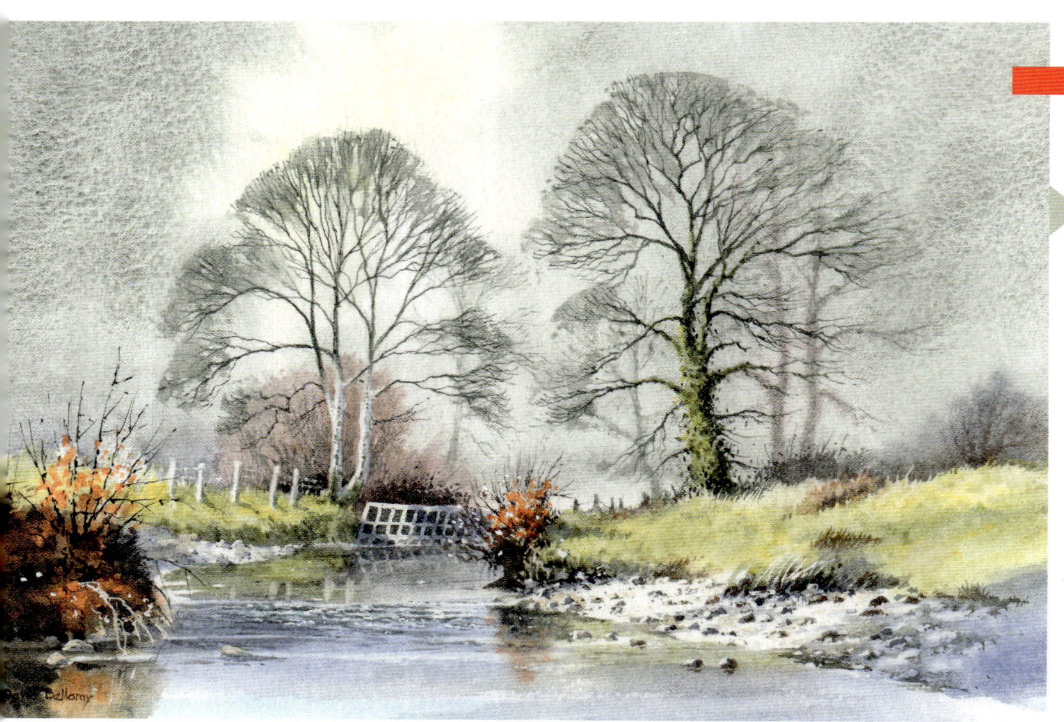

River Chwefri – initial completed painting

27 × 19cm (10½ × 7½in) Saunders Waterford 300gsm (140lb) Not surface paper

The hanging gate across the river was a striking feature of the scene, but after completing the painting I was not happy with it and decided to remove the gate. I also felt that introducing a darker, moody mass into the background would enhance the mood of the work.

Tips for success with sponging out

- Sponging out ugly or unwanted features is an extremely useful method, although it can be almost impossible with staining colours such as alizarin crimson or many of the greens.

- If the sponging does not work because staining colours are involved, then a strong glaze, or a covering with gouache or Daniel Smith watercolour ground are possible alternatives.

- Vigorous scrubbing of watercolour paper can destroy the fibres of the paper and possibly mess up the entire work, so if you are uncertain about the effects then test it by sponging in this way on the side of the paper, or on similar paper.

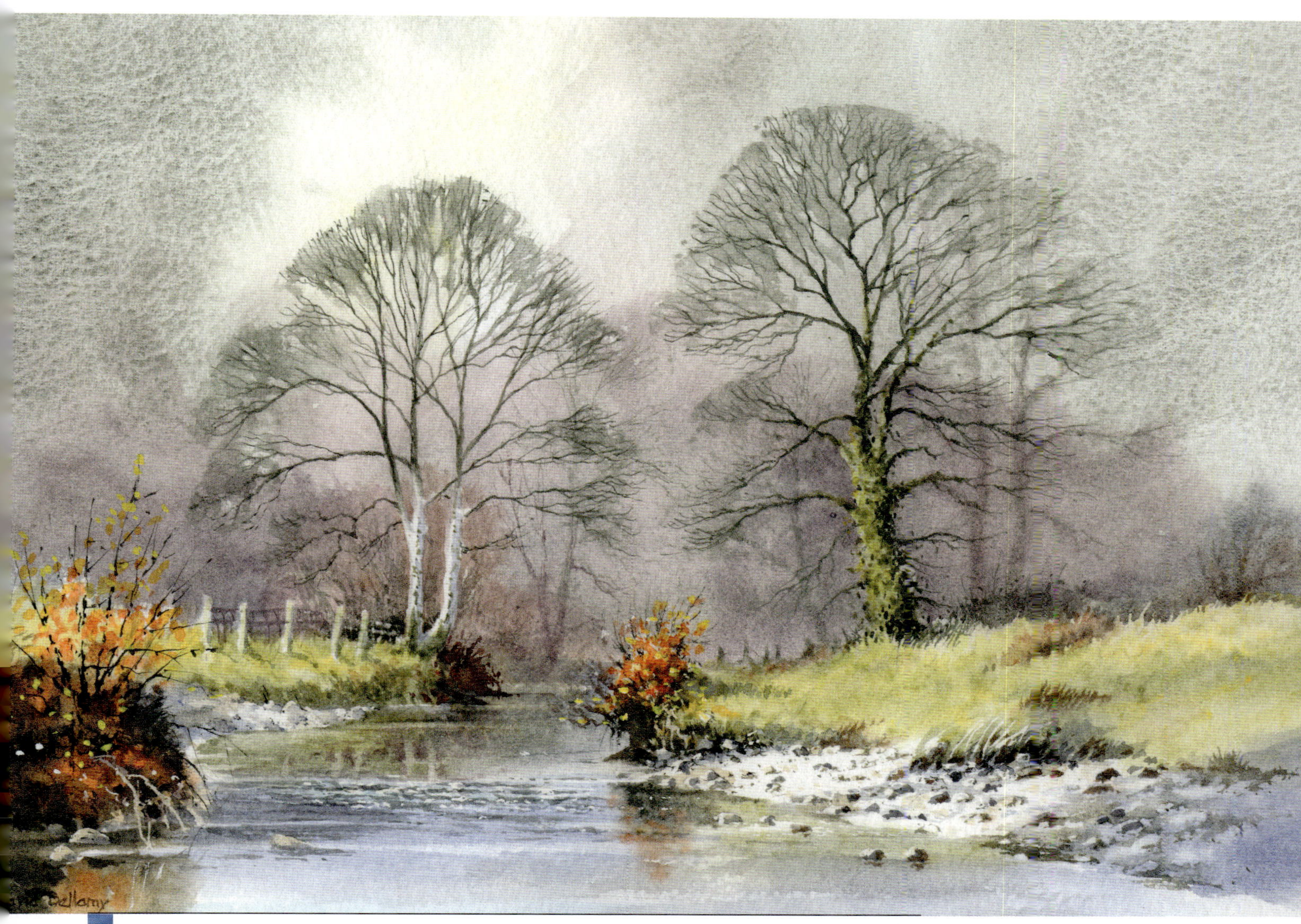

Improving *River Chwefri*

Saunders Waterford paper is sized both internally and externally. As a result, it is extremely robust and stands up well to sponging and scrubbing – just what was needed here.

- With a natural sponge I rubbed out the gate fairly easily, including part of the dark bush behind it. While I did this I masked off the birch trees with a scrap of cartridge paper so that they were not affected by the scrubbing.

- One or two recalcitrant bits had to be encouraged to leave by lifting out with a small flat brush, and the paper left to dry.

- Once all was dry I laid a wash of moonglow over the background areas, avoiding the prominent trees, and then worked on the left-hand bank where the original gate was located, to suggest the bend in the river, then reflections in the water.

- Finally I added some extra detail on the left-hand bush with gouache.

Make good a disaster

We all find that sometimes a painting simply doesn't work, and perhaps end up tearing it to shreds. Occasionally, however, we can see that a part of the composition has potential, and this example is one such work where I have taken around a quarter of the overall picture and turned it into a decent composition of its own. There is something of a fun challenge in this.

Trimming the fat – cropping a composition

Sunny Interval, below, is a sawn-off composition from a larger work done as a demonstration. Before consigning a poor painting to the bin, I sometimes reassess and cut it down to create a better composition, especially some of my demonstration paintings.

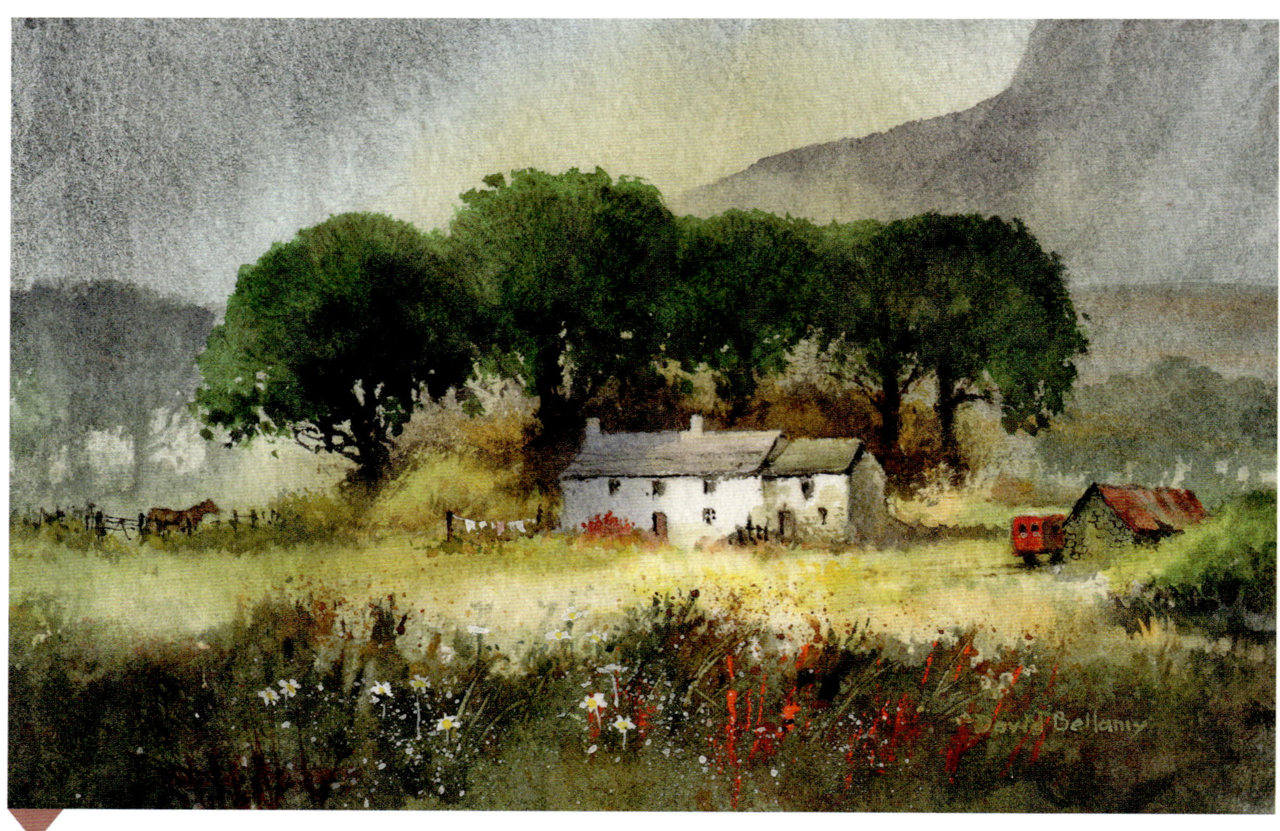

Sunny Interval

23 × 15cm (9 × 6in) Saunders Waterford 640gsm (300lb) Rough surface paper

After making the cut, I added cast shadow over the left-hand end of the house, and this gives a strong suggestion of sunlight on the rest of the building.

I introduced a pony on the left and a van on the right, then a clothesline using white gouache. Both white and orange gouache were also used to spatter and define flowers in the foreground. I loved the end result and the challenge proved to be great fun.

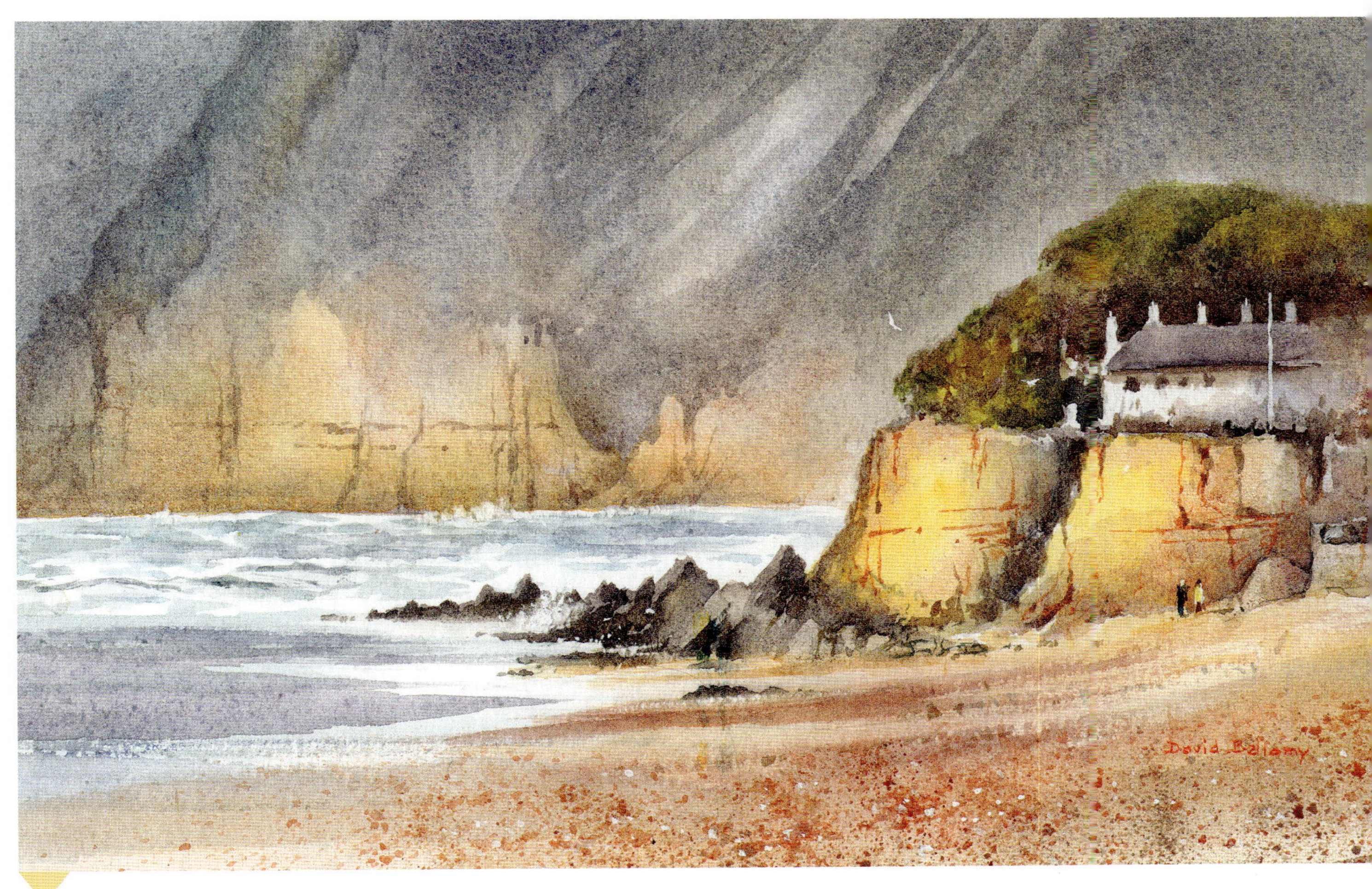

Rising Tide, Sidmouth

23 × 15cm (9 × 6in) Saunders Waterford 425gsm (200lb) Not surface paper

This is another demonstration painting which I've cut down considerably. I subdued the background cliff structures, cut off the sky area, and added two figures on the sand below the building. The dark figure was easy to render, but the right-hand lighter figure was created by first painting in white gouache, then overlaying this with nickel titanate yellow – a technique that often gets me out of trouble. One easy way to create a simple but effective foreground is to employ heavy spatter. In this scene I have applied a variety of colours spattered with a toothbrush, including white gouache.

NEW ROUTES:
Beyond wall art

Most artists find after some time that they are increasingly having to store away their creations, or that unsold paintings accumulate in their plan chests. For some this can become really depressing, and they wish they had another outlet for their art.

One way of tackling this is to produce artwork designed not to hang on the wall, but rather to be kept in volume form as a record of family events, the holiday of a lifetime, local history, community activities or personal highlights in your life, or perhaps a particular aspect of your life. You might also try painting a collection of scenes to be printed as postcards or calendars, whether for personal use or to sell.

The painting here shows another idea: it is an example of recreating a scene out of the past, and you may like to consider doing this type of work on some aspect of your local community. The resulting painting – or paintings – could be exhibited in a permanent local collection, or used to illustrate a local guidebook or greetings card. Such community projects also offer an opportunity for you to have a permanent display of the work in the village hall, or on notice/display boards in the village or town, information centre, or wherever.

This chapter covers a mixture of ideas to set you off on projects of this nature to make the most of your creativity.

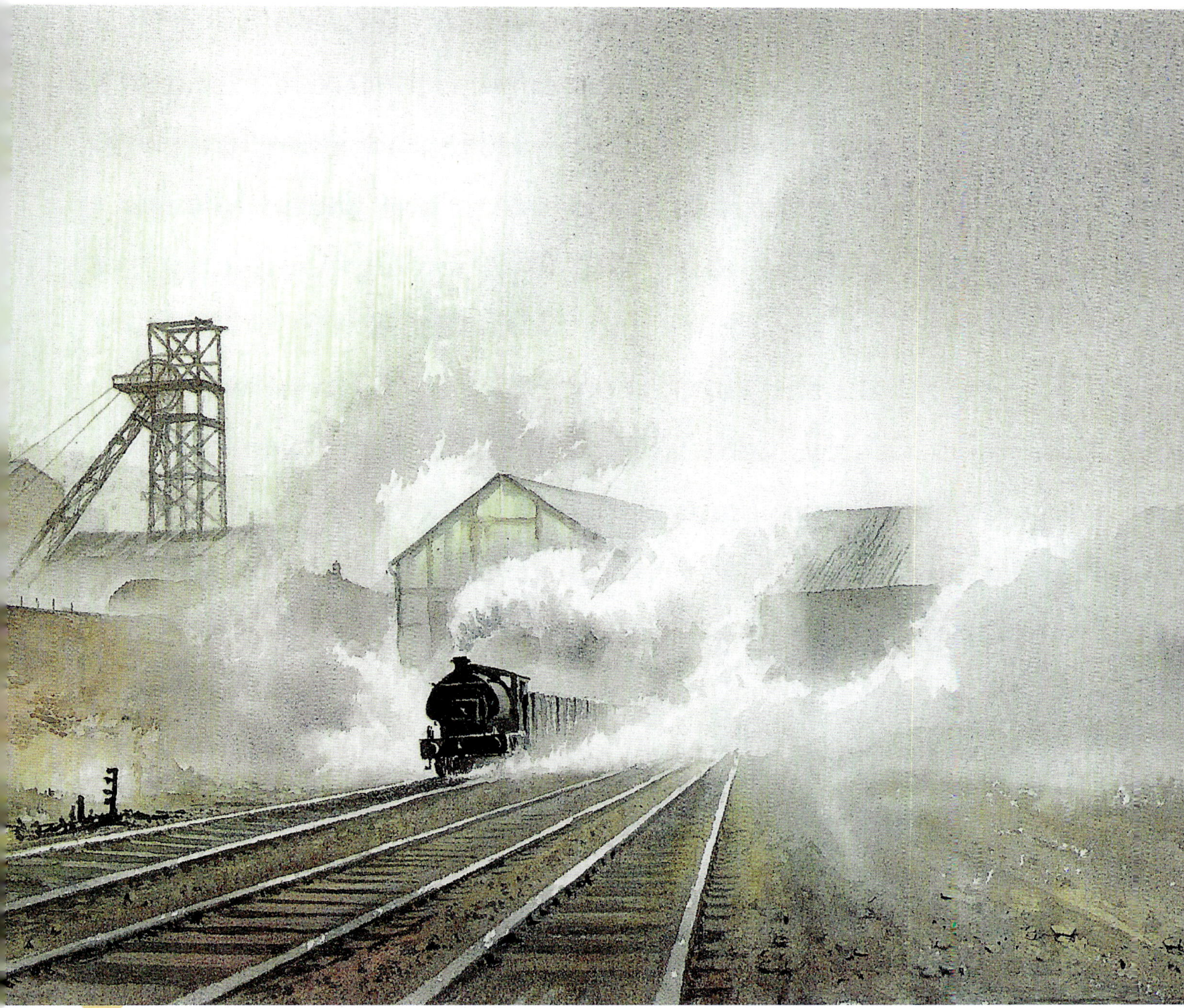

Steam at Cefn Coed

43 × 25.5cm (17 × 10in) Saunders Waterford 300gsm (140lb) Not surface paper

When I visited the Cefn Coed Mining Museum some of the old buildings still existed, including the pithead gear, while others were part-demolished. A site plan enabled me to work out the line of the railways, and old photographs helped to suggest the structure of the half-demolished buildings. I added in pithead details where they had been lost, and included steam or smoke to obscure parts of which I was unsure.

I found and sketched the type of locomotive that worked at the site at the Dean Forest Railway Centre. In the studio sketch that I drew in 1992, I included a note to bring in swirling snow from the right, but in the end decided I had obscured enough already. One of the points I bore in mind when visiting this old site was that everything looked fresher and greener – to inject an authentic look to the painting I had to introduce a lot more muck and debris.

Illustrating family events

Family events can easily be forgotten and a project like this can bring to life family history for future generations. I decided to create an illustrated record of some of the more interesting events in our family history, with my granddaughters in mind. An A4 (21 × 29¾cm/8¼ × 11¾in) hardback sketchbook with Bockingford paper proved to be an excellent choice for this account of my paternal grandfather's adventures in the Boer War in 1901, as I could not only paint directly onto it, but add collage, maps, photographs, diagrams and all manner of images, as well as the text.

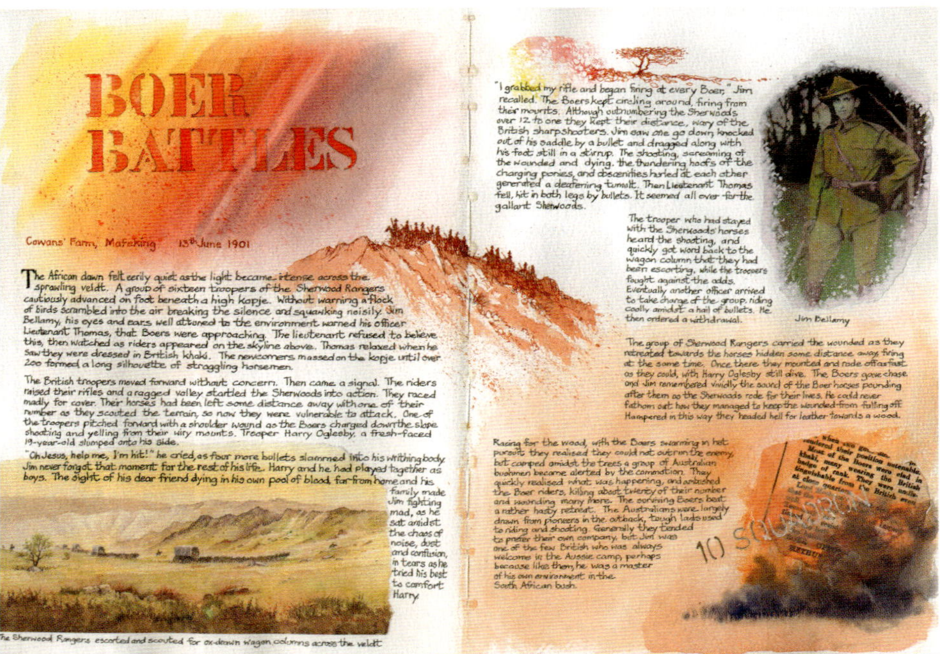

Boer Battles

- For the heading I used a lettering stencil after laying down the background, while the Boer group on the *kopje* (ridge) were drawn directly across the centre of the two pages and coloured in light red.

- At the bottom left is a reduced print of a watercolour I painted of a wagon column pulled by oxen: a common duty of the Sherwood Rangers was to act as out-riders and scouts to such wagon trains, and warn of Boer ambushes.

- On the top right is a copy of a photograph of my grandfather in his uniform. I used white gouache to disguise the edges of the photograph.

- The collage at the bottom of the page is from a contemporary newspaper over which I have stencilled the unit identity and lost part of the irrelevant newspaper piece with some watercolour depicting battle smoke.

- Finally I washed warm colours over the pages to bring it all together. It pays to carefully plan each page, sometimes as a double-page spread like this, and work out how much space the text is likely to need. Running some of the text over less important parts of an illustration can be very effective.

Boer Battles

The two pages shown here give some idea as to how I went about producing the story. I began with research: the Sherwood Rangers Museum in Nottingham kindly provided information and cuttings from contemporary newspapers that were useful to fill up a page where needed – and I found one or two humorous anecdotes that provide some relief from tragic events.

The facing page shows a two-page spread, the narrative describing how sixteen troopers of the Sherwood Rangers were attacked by over 200 Boers in June 1901. My grandfather lost his best friend in the action, but otherwise the troopers managed to extricate themselves from potential disaster.

The account brings back memories of many happy moments as a young boy listening to my grandad's tales, and I have much anticipation of further adventures seeking out the exploits of my other, maternal grandfather.

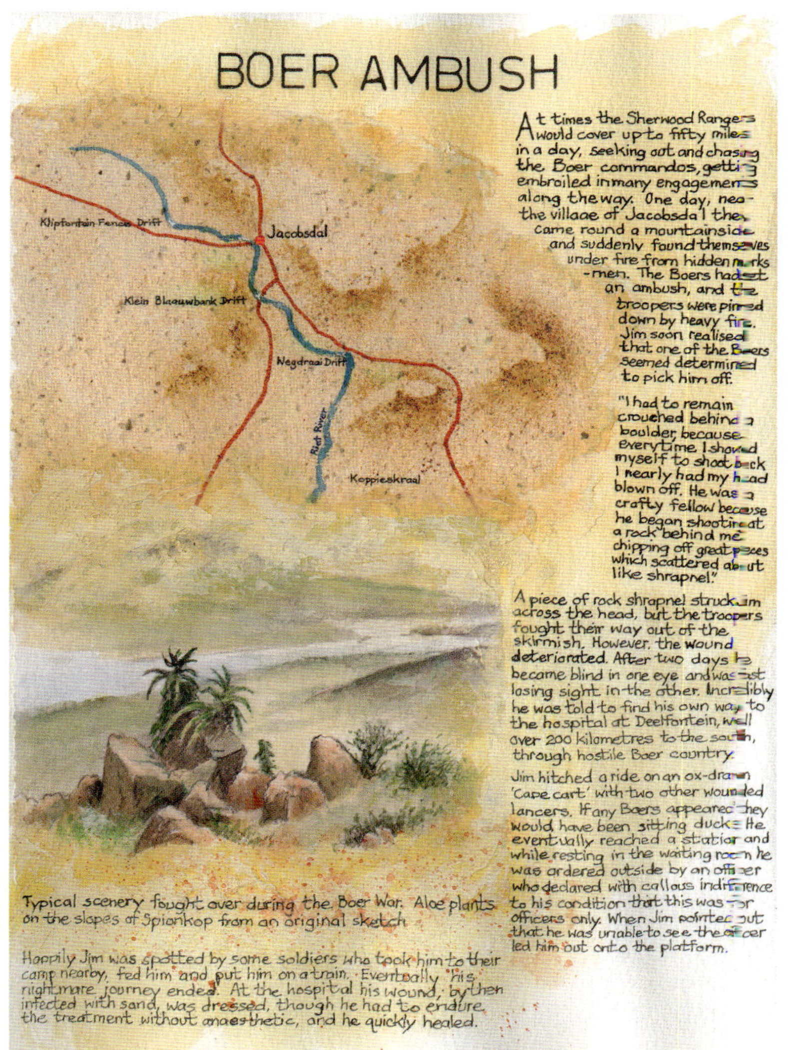

Typical scenery fought over during the Boer War. Aloe plants on the slopes of Spionkop from an original sketch

Boer Ambush

This map shows the area where the ambush took place. The map was drawn on Khadi speckled watercolour paper with a buff tint that well suited the rough scrub-covered ground.

- To define the hills I spattered raw umber from a toothbrush, using a small shaped mask to make out the sharper *kopje* edges.

- For the left-hand map edge I used a deckle-edge ripper – a ruler-like and rather vicious instrument that allows you to create deckle edges. The other three sides were torn carefully to produce the optimum shape, and then it was glued down. Once the paper had dried I covered the edges with watercolour ground, and when this had dried painted Naples yellow over the edges and much of the page where the text would appear.

- The sketch below the map is a copy of one of my sketches done at Spion Kop. The text describes the Boer ambush in which my grandfather was wounded and how he had to travel vast distances across South Africa to reach a hospital.

Journal sketching

Whenever I look through photographs, sketches and journals of my holidays, trips and expeditions I become carried away into past adventures and exciting worlds so different from normal life. Some of it truly amazes me, especially when I have forgotten about the details.

Bavarian Sunshine

Recently it struck me that I should create an illustrated record of some of the more fascinating trips – both for my own interest, but also for my enjoyment, as I am unable any longer to scale the heights.

I began the project covering a series of trips to the Bavarian Alps, and here I include a few pages from these memorable winter days. This sort of project can be a record of your 'holiday of a lifetime', highlights of an expedition, or perhaps just a quiet day out in the countryside. It's an excellent idea to include local colour where you can, such as customs and culture (as you will see in the following illustrations), as well as bits of humour, interesting characters and odd events.

I chose a journal specifically for this project, a large hard-back sketchbook with Saunders Waterford Not surface paper. It measures 25.5 × 35.5cm (10 × 14in).

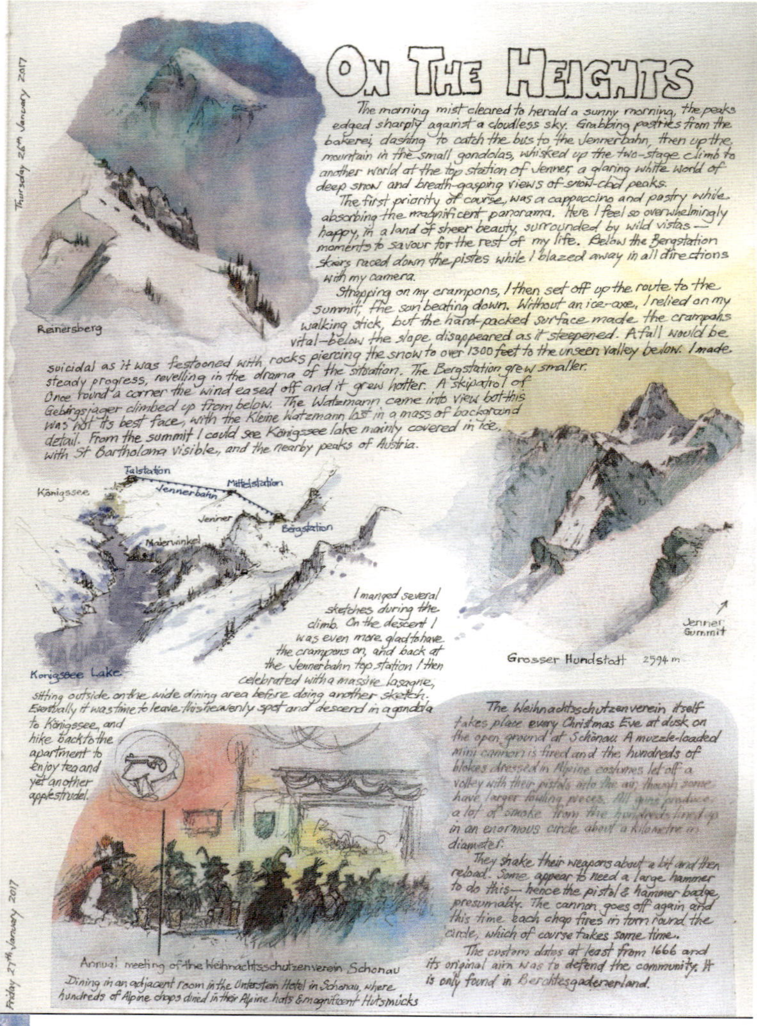

On the Heights

This page is one from a winter trip to the Berchtesgaden area where I have attached copies of two sketches of the spectacular mountain scenery that I carried out on the day, plus a diagram of the area.

- This type of diagram is an excellent alternative to a map as it gives a good idea of the sort of topography encountered, from a bird's-eye viewpoint.

- At the bottom of the page is a rough sketch I did in the Unterstein Hotel dining room in Schonau showing a meeting of the local Weihnachtsschützenverein (Christmas shooting club) taking place in an adjacent room. I carry a pocket sketchbook even when in a restaurant on these trips, as you never know what might happen. Later I researched into their activities and have included this at the bottom right.

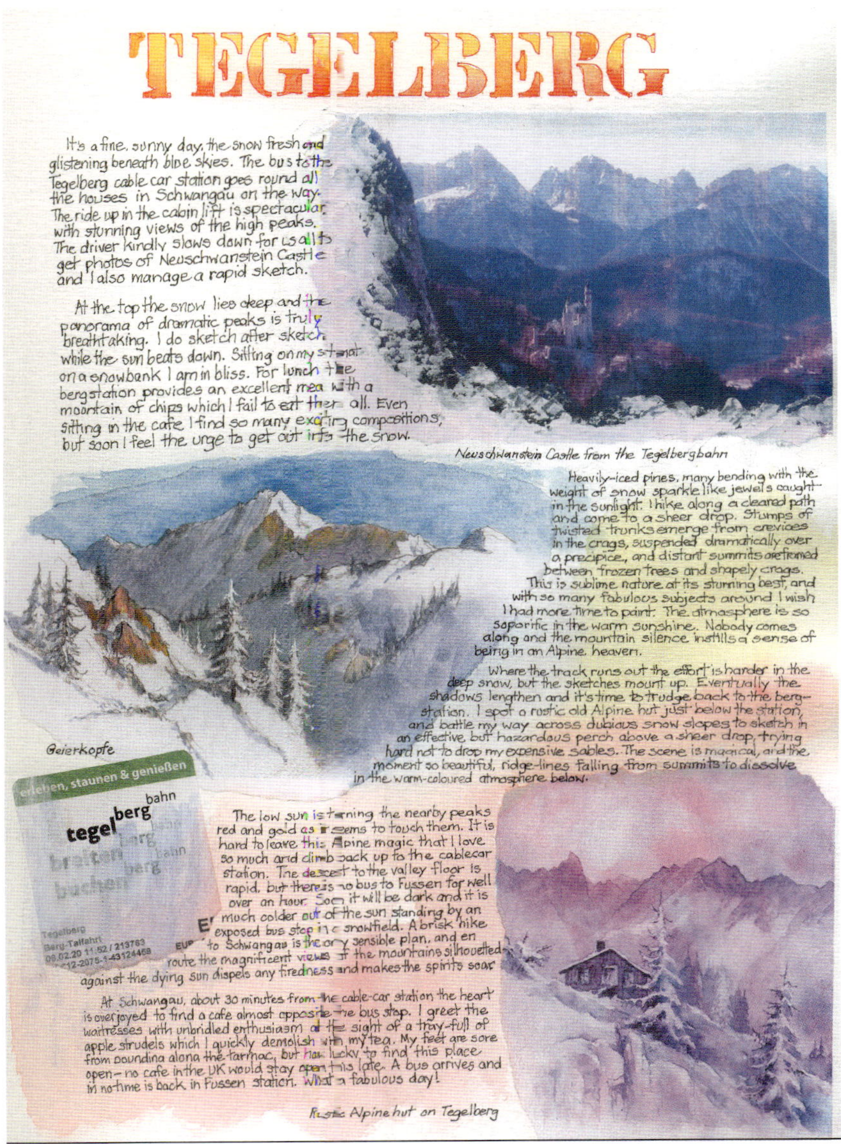

Tegelberg

This is an episode from another Bavarian trip, depicting a memorable day on the Tegelberg Mountain near Füssen in the most brilliant of winter conditions. Here I used a stencil to draw the title.

- My photograph of Neuschwanstein Castle from the Tegelbergbahn is not great, and I could have used better images from postcards and other tourist literature, but this seemed more personal.

- On the left and bottom of the image I roughly plastered Daniel Smith watercolour ground which hid the stark dark edge and at the same time suggested snow.

- The two copies of sketches remind me of what a fabulous day it was, in warm sunshine with a magnificent subject every few metres.

- I have also included the cable-car ticket, subduing part of it that referred to other services with white gouache.

Enhanced sketchbooks

Sketchbooks made while on a trip can be works of art in themselves, and you can take this further by enhancing them on your return. While the Bavarian examples on the previous pages were created as a separate album from the sketchbooks, there is an obvious overlap in content.

If you intend to make your travel sketchbooks into more than just rough sketches from which to work up paintings, then it's worth considering your approach before leaving home for the trip. I love maps and leave pages clear in my sketchbooks for these. Maps can show my route, wild campsites and even where I did each sketch if necessary, but you can leave pages blank for photographs, leaflets and all manner of scraps of paper you collect along the way that have some meaning for you and can be collaged into the journal or sketchbook. You can include complete paintings, not necessarily completed in the field, as well as notes, anecdotes and items of interest that you encounter.

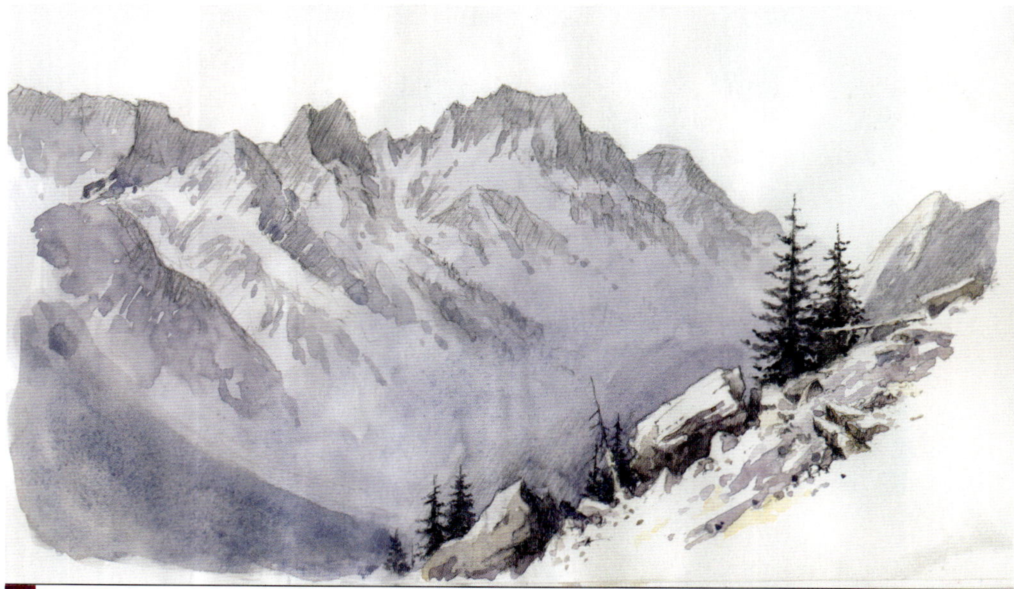

Sundance Mountains, Canadian Rockies

One of the greatest benefits of practising watercolour sketching is that you are learning to paint in watercolour in a more relaxed way than at a table at home on a large sheet of more expensive watercolour paper. Many people, including myself, have found this to improve their watercolour techniques more rapidly than other methods.

- Although this is a watercolour sketch done in an A4 (21 × 30cm/8¼ × 11¾in) cartridge sketchbook, it is virtually a complete watercolour painting.

- The foreground has been left as a vignette, giving the work a strong feeling of spontaneity.

- This is the sort of sketch that you might like to include when your outdoors work is aimed at creating an illustrated journal that is a work of art itself, perhaps even taking the composition over a double-page spread in a bound sketchbook.

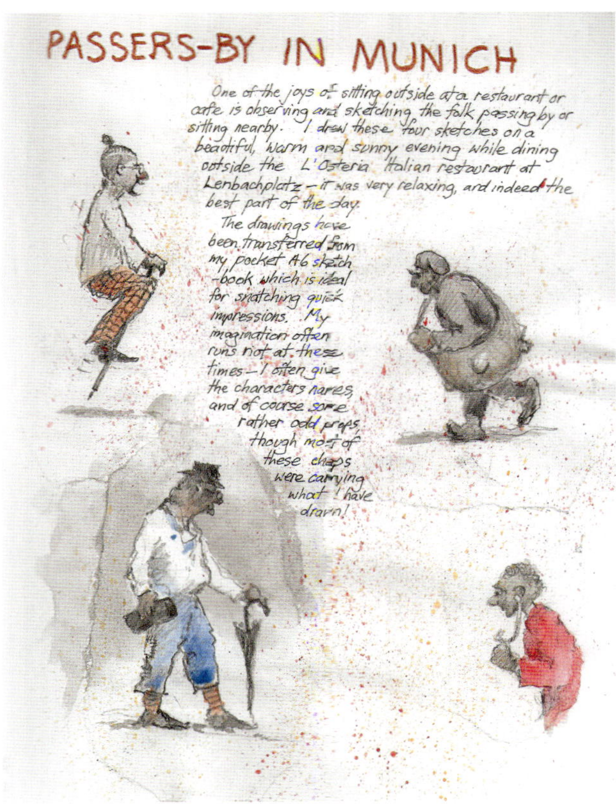

People-watching

These four characters were originally drawn in my A6 (10.5 × 14.5cm/4¼ × 5¾in) pocketbook, so I transferred them to the main book and then coloured them in.

I love sitting outside a café watching the passers-by with my sketchbook primed ready for action. Occasionally I am rewarded with a never-ending stream of fascinating characters, with some carrying the most peculiar contraptions, and if not then I sometimes give them something appropriate, such as a pogo stick. We all need laughter in this crazy world, and injecting some humour into your sketchbooks and journals can be extremely therapeutic.

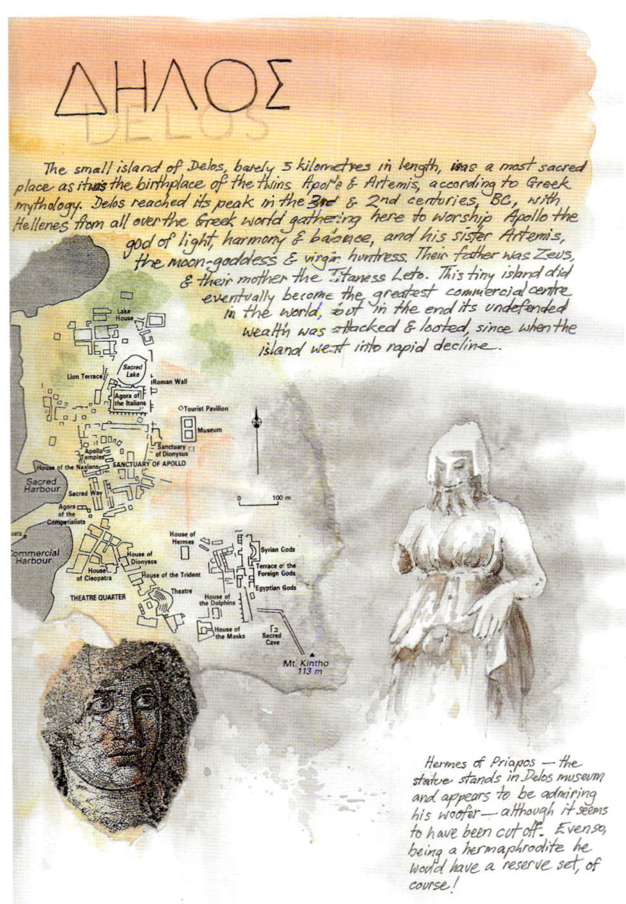

Delos Antiquities

The visit to Delos was a day excursion from the Greek island of Mykonos and this page in my A4 (21 × 30cm/8¼ × 11¾in) sketchbook shows the site map of Delos ruins, and below it a mosaic of the god Dionysus. On the right is a monochrome watercolour sketch of the hermaphrodite Hermes of Priapos. Occasionally, on location I position a small sketch in one part of the page deliberately so that I can add further illustrations, collage or text elsewhere, as in this example. At the top I drew in the Greek word for Delos, with the English version echoed beneath in a lighter tone.

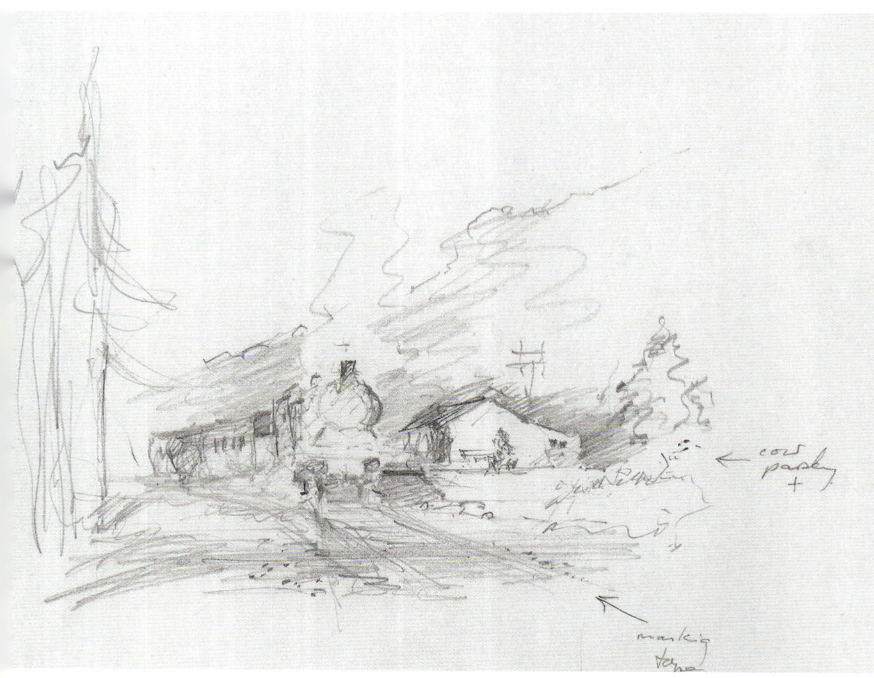

Rough studio sketch of Aberedw Railway Station

The station no longer exists, thus creating quite a challenge to reconstructing a faithful rendering of the scene as it was in the early 1960s. This studio sketch helped me work out the composition, the relationships of the various features, and the perspective on the train and railway as well as the building. I wanted the rising vapour to break up the long diagonal line of the massed trees.

Re-creating history

One genre I particularly enjoy is that of re-creating history, as it needs some research and can be a fascinating challenge.

Steam at Aberedw

My book on the South Wales coalmines was published in 1993. Many of the illustrations therein were created using this approach.

In each case I visited the sites, which sometimes still featured some of the old buildings, and did sketches and took photographs from various angles.

Mining museums and railway preservation places with industrial locomotives also provided a wealth of material to work from, and figures dressed in the clothes of that time brought the image to life.

Locomotive detail

The class 2 2-6-2 type was the main engine used on this section of the Mid-Wales line during the post-war period, and as so often I have employed the devious method of introducing steam to obscure much of the lower part. While this does hide a lot of complicated bits which you may not wish to include, it also lends a sense of atmosphere, almost bringing the metal beast to life, and of course simplifies the scene. The softness of the steam juxtaposed against the hard lines of the engine always works well, and too much detail can overwhelm.

Railway preservation centres are excellent places to gather information about locomotives, with many of them in use and thus showing how the steam and smoke affects various parts. You can never take too many photographs of these amazing subjects from various angles. I well remember, at Brecon Station as a young lad, being shocked out of my skin when the engine next to me let out its noisy steam-blast.

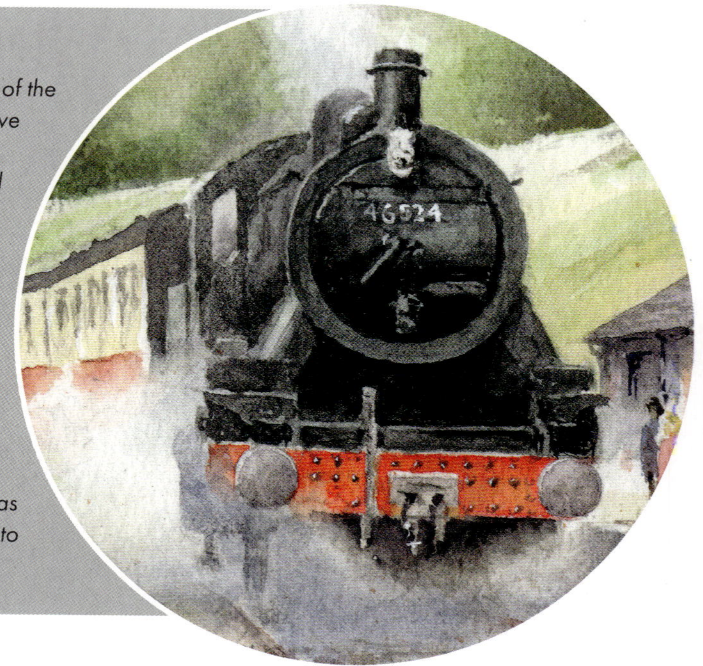

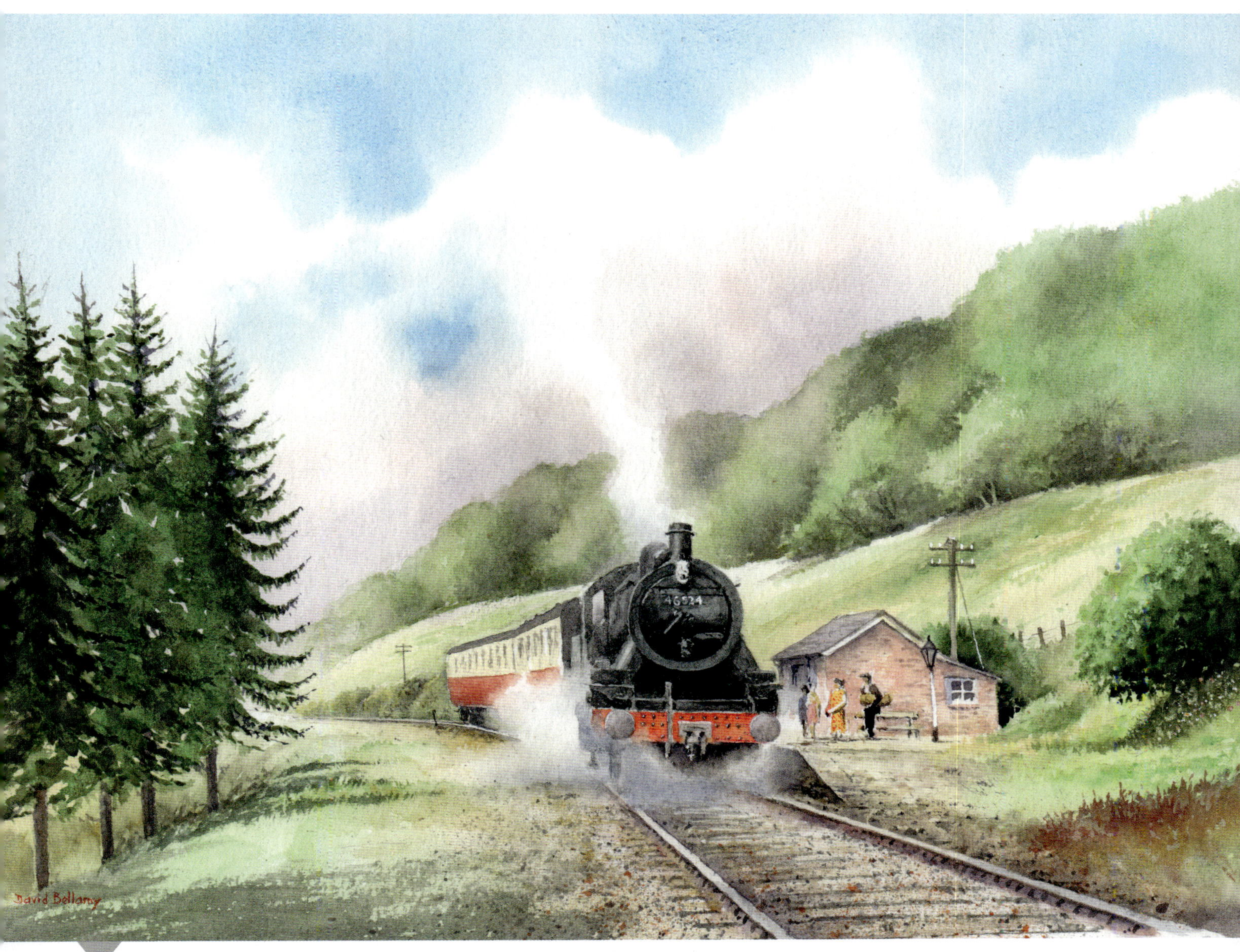

Steam at Aberedw Station

38 × 28cm (15 × 11in) Saunders Waterford 640gsm (300lb) Not surface paper

The painting depicts a sunny summer afternoon in the early 1960s before the railway line was closed down, with four passengers waiting to board the train.

In a scene like this perspective and scale can be critical: the size of the station building – hardly more than a bus shelter – vis-à-vis the locomotive and the figures needs special care; as do the perspective and curve of the railway line, carriages and station building. This is where the studio sketch should be as comprehensive as you need in order to work out these issues.

The platform still exists, now a repository for silage bales, but only a few of the lower bricks of the building remain. I find it important to visit the site in a project like this, to get the feel of the setting. Many trees have grown up to the right of the line. I was lucky with this painting, as many of my neighbours came forward with information and photographs as it was in those days.

Index

First published in 2025

Search Press Limited,
Wellwood, North Farm Road,
Tunbridge Wells, Kent TN2 3DR

Text copyright © David Bellamy,
2025
Photographs by Mark Davison and
the author.
Photographs and design copyright
© Search Press Ltd. 2025

ISBN: 978-1-80092-300-3
ebook ISBN: 978-1-80093-290-6

The imperial measurements in this
book are rounded to the nearest ¼in.
Always use either metric or imperial
measurements, not a combination
of both.

Suppliers
If you have difficulty in obtaining
any of the materials and equipment
mentioned in this book, then please
visit the Search Press website for
details of suppliers:
www.searchpress.com

Bookmarked Hub
For further ideas and inspiration, and
to join our free online community,
visit: www.bookmarkedhub.com

You are invited to visit the author's
website: www.davidbellamy.co.uk

Publishers' note
All the step-by-step photographs
in this book feature the author,
David Bellamy, demonstrating how
to paint with watercolour. No models
have been used.

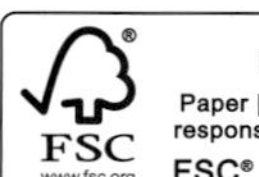